EDUCATION

LAW, POLICY AND PRACTICE

IN

NORTHERN IRELAND

THE QUEEN'S
ANNIVERSARY PRIZES

1996

The Queen's Anniversary Prizes for Higher and Further Education recognise the contribution of universities and colleges to the social, economic, cultural and intellectual life of the nation.

In 1994, the inaugural year of the competition, The Queen's University of Belfast was awarded a prize for the work of Servicing the Legal System.

The prize citation for SLS in 1994 read:

"This is an outstanding service to overcome the special problems of distributing knowledge about new law inside a small jurisdiction. It is an international exemplar."

The Servicing The Legal System Programme

This programme was inaugurated in August 1980 in the Faculty of Law at Queen's University, Belfast to promote the publication of commentaries on various aspects of the law and legal system of Northern Ireland. Generous financial and other support for the programme has been provided by the Northern Ireland Court Service, the Inn of Court of Northern Ireland, the Bar Council of Northern Ireland, the Law Society of Northern Ireland and Queen's University. Details of other SLS publications may be obtained from the SLS Office, School of Law, The Queen's University of Belfast, Belfast BT7 1NN.

Education
Law, Policy and Practice in Northern Ireland

Laura Lundy, LL.B., LL.M., B.L.
Senior Lecturer, School of Law,
Queen's University, Belfast

SLS Legal Publications (NI)
2000

© Laura Lundy

All rights reserved.
No part of this publication may be reproduced, stored in a retrieval system, or transmitted in any form or by any means, including photocopying and recording, without the prior written permission of the publisher.

The reproduction of Crown Copyright material is in accordance with the requirements of Her Majesty's Stationery Office; all sources are indicated in the text.

The author has expressly asserted her moral right of paternity in this work.

First published 2000 by SLS Legal Publications (NI), School of Law, Queen's University, Belfast BT7 1NN.

ISBN 0 85389 790 5

Typeset by SLS Legal Publications (NI)
Printed by MPG Books Ltd., Cornwall

For my mother and father

PREFACE

Education: Law, Policy and Practice in Northern Ireland is the first and only book whose main focus is the law relating to schools in Northern Ireland. Twenty years ago there would have been no need for a book devoted to education law as the area was largely unregulated. Today, there are six major Orders in Council detailing the rules and procedures which affect schools. The book's primary focus is on these Education Orders - the public law aspects of schooling. The education legislation provides fertile ground, not just for analysis but for litigation. Recent years have seen an unprecedented rise in the number of legal challenges involving schools. This has been fuelled by two things. The first is an increased willingness on the part of parents to exercise their rights in relation to their child's education. This has been encouraged by a series of education policies aimed at securing parental involvement in children's schooling. The second factor which has contributed to the increase in litigation has been the availability of legal aid to children in their own right (i.e. not subject to a parental means test). Most recently, the Human Rights Act 1998 has brought increased significance to the United Kingdom's international obligations under the European Convention on Human Rights and opened the doors to new types of legal challenge in the domestic courts.

The objective of the book is to provide an account of education law in Northern Ireland in key areas, including: school government, admissions, the curriculum, attendance, discipline, special educational needs and transport to school. The book is primarily a legal text, aimed at increasing understanding of the legal aspects of the school system so that lawyers and other professional advisers can provide children, parents and teachers with accurate advice as to their rights. However, like other parents whose children are going through the state education system, I have a vested interest in hard-pressed educational resources being used to pay for education and not for legal costs or damages. It is therefore my hope that the book will also be used by schools, school governors and those involved in educational administration as a benchmark for good practice which will help to keep them on the right side of the law. Statutory references and case citations have been consigned to footnotes in the hope that the text will be rendered more accessible to non-lawyers. Finally, the book is also intended to accommodate the significant level of academic interest in this area. The text goes beyond a black letter account of the law, sets the key legal provisions in their social and policy context and assesses how they are operating in practice. In particular, the first chapter examines the key influences on the development of the law in this jurisdiction and provides an assessment of the potential impact of devolution. Moreover, each chapter starts with a broad introduction which examines the historical position and policy objectives of the law in that area and provides a critique as to how well the law is meeting those objectives.

Many people have provided me with invaluable assistance in the course of writing this book. Two, in particular, merit special mention. Sara Gamble, Publications Editor of SLS, has supported me from the very beginning -

establishing contacts, encouraging my progress and finally subjecting my unruly drafts to an exceptionally thorough and thoughtful editing process. All of this was carried out with consistent good humour and in a spirit of friendship and I am much indebted to her. The second is Gemma Loughran, Barrister at Law, who read the complete book in draft and made many valuable improvements to the substance. Gemma brought both a fine legal mind and intimate knowledge of the education system to the text and the book is much improved as a result. I am truly grateful for her generosity in sparing some time from her busy professional life to read such a long manuscript. In addition, many individuals commented on specific chapters in the book and I am most grateful to them for their insight and expertise. These include: Alex Barr, Chief Education Welfare Officer at the Southern Education and Library Board, Aidan Canavan, President of the Special Education Appeals Tribunal, Tara Caul of the Children's Law Centre, Christine Jendoubi of the Department of Education; Brigid Hadfield, Professor of Public Law at the University of Essex; Ruth Lavery (formerly Senior Lecturer in Law at Queen's University, Belfast), Imelda McAuley of the School of Law at Queen's, Geraldine McEvoy of IPSEA, Colin McGuigan, Secretary to the Special Education Appeals Tribunal, Hilary Mc Laughlin of the Department of Education; G. I Millar of Translink, Chris Moffat, Stanley Smith (formerly of the Department of Education for Northern Ireland) Nadine Kirke of IPSEA. I would also like to thank former students who provided me with research assistance. In particular, I am grateful to Ryan Williams, Grainne McKeever and Louise Smylie. Thanks are also due to my "Education, the Law and Children's Rights" class on the Masters in Education degree offered by the Graduate School of Education at Queen's University who, in the spring of 2000, offered me an honest insight into what it was like to be a hard-working and conscientious teacher struggling to keep yourself within the boundaries of legality. Their perspective and questions prompted many useful last minute amendments to the text. Finally, my thanks are to my family who have had to endure the long book's long gestation: to James whose birth inspired my interest in education law; to Ellen who arrived in the middle of it all; and to Paul who is always there for me.

The law is as stated on the 28 October 2000. Any errors which may remain in the text are my own.

Laura Lundy
November 2000

CONTENTS

Preface vii
Table of Cases xiii
Table of Legislation and Rules xvii
Abbreviations xxxii

CHAPTER 1 **EDUCATION LAW IN NORTHERN IRELAND - AN ANALYSIS AND OVERVIEW** 1
    INTRODUCTION 1
    INFLUENCE OF EDUCATIONAL POLICY IN GREAT BRITAIN 2
    DISTINCTIVE ELEMENTS OF THE NORTHERN IRELAND EDUCATION SYSTEM 4
    FACTORS WHICH IMPACT ON EDUCATIONAL POLICY IN NORTHERN IRELAND 8
    EDUCATION LAW UNDER DEVOLUTION 11
    SCRUTINY AND CHALLENGE UNDER THE NORTHERN IRELAND ACT 1998 13
    THE DOMESTIC LEGAL FRAMEWORK 22
    INTERNATIONAL OBLIGATIONS 26

CHAPTER 2 **THE NORTHERN IRELAND SCHOOL SYSTEM** 35
    INTRODUCTION 35
    ORGANISATIONS WITH A STATUTORY REMIT 36
    CATEGORIES OF SCHOOL IN NORTHERN IRELAND 41
    FORMS OF EDUCATIONAL PROVISION 43
    DUTY TO PROVIDE SUFFICIENT SCHOOLS 44
    PROVISION OF EDUCATION OTHERWISE THAN AT SCHOOL 48
    PROPOSALS FOR CHANGES IN SCHOOLS 49
    DISCRIMINATION IN THE PROVISION OF SCHOOLS 54
    ACCOUNTABILITY 58

CHAPTER 3 **SCHOOL GOVERNMENT** 65
    INTRODUCTION 65
    COMPOSITION OF THE BOARD 68
    METHOD OF APPOINTMENT 69
    ELIGIBILITY FOR APPOINTMENT 76
    DURATION AND TERMINATION OF APPOINTMENTS 77
    OPERATION OF THE BOARD 77
    FUNCTIONS OF THE BOARD 82
    GOVERNORS' RESPONSIBILITY FOR FINANCE 84
    LEGAL STATUS 89
    DISPUTES WITH EDUCATION AND LIBRARY BOARDS AND/OR THE DEPARTMENT 90

CHAPTER 4 **ADMISSIONS** 91
    INTRODUCTION 91
    INFORMATION ON ADMISSIONS 95

NORMAL AGE OF ADMISSION TO PRIMARY AND SECONDARY
SCHOOLS 95
LEGAL REGULATION OF THE NUMBERS OF PUPILS ATTENDING
EACH GRANT-AIDED SCHOOL 97
SIGNIFICANCE OF PARENTAL PREFERENCE........................... 99
PROCEDURE FOR ADMISSION 100
DUTY TO DRAW UP ADMISSION CRITERIA 102
SPECIFIC ADMISSIONS CRITERIA 105
RESTRICTIONS ON CRITERIA IN NURSERY SCHOOLS 116
RESTRICTIONS ON CRITERIA IN PRIMARY SCHOOLS 116
RESTRICTIONS ON CRITERIA IN SECONDARY SCHOOLS 117
RESTRICTIONS ON CRITERIA IN GRAMMAR SCHOOLS 119
ADMISSION OF CHILDREN WITH DISABILITIES 123
ADMISSION APPEAL TRIBUNALS 123
OTHER COMPLAINTS ABOUT ADMISSIONS 127

CHAPTER 5 THE CURRICULUM 129
INTRODUCTION 129
THE CURRICULUM IN GRANT-AIDED SCHOOLS 132
EXEMPTIONS FROM THE NORTHERN IRELAND CURRICULUM 137
SEX EDUCATION 140
IRISH LANGUAGE 143
DISCRIMINATION IN THE CURRICULUM 147
POLITICAL/CULTURAL ISSUES 149
RELIGIOUS EDUCATION IN THE CURRICULUM 149
CHARGING FOR THE CURRICULUM 154
PROVISION OF INFORMATION ON INDIVIDUAL PUPIL'S
ACHIEVEMENT 161
PUPIL RECORDS 163
THE CURRICULUM COMPLAINTS TRIBUNAL 165
INSPECTIONS 169
TARGET SETTING 170
REDRESS FOR POOR QUALITY EDUCATION 171

CHAPTER 6 SECURING EDUCATION: SCHOOL ATTENDANCE OR OTHERWISE 173
INTRODUCTION 173
REGISTRATION AND THE MONITORING OF ATTENDANCE 175
PARENTAL DUTY TO SECURE THE CHILD'S EDUCATION 177
REGULAR ATTENDANCE AT SCHOOL 179
EDUCATION AT HOME 183
FAILURE TO COMPLY WITH THE PARENTAL DUTY TO SECURE
EDUCATION 185
ATTENDANCE ORDERS 187
CRIMINAL PROSECUTION 189
EDUCATION SUPERVISION ORDERS 190
CARE ORDERS 194
GENERAL PRINCIPLES TO BE CONSIDERED WHEN MAKING EDUCATION
SUPERVISION ORDER AND CARE ORDERS 195

CHAPTER 7 DISCIPLINE 199
INTRODUCTION 199
GENERAL LEGAL PRINCIPLES 201
THE SCHOOL'S STATEMENT ON DISCIPLINE 204
ACTIONS GIVING RISE TO DISCIPLINARY MEASURES 206
DETERMINING WHAT IS UNACCEPTABLE BEHAVIOUR 206

INVESTIGATING AN INCIDENT OF MISBEHAVIOUR 208
PARTICULAR FORMS OF DISCIPLINE 213
EXCLUSIONS 219
GROUNDS FOR EXCLUSION 220
SUSPENSIONS 223
EXPULSIONS 224
EXPULSION APPEAL TRIBUNAL 226
EDUCATIONAL ARRANGEMENTS FOR EXPELLED PUPILS 227
DISCIPLINARY RECORD 229
PROVISION FOR CHILDREN WITH BEHAVIOURAL DIFFICULTIES 229
INDEPENDENT SCHOOLS 230

CHAPTER 8 SPECIAL EDUCATIONAL NEEDS 233
INTRODUCTION 233
LEGAL RESPONSIBILITIES 236
DEFINITION OF SPECIAL EDUCATIONAL NEED 239
THE CODE OF PRACTICE 242
IDENTIFICATION OF CHILDREN WITH SPECIAL
   EDUCATIONAL NEEDS 245
STATUTORY ASSESSMENT... 246
THE STATEMENT 251
PROCEDURE FOR MAKING A STATEMENT 252
FORM AND CONTENT OF THE STATEMENT 255
CHANGES TO THE STATEMENT: REVIEW, AMENDMENT AND
   TERMINATION 256
SPECIAL EDUCATIONAL NEEDS TRIBUNAL 257
APPEAL FROM THE TRIBUNAL 265
CHILDREN FOR WHOM NO STATEMENT IS MAINTAINED 266
THE RESOURCE ISSUE 268
ACTIONS FOR NEGLIGENCE 271
ASSISTANCE WITH EDUCATION AT NON GRANT-AIDED SCHOOLS . 274

CHAPTER 9 INTEGRATED EDUCATION 277
DEFINITION 277
INTRODUCTION 278
CATEGORIES OF INTEGRATED SCHOOL 282
PROCEDURE FOR ACQUIRING INTEGRATED STATUS 284
MANAGEMENT ISSUES SPECIFIC TO AN INTEGRATED SCHOOL 294

CHAPTER 10 SCHOOL TRANSPORT 297
INTRODUCTION 297
OBLIGATION TO PROVIDE FREE TRANSPORT 300
TYPE OF PROVISION WHICH MUST BE MADE 308
WITHDRAWAL OF ASSISTANCE 311
COMPLAINTS 314

Appendix 315
Index 317

TABLE OF CASES

Albert and Le Compte v Belgium (1983) 13 EHRR 415 .... 1.57
Armagh District Council v Fair Employment Agency [1983] NI 346 .... 1.37
Associated Provincial Picture Houses Ltd v Wednesbury Corporation
  [1948] 1 KB 223 .... 7.09
B and G, Re [1985] FLR 493 .... 6.27
Belfast Port Employers' Association v Fair Employment Commission
  [1994] NIJB 36 (CA) 1.37
Belgian Linguistic Case, The (1968) 1 EHRR 252 ....
  .... 1.51, 1.52, 1.58, 2.36, 5.37, 9.04
Bevan v Shears [1911] 2 KB 936 .... 6.26
Bolam v Friern Hospital Management Committee [1957] 1 WLR 582 .... 8.99
Bostock v Kay, *The Times*, 20 April 1989 .... 3.33
Bradbury v London Borough of Enfield [1967] 1 WLR 1311 .... 2.52, 2.70
Brungate v ILEA [1989] 2 All ER 417 .... 3.17, 3.19, 3.24
Campbell and Cosans v United Kingdom (1982) EHRR 293 ....
  .... 1.51, 1.53, 1.54, 1.60, 5.11, 6.23, 7.02, 7.07, 7.10, 7.33
Cecil, *In re*, unreported, 27 January 1989, High Court NI ....
  .... 1.37, 2.34, 2.35, 2.38, 2.72, 2.80, 5.51
Christmas v Hampshire CC [1998] ELR 1 .... 8.98
Cleary v Booth [1929] 2 KB 416 .... 7.21
Collins v Willcock [1984] 1 WLR 1172 .... 7.33
Costello and Roberts v UK (1995) 24 EHRR 238 .... 7.77
Crump v Gilmore [1969] 68 LGR 56 .... 6.39
Cunningham, *In re*, unreported, 25 August 1995, High Court NI ....
  .... 4.34, 4.75, 4.76, 4.77, 4.78, 4.87, 4.91
DPP v G, *The Times*, 24 November 1997 .... 7.26
DJMS (a minor), Re [1977] 3 All ER 582 .... 6.42, 6.53
Daly, *In re*, unreported, 5 October 1990, High Court NI ....
  .... 1.37, 2.59, 2.80, 9.05, 9.09, 9.38
Dutch Sex Education Case, The (1976) 1 EHRR 711 .... 1.51, 1.54, 1.59
EOC's Application (No. 2), *In re* [1988] NI 44 .... 2.80, 4.40
Essex CC v B [1993] 1 FLR 866 .... 6.45, 6.48, 6.55, 6.57
Fagan v Metropolitan Police Commissioner [1969] 1 QB 439 .... 7.35
Farren, *In re* [1990] NIJB 72 or [1990] NI 70 .... 4.31, 4.32, 4.91, 4.95
Fenton, *In re*, unreported, September 2000, High Court NI 4.35, 4.50, 4.61
George v Devon CC [1988] 3 All ER 1002 ....
  .... 6.19, 10.01, 10.09, 10.19, 10.20, 10.21, 10.29
Gillick v West Norfolk and Area Health Authority [1986] 1 AC 112 .... 5.31
Graeme v United Kingdom (1990) 64 DR 158 .... 1.56
Gribbon's Application, *In re* [1990] NI 15 .... 2.79, 4.47
H v United Kingdom (1984) 37 DR 105 .... 6.02, 6.23, 6.28
H (minors) (Sexual Abuse: Standard of Proof), Re [1996] AC 563 .... 7.26
Hares v Curtin [1913] 2 KB 328 .... 10.10, 10.26
Harris v Gwent CC, unreported, 6 April 1995 .... 10.28
Hinchley v Rankin [1961] 1 All ER 692 .... 6.07
Holmes, *In re*, unreported, 27 September 1991, High Court NI ....
  .... 4.06, 4.33, 4.47, 4.83, 4.90
Jacques v Oxfordshire CC (1967) LGR 440 .... 10.27
James v Eastleigh Borough Council [1990] 2 All ER 607 .... 1.37

Jenkins v Howells [1949] KB 218 .... 6.16, 6.17
Joyce v Dorset County Council, unreported, 25 January 1996 .... 8.83
Kean, *In re*, [1997] NIJB 109 .... 2.76, 2.78, 7.25, 7.50, 7.58, 7.59
Kerr, *In re*, unreported, 31 July 1996 .... 4.75, 4.79, 4.94
Kjelsden, Busk Masden and Peterson v Denmark (1976) EHRR 711 ....
.... 1.54, 5.21, 5.30, 5.45
L v Salford CC [1998] ELR 28 .... 8.59
Lagan College, *In re*, unreported, 1992, High Court NI 2.78, 4.29, 4.69
McAteer v DENI 10.17
McGurk, *In re*, [1992] 11 NIJB 10 .... 4.83, 4.90, 4.95
McIntyre v United Kingdom (1998) Application No. 29046/95 .... 8.11
Mandla v Lee (Dowell) [1983] 1 All ER 1062 .... 4.45, 5.42, 7.20
Mansell v Griffin [1908] 1 KB 160 .... 7.07, 7.08, 7.43
Martin's Application, *In re*, unreported, 8 May 2000, High Court NI ....
.... 5.38, 10.01, 10.08
Meade v Haringey LBC [1979] 2 All ER 1016 .... 2.33, 2.71
Moore, *In re*, [1994] NIJB 111 (CA) 2.78, 4.06, 4.22, 4.23, 4.52, 4.64, 4.67-4.68
Moore, *In re*, [1994] NIJB 99 (High Court NI) 4.32, 4.35, 4.51, 4.68
Noble v ILEA (1984) 83 LGR 291 .... 3.32
O (a minor) *In re* [1992] WLR 912 .... 6.52, 6.53, 6.55
Patton, *In re*, unreported, 30 September 1994, High Court NI 4.33, 4.95, 9.37
Phelps v London Borough of Hillingdon, Anderton v Clyde CC,
  G (a minor), *In re*, Jarvis v Hampshire CC, unreported, 27 July 2000 (HL) ....
.... 5.101, 8.98, 8.99, 8.100, 8.101, 8.102
Phelps v London Borough of Hillingdon [1998] ELR 38 (High Court) 8.98
  [1998] ELR 587 (CA) 8.98, 8.99, 8.100
Phillips v Brown, unreported (1980) 6.28
PD v United Kingdom (1989) 62 DR 292 .... 1.54, 8.67
R v Bedfordshire County Council, *ex parte* DE, unreported, 1 July 1996 ....
.... 10.13, 10.21
R v Brent London Borough Council, *ex parte* Gunning [1985] 84 LGR 168 .... 2.44
R v Buckinghamshire CC, *ex parte* Milton Keynes [1997] Admin LR 158 .... 2.44
R v Camden LBC, *ex parte* H, *The Times*, 15 August 1996 .... 7.24, 7.50, 7.51, 7.53
R v Cheshire CC, *ex parte* C, *The Times*, 1 August 1997 .... 8.105
R v Cleveland CC, *ex parte* Commission for Racial Equality ....
  [1993] 1 FCR 597 .... 2.62, 4.45
R v Coupland, unreported, 7 June 1996 .... 8.59
R v DENI, *ex parte* Campbell College [1982] NI 123 .... 2.50, 2.53, 2.54, 2.79
R v Dunraven School , *ex parte* B [2000] ELR 156 .... 7.25, 7.26, 7.29
R v Dyfed CC, *ex parte* S [1995] 1 FCR 143 .... 10.01, 10.13, 10.16
R v East Sussex CC, *ex parte* Tandy [1998] ELR 80 .... 2.39, 8.95, 8.96
R v East Sussex CC, *ex parte* D unreported, 15 March 1991 .... 10.13
R v Essex CC, *ex parte* C [1994 Fam Law 128 .... 10.01, 10.13, 10.14, 10.18
R v Essex CC, *ex parte* Bullimore, unreported, 26 March 1999 .... 10.01, 10.39
R v Fernhill Manor School, *ex parte* A [1993] 1 FLR 620 .... 2.24, 7.75, 7.76
R v Gloucestershire CC, *ex parte* Barry [1997] 2 All ER 1 .... 8.93, 8.94, 8.95, 8.96
R v Governing Body of Irlam and Cadishead Community High School, ...
  ex parte Salford CC, unreported (1992) 9.23
R v Governors of St Gregory's RC Aided High School, *ex parte* M, ...
  The Times, 27 January 1994 .... 7.08, 7.17, 7.51
R v Governors of London Oratory, *ex parte* Regis, *The Times*,
  17 February 1988 .... 7.03, 7.22, 7.25, 7.62, 7.63
R v Governors of Small Heath School, *ex parte* Birmingham CC,
  The Times, 14 August 1989 .... 3.33, 9.16
R v Gwent CC, *ex parte* Perry [1985] 129 Sol J 737 .... 6.25, 6.29

R v Hampshire Education Authority, *ex parte* J [1985] 84 LGR 547.................................
....8.14, 8.16, 8.67
R v Hereford and Worcester CC, *ex parte* P [1992] 2 FLR 207.................10.24. 10.25
R v Hillingdon LBC, *ex parte* Governing Body of Queensmead School,....................
[1997] ELR 331 ....8.93, 8.94
R v Hopley [1860] 2 F&F 202 ....7.08, 7.11
R v ILEA, *ex parte* Ali [1990] COD 317 ....2.33
R v Kent, *ex parte* W [1995] ELR 362 ....8.105
R v Lancashire CC, *ex parte* M [1989] FLR 279 ....8.18
R v London Borough of Newham, *ex parte* X, *The Times*, 15 November 1994............
....7.21, 7.51, 7.71, 10.37
R v London Borough of Sutton, unreported (1986)...2.43
R v Neale, *ex parte* S [1995] ELR 198 ....7.54
R v Newport Salop Justices, *ex parte* Wright [1929] 2 KB 416.................................
....7.07, 7.08, 7.10, 7.21, 10.37
R v Northampton CC, *ex parte* Gray, *The Times*, 10 June 1986 ....3.18
R v Northamptonshire CC, *ex parte* K [1994] ELR 397...2.58
R v Oxfordshire CC, *ex parte* W, *The Times*, 12 November 1986.............................8.18
R v Rahman [1985] 81 Cr App R 340 ....7.38
R v Rochdale Metropolitan B C, *ex parte* Schemet [1993] 91 LGR 425 ....
....10.13, 10.14, 10.18, 10.35
R v Roman Catholic Schools, *ex parte* S [1998] ELR 304 ....7.23, 7.30
R v Rotherham MBC, *ex parte* Clark and others [1998] ELR 152...........................4.22
R v Secretary of State for Education, *ex parte* Chance, unreported, 1982.............2.70
R v Secretary of State for Education, *ex parte* Cumbria CC....................................
[1994] ELR 220 ....2.43
R v Secretary of State for Education, *ex parte* R and D [1994] ELR 495...............5.48
R v Secretary of State for Education and Employment, *ex parte* E
[1996] ELR 312 ....8.18
R v Secretary of State for Education and Science, *ex parte* E..................................
[1992] 1 FLR 377..8.07, 8.48, 8.58, 8.67
R v Secretary of State for Education and Science, *ex parte* Keating ....
[1985] 84 LGR 469 ....2.58
R v Secretary of State of Education and Science, *ex parte* Lashford
[1988] 1 FLR 72..8.67
R v Secretary of State for Education and Science, *ex parte* Russell, unreported,
28 June 1983 ....2.41
R v SENT, *ex parte* South Glamorgan [1996] ELR 326...8.83
R v SENT, *ex parte* F [1996] ELR 213...8.83
R v South Glamorgan Appeals Committee, *ex parte* Evans, unreported, ...
10 May 1984 ....4.23
R v Staffordshire CC, *ex parte* A, *The Times*, 29 August 1996...............................7.71
R v Stoke Newington School, *ex parte* M, unreported 7.63
R v Surrey CC, *ex parte* H [1983] LGR 219.......................................8.05, 8.53, 8.92
R v Surrey CC, *ex parte* P [1997] ELR 516..8.91
R v Surrey Quarter Sessions Appeals, *ex parte* Tweedie [1963] LGR 464............6.28
R v Taylor, *The Times*, 28 December 1983..7.08
R v Turnbull [1977] QB 244...7.30
Rogers v Essex County Council [1986] 3 All ER 321............6.17, 6.18, 10.01, 10.10
Rootkin v Kent [1981] 2 All ER 227...10.32, 10.33
Russell v London Borough of Kingston [1996] ELR 400..8.83
S v SENT [1995] 1 WLR 1627 ....4.94, 8.83, 8.84, 8.105
S and C v SENT [1997] ELR 242 ....8.82
SP v United Kingdom (1997) 23 EHRR 139 ....8.67
Salomon v Commissioners of Customs and Excise [1966] 3 All ER 871..............1.50

Scullion, *In re*, unreported, 1995, High Court NI 2.46
Secretary of State for Education and Science *v* Tameside Metropoliton Borough ....
  [1976] 3 All ER 665 .... 2.35, 2.70
Shaxted *v* Ward [1954] 1 All ER 336 .... 10.10
Simpson *v* United Kingdom (1989) 64 DR 188 .... 1.52, 1.57, 8.67, 8.106
Smith *v* LEA [1978] 1 All ER 411 .... 2.35
Smith *v* Safeway [1996] IRLR 456 .... 7.19
Spears *v* Warrington Corporation [1954] 1 QB 61 .... 7.19
Surrey CC *v* Ministry of Education [1953] 1 All ER 705 .... 10.26
T and M, *Re* [1995] ELR 1 .... 5.50
Terrington *v* Lancashire CC, 26 June 1986 .... 7.31
Tinker *v* Des Moines Independent Community School District (1960) ....
  393 US 503 .... 7.20
Trainor, *In re* unreported, 28 August 1996, High Court NI 4.73, 4.75, 4.77, 4.93
Tucker, *In re* [1995] NI 14 .... 4.31, 4.75, 4.91, 4.93
Tyrer *v* UK (1992) 17 EHRR 1 .... 7.43
Valsamis *v* Greece (1997) 24 EHRR 294 .... 1.51, 1.55, 1.59
W and DM *v* United Kingdom (1984) 37 DR 96 .... 1.53, 1.56, 6.23
Walsh, *In re*, unreported, 8 May 2000, High Court NI 2.48
Warwick *v* UK (1986) 60 DR 5 .... 7.43
Watt *v* Kesteven CC [1955] 1 All ER 473 .... 2.71
X *v* Bedfordshire CC [1995] 3 All ER 353 .... 5.101, 8.05, 8.25, 8.97
X *v* United Kingdom (1978) 14 DR 179 .... 1.60
X, Y and Z *v* Germany (1982) 29 DR 224 .... 1.53
Y *v* UK (1992) 17 EHRR 238 .... 7.43, 7.77

TABLE OF LEGISLATION AND RULES

Children and Young Person Act 1968
   s 74 (1)(c) 6.50
Children (NI) Order 1995 .... 1.38, 1.42, 6.04, 9.20
   art 2 .... 6.53
   art 3 .... 6.43, 6.45, 6.51
   art 3(1) 6.54
   art 3(3) 6.54, 6.55
   art 3 (5) 6.53, 6.57
   art 6 .... 7.07
   art 8 .... 5.31
   art 50 .... 6.52
   art 50(1) 6.53
   art 50(3) 6.53
   art 55 .... 1.42
   art 55(1) 6.44
   art 55(2) 6.45
   art 55(3) 6.45
   art 55(6) 6.47
   art 55(7) 6.44
   art 128 .... 1.42, 6.11
   art 130 .... 6.44
   art 131 .... 6.41, 6.44
   Sch 4 .... 6.47
   Sch 4, para 4 .... 6.50
   Sch 4, para 5 .... 6.50
   Sch 4, para 6 .... 6.49, 6.50
   Sch 4, para 7 .... 6.50
   Sch 4, para 7 (1)(c) 6.50
   Sch 4, para 7(2) 6.50
   Sch 4, para 8 .... 6.50
   Sch 4, para 9 .... 6.50
   Sch 10 .... 6.41
Commissioner for Complaints (NI) Order 1996
   art 7 .... 2.73
Data Protection Act 1998 .... 5.86, 7.72
Departments (NI) Order 1999
   art 3 (7) 1.18
Disability Discrimination Act 1995 .... 1.31, 4.56, 4.85, 5.43
   s 29 .... 4.85, 5.43
   Sch 8, para 15 .... 4.85
Education Act (Ireland) 1831 .... 1.02
Education Act (NI) 1923 .... 3.10, 3.12
   s 2 .... 2.07
   s 14 .... 1.09
   s 15 .... 1.09
   s 26 .... 5.47
   s 27 .... 5.47
   s 28 .... 5.47
   s 30 .... 10.04
Education Act (NI) 1930 .... 3.03, 3.10, 5.47

s 4 (3) 5.54
s 4 (5) 5.49
s 5 .... 5.54
Education Act 1944 .... 1.34, 5.46
   s 39(2)(b) 6.23
Education Act 1993 .... 1.43, 8.01
   s 241 .... 5.33
Education Act 1996 .... 1.38
   s 19 .... 2.39
   s 35 .... 2.43
   s 186 .... 9.16, 9.21
   s 189(6) 9.19
   s 192 .... 9.22
   s 346 .... 9.14
   ss 353-376 .... 5.02
   s 354(1)(b) 5.39
   s 354(2)(d) 5.39
   s 354(5) 5.39
   s 403 .... 5.33
   s 404 .... 5.33
   s 405 .... 5.33
   s 406 .... 5.45
   s 407 .... 5.45
   s 411 .... 4.23
   s 509 .... 10.02
   s 573(5) 2.50
Education Act (NI) 1947 .... 3.12, 5.01
Education Act 1997 .... 7.05
   s 154(3)(b) 7.15
   s 154(7)(a) 7.14
Education and Libraries (NI) Order 1972 .... 1.38, 1.39, 2.09, 3.12, 5.47, 8.01
   art 3 .... 2.07, 2.08
   art 3 (3) 2.08
   Sch 2, para 1 (1)(a) 1.07
Education (NI) Order 1976
   art 13 .... 1.09
Education (NI) Order 1984
   art 16 .... 8.01
Education and Libraries (NI) Order 1986 .... 1.39, 2.08
   art 2 .... 2.24, 2.26, 2.27, 2.29, 3.12, 3.13, 6.11, 10.08
   art 3 .... 2.07
   art 3(1)(b) 2.06
   art 4 (1) 6.02
   art 5 .... 2.11, 2.32
   art 6 .... 2.11, 2.32, 2.34, 2.35
   art 6(1) 2.34, 2.58
   art 6(3) 2.37, 7.70
   art 8 .... 4.17
   art 9A 3.26, 3.35
   art 9B(1) 3.26
   art 9B(2) 3.26
   art 9B(4) 3.26
   art 9B(5) 3.26
   art 9B(6) 3.26
   art 9C 3.27

art 9D	3.27
art 10	2.20, 3.08
art 10(2)	3.36
art 10(4)	3.23
art 11(3)(a)	3.36
art 11(3)(b)	3.36
art 12	3.23
art 13	3.28
art 13(1)	3.13
art 13(3A-D)	3.20
art 13(4)	3.24
art 13(5)	3.24
art 13(6)	3.22
art 14	2.40, 2.41, 2.47, 2.48, 9.35
art 14(1)(c)	9.35
art 14(1)(d)	2.49, 9.35
art 14(1)(e)	9.35
art 14(2)	2.42
art 14(2)(d)	2.49
art 14(3)	2.42
art 14(5)	2.42, 2.43
art 14(6)(a)	2.43
art 14(6)(b)	2.43
art 14(6)(c)	2.43
art 14(7)	2.45
art 14(9)	2.45
art 14(10)	2.49, 2.54
art 15	2.46, 2.47
art 15(1)	2.46
art 15(2)	2.46
art 15(3)	2.46, 2.47
art 15(4)	2.47
art 16	2.48
art 16(1)	8.47
art 16(3)	2.48
art 16(4)	2.48
art 16(5)	8.48
art 16(5)(a)(ii)	8.48
art 17(6)	3.12
art 18	4.18
art 20(2)	8.30
art 21	2.34, 5.48, 9.04
art 21(1)	5.01, 5.48
art 21(2)	5.48, 5.49, 9.39
art 21(4)	5.51
art 21(5)	5.49
art 21(7)	5.49
art 22	2.34
art 22(1)	5.54
art 22(2)	5.54
art 22(4)	5.54
art 23	2.43
art 23(2)	5.90
art 25	5.49
arts 29-32	5.91
arts 29-36	8.01

art 44	5.11, 5.30, 5.45, 6.27, 10.02, 10.14
art 45	2.38 6.01, 6.10, 6.24, 6.33, 7.69, 10.02
art 45(1)	6.10
art 46	4.11, 4.12, 4.65
art 46(1)	6.12
art 46(2)	6.12, 6.13
art 46A	4.13, 4.15, 5.90
art 46A(2)	4.15
art 46A(3)	4.15
art 46A(4)	4.15
art 47	6.12
art 48	6.05
art 49	7.03, 7.47, 7.77
art 49(9)	7.67
art 49A	7.34, 7.36, 7.37
art 49(1A)	7.34, 7.77
art 52	5.38, 5.67, 6.19, 10.02, 10.07, 10.08, 10.09, 10.17, 10.20, 10.23, 10.38
art 52(1)	10.08
art 52(1)(a)	10.08
art 52(3)	10.07
art 52(4)	10.07
art 63(2)	6.20
art 100	3.60
art 101	2.61, 2.63, 2.65, 2.66, 2.70, 2.71, 2.72, 4.86, 4.87, 4.96, 5.85, 5.94, 5.98, 7.57, 7.60, 8.79, 8.89, 10.39
art 101(2)	2.66
art 101(3)	2.65
art 101(4)	2.64, 3.60, 5.94, 5.98
art 101(5)	2.67, 2.68, 5.98
art 101(6)	2.69
art 102	3.43, 5.95
art 102(1)	5.96
art 102(5)	5.96
art 102(7)	5.96
art 102(8)	5.98
art 102A	5.95, 5.97
art 102A(4)	5.97
art 102 B	5.98
art 116	1.16
Sch 1, para 2(4)	3.33
Sch 2	2.10
Sch 2, para 1(2)(b)	1.07
Sch 2, para 2(1)	1.07
Sch 2, para 2(1)(a)	2.10
Sch 4	2.20, 2.21
Sch 4, para 1	3.36
Sch 4, para 1(2)	3.29, 3.37
Sch 4, para 3(2)(A)	3.13
Sch 4, para 2(2)(a)	1.10
Sch 4, para 5	1.10
Sch 4, para 5(1)(c)	3.13
Sch 4, para 5(1)(d)	3.13
Sch 4, para 5(4)	3.16
Sch 4, para 6	3.13, 6.44
Sch 4, para 6(1)	3.13, 9.12

Sch 4, para 6(2)	3.13
Sch 4, para 6(2)(a)	3.13, 9.12
Sch 4, para 6(3)	3.13
Sch 4, para 6(4)	3.18
Sch 4, para 6(5)	3.13
Sch 4, para 7	3.19
Sch 5	1.10
Sch 5, para 1(2)	3.08, 3.26
Sch 5, para 2(1)	3.13
Sch 5, para 2(2)	3.13
Sch 5, para 2(3)	3.37
Sch 5, para 2(4)	3.18
Sch 5, para 3(2)	3.13
Sch 5, para 3(4)	3.37
Sch 5, para 4(3)	3.13
Sch 5, para 7(1)	3.12
Sch 6	2.47
Sch 6, para 1(2)	3.08
Sch 6, para 2	3.14
Sch 6, para 3(8)	3.34
Sch 6, para 4(4)(B)(ii)	3.15
Sch 6, para 5(2)(B)(i)	3.15
Sch 7, para 2(6)	3.34
Sch 11	8.64
Sch 13	10.09, 10.18
Sch 13, para 1(1)	6.28, 6.33
Sch 13, para 1(2)	6.33
Sch 13, para 1(3)	6.35
Sch 13, para 1A(2)	6.33
Sch 13, para 1B	6.37
Sch 13, para 3	6.38, 10.12, 10.23
Sch 13, para 3(1)	6.14
Sch 13, para 3(2)	6.14, 6.36, 10.02, 10.14
Sch 13, para 3(2)(a)	6.16, 6.17
Sch 13, para 3(2)(c)	6.20
Sch 13, para 3(3)	6.21
Sch 13, para 3(4)	6.21, 6.36
Sch 13, para 3(5)	6.16, 6.18
Sch 13, para 3(6)	6.14, 6.18
Sch 13, para 4	6.38
Sch 13, para 4(1)	6.44
Sch 13, para 4(6)	6.44
Sch 13, para 5(1)	6.44
Sch 13, para 6	6.41, 10.10
Sch 14	6.33
Education (No 2) Act 1986	3.02
s 44	5.45
Education (Corporal Punishment) (NI) Order 1987	7.02, 7.33
Education (NI) Order 1993	1.41
art 28	1.09, 1.17, 1.41
art 36	7.70
art 37	3.23
art 39	1.41, 7.04, 7.47
art 47	1.41, 5.90
Sch 2	2.22, 3.08, 3.12, 3.13, 3.15, 3.18, 3.36
Sch 3	2.21

Sch 4 .... 2.65, 5.91
Education (NI) Order 1996 .... 1.43, 2.75, 4.15, 8.01, 8.64
   art 3 .... 2.28, 8.13, 8.85
      art 3(2)(a) 8.14
      art 3(2)(b) 8.14
      art 3(2)(c) 8.14
      art 3(3) 8.15
      art 3(4)(a) 8.16
      art 3(6) 8.13
      art 3(7) 8.13
      art 4(1)(4) 8.19
      art 4(2) 8.19, 8.24
      art 4(3) 8.25
      art 5 .... 8.19
      art 6 .... 8.07
      art 7 .... 8.05, 8.53, 8.67, 8.91
      art 7(1) 8.11
      art 7(2) 8.11
      art 8 .... 8.05
      art 8(1)(a) 8.09
      art 8(1)(b) 8.09
      art 8(1)(c) 8.27
      art 8(2) 8.11
      art 8(3) 8.08
      art 8(4) 8.08
      art 9 .... 8.08
      art 9(3) 8.08
      art 9(4) 8.08
      art 11 .... 8.67
      art 11(1) 8.103
      art 11(3) 8.104
      art 12 .... 8.67
      art 12(1) 8.103
      art 12(2) 8.104
      art 13 .... 8.26
      art 13(3)(b) 8.26
      art 15 .... 8.28, 8.32, 8.67
      art 15(1) 8.29, 8.31, 8.51
      art 15(1)(d) 8.31
      art 15(3) 8.31
      art 15(4) 8.31
      art 16 .... 7.74, 8.57, 8.94, 8.95, 8.96
      art 16(1) 8.07, 8.67
      art 16(3) 8.57
      art 16 .... 8.85
      art 16(4)(b) 8.33
      art 17 .... 8.89
      art 17(2) 8.67
      art 17(3) 8.67
      art 18 .... 5.22, 8.67
      art 18(1) 8.67
      art 19(5)(b) 8.60
      art 20 .... 8.30
      art 20(1) 8.51
      art 20(2) 8.67
      art 20(3) 8.67

art 22(2) 8.66
art 22(2)(b) 8.66
art 22(2)(c) 8.66
art 24 .... 8.82
art 26 .... 8.103
art 27 .... 6.33
art 31 .... 4.13, 5.90
art 32 .... 7.34
art 33 .... 5.95
art 34 .... 5.12
art 35(3) 5.19
art 36 .... 9.16
art 37 .... 9.25
art 40(6) 3.58
art 42 .... 7.70
art 56 .... 4.19
Sch 1, para 4 .... 8.43
Sch 1, para 4(3) 8.43
Sch 1, para 5 .... 8.43
Sch 2, para 2 .... 8.50
Sch 2, para 3 .... 8.67
Sch 2, para 3(1) 8.52
Sch 2, para 3(2) 8.52
Sch 2, para 3(3)(b) 8.91
Sch 2, para 3(4) 8.54
Sch 2, para 4(2) 8.55
Sch 2, para 4(6) 8.55
Sch 2, para 5 .... 8.56
Sch 2, para 5(1) 8.67
Sch 2, para 6 .... 8.56
Sch 2, para 8 .... 8.62, 8.67
Sch 2, para 8(5) 8.67
Sch 2, para 9 .... 8.61
Sch 2, para 10 .... 8.61
Sch 2, para 11 .... 8.63, 8.67
Sch 2, para 11(3) 8.67
Sch 3 .... 5.13, 5.35, 5.36
Sch 3, para 3(3) 8.52
Sch 4 .... 3.58
Sch 5 .... 5.90
Education (NI) Order 1997 .... 1.44, 2.80, 4.05, 4.31
art 9(1) 4.22
art 9(2) 4.22
art 9(3) 4.22
art 10 .... 4.29, 8.49
art 10(2)(a) 4.19
art 10(3) 4.19
art 10(4) 4.19
art 11 .... 2.51, 4.17
art 12 .... 4.18
art 12(2) 4.18
art 12(3) 4.21
art 12(4) 4.21
art 12(5) 4.21
art 12(6) 4.21
art 12(7) 4.21

art 13 .... 4.24, 4.26
art 13(2) 4.26
art 13(3) 4.27, 4.86
art 13(4) 4.28, 4.85
art 13(5) 4.86
art 14 .... 4.24, 4.26
art 14(2) 4.26
art 14(3) 4.26
art 14(4) 4.26
art 14(5) 4.27, 4.86
art 14(6) 4.28, 4.85
art 14(7) 4.86
art 14(7)(a) 4.28, 4.86
art 15(1) 4.86
art 15(2) 4.86
art 15(4) 4.87
art 16 .... 4.29, 4.37
art 16(4) 4.29, 4.53
art 16(5) 4.34, 4.57
art 16(6) 4.81
art 16(8) 4.50, 4.61
art 17 .... 4.09
art 17(2) 4.09
art 17(3) 4.09
art 17(4) 4.09
art 19(2)(b) 4.19
art 21(1)(g) 4.25
art 21(2) 4.28
art 22(2) 4.27
art 23 .... 6.18, 10.07
art 23(2) 10.09
Education (NI) Order 1998 .... 1.04, 1.22, 1.45, 2.11, 2.19,
 .... 2.22, 2.23, 3.14, 3.45, 5.36, 7.05, 9.08
art 3 .... 7.12
art 3(1) 7.12
art 3(2) 7.12
art 3(2)(b) 7.12
art 3(3) 7.13
art 3(3)(a) 7.13
art 3(3)(c) 7.14
art 4 .... 7.28, 7.36
art 4(1) 7.36
art 4(3) 7.37
art 4(4) 7.37
art 5 .... 7.08, 7.38, 7.41
art 5(2)(b) 7.41
art 5(3) 5.39
art 5(3)(a) 7.39
art 5(3)(b) 7.39
art 5(3)(d) 7.39
art 6 .... 7.73
art 6(3) 7.74
art 7 .... 5.05
art 8 .... 5.05
art 9 .... 5.05
art 13 .... 3.26

art 13(1)	3.43
art 13(2)(a)	3.43
art 13(2)(b)(i)	3.43
art 14	5.99
art 14(1)	5.99
art 14(2)	5.99
art 14(4)	5.99
art 14(5)	5.99
art 15	3.40
art 16	4.18
art 16(7)	4.18
art 44	3.44
art 47	3.44
art 48	3.44
art 50	3.44
art 53	3.47
art 54(5)(a)	3.47
art 54(5)(b)	3.47
art 55(1)	3.48
art 55(4)	3.48
art 56	3.49
art 57	3.49
art 59	3.50
art 60(1)	3.51
art 60(2)	3.51
art 60(3)	3.51
art 60(6)	3.51
art 60(7)	3.51
art 60(8)	3.51
art 60(9)	3.51
art 60(10)	3.51
art 60(11)	3.51
art 61(4)	3.52
art 61(6)	3.52
art 61(7)	3.52
art 62(2)	3.53
art 62(3)	3.53
art 62(4)	3.53
art 62(6)	3.54
art 62(7)	3.54
art 62(8)	3.54
art 62(9)	3.54
art 62(10)	3.54
art 63	3.56
art 63(2)	3.56
art 63(3)	3.56
art 63(4)	3.55, 3.56
art 63(6)	3.55, 3.57
art 63(7)	3.55, 3.57
art 63(8)	3.57
art 63(9)	3.57
art 63(10)	3.57
art 86	2.37, 2.39, 8.95, 8.96
art 70(5)	3.45
art 70(6)	3.45
art 70(8)	3.45

art 86(1) 2.38
art 86(2) 2.38
art 86(5) 2.37
art 89 .... 5.38
Part VII 3.45
Education Reform Act 1988 .... 1.04, 1.06
   ss 2-4 .... 5.02
   s 2(1) 5.33
   s 7(1) 5.48
Education Reform (NI) Order 1989 .... 1.04, 1.06, 1.08, 1.15, 1.40, 2.13,
                        .... 2.65, 2.75, 3.01, 3.02, 3.04, 3.05, 4.05, 5.10, 9.03, 9.13
   art 3 .... 2.06
   art 3(a) 2.32
   art 3(b) 2.32
   arts 4-35 .... 5.90
   art 4 .... 5.09, 5.27, 5.45, 5.90
   art 5 .... 5.12, 5.21, 5.22, 5.26
   art 5(1) 5.49
   art 5(1)(a) 5.06
   art 5(2) 5.13
   art 5(6) 5.12
   art 5(6A) 5.12
   art 6 .... 5.14, 5.21, 5.22, 5.26, 8.89
   art 7(1) 5.20
   art 7(3)(a) 5.17
   art 7(3)(b) 5.16
   art 7(3)(c) 5.19
   art 7(6) 5.20
   art 8 .... 5.10, 5.21, 5.22, 5.26, 5.27
   art 10 .... 5.08
   art 10(5) 5.08
   art 11(1) 5.89
   art 11(1)(a) 5.49, 5.62
   art 11(1)(b) 5.14, 5.18, 5.62
   art 13 .... 5.49
   art 13(1)(b) 9.39
   art 14(1) 5.26
   art 14(3) 5.26
   art 14(4) 5.26
   art 14(6) 5.26
   art 15 .... 5.21
   art 16 .... 5.22
   art 17(7) 5.25
   art 17(8) 5.25
   art 17(9) 5.25
   art 21(1)(b) 4.84
   art 30 .... 5.95
   art 33 .... 2.66, 5.87, 5.88, 8.89
   art 33(2) 5.90
   art 33(4) 5.89
   art 33(8) 2.66
   art 35 .... 2.31
   art 35(2) 5.36
   art 35(6) 5.91
   art 36 .... 4.05, 6.47
   art 36(3) 4.23

art 37	6.47
art 39(a)	2.32
art 42	4.02
art 44	4.01
art 60	5.73
art 64	2.23, 2.30, 9.01, 9.04
art 66	9.01, 9.36
art 68	9.14
art 69(1)(a)	9.16
art 69(1)(b)	9.17
art 69(2)	9.17
art 69(5)	9.21
art 69(10)	9.20
art 70	9.18, 9.22
art 70(3)	9.19
art 70(4)	9.19
art 70(5)	9.19
art 70(6)	9.20
art 70(7)	9.20
art 70(8)	9.20, 9.21
art 70(11)	9.22
art 71	9.24
art 71(6)	9.25
art 71(7)	9.26
art 71(8)	9.28
art 71(12)	9.31
art 72	3.58, 9.32
art 73(3)	9.33
art 73(4)	9.33
art 73(7)	9.34
art 73(9)	9.34
art 74	9.35
art 75(1)	9.32
art 75(8)	9.32
art 75(9)	9.32
art 75(10)	9.32
art 79	9.35
art 83(1)	9.32
art 88	9.01, 9.36
art 89	2.20, 3.13, 3.16, 9.12
art 90	8.14
art 91	9.16, 9.17, 9.18
art 92(4)	9.25
art 92(5)	9.26
art 92(6)	9.27
art 92(9)	9.31, 9.32
art 93(3)	9.33
art 93(4)	9.33
art 93(7)	9.34
art 93(9)	9.34
art 93(10)	9.34
art 94	9.35
art 97	9.35
art 101	3.35
art 121	3.20
art 122	3.21

art 123	3.26, 3.35
art 124	3.26, 7.12
art 125	3.26, 3.40
art 125(2)(a)	3.40
art 126	3.42
art 127	5.74
art 127(6)	5.74
arts 128-138	5.90
art 128	5.56, 5.58, 5.59, 5.60, 5.61, 5.70, 5.72, 5.73
art 128(1)	5.60
art 128(2)	5.61, 5.62
art 128(4)(a)	5.63
art 128(4)(b)	5.64
art 128(6)	5.65
art 128(7)	5.66
art 128(8)	5.66
art 128(9)	5.68
art 128(10	5.68
art 128(11	5.63
art 129	5.56, 5.58, 5.60, 5.61, 5.72, 5.73
art 129(3)	5.68
art 129(4)	5.68
art 129(5)	5.68
art 129(6)	5.68
art 130	5.56, 5.58, 5.59, 5.60, 5.61, 5.72, 5.73
art 131	5.56, 5.57, 5.58, 5.60, 5.61, 5.72, 5.73
art 131(2)	5.57
art 131(3)	5.68
art 132	5.56, 5.72
art 133	5.56
art 134	5.56
art 135	5.56, 5.75
art 136	3.26, 5.56
art 137	5.56
art 137(1)	5.76
art 137(2)	5.76
art 141	1.08, 2.12
art 142	1.08, 2.17
art 143	1.08
art 144	1.08
art 145	1.08
art 146	1.08
arts 147-149	5.90
art 156	4.12, 4.13, 4.65, 6.12
art 158	2.63
art 173(3)	5.65
Part III	5.90
Sch 2	5.13, 5.35, 5.36
Sch 5	1.10, 2.23, 3.08
Sch 5, para 2(1)(a)	3.13
Sch 5, para 2(2)	3.12
Sch 6	5.71, 9.31
Sch 7	3.18
Sch 8, para 1(2)	2.15
Sch 8, para 1(3)	2.15, 2.16
Education Reform (Amendment) Order (NI) 1998	5.13, 5.36

European Communities Act 1972 .... 1.22, 1.25
Fair Employment (NI) Act 1976
    Part V 1.25
Fair Employment and Treatment (NI) Order 1998 .... 1.29, 1.31, 2.59, 9.40
    s 71 .... 1.35
    s 71(3) 1.35
Human Rights Act 1998 .... 1.22, 1.25, 1.61, 1.62
    s 1 .... 1.61
    s 3 .... 1.61
    s 4 .... 1.61
    s 6 .... 1.61
    Sch 3 .... 1.62
Judicature (NI) Act 1978
    s 18(1) 2.79
Local Government Act 1986
    s 2A 5.33
Magistrates' Courts (Children and Young Persons) Rules (NI) Order 1969 .... 5.86
Northern Ireland Act 1974
    s 1 .... 1.03
    Sch 4 .... 1.03
Northern Ireland Act 1998 .... 1.07, 1.21, 1.22, 1.25, 1.50, 1.61, 5.40
    s 4(5) 1.24
    s 6 .... 1.23
    s 6(1) 1.22
    s 6(2)(a) 1.22
    s 6(2)(b) 1.22
    s 6(2)(c) 1.22
    s 6(2)(d) 1.22
    s 6(2)(e) 1.22
    s 6(2)(f) 1.22
    s 9 .... 1.23
    s 10 .... 1.23
    s 11 .... 1.23
    s 24 .... 2.56, 2.59
    s 24(1) 1.25
    s 26 .... 1.26, 1.50, 2.56
    s 26(1) 1.26
    s 26(2) 1.26
    s 26(3) 1.26
    s 26(4) 1.26
    s 26(4)(b) 1.26
    s 29 .... 1.25
    s 42(2) 1.24
    s 69 .... 1.50
    s 69(1) 1.28
    s 69(3) 1.28, 2.56
    s 69(4) 1.28
    s 69(5) 1.30
    s 69(11)(b) 1.28
    s 70(2) 1.30
    s 70(3) 1.30
    s 71(1) 1.30
    s 72 .... 1.28
    s 73 .... 1.31
    s 74 .... 1.31
    s 75 .... 1.32, 1.34, 1.37, 2.55, 2.55, 4.38, 4.56

s 75(1)	1.33
s 75(2)	1.33
s 75(3)	1.33
s 76	1.29, 1.36, 1.37, 2.59, 4.37, 4.38, 9.38
s 76(2)	1.36
s 76(5)	1.36
s 76(7)	1.36
s 98(1)	1.26
s 98(4)	1.37
s 98(5)	1.37
s 134	1.23
s 143	1.23
Part VIII	1.23
Sch 3	1.27
Sch 9, para 1	1.34
Sch 9, para 3	1.34
Sch 9, para 4	1.34
Sch 9, para 10	1.34
Sch 9, para 11	1.34
Sch 9, para 11(1)(b)	1.34
Northern Ireland Constitution Act 1973	1.16, 2.72
s 17	1.37, 2.59
s 19	1.29, 1.37, 2.59, 4.37, 4.38
Ombudsman (NI) Order 1996	
art 8	2.73
Police and Criminal Evidence (NI) Order 1989 (PACE)	7.26
Race Relations (NI) Order 1997	1.31, 7.20
art 3	4.45
art 5	2.62
art 5(3)	5.42
art 18	2.61, 5.42
art 18(1)	4.45
art 19	2.61, 5.42
art 20	2.61, 5.42
art 20(2)	2.61
art 20(3)	2.61
Road Traffic (NI) Order 1981	10.28
Road Traffic (NI) Order 1991	
art 3	10.28
Rules of the Supreme Court (NI) (Amendment) Order 1999	
art 7	8.82
School Standards and Framework Act 1998	1.04, 1.05, 1.22, 5.05
Sex Discrimination (NI) Order 1976	1.31, 7.49
art 24	2.57, 4.40, 5.41, 7.19
art 24(a)	4.41
art 24(b)	4.41
art 25	2.57, 2.58, 4.40
art 26	2.57
art 27(1)	4.42
art 27(2)	4.42
art 28	4.43
art 40	4.40
Theft Act (NI) 1969	
s 1	7.42

SECONDARY LEGISLATION

Class Sizes in Primary Schools Regulations (NI) 2000	4.18
Curriculum (Complaints Tribunal) Regulations (NI) 1992	
Sch 1	5.92
Sch 2	5.93
Sch 2, para 6	5.94
Curriculum (English in Irish-Speaking Schools) Exception Regulations (NI) 1996	5.36
Curriculum (Programme of Study and Attainment Targets in Irish in Irish-Speaking Schools at Key Stages 3 and 4) Order (NI) 1998	5.36
Education (Curriculum) (Temporary Exceptions) Regulations (NI) 1990	
reg 3(1)(a)	5.23
reg 3(1)(b)(i)	5.23
reg 3(1)(b)(ii)	5.23
reg 4	5.24
reg 5	5.24
reg 6	5.24
reg 12(1)	5.24
reg 12(2)	5.24
reg 12(3)	5.24
reg 12(4)	5.24
Education (Groups of Grant-Maintained Schools) Regulations 1994	9.14
Education (Individual Pupil's Achievements) Information Regulations (NI) 1998	5.77
reg 5(2)	5.77
reg 6(3)	5.80
reg 6(4)	5.80
reg 7(1)(d)	5.78
reg 7(2)	5.78
reg 8(1)	5.78, 5.79
reg 8(2)	5.78, 5.79
reg 9(1)	5.79
reg 9(2)	5.79
reg 10	5.80
reg 11(1)	5.81
reg 11(2)	5.81
reg 11(3)	5.81
Sch 1	5.79
Sch 2	5.79
Sch 3	5.79
Sch 4	5.80
Sch 5	5.79, 5.80
Sch 6	5.80
Sch 7	5.80
Sch 8	5.80
Education (National Curriculum) (Attainment Targets and Programmes of Study in Welsh) Order 1995	5.39
Education (Pupil Records) Regulations (NI) 1998	5.82, 7.72
reg 3	5.82
reg 6(1)(c)	5.83
reg 6(1)(d)	5.82
reg 6(2)	5.82
reg 6(3)	5.82
reg 6(4)	5.83
reg 7 (3)	5.84

reg 8.. 5.85
reg 10.. 5.86
Sch 1... 5.82
Sch 2... 5.82
Education (Pupil Registration) Regulations (NI) 1995
   reg 9(1)(c)... 6.25
Education (Registration and Attendance of Pupils) Regulations (NI) 1974 .... 6.05
   reg 4... 6.06
   reg 5... 6.06
   reg 6...
   reg 6(1)... 6.06
   reg 6(3)... 6.06
   reg 7... 6.06
   reg 8... 6.08
   reg 9... 6.08
   reg 14... 6.29
   reg 18... 6.08
Education (School Government) Regulations 1989................................3.25, 3.33
Education (School Information and Prospectuses) Regulations (NI) 1993
   reg 10 (g).. 6.09
Education (Special Educational Needs) Regulations 1994
   reg 11...8.30, 8.45
   reg 14... 8.56
   reg 14 (5)... 8.62
Education (Special Educational Needs) Regulations (NI) 1997
   reg 4(3).. 8.30
   reg 5... 8.51
   reg 5(1).. 8.32
   reg 5(1)(c)... 8.40
   reg 5(1)(e)... 8.40
   reg 5(2).. 8.33
   reg 5(3).. 8.33
   reg 5(4).. 8.33
   reg 5(5).. 8.33
   reg 6(5).. 8.37
   reg 8... 8.41
   reg 9... 8.44
   reg 9A(1)... 8.51
   reg 9A(2)... 8.51
   reg 9A(3)... 8.51
   reg 9A(4)... 8.40
   reg 9A(5)... 8.40
   reg 10... 8.50
   reg 13... 8.60
   reg 14... 8.60
   reg 15... 8.60
   Sch Part A... 8.50
   Sch Part B... 8.57
Education (Special Educational Needs) (Amendment) Regulations (NI) 1998
   reg 2...8.40, 8.51
Education (Target-Setting in Schools) Regulations (NI) 1998
   reg 3... 5.100
   reg 4... 5.100
   Sch 1... 5.100
   Sch 2, para 1... 5.100
   Sch 2, para 2... 5.100

Sch 2, para 3	5.100
Sch 2, para 4	5.100
Grammar Schools (Charges) Regulations (NI) 1992	5.72
reg 4	5.73
reg 4(4)	5.73
reg 5	5.74
Grammar Schools (Charges (Amendment) Regulations (NI) 1995	5.72
Pre-School Education in Schools (Admissions Criteria) Regulations (NI) 1998	4.62
Pre-School Education in Schools (Admissions Criteria) (Amendment) Regulations (NI) 1999	4.62
Primary Schools (Admissions Criteria) Regulations (NI) 1997	4.63
reg 4(d)	4.65
reg 5	4.54, 4.64
Public Service Vehicles (Carrying Capacity) Regulations (NI) 1995	
reg 61(2) (b)	10.28
Registration and Attendance of Pupils Regulations (NI) 1974	
reg 6	6.25
Road Vehicles Lighting (Amendment) Regulations (NI) 1995	
reg 17	10.28
Road Vehicles Lighting (Amendment) Regulations (NI) 1997	
reg 4	10.28
Rules of the Supreme Court (NI)1980	
ord 53	2.77
ord 55	8.83
ord 56	8.82
ord 94	8.82
School Admissions (Appeal Tribunals) Regulations (NI) 1998	
Sch 1, para 1	4.88
Sch 1, para 2	4.88
Sch 1, para 3	4.88
Sch 1, para 4	4.88
Sch 1, para 5	4.88
Sch 1, para 6	4.88
Sch 1, para 7	4.88
Sch 2, para 1	4.89
Sch 2, para 3	4.89
Sch 2, para 4	4.89
Sch 2, para 6	4.89
Sch 2, para 7	4.89
Sch 8	4.93
Sch 8, para 9	4.93
Schools (Expulsion of Pupils) (Appeal Tribunals) Regulations (NI) 1994	7.64
Sch 1	7.65
Sch 2	7.66
Sch 2, para 5	7.53
Schools (Expulsion of Pupils) (Appeal Tribunals) (Amendment) Regulations (NI) 1998	
reg 2	7.53
Schools (Suspension and Expulsion of Pupils) Regulations (NI) 1985	7.03
Schools (Suspension and Expulsion of Pupils) Regulations (NI) 1995	
reg 3	7.61, 7.69
reg 3(A)	7.55
Sch 2, para 5	7.66, 7.67
Schools (Suspension and Expulsion of Pupils) (Amendment) Regulations (NI) 1998	
reg 2	7.66, 7.67

reg 3(c) 7.55
Secondary Schools (Admissions Criteria) Regulations 1995 .... 4.05, 4.71
Secondary Schools (Admissions Criteria) Regulations (NI) 1997
.... 4.05, 4.70, 4.71, 4.83
    reg 4(a) 4.73
    reg 5 .... 4.54, 4.55
    reg 5(a) 4.66
    reg 5(a) 9(ii) 4.69
    reg 5(a) 9(iii) 4.69
    reg 5(b) 4.84
    reg 5(c) 4.55
    reg 6 .... 4.54, 4.80
Special Educational Needs (Tribunal) Regulations (NI) 1997
    reg 4 .... 8.66
    reg 7(1)(a) 8.68
    reg 7(1)(b) 8.68
    reg 7(1)(c) 8.69
    reg 7(3) 8.68
    reg 8 .... 8.71, 8.78
    reg 9 .... 8.68
    reg 11 .... 8.69
    reg 12 .... 8.70, 8.78
    reg 13 .... 8.70, 8.78
    reg 14 .... 8.70
    reg 16 .... 8.72
    reg 17 .... 8.72
    reg 17(b) 8.75
    reg 20 .... 8.72
    reg 21 .... 8.72
    reg 22 .... 8.72
    reg 23 .... 8.72
    reg 25 .... 8.73
    reg 26 .... 8.74
    reg 26(4) 8.74
    reg 27 .... 8.76
    reg 27(2) 8.73
    reg 28 .... 8.77
    reg 28 (5) 8.66
    reg 29 .... 8.78
    reg 31 .... 8.80
    reg 32 .... 8.81

INTERNATIONAL CONVENTIONS

European Convention on Human Rights
    Art 3 .... 1.59, 7.08, 7.34, 7.43, 7.77
    Art 6(1) 1.57
    Art 8 .... 1.59
    Art 9 .... 1.55, 1.57, 1.59, 5.53, 7.20
    Art 10 .... 1.59, 7.20
    Art 14 .... 1.25, 1.58, 2.56, 2.59, 4.39, 4.54, 5.40, 5.44, 5.53
    Art 34 .... 1.30
    Art 2 of First Protocol 1.25, 1.52, 1.53, 1.55, 1.56, 1.58,
    .... 1.59, 1.60, 1.62, 2.33, 2.36, 2.59, 4.54, 5.11, 5.21, 5.31,
    .... 5.40, 5.44, 5.45, 5.53, 6.02, 6.23, 6.27, 7.02,
    .... 7.10, 7.70, 8.11, 8.67, 8.106, 9.04

UNESCO Convention against Discrimination in Education
    Art 2(b) 9.04
United Nations Convention on the Rights of the Child
    Art 2 (1) 2.56
    Art 12 .... 1.48, 5.32, 5.53, 7.15, 8.42, 8.75, 9.23
    Art 14 .... 5.53
    Art 23(1) 8.10
    Art 26(1) 6.01
    Art 28 .... 1.47, 5.56
    Art 28(1)(e) 6.01
    Art 28(2) 1.47
United Nations Universal Declaration of Human Rights
    Art 26(1) 1.46
    Art 26(2) 5.11
    Art 26(3) 6.02
Treaty of Rome (EU Treaty) 1957
    Art 119 .... 1.25

ABBREVIATIONS

CCMS	Council for Catholic Maintained Schools
CI	Controlled Integrated
DE	Department of Education
DEFHETE	Department of Further and Higher Education and Training
DENI	The Department of Education for Northern Ireland
ECHR	The European Convention on Human Rights
ELB	Education and Library Board
EMU	Education for Mutual Understanding
GM	Grant-maintained
GMI	Grant-maintained integrated
LEA	Local Education Authority
NIHRC	Northern Ireland Human Rights Commission
SACHR	Standing Advisory Commission on Human Rights
SEN	Special educational needs
SENT	Special Educational Needs Tribunal
UNCRC	The United Nations Convention on the Rights of the Child
The 1986 Order	The Education and Libraries Order (NI) 1986
The 1989 Order	The Education Reform (NI) Order 1989
The 1993 Order	The Education (NI) Order 1993
The 1996 Order	The Education (NI) Order 1996
The 1997 Order	The Education (NI) Order 1997
The 1998 Order	The Education (NI) Order 1998

CHAPTER ONE

EDUCATION LAW IN NORTHERN IRELAND - AN ANALYSIS AND OVERVIEW

INTRODUCTION

1.01 The law in Northern Ireland is shaped by a number of disparate influences. These include policy developments at Westminster, the political situation in Northern Ireland, the churches, public opinion and the United Kingdom's international obligations. On different issues, different influences predominate. This chapter provides an analysis and overview of the factors which have influenced the content of education law in Northern Ireland. Undoubtedly the factor which has had the single biggest impact on the law in this jurisdiction has been educational policy in Great Britain: there are several areas where the law in Northern Ireland is virtually indistinguishable from that of its neighbouring jurisdiction.[1] However, in contrast to other areas of social provision such as social security, Northern Ireland education law is more often than not quite distinctive from England and Wales. The objectives of this chapter are: (i) to describe the influence of educational policy in Great Britain on law reform in Northern Ireland; (ii) to detail the factors which distinguish the Northern Ireland education system from that of its neighbouring jurisdiction; and (iii) to provide an analysis of the social, cultural and political factors which have influenced the development of education law in Northern Ireland.[2] The intention is to give a general overview of the factors which have shaped the law to date and to assess the impact which devolution may have on education law in Northern Ireland in the future.

1.02 The chapter concludes with a description of the key sources of education law, both national and international. The law relating to education is largely statute-based, the area always having been considered too important to leave to the vagaries of the common law.[3] The seven statutes described at the end of this chapter, along with the delegated legislation made under them, form the main body of education law. The specific content of these statutes is considered in detail in the subsequent chapters of this book along with the policy objectives which engendered the particular initiatives that they represent. The objective of the final section of this chapter is to provide a chronological description of the primary sources of legislation which will act as a point of reference for the rest of the book. The chapter finishes with an analysis of the two main international obligations which impact on education

---

[1] See, for instance, the legislative provision in relation to special educational needs, attendance and discipline.
[2] Much of this analysis is derived from a previous article by the author. Lundy, 'From Act to Order: The Metamorphosis of Education Legislation' [1998] Vol. XX(1) *Liverpool Law Review* p. 63.
[3] State education in Ireland was established by Education Act (Ireland) 1831.

law in Northern Ireland: (i) the United Nations Convention on the Rights of the Child (UNCRC) and (ii) the European Convention on Human Rights (ECHR).

INFLUENCE OF EDUCATIONAL POLICY IN GREAT BRITAIN

1.03 The major factor which has determined the content of education legislation in Northern Ireland has been policy developments in England and Wales. Since the beginning of the 1980s education has been a key issue in all elections to Westminster. There has been an unprecedented amount of change. These developments have inevitably impacted on the content of the law in Northern Ireland. At the time of writing the power to make legislation in education has been devolved to the Northern Ireland Assembly which may well chart a distinctive course.[4] However, this has not been possible during the period in which most of the legislation which is described in this book was enacted. Since the Northern Ireland Parliament was abolished in 1973, legislation for Northern Ireland on various matters including those pertaining to education has been by way of Order in Council at Westminster.[5] Debate on this legislation has been limited and possibly as a consequence of this, the general approach taken to law reform has been to reproduce the legislative proposals which had previously been adopted in Great Britain.[6] The last two decades have seen an unprecedented increase in the legislation affecting schools in the United Kingdom.[7] This legislation might be seen to have had two basic aims: first, to increase choice and parental rights in education and secondly, to transfer decision-making from local education authorities to schools.

Parental rights

1.04 Much of the educational reform of the past decade has been designed to increase the say of parents in decisions which are made about their children's schooling. Perhaps the most notable of these reforms have been the introduction of a common curriculum and the policy known as 'open enrolment' whereby parents were given a right to express a preference as to the school that they wish their child to attend. These, coupled with a series of measures aimed at giving parents greater information about their child's school and individual performance, have radically changed the expectations of parents and therefore the culture in which most schools operate.[8] Each of the statutory initiatives in Great Britain soon appeared in Northern Ireland in the

---

[4] For an assessment of this, see para. 1.20.
[5] Northern Ireland Act 1974, s. 1 and Sch. 1.
[6] For a description of the legislative process and an analysis of its limitations, see Hadfield 'Legislating for Northern Ireland: Options for Reform', Annex D of the *Eighteenth Annual Report of the Standing Advisory Commission for Human Rights (1992-3)*, (1993, HMSO), pp. 111.128.
[7] For an analysis of the reforms, see Harris, 'Education reform and the law in England and Wales' (1997) 1 *Australia and New Zealand Journal of Law and Education* 3.
[8] For an analysis of the reforms see Harris, *Law and Education: Regulation, Consumerism and the Education System* (1993).

form of an Education Order: for instance the key provisions of the landmark Education Reform Act 1988 were replicated in the Education Reform (NI) Order 1989. This emphasis on parental rights has continued with the new Labour government who were elected in 1997 on a manifesto which proclaimed that their priorities were "Education, Education, Education". The new administration has taken up the mantle of parental rights, placing its focus on the quest for improved standards in schools. One of its first pieces of legislation was the School Standards and Framework Act 1998 which introduced baseline assessments for all children in primary one, school development plans and new roles for Local Education Authorities (LEAs) in the maintenance of quality. As in the past, similar proposals for Northern Ireland were introduced soon after by the Education (NI) Order 1998.

The management of schools

1.05 The second area which has seen trenchant reform has been the provisions relating to the management of schools. In England and Wales, the Conservative government introduced a series of reforms designed to reduce the influence of politically controlled LEAs (most of which had Labour majorities) by transferring responsibility to schools themselves. One of the major initiatives in this regard was the introduction of a new category of school - the grant-maintained school - to which schools could "opt out" of local authority control via a ballot of parents. While the concept of grant-maintained schools was hotly contested in Great Britain, the issue failed to excite the same controversy in Northern Ireland. This was because the original proposals to extend grant-maintained status to all schools in Northern Ireland were shelved following local objections and in the end the option was restricted to those schools wishing to attain integrated status.[9] Likewise, the recent restructuring of school categories in England and Wales introduced by the School Standards and Framework Act 1998 has not been proposed for Northern Ireland.[10] It will be seen that many of these reforms had a politically-inspired agenda which is simply not relevant in Northern Ireland's different political context. However, while the major organisational changes in Great Britain have not affected Northern Ireland's educational system, many of the attendant changes in terms of the internal management of schools have been transferred. Most notable among these were the new obligations on Boards of Governors introduced by the Education Reform (NI) Order 1989 in relation to admissions, discipline, and special educational needs as well as increased responsibility for financial management.

The impact in Northern Ireland

1.06 In many respects, it has been the norm for education law reform for Northern Ireland to begin at the point where the legislative process for England and Wales has ended. Once an Education Act was enacted at Westminster, the policy process appeared to kick-start across the Irish sea with the Department of Education for Northern Ireland (DENI) formulating similar

---

[9] See further Chapter 9.
[10] School Standards and Framework Act 1997 and the DfEE, *Excellence in Schools* (1997) Cm. 3681, Chapters 3 and 7.

proposals for Northern Ireland. The Northern Ireland proposals have been often identical to their British counterparts save for those adaptations which were necessary in view of the different administrative systems pertaining in the two jurisdictions. Thus in areas such as school attendance, discipline and special educational needs, the law in Northern Ireland is virtually identical to that in England and Wales. However, in other areas there have been a number of forces at play which have frequently resulted in the implementation of distinctively different legislative provisions.[11] For instance, three of the key educational policy reforms of the last decade have ended up distinctly different in Northern Ireland from their counterparts in England and Wales, albeit in different ways and for different reasons. The Northern Ireland curriculum was tailored from the outset to reflect the different political and cultural context pertaining in Northern Ireland.[12] The proposals for the introduction of grant-maintained schools began the same way as in England and Wales but, following the pre-legislative consultation process, were fashioned into a distinctive category of school to service a demand for a particular form of education (integrated education), which is peculiar to Northern Ireland.[13] The legislation which gave effect to open enrolment was initially identical but was forced to change following a spate of litigation involving grammar school admissions.[14] In each case, the end result is that Northern Ireland now has legislation which is distinctive from that of its neighbouring jurisdiction. The objective of the next section is to analyse some of the factors which may have facilitated or engendered these changes and to consider what changes, if any, will result under the new arrangements for the government of Northern Ireland.

DISTINCTIVE ELEMENTS OF THE NORTHERN IRELAND EDUCATION SYSTEM

Educational organisation

1.07 Under Direct Rule, DENI performed the same statutory functions as the Secretary of State for Education in England and Wales. Under the new political arrangements in the Northern Ireland Act 1998, the Department of Education ('the Department') is headed by a Minister for Education responsible to the Assembly, a position which reflects more closely the position in England and Wales. Likewise, local Education and Library Boards (ELBs) perform many of the same functions as the Local Education Authorities (LEAs) in England and Wales. The key distinction between LEAs and ELBs lies in their composition. In particular, ELBs are not subject to the same political influences as their counterparts in England and Wales. In Northern Ireland all appointments to ELBs are made by the Department. Moreover, whereas LEAs are composed of directly elected local

---

[11] A good illustration of this is the Education Reform (NI) Order 1989 which was intended to mirror many of the changes introduced in England and Wales by the Education Reform Act 1988.
[12] See Chapter 5.
[13] See Chapter 9.
[14] See Chapter 4.

representatives, legislation in Northern Ireland provides that ELBs should not have more than two-fifths of their members nominated by local district councils.[15] This measure, which was designed to ensure that no one political grouping could have overall control of an education authority, was introduced following a major review of local government in Northern Ireland in 1970.[16] The review had been planned as a tidying-up exercise but was hastened by the commencement of civil unrest and in particular allegations that unionists were using their majorities on local authorities to discriminate against the minority Catholic population of Northern Ireland.[17] Education had not been one of the major areas of concern. However, it was considered that educational administration would benefit from the same changes which were taking place throughout local government. In an effort to ensure that ELBs were broadly representative of the main sectional interests, provision was made for the representatives of the 'transferors' (the Protestant churches who had transferred their schools to the state in the 1920s and 1930s) and the trustees of maintained schools (normally the Catholic Church) authorities to have members appointed to the area boards.[18] The presence of the churches and the reduced influence of political representatives on ELBs is of some significance given that many of the Conservative reforms in Britain in the 1980s were designed to reduce the powers of LEAs on account of their tendency to reflect the political persuasion of the local council. It will be seen that, although many of these reforms were also proposed in Northern Ireland, the different political context may have affected the government's resolve to see the changes right through to the statute book.

1.08 Northern Ireland's education system can also be distinguished from England and Wales in relation to the categories of schools in operation. In England and Wales, the categories of school have seen major re-organisation. The key reform introduced by the Conservative government was the grant-maintained school, created through an election by parents to 'opt-out' of local authority control. In 1998 the Labour government restructured the categories of schools in England and Wales in a way that restored some of the influence of LEAs.[19] Similar reforms were not proposed for Northern Ireland. Until 1989 Northern Ireland had basically only two categories of school: (i) controlled schools (managed by the ELB for the area) and (ii) voluntary schools (owned and managed by trustees who are normally the local

---

[15] Education and Libraries (NI) Order 1986, Sch. 2, para.1(2)(b). The remaining members are representatives of the churches, teachers and those working in the library service.

[16] *Review Body on Local Government in Northern Ireland* (Belfast: HMSO, 1970), Cmd. 546. This is commonly referred to as the 'McCrory Report'.

[17] See further, J. Loughlin, 'Administering Policy in Northern Ireland', in *Northern Ireland: Politics and the Constitution*, ed. B. Hadfield (Buckingham: Open University Press, 1992), 66 - 69.

[18] Education and Libraries (NI) Order 1972, Sch.2, para.1(1)(a). This provision is now contained in the Education and Libraries (NI) Order 1986, Sch.2, para.2(1).

[19] See Meredith, 'The Fall and Rise of Local Education Authorities' (1998) Vol. XX(1) *Liverpool Law Review* 41.

churches).[20] There are two types of voluntary school; (i) maintained schools (which include all voluntary primary and secondary schools) and (ii) voluntary grammar schools.[21] The majority of voluntary maintained schools are controlled by the Catholic Church. In order to facilitate the management of these schools, the Education (Reform) (NI) Order 1989 transferred responsibility for all Catholic maintained schools to a statutory body, the Council for Catholic Maintained Schools (CCMS).[22] The 1989 Order also introduced a new category of school, the grant-maintained integrated school. Thus Northern Ireland has three basic categories of school: (i) controlled schools; (ii) voluntary schools; and (iii) grant-maintained integrated schools and there are no plans to radically alter these structures at present.

Religious segregation

1.09 Administrative differences aside, the most distinctive factor about Northern Ireland's school system is that it is *de facto* although not necessarily *de iure* religiously segregated. The reason for this is historical, due to a large extent to the churches' response to legislative reform in the 1920s and 1930s.[23] After the partition of Ireland in 1921, Northern Ireland's education system was subject to a major programme of administrative reform. Schools which had previously operated on a voluntary and charitable basis were offered the opportunity to transfer their capital assets to the state in order to secure full funding for both capital and maintenance.[24] Many Protestant owned schools availed of this opportunity in return for guaranteed management positions on the school Board. Today, these transferred schools constitute the controlled sector in Northern Ireland and continue to be managed under the auspices of the local Education and Library Boards. In contrast, the Catholic Church was suspicious of the new Northern Ireland state and viewed the process of transfer as a threat to Catholic education. As a result of this, Catholic schools chose to retain their voluntary status thereby receiving a reduced level of capital funding.[25] These Catholic schools, along with a smaller number of Protestant and non-denominational schools which did not transfer their assets to the state, now make up the voluntary education sector.

---

[20] Controlled schools in Northern Ireland are similar to county schools in England and Wales and should not therefore be confused with the voluntary controlled schools in the latter jurisdiction.
[21] Voluntary grammar schools are funded by a direct grant from the Department rather than through ELBs.
[22] Education Reform (NI) Order 1989, arts. 141. 146. The CCMS is under a duty to "promote the effective management and control of Catholic maintained schools" (art. 142). Voluntary grammar schools do not fall within the remit of the CCMS.
[23] For an account of this, see S. Dunn, 'A short history of education in Northern Ireland, 1920 – 1990', Annex B in the *Fifteenth Report of the Standing Advisory Committee on Human Rights (1989 - 1990)* (London: HMSO, 1990), 49-96.
[24] Education Act (NI) 1923, s.14.
[25] Voluntary schools were initially provided with 50% of their capital costs (Education Act 1923, s.15). This increased over time to 85% in 1976 (Education (NI) Order 1976, art.13). The Education (NI) Order 1993 created a new category of voluntary school which is eligible for 100% of its capital costs (art.28).

1.10 The transfer process has had two lasting effects. First, Protestant pupils generally attend controlled schools and Catholic pupils generally attend voluntary schools. The religious divisions in Northern Ireland are such that few Protestant parents will send their child to a school with a Roman Catholic ethos and few Catholic parents wish to send their child to a school attended by mainly Protestant pupils. The numbers of pupils attending each type of school are such that the school system effectively divides into two along religious lines.[26] The second consequence is that the majority of schools in Northern Ireland have a management body on which the local churches are in a majority. In the controlled sector, the largest single group of governors is the transferors' representatives (the main Protestant churches).[27] In voluntary schools, it is the trustees of the school's capital assets (usually the Catholic church).[28] Thus, with few exceptions, Boards of Governors in Northern Ireland have a significant proportion of their membership drawn from the local clergy or from those whom they have chosen to represent them.[29] It is largely through these guaranteed positions on the management committees of individual schools that the churches in Northern Ireland have been able to exercise a significant influence on the development of the education system and indeed the legal provisions which govern it.

Selection on ability

1.11 The third major difference in the Northern Ireland education system is that there is a selective system of education at secondary level. At the age of 11, pupils undertake a centrally organised aptitude test which is used to determine which children will attend grammar schools and which will attend non-selective secondary schools. This is officially called the transfer procedure test although it is still referred to locally as the '11 plus'. The major policy of comprehensive education which took place in England and Wales in the 1960s and 1970s failed to take hold in Northern Ireland. This can be partly attributed to the fact that, until 1972, responsibility for such a change lay with the Northern Ireland Parliament rather than Westminster. At the time when England and Wales began to introduce comprehensive schools, a Northern Ireland White Paper reiterated the arguments against the elimination

---

[26] In 1998/99 there were 545 controlled schools attended by mainly Protestant pupils and 506 Catholic maintained primary and secondary schools. There was a small number (11) of non-Catholic voluntary primary schools. There were also 54 voluntary grammar schools which include a mixture of denominational and non-denominational schools.

[27] In controlled primary and secondary schools, transferors' representatives constitute 4/9 of the total membership (Education and Libraries (NI) Order 1986, Sch. 4, para. 2(2)(a)).

[28] In voluntary maintained schools, the trustees hold 6/9 of the total membership (4/9 if the school has opted for full capital funding) (Education and Libraries (NI) Order 1986, Sch. 5).

[29] The major exception to this relates to grant-maintained integrated schools, a new category of school created by the 1989 Order. These have broken the tradition of church representation in that the largest group of governors on the Board are foundation governors who are normally the parents of pupils who worked originally to establish the school (Education Reform (NI) Order 1989, Sch.5). In controlled integrated schools, the legislation attempts to strike a balance between both religions by providing equal nomination rights to the transferors' representatives and the trustees of Catholic-maintained schools (Education and Libraries (NI) Order 1986, Sch. 4, para.5).

of selection and instead proposed a gradual move to a system where grammar schools remained but the effects of selection were minimized in the other secondary schools.[30] More radical proposals for the abolition of grammar schools appeared in the early 1970s.[31] However, it was the major upheaval in the system of government of Northern Ireland in 1972 which paved the way for renewed attempts to introduce a system of comprehensive schools. In 1976, the Labour government published a consultation document which contained firm proposals for the abolition of the selective system in Northern Ireland.[32] Interim measures were put in place for 1978-1980. However these temporary arrangements, along with the proposals for the full move to comprehensive schooling, were abandoned following the Conservative success in the 1979 general election. No further proposals were forthcoming from successive Conservative governments. New Labour did not revive the issue other than to approve the commissioning of research by DENI into the operation of selection at the age of 11. This research was published in September 2000 and it remains to be seen what approach will be taken by the new Assembly.[33]

FACTORS WHICH IMPACT ON EDUCATION LAW IN NORTHERN IRELAND

1.12 One possible explanation of the differences between education law in Northern Ireland and that in Great Britain may lie in the general public attitude towards the education system in Northern Ireland. Put simply, there is not the same level of disquiet which appears prevalent in Great Britain. Statistics bear the public confidence out. Northern Ireland has the highest levels of performances at GCSE Level in the United Kingdom as well as the lowest percentage of school leavers with no qualifications.[34] The reality is that, apart from ongoing concerns about funding, most parents in Northern Ireland are happy with the education being provided. This is partly evidenced by the lack of a sizeable independent sector in Northern Ireland. Independent schools here are generally integrated schools or Irish medium schools which are in the process of seeking public funding or schools run by independent churches. The lack of demand for a private education is indicative of the fact that educational standards in state schools are simply not perceived to be a problem by parents. Moreover, the types of disciplinary problems which

---

[30] Government of Northern Ireland, Ministry of Education, *Educational Development in Northern Ireland* (Belfast: HMSO, 1964), Cmd. 470.

[31] Ministry of Education for Northern Ireland, *A Report of the Advisory Council for Education in Northern Ireland, The Existing Selection Procedure for Secondary Schools in Northern Ireland* (Belfast: HMSO,1971), Cmd. 551. Ministry of Education for Northern Ireland, *A Report of the Advisory Council for Education in Northern Ireland, Reorganisation of Secondary Education in Northern Ireland* (Belfast: HMSO, 1973), Cmd. 574.

[32] Department of Education for Northern Ireland, *Reorganisation of Secondary Education in Northern Ireland, A Consultation Document* (London: HMSO, 1976).

[33] See further para 1.20.

[34] In Northern Ireland in 1996 51.3% of pupils achieved grades A* - C at GCSE level, compared to 43.5% in England and 40.9% in Wales. 4.4 % of pupils left school with no qualifications compared to 8.1% in England and 10.7% in Wales, *Regional Trends 32* (London: The Stationery Office, 1997), Table 4.6, p. 54.

featured so openly in England are unheard of. Although Northern Ireland's teachers report growing problems in indiscipline, concern is focused on the behaviour of individual children rather than whole schools.[35] Because of the general perception that the system is working, parents are persuaded readily by the 'if it isn't broken, don't fix it' arguments put forward by local educational bodies when faced with change.

1.13 This general sense of satisfaction has meant that there has not been the same drive for reform that has been apparent in England and Wales. The Conservatives won the 1987 general election on a manifesto which promised sweeping educational reform. They were returned in 1992 with similar promises. Labour replaced them in 1997 with its promise to make its priorities "Education, Education, Education". This political agenda is simply not apparent in Northern Ireland. The reality of the Northern Ireland political system has been that all of the parties which held seats at Westminster campaigned on the key constitutional issue: unionism or nationalism.[36] Although their election manifestos set out general commitments in relation to issues such as social security, health and education, they were all remarkably similar. Local political representatives were in an interesting position in this respect. Until now, they did not have responsibility for budget commitments or spending decisions and the tendency was for them to seek to get the most they could get for Northern Ireland. The result was that they normally presented a united front on key social issues. This was apparent in the response to plans to slim down the number of Education and Library Boards from five to four in 1997.[37] It was difficult for DENI led by a British-based politician to introduce change which was contested by all of the democratically-elected representatives in the jurisdiction. It remains to be seen whether local politicians will take different decisions on some of the issues when they are holding the purse strings at Stormont.

1.14 From a policy perspective, it has been the norm for local politicians to seek parity with the rest of the United Kingdom in most aspects of social provision. This was the explicit approach of the first Northern Ireland Parliament and continues to guide thinking today. Battles have been fought to achieve equality in matters such as social security and health services.[38] However, educational issues stand as an interesting exception to this. Rather than pushing for parity in all aspects of provision, local politicians have actively supported the case for sustaining Northern Ireland's unique system of education. Moreover, this support for the status quo has been evident whatever the party in power at Westminster. Plans for comprehensive schools were resisted just as vigorously as the proposals on grant-maintained schools. One reason for the politicians' adherence to the existing structures may stem

---

[35] See, *The Report of the Working Party on Discipline in Schools in Northern Ireland* (DENI, 1990).
[36] The major political parties at Westminster do not have any elected representatives from Northern Ireland. The Labour party does not even put candidates forward in local elections.
[37] The Draft Education and Library Boards (NI) Order 1997 has not made it past the proposal stage.
[38] See, for instance, Lundy, 'Parity, Parrotry or Plagiarism: Unemployment Benefit in Northern Ireland 1846 - 1996' , Chapter One in Dawson, Greer, and Ingram (eds), *One Hundred and Fifty Years of Irish Law* (1996, SLS and Roundhall).

from the fact that their constituents are generally happy with what has been happening as discussed above. However, another factor is almost certainly the close link between the churches and schools. Politicians in Northern Ireland, whose votes often divide along religious lines, do not wish to go against the express wishes of the churches at the risk of isolating themselves from their electorate who attend them.

1.15 This brings us to what is arguably the single biggest influence on the development of Northern Ireland education law - the role of the main religious bodies. Their imprint can be seen on the reforms discussed earlier in this chapter. They have also been significant in a number of other key areas. For instance, the 1989 Order saw the establishment of the CCMS, a statutory body established to oversee the management of all Catholic primary and secondary schools. During the consultation process the Catholic church successfully campaigned for the right to be consulted on a wide range of matters including admission, expulsions etc thus extending their legal position and influence. The Protestant churches have argued for a similar statutory body to represent the interests of the transferors in controlled schools. While this has not been acceded to, the voluntary Transferors Representatives' Council has still managed to secure a number of legal provisions which reinforce its position in controlled schools.[39] The influence of the churches on the education system in Northern Ireland is such that the government must at the very least consider their views carefully and is in fact often prepared to concede or at least compromise on major reforms. However, this willingness to concede cannot be attributed simply to a reluctance on the part of the government to come into conflict with the churches.[40] In order to understand the churches' capacity to sway education law reform in Northern Ireland, consideration must be given to the wider social context prevailing.

1.16 In Northern Ireland religion is always closely connected with other related issues such as discrimination and minority rights. Opposing the churches in the area of education can readily be interpreted as a form of discrimination against the communities which they represent. The Catholic church has been particularly successful in promoting the importance of a Catholic education and portraying unwelcome developments as an attack on the Catholic community. The case of *In re Daly*, in spite of its lack of success, is a key illustration of this strategy.[41] The case was founded on the anti-discrimination provisions of the Northern Ireland Constitution Act 1973. This Act also established the Standing Advisory Commission on Human Rights (SACHR). One of SACHR's notable successes was the increase in the level of capital funding offered to voluntary schools. Prior to 1993 the maximum available was 85 per cent.[42] However, research commissioned by SACHR indicated that the reduced capital funding in voluntary schools may

---

[39] For instance, they have the right to positions on the Boards of Governors of new controlled schools (i.e. schools which have never transferred).
[40] It is notable that that church schools in England and Wales have not been able to exercise the same degree of influence.
[41] *In re Daly* unreported decision of the High Court of Northern Ireland, 5 October 1990. See further para. 9-05.
[42] Education and Libraries (NI) Order 1986, art. 116.

have had an impact on the curriculum and levels of attainment in these schools, the majority of which were Catholic.[43] The government responded by allowing voluntary schools to opt for full capital funding in return for increased Departmental representation on the Board of Governors.[44] In this instance, significant legislative change was forthcoming not simply because of the religious dimension to the discussion. In fact, it was a long-standing and widely accepted principle that voluntary schools should receive less capital funding than fully controlled schools in return for greater autonomy and in particular, the freedom to pursue denominational religious education.[45] The government's willingness to depart from this principle can be attributed to the fact that the argument was couched in terms of discrimination and minority rights.

1.17 The need to ensure equality is particularly acute in Northern Ireland because of the civil unrest which has afflicted the region for over 30 years. It is widely recognised that social provision is inextricably tied into the attainment of political stability and that the education system has a pivotal role to play in this. Thus it was in this very different social and political context that legislation which emanated from England and Wales passed through the Northern Ireland legislative process and emerged looking distinctively different. The question now is what direction the law will take when it is determined through a locally-based legislative process.

EDUCATION LAW UNDER DEVOLUTION[46]

1.18 At the time of writing, Northern Ireland has entered into a new political settlement. For the first time since 1974, the law relating to schools will be enacted through an Act of the Northern Ireland Assembly and the system will be administered by the Department of Education led by a local Minister for Education. Prior to devolution, all educational issues within Northern Ireland fell within the remit of the Department of Education for Northern Ireland (DENI). Under devolution the education functions have been split with further and higher education going to a new Department of Further and Higher Education and Training and Employment (DEFHETE) while responsibility for schools vests in a reconstituted Department of Education ('the Department'). The legislation which gave effect to this change simply requires the DENI to drop the "for Northern Ireland" from its title, a move which symbolises the transition from power at Westminster

---

[43] Cormack, Gallagher and Osborne, 'Religious Affiliation and Educational Attainment in Northern Ireland: The Financing of Schools in Northern Ireland' Annex E in the *Sixteenth Report of the Standing Advisory Commission on Human Rights (1990- 1991)* (London: HMSO, 1991), pp. 117-212.

[44] Education (NI) Order 1993, art. 28. The concession on the membership of the Board of Governors is not as significant as it might appear because the Department will consult the Board of Governors before making nominations to the Board.

[45] See Dunn, *op cit* n.23 at pp. 62-64.

[46] The analysis in this section is derived largely from a previous article by the author: Lundy, 'Education Law under Devolution, the Case of Northern Ireland' [2000] *Education Law Journal* 81.

(where Northern Ireland departments need to be distinguished from their counterparts in England and Wales) to self-contained government.[47]

1.19 Ministerial posts in the Northern Ireland executive do not go straight to the majority party but instead are spread between the political parties under a system known as D'Hondt.[48] The first Minister for Education is Martin McGuinness of Sinn Fein, a person alleged to have links with the Irish Republican Army (IRA). It was also considered to be relevant to his appointment that he had left school at the age of 15 with no formal qualifications. Mr McGuinness's decision to opt for education was a complete surprise and exceptionally controversial. Although there was no guarantee which parties would choose which Department, it had been widely speculated that Sinn Fein would opt for the Ministry of Education if it remained but that it would have proposed Bairbre de Brun, an ex-teacher with no IRA connections, for the post of Minister for Education. The reason why Sinn Fein put Martin McGuinness forward is unclear, although there was some press speculation that it was in retaliation for David Trimble's decision to place a February 2000 deadline on the commencement of arms decommissioning. The public reaction to the appointment was immediate. In addition to a flood of letters to the local papers objecting in strong terms to the placing of children's development in the hands of a person with connections to paramilitaries, in several schools pupils walked out of classes in protest.

1.20 Given that there is now a realistic prospect that educational reform will be determined by locally-based politicians for the first time in over 20 years, it will be interesting to see whether the law in Northern Ireland will continue to follow the pattern of England and Wales or whether something wholly distinctive will emerge. Changes may well occur at the organisational level. In spite of the reorganisation of the Departments under devolution, the Department of Education is unaffected in its obligations to schools.[49] However, the fate of the ELBs may be less secure. Although their amalgamation was contested when it was proposed via Westminster, economic pressures may force a rethink when the issue is considered locally: re-organisation was mentioned in a number of the manifestos for the 1998 election to the Assembly. The categories of school are unlikely to be affected: public opinion and the influence of the churches are likely to sustain the existing structures. However, it will be interesting to see how certain types of school such as integrated and Irish-medium fare given that they have the specific support of political parties who for the first time have a say in the operation of the education system. The single biggest issue which faces the Assembly in the context of education is the question of selection at 11. The Minister for Education, Martin McGuinness, is openly opposed to selection. However, the various political parties with seats in the Assembly hold different views. Much will depend on the response to the research report

---

[47] Departments (NI) Order 1999, art. 3(7).
[48] The system is named after Viktor D'Hondt who invented it. It allows the party with the largest number of MLAs to choose a Department and appoint a Minister in turn until all posts have been filled. The system is designed to ensure that executive power is spread across the major political parties in the Assembly.
[49] Responsibility for higher and further education has been transferred to a new Department.

compiled by Queen's University, Belfast and the University of Ulster and published in September 2000.[50] On other matters it is likely that the Assembly will keep a close watch on developments in England and Wales to ensure that Northern Ireland does not fall too far out of line. For instance, as regards the common curriculum, many pupils in Northern Ireland take examinations organised by the English examination boards and there will therefore be a pressure to co-ordinate the substance of what is taught. In contrast, in other areas such as discipline, attendance and special educational needs, there may be more scope for differentiation to reflect the different context in Northern Ireland. Experience of the previous Northern Ireland Assembly (1982-1986) suggests a willingness on the part of local politicians to consider differing options.[51] Likewise, the reports of the Northern Ireland Forum for Political Dialogue also indicate a willingness to depart from the British norms.[52]

SCRUTINY AND CHALLENGE UNDER THE NORTHERN IRELAND ACT 1998

1.21 The Belfast Agreement is founded on principles which include "the protection and vindication of the human rights of all" and "partnership, equality and mutual respect".[53] The Northern Ireland Act 1998, which is intended to implement the agreement, contains a number of provisions which are designed to ensure equal treatment and compliance with general human rights standards both in terms of the law-making process and the actions of public bodies. The implications of the 1998 Act are considered below under the following categories: (i) Acts of the Assembly; (ii) Ministers and departments; (iii) the protection of human rights; and (iv) the promotion of equality of opportunity (and non-discrimination).

Legislation: Acts of the Northern Ireland Assembly

1.22 The last major piece of education legislation to be introduced in Northern Ireland was the Education (NI) Order 1998.[54] Legislative reform appears to have been put on hold pending the establishment of the Assembly and no new education legislation was initiated in the Assembly's short life prior to suspension. With the resumption of devolution, education law for Northern Ireland will be made by Acts of the Assembly. However, an Act of the Assembly is not law if it is "outside the legislative competence of the Assembly".[55] An Act will fall foul of this provision in a number of instances. These include: where it would form part of the law of a country or territory

---

[50] See DE, *The Effects of the Selective System of Secondary Education in Northern Ireland*, Main Report, September 2000.
[51] See generally, O'Leary, Eliott and Wilford, *The Northern Ireland Assembly 1982-1986: A Constitutional Experiment* (1988) pp.87-94 for the work of the statutory committee on education. It is worth noting, however, that this Assembly did not have the power to legislate.
[52] See, for example, its recommendations on special educational needs, *Special Educational Provision for School-age Children in Northern Ireland* (1998).
[53] *The Agreement* (1998) p. 1, Declaration of Support.
[54] This parallels many of the school discipline and standard setting provisions in the School Standards and Framework Act 1998.
[55] Northern Ireland Act 1998, s.6(1).

other than Northern Ireland;[56] deals with an excepted matter; or modifies an enactment in section 7 (specified provisions of the European Communities Act 1972, the Human Rights Act 1998 and specified provisions of the Northern Ireland Act 1998).[57] From the point of view of education law there are three other significant instances when an Act of the Assembly will be considered to be outside its legislative competence. These are where it is incompatible with European Convention rights or Community law or where it discriminates against any person or class of person on the grounds of religious belief or political opinion.[58]

1.23 Acts of the Assembly are subject to a detailed scrutiny procedure which is designed to ensure that an Act will not receive Royal Assent if it is outside the legislative competence of the Assembly. Firstly, the Minister in charge of the Bill must make a statement to the effect that the Bill is within the Assembly's legislative competence.[59] Secondly, standing orders shall ensure that a Bill is not introduced in the Assembly if the Presiding Officer decides that any provision of it would be outside the legislative competence.[60] Thirdly, the Attorney-General for Northern Ireland may refer the issue of a Bill's legislative competence to the Judicial Committee of the Privy Council for a decision.[61] If the Judicial Committee decides that a provision of the Bill would be outside the legislative competence of the Assembly, the Secretary of State will not submit the Bill in its unamended form for Royal Assent.[62] Finally, standing orders are required to include provision that each Bill must be sent to the Human Rights Commission as soon as is reasonably practicable after its introduction and that the Assembly may ask the Human Rights Commission, where it thinks fit, to advise whether a Bill is compatible with human rights (including the Convention rights).[63] The combined effect of these provisions is that it should be difficult for an Act to make it onto the statute book with a provision which is outside the legislative competence of the Assembly. That said, it remains possible that an Education Act might include a provision which is in contravention of an interpretation of a provision of the ECHR or of Community law or of one of the other grounds specified in section 6 of the 1998 Act. In such cases, it will be possible to argue in court that the provision is not legally valid and consequently not binding.[64]

1.24 Most Acts of the Northern Ireland Assembly will be enacted by a simple majority of members voting. However, certain issues which are deemed to require cross-community support (such as the making, amendment or repeal of standing orders) have extraordinary rules on voting. These special voting arrangements can also be triggered on any issue by a "petition of concern"

---

[56] *Ibid* subject to exceptions.
[57] *Ibid* s.6(2)(a)(b) and (f)
[58] *Ibid* s.6(2)(c)-(e).
[59] *Ibid* s.9.
[60] *Ibid* s10.
[61] *Ibid* s.11.
[62] *Ibid* s.143.
[63] *Ibid* s.134.
[64] The procedures for court challenges on these issues are set out in Part VIII of the 1998 Act.

brought by at least 30 of the 108 MLAs.[65] In such cases, a vote will only pass with a majority of both the unionist and national designations present and voting or by a weighted majority (60%) of members voting including at least 40 per cent of each of the nationalist and unionist designations present and voting.[66] While it might be anticipated that much education legislation could pass through the Assembly in the normal manner, any changes to school structures, finance or the curriculum may be matters on which a petition of special concern would be brought forward. Once again, the fact that it would be Mr McGuinness who would be promoting the legislation serves to heighten the possibility of a "petition of concern" being instigated.

Executive decision-making: Ministers and Departments

1.25 As a result of the Northern Ireland Act 1998, executive powers are exercised by Ministers and Northern Ireland departments on transferred matters such as education. The division within Northern Ireland's political parties is such that it had been anticipated that there would be occasions when it would be difficult for a Minister to command the trust of his or her opponents (either at all or on certain contentious issues). In view of this the 1998 Act contains a series of safeguards to ensure that the actions of Ministers are not party-political and that decisions on potentially contentious issues have the backing of both communities. First among these checks and balances is the system of cross-party statutory committees. These have the power to: consider and advise on departmental budgets; approve secondary legislation and take the committee stage of relevant primary legislation; call for persons and papers; initiate enquiries and make reports; and to consider and advise on matters brought to the committee by the Minister.[67] More generally, there is a series of legal requirements imposed upon executive decision-making. In particular, a Minister or department does not have the power to make, confirm or approve any subordinate legislation, or to do any act, in so far as the legislation or act: is incompatible with Convention rights; is incompatible with community law; discriminates against a person or class of person on the ground of religious belief or political opinion; and, in the case of an act, aids or incites another person to discriminate on the grounds of religious belief or political opinion; or, in the case of subordinate legislation, modifies specific enactments including specified parts of the European Communities Act 1972, the Human Rights Act 1998 and specified parts of the Northern Ireland Act 1998.[68] These obligations mean that all education regulations and acts of the Minister for Education and the Department of Education will be considered to be invalid unless they comply with these provisions. For example, if a

---

[65] Northern Ireland Act 1998, s.42(2).
[66] *Ibid* s.4(5)
[67] Northern Ireland Act 1998, s. 29. Strand One, para. 9 of the Agreement Reached in the Multi-Party Negotiations. The allocation of committee chairs is conducted according to the d'Hondt system and results in the chair being drawn from a political party in an "opposed" position to that of the Minister. Membership of the committee is proportionate to party strength in the Assembly.
[68] *Ibid* s.24(1). The provisions relating to religious or political discrimination do not apply to any act which is unlawful by virtue of the Fair Employment (NI) Act 1976 or would be unlawful but for some exception made by Part V of that Act.

departmental policy could be shown to discriminate on the grounds of sex it might be considered to be invalid because of its failure to comply with Article 119 of the Treaty of Rome or Article 14 of the ECHR (if the child's right to education under Article 2 of the First Protocol is affected).

1.26 Section 26 of the 1998 Act contains a number of provisions which are intended to ensure that the actions of Ministers and departments (including the making, confirming or approving of subordinate legislation) are compatible with the United Kingdom's international obligations, with the interests of defence or national security or with the protection of public safety or order. International obligations are defined as "any international obligations of the United Kingdom other than obligations to observe and implement Community Law or the Convention Rights."[69] The Secretary of State has the power to issue orders: directing that proposed action will not be taken: directing that action required to give effect to the international obligations etc. will be taken; and revoking incompatible subordinate legislation.[70] Subordinate legislation may also be revoked if it would have an adverse effect on the operation of the single market in goods and services in the United Kingdom.[71]

1.27 The legal provisions provide a restrictive framework and the statutory committees a watchdog to ensure that Ministers and departments do not abuse power for party-political ends. However, in the context of division and suspicion which characterises Northern Ireland politics, it will be interesting to see whether the parties will be able to buckle down to government or whether long-standing hostilities will ultimately frustrate normal political engagement. Reaching agreement may be difficult where decisions are uncontentious but possibly unattainable where the issues under consideration attract significant cross-community differences.[72] Some of the most politically controversial issues such as policing have been "excepted" or "reserved" at Westminster.[73] Of the issues which have been transferred it is arguable that the one which is most likely to generate cross-community division is education. The possibility of conflict occurring in the sphere of education is high primarily because of the religiously segregated nature of the school system. The polarisation of interests within the education system may well send individuals scuttling into their opposing corners at the first hint of preferential treatment being afforded to one community over the other. Moreover, there can be little doubt that the potential for conflict is aggravated by the identity of the first Minister for Education. Within minutes of the appointments being finalised, the deputy chair of the education committee, Mr Sammy Wilson, (a member of Ian Paisley's Democratic Unionist Party who will not directly address members of Sinn Fein) declared that he saw his role on the committee to be "Dobermann at McGuinness's heels"[74]. It remains to

---

[69] *Ibid* s.98(1).
[70] *Ibid* s.26(1)-(4).
[71] *Ibid* s.26(4)(b)
[72] Opponents of the agreement have described the arrangements as a "recipe for political stalemate". See I. Paisley, 'Peace Agreement – or Last Piece in a Sellout Agreement', (1999) 4/22 *Fordham International Law Journal* 1273 at p. 1303
[73] Northern Ireland Act 1998, Sch. 3.
[74] To which Mr Mc Guinness retorted in the Assembly on 31 January 2000 that "the place for a Dobermann is at the heel of the Master".

be seen whether the Minister for Education will be able to command sufficient support to carry other members of the committee with him on key decisions, policy initiatives and legislation.

The protection of human rights

1.28 The 1998 Act has a number of provisions designed for the protection of human rights. Human rights is not defined apart from the fact that it is stated to *include* "Convention rights".[75] This definition must therefore embrace other rights such as those set out in the United Nations Convention on the Rights of the Child (UNCRC) which is considered at the end of the chapter. Responsibility for ensuring that Northern Ireland law and practice is in accordance with human rights rests with a new body – the Northern Ireland Human Rights Commission (NIHRC).[76] The NIHRC's general function is to: "keep under review the adequacy and effectiveness in Northern Ireland of law and practice relating to the protection of human rights."[77] The NIHRC has an important role in advising the Assembly of legislative and other measures which ought to be taken to protect human rights and as to whether Bills are compatible with human rights.[78]

1.29 One of the first tasks of the NIHRC is to make recommendations on a new Bill of Rights for Northern Ireland. The Bill of Rights is intended to supplement the European Convention on Human Rights.[79] The agreement suggests that two issues, both of which have potential ramifications for education, require particular consideration in the context of a new Bill of Rights. The first is an obligation on government and public bodies to "respect on the basis of equality of treatment, the identity and ethos of both communities in Northern Ireland". Any enhancement of Convention rights in this regard could have significant implications for issues such as language and religion in schools. Secondly, the NIHRC will consider the need for "a clear formulation of the rights not to be discriminated against and to equality of opportunity in both the public and private sectors". A review of anti-discrimination law would almost certainly entail a consideration of the need to extend the application of section 76 of the Northern Ireland Act 1998 (which prohibits public bodies from discriminating on the grounds of religious belief or political opinion) to cases of indirect discrimination.[80] Because schools are so religiously segregated, potential issues of indirect discrimination abound. In particular, key questions arise in relation to school admissions since many schools use admissions criteria based on catchment area or contributory primary schools which have indirectly discriminatory effects.[81] A further

---

[75] Northern Ireland Act 1998, s. 69(11)(b).
[76] This replaces the Standing Advisory Commission on Human Rights (SACHR), *ibid* s. 72.
[77] *Ibid* s. 69(1).
[78] *Ibid* s. 69(3)-(4).
[79] *The Agreement* (1998), 'Rights, Safeguards and Equality of Opportunity' para. 4.
[80] S. 76 replaced s.19 of the Northern Ireland Constitution Act 1973. The case law on s. 19 of the 1973 Act makes it clear that s.76 does not apply to cases of indirect discrimination. See B. Hadfield, 'The NI Constitution Act – lessons for minority rights' in P. Cumper and S. Wheatley (eds) *Minority Rights in the New Europe* (1999) 129-146.
[81] For instance, admission criteria in controlled secondary schools which prioritise children from specified controlled contributory primary schools (attended by mainly Protestant pupils)

issue for consideration might be the current exemption of education from the Fair Employment and Treatment (NI) Order 1998 which fails to prohibit religious discrimination in relation to teachers. The exception is in practice an endorsement of the Catholic Church's desire to employ Catholic teachers in its schools. However, the legislation requires the exception to be kept under review and the consultation on the Bill of Rights may well revive this issue.[82]

1.30 The NIHRC is also empowered to bring proceedings involving law or practice relating to the protection of human rights.[83] The NIHRC may also assist individuals who have commenced or wish to commence proceedings relating to the protection of human rights. Assistance may be given where the case raises a question of principle; it is unreasonable to expect the person to deal with the case without assistance because of its complexity or because of the person's position in relation to another person involved or for some other reason; or where there are other special circumstances which make it appropriate for the NIHRC to provide assistance.[84] The NIHRC may provide or arrange for the provision of legal advice; arrange for the provision of legal representation; or provide any other assistance which it thinks appropriate.[85] This would enable parents who believe that the action of their child's school or ELB or the Department is in breach of human rights to apply to the NIHRC for assistance to take a case.[86] The NIHRC has already shown itself willing to step into existing litigation, producing a series of *amicus* briefs in cases where there is a human rights dimension. However, given the Commission's limited budget[87] and the fact that there is likely to be high level volume of demand for assistance on a wide range of issues, decisions to assist will need to be strategically focused. The Commission suggests that it is likely to intervene where there would be a "significant impact", that is it would affect a large number of people or involve an "egregious violation of human rights".[88] Its predecessor, the Standing Advisory Commission on Human Rights (SACHR) maintained a particular interest in the education system throughout its existence.[89] In fact, one of SACHR's most notable successes might be considered to be the changing of the funding arrangements for voluntary schools (most of which are Catholic) in the light of research which linked lower attainments in these schools to the reduced levels of capital funding.[90]

---

would undoubtedly disadvantage children who had attended a Catholic maintained primary school.

[82] The Chief Commissioner, Professor Brice Dickson has recently said that "a person's religion, in my view at least, should not determine his or her capacity to educate children". 'Human Rights as Society's Gel', Address at St Patrick's Cathedral Dublin, 2 April 1999.
[83] Northern Ireland Act 1998, s.69(5).
[84] *Ibid* s. 70(2).
[85] *Ibid* s. 70(3).
[86] The applicant must be able to show "victim" status according to Article 34 of the ECHR. *Ibid* s.71(1).
[87] Currently £750 000 which represent approximately 50 pence per person in Northern Ireland and is approximately half of the budget of the Equal Opportunities Commission for Northern Ireland before it was merged into the Equality Commission.
[88] NIHRC, *Draft Strategic Plan*, (2000).
[89] The NIHRC replaces SACHR but has a wider remit and more powers than its predecessor.
[90] See, R. Cormack, A. M. Gallagher and R. Osborne, 'Religious Affiliation and Educational Attainment in Northern Ireland: The Financing of Schools in Northern Ireland' Annex E in

The NIHRC's strategic plan expressly highlights children's rights (including "inequality of access to education.") as one of its priority areas.[91] On education, the Commission may wish to focus on issues unique to Northern Ireland such as Irish language education or religious discrimination issues. However, it is to be hoped that the NIHRC will be able to use the new legal framework to test issues which would also be of national concern such as those in relation to school exclusions and special educational needs. It has been observed that the NIHRC will have to tackle some of the most politically controversial issues in Northern Ireland in order to gain credibility.[92] It is also true that an effective way of gaining popular support would be to have an impact on the issues which affect most people in their everyday lives.[93] The educational sphere provides an opportunity to engage the majority of both sides of the community on issues to which they can relate, that is their children's education.

Equality of opportunity

1.31 The Northern Ireland Act 1998 established a new body, the Equality Commission, to replace the existing Fair Employment Commission, Equal Opportunities Commission, Commission for Racial Equality and the Northern Ireland Disability Council.[94] The Equality Commission will exercise the various statutory functions of the previous bodies.[95] These include, in the respective areas of religion, political opinion, sex and marital discrimination, race and disability, the powers to provide advice and training, assist applicants with complaints, undertake research and conduct investigations where there appears to be discrimination. The Equality Commission also has a new role in terms of the enforcement of the statutory equality duty on public authorities considered in the following section.

The statutory duty on public authorities

1.32 One of the new aspects of the Northern Ireland Act is the duty on public authorities to "have regard to the need to promote equality of opportunity" under section 75. This statutory duty replaces the Policy and Fair Treatment (PAFT) guidelines which had been in operation since 1994.[96] These guidelines required public authorities to consider the impact of newly

---

the *Sixteenth Report of the Standing Advisory Commission on Human Rights (1990-1991)* (London: HMSO, 1991), pp. 117 - 212.
Voluntary schools can now opt to have their capital funding raised from 85% to 100% in which case state representation on the Board of Governors increases.
[91] NIHRC, *Strategic Plan* (2000).
[92] See S. Livingstone, 'The Northern Ireland Human Rights Commission' (1999) 4/22 *Fordham International Law Journal* 1465 at 1498.
[93] The NIHRC's Chief Commissioner has previously expressed a need to convince people "especially perhaps those of a unionist disposition that human rights are for all, not just for one particular community." See, B. Dickson, 'Northern Ireland and the Human Rights Act', Chapter 6 in Lester and Pannick, *Human Rights Law and Practice* 287, at para. 6.39.
[94] Northern Ireland Act 1998, ss.73 and 74.
[95] The obligations arise under the Fair Employment and Treatment (NI) Order 1998, the Sex Discrimination (NI) Order 1976, the Race Relations (NI) Order 1997 and the Disability Discrimination Act 1995 respectively.
[96] These replaced an initial set of guidance which had been in operation from 1990.

proposed or established policies on specific groups such as people of different religious belief or political opinion, men and women, people with and without disabilities etc. The PAFT guidelines had been criticised on the basis that they were too broad, arbitrarily implemented and did not provide individuals with an effective means of complaint.[97] The statutory duty, which replaces the PAFT guidelines, is intended to be an "effective means of injecting equality considerations into the mainstream of public sector activities".[98]

1.33   Public authorities are required to have regard to the need to promote equality of opportunity between: (i) persons of different religious belief, political opinion, racial group, age, marital status or sexual orientation; (ii) men and women generally; (iii) persons with a disability and persons without; and (iv) persons with dependants and persons without.[99] Moreover in carrying out their functions public authorities shall have regard to the "desirability of promoting good relations between persons of different religious belief, political opinion or racial group".[100] Public authorities are defined to include the Department, ELBS and the CCMS.[101] It does not include Boards of Governors.

1.34   The statutory duty under section 75 is intended to be enforced in a number of ways. First, the Equality Commission is required to keep under review the effectiveness of the duties imposed by section 75.[102] Secondly, public authorities may be required to submit an equality scheme which shows how the authority proposes to fulfil the duties imposed by section 75 to the Equality Commission for approval.[103] The scheme must include a number of prescribed matters including the authority's arrangements for assessing its compliance with section 75 and for assessing and consulting on the likely impact of policies adopted or proposed to be adopted on equality of opportunity. Finally, a person who claims to have been affected by a failure of the authority to comply with its scheme may complain in writing to the Equality Commission within 12 months of the day on which the complainant first knew of the matters alleged.[104] Before making a complaint the complainant must bring the complaint to the notice of the authority and give the authority a reasonable opportunity to respond. The Commission must investigate the complaint or give the complainant reasons for not investigating. The Equality Commission may carry out investigations on its own initiative if it believes that a public authority may have failed to comply with an equality scheme.[105] If it conducts an investigation, a copy of its report will be sent to the Secretary of State as well as the authority and complainant (if any). If the report recommends action by the authority and that action is not taken within a reasonable time, the Commission may refer the matter to

---

[97] See SACHR *Employment Equality: Building for the Future* (HMSO, 1997) Cm 3684 and further, Hadden, Rainey and McGreevy, *Equal But Not Separate* (FET, 1998) pp. 9-11.
[98] *Partnership for Equality* (HMSO, 1998) Cm 3890 p.28.
[99] Northern Ireland Act 1998, s.75(1).
[100] *Ibid* s. 75(2).
[101] *Ibid* s. 75(3).
[102] *Ibid* Sch.9, para. 1.
[103] *Ibid* Sch. 9, paras. 3-4.
[104] *Ibid* Sch. 9, para. 10.
[105] *Ibid* Sch. 9, para. 11(1)(b).

the Secretary of State who may give directions to the public authority in respect of any matter referred.[106]

1.35 The statutory equality duty has far reaching implications for the public bodies involved in the delivery of education. Apart from the fact that the duty is now on a statutory basis, it includes consideration of issues going beyond that of the existing anti-discrimination legislation. In particular, it extends to age and sexual orientation. Moreover the statutory duty applies to a wide range of public bodies. From now on the Department, the ELBs and CCMS will have to consider the impact that their policies, and /or proposed legislation might have on the specified groups. The operation of section 75 will be particularly important in schools in relation to religious discrimination since education is specifically exempt from the traditional anti-discrimination legislation.[107] Equality issues might arise in relation to the operation of school admission policies where the application of specific criteria may have differential impacts on children of different religions, gender or race. There may also have to be a reconsideration of policy in relation to children with disabilities, particularly those who do not have a statement of special educational need.[108] These issues will need to be re-evaluated in the light of section 75. This is not to say that education authorities will not be able to implement policies which have differential impact. They will, however, have to direct their attention to the nature and scale of the impact and to the reasons why the course of action is justified notwithstanding. If it is properly implemented and rigorously enforced, section 75 provides an opportunity for the active mainstreaming of equality issues, a position which offers much potential over litigation-based strategies for reform.[109]

Discrimination by public authorities on the grounds of religious belief or political opinion

1.36 Section 76 of the 1998 Act makes it unlawful for a public authority "in carrying out functions relating to Northern Ireland to discriminate, or aid to incite another person to discriminate, against a person or class of person on the ground of religious belief or political opinion." In this context, public authorities include the Minister for Education, the Department, CCMS and ELBs.[110] Any person adversely affected by such an act may take legal action which includes actions for damages or for an injunction restraining the defendant from further contraventions.[111] Section 76 can also be used to challenge actions relating to the making, confirmation or approval of subordinate legislation (e.g. education regulations) if the legislation contains a

---

[106] *Ibid* Sch. 9, para. 11. The Assembly must be notified of any reports or referrals to the Secretary of State and any directions issues by the Secretary of State as a consequence.
[107] Fair Treatment and Employment (NI) Order 1998, s. 71. The Commission does have the power to conduct investigations into religious discrimination in schools (s.71(3)).
[108] See L. Lundy, 'Stating a case for the un-statemented: children with special needs in mainstream schools' (1998) 1 *Child and Family Law Quarterly* 61.74.
[109] See generally, C. Mc Crudden, 'Mainstreaming Equality in the Governance of Northern Ireland', (1999) 4/22 *Fordham International Law Journal* 1696, at p. 1769.
[110] Northern Ireland Act 1998, s.76(7).
[111] *Ibid* s.76(2).

provision which discriminates against a person or class of person on the grounds of religious belief or political opinion.[112] In such cases, an individual adversely affected cannot commence proceedings on the basis of the contravention alone but the contravention may be relied on in legal proceedings relating to the validity of the subordinate legislation.

1.37 Section 76 has replaced section 19 of the Northern Ireland Constitution Act 1973. However, the case authority from section 19 remains valid.[113] In practice, section 19 was of limited application unless there was a clear instance of direct discrimination. Legislation is considered to discriminate if it treats a person or class of persons "less favourably in any circumstances than other persons are treated in those circumstances by the law...".[114] A person is considered to have discriminated against another person if he treats that other person or class of persons less favourably in any circumstances than he treats or would treat other persons in those circumstances.[115] The courts have not been prepared to find that section 19 extended to cases of indirect discrimination (i.e. where the proportion of people of a particular religious belief/political opinion who can comply with a particular requirement is significantly smaller than others). In fact until recently the courts focused on whether the respondents actually intended to discriminate.[116] However, following the House of Lords' decision in an English case, *James* v *Eastleigh Borough Council,* the test for direct discrimination is now applied according to the so-called 'but for' test. This asks whether the applicant would have received the same treatment 'but for' his religion/political opinion.[117] Even so, there are not many instances where this type of discrimination can be shown to have occurred in the context of public law decision-making. Education law is no exception. There have been two high profile cases under the Northern Ireland Constitution Act 1973, *In re Daly* and *In re Cecil*.[118] Neither was successful in establishing discrimination. That said, section 76 challenges to delegated legislation and the actions of public authorities remain possible in the context of education and are highlighted in the book where they arise.[119] Moreover, it is possible that section 76 will be interpreted differently by the courts in the light of section 75.

THE DOMESTIC LEGAL FRAMEWORK

1.38 The objective of this section is to provide a description of the key pieces of legislation which form the body of education law in Northern

---

[112] *Ibid* s.76(5). The provision extends only to the whole or any part of Northern Ireland (i.e. presumably it must not affect any territory outside of Northern Ireland).
[113] See further Hadfield, 'The Northern Ireland Constitution Act 1973 - Lessons for Minority Rights' in Cumper and Wheatley (eds) *Rights in the New Europe* (1999) pp. 129-146.
[114] Northern Ireland Act 1998, s. 98(4).
[115] *Ibid* s.98(5).
[116] *Armagh District Council* v *Fair Employment Agency*[1983] NI 346.
[117] [1990] 2 All ER 607. This was applied in the Northern Ireland case of *Belfast Port Employers' Association* v *Fair Employment Commission* [1994] NIJB 36(CA).
[118] For discussion of *In Re Daly* (which involved s.17 of the 1973 Act) see para. 9.07. For discussion of *In Re Cecil* see para. 2.74.
[119] See the discussion in paras. 4.36-4.39 on admissions.

Ireland, to highlight the policy initiatives behind them and to give a summary of their main reforms. There are seven Orders in total (six education Orders and the Children (NI) Order 1995), each of which contains significant amendments to the Orders which precede it. This makes it difficult for anyone who wishes to find out which provisions are currently in force. In England and Wales the nettle has already been grasped: the Education Act 1996 consolidated education legislation going back to the Education Act 1944. Although the provisions in force in Northern Ireland do not go back quite as far (there was a consolidating Order in 1972 and another in 1986), the pace of legislative change in the past 20 years has been such that the area is calling out for a tidy up. This very point was made by Mac Dermott LJ in *In re Daly* where he said:

> "It may be possible for those in daily contact with educational issues to be familiar with and understand all the relevant legislation but as parents become increasingly involved in educational matters they as well as teachers and members of Boards of Governors must face a daunting task when they read the various statutory provisions, seek to find what is relevant and then try to understand articles containing numerous paragraphs and sub-paragraphs. . . .Where individual members of the public are expected to participate in the administration of the education system it would seem to me to be desirable that they should only have to refer to one document and that document should be expressed in crisp and easily understood language."[120]

Lord Justice MacDermott was writing just after the implementation of the 1989 Order. There have been five major Orders affecting education since then as well as the Northern Ireland Act 1998.[121]

Education and Libraries (NI) Order 1986

1.39 The Education and Libraries (NI) Order 1986 is referred to as the "principal Order" as it provides the basis of most of the current education legislation. It was introduced as consolidating legislation replacing the Education and Libraries (NI) Order 1972 and subsequent amendments (the Education (NI) Orders 1976, 1978 1980 and 1984). The 1986 Order has been repeatedly amended but contains the provisions on the obligations of ELBs, the management of individual schools, changes to the status and character of schools, the rights and duties of parents and administration in ELBs.

Education Reform (NI) Order 1989

1.40 The Education Reform (NI) Order 1989 was the most far-reaching piece of education legislation since the 1947 Butler reforms. The changes that it introduced were based on provisions which had been implemented in England and Wales by the Education Reform Act 1988.[122] The government's

---

[120] Unreported decision of the High Court of Northern Ireland, 5 October 1990.
[121] This does not include the Education (NI) Order 1987 which made various miscellaneous amendments.
[122] For a discussion of these reforms, see Flude and Hammer, *The Education Reform Act 1988: Its Origins and Implications* (1990).

stated objectives were to raise educational standards, give parents a greater say in the education of their children and to devolve power in the running of schools to a local level.[123] In furtherance of this, the 1989 Order introduced the following major changes: the implementation of a common curriculum; a system of open enrolment for admission to schools; financial delegation to schools; an enhanced role for Boards of Governors in the management of schools and new procedures for establishing integrated schools including grant-maintained integrated schools. It also established the Catholic Council for Maintained Schools (CCMS). Most of the provisions in the 1989 Order came into operation in February 1990. However, some of the reforms were implemented more gradually, (for instance, those relating to assessment in the common curriculum are not yet fully in force).

Education (NI) Order 1993

1.41 The key change introduced by the 1993 Order for schools relates to the provision of capital grants to voluntary schools, both maintained and voluntary grammar. Prior to the implementation of the Order, such schools were eligible only for up to 85 per cent of their capital expenditure costs. This could be contrasted with controlled schools who received full funding for capital costs. Research commissioned by SACHR indicated that this differential level of funding had an impact on levels of attainment in voluntary schools, the majority of which were attended by Catholic children.[124] The 1993 Order introduced a procedure whereby voluntary schools could opt for full capital funding. If voluntary schools opt for this, state representation on the Board of Governors increases with the result that the school trustees no longer represented a majority on the Board.[125] The 1993 Order also contained a number of other reforms. For instance, it introduced a system for appealing against a decision to expel a pupil and extended the remit of the curriculum complaints tribunal to complaints about religious education.[126]

Children (NI) Order 1995

1.42 The Children (NI) Order 1995 made wide-ranging changes to the law relating to children. Its provisions mirror those implemented in England and Wales by the Children Act 1989. Although the Order is not specifically concerned with education, there are a number of provisions which impact on schools. Two in particular are worthy of note. First, the Children Order redefined the term "parent" to include all those with parental responsibility for the child.[127] This definition replaced the definition of parent in the 1986 Order and is now the key definition when considering legal responsibilities under all of the Education Orders. Secondly, the Children Order introduced a new procedure for dealing with persistent absenteeism from schools. The

---

[123] *Education Reform in Northern Ireland - the Way Forward* (DENI, 1988).
[124] Cormack, Gallagher and Osborne, *Religious Affiliation and Education Attainment in Northern Ireland: The Financing of Schools in Northern Ireland* in the Sixteenth Report of the Standing Advisory Committee on Human Rights (1990-91).
[125] Art. 28 of the 1993 Order.
[126] *Ibid* Arts. 39 and 47.
[127] Art. 128 of the Children (NI) Order 1995.

Education Supervision Order, which came into force in November 1996, allows courts to transfer responsibility for ensuring the child's education from his or her parents to the ELB working through their education welfare officers.[128]

Education (NI) Order 1996

1.43 The main reforms introduced by the Education (NI) Order 1996 relate to the provision which must be made for children with special educational needs. The 1996 Order, which replaced the previous provision in the 1986 Order, contains reforms similar to those implemented in England and Wales by the Education Act 1993. The objective of those reforms was to "allow the mothers and fathers of children with special educational needs to play as full a part in the decisions about their child's education".[129] In order to achieve this, the 1996 Order made two key changes to the system. First, it introduced a new tribunal, the Special Educational Needs Tribunal (SENT), to hear appeals concerning educational provision for children with special needs. Secondly, it provides for a Code of Practice on special educational needs which schools are required to "have regard to" when taking decisions about children with special needs. The SENT began operating in September 1997. The implementation of the Code of Practice was postponed to September 1998. The 1996 Order also contains a number of other significant amendments. These include: the establishment of an Independent Schools Tribunal; the simplification of the procedures for establishing an integrated school; provision for the incorporation of all Boards of Governors and the conferment on ELBs of a power to direct a grant-aided school to admit a child who has been expelled from another school.

Education (NI) Order 1997

1.44 The 1997 Order made changes in two key areas: (i) admissions and (ii) home to school transport. In relation to admissions, the Order attempted to clarify and simplify the provisions on parental preference and admissions criteria. There was a need for clarification because admissions had been the most litigious area of education law since the introduction of open enrolment in 1990. There were a series of judicial review actions concerning refusals to admit to grammar schools. These had exposed some ambiguities in the legislation as well as practices which although not illegal could operate unfairly for parents. The changes to admissions were also to be read alongside changes to the provisions on home to school transport. In a departure from previous policy, it was decided that ELBs would only pay transport to the nearest suitable school and not any school of the parent's choice as had previously been the case. The 1997 Order also gave ELBs the power to charge pupils for transport costs in certain instances.

---

[128] *Ibid* art. 55.
[129] *Choice and Diversity* (DfEE, 1992), para. 1.53.

Education (NI) Order 1998

1.45 The 1998 Order contains several reforms which bring Northern Ireland into line with recent developments in England and Wales. First, it contains a number of provisions on discipline which are similar to those contained in the Education Act 1997, that is new responsibilities for Boards of Governors and clarification of the law in relation to detention and restraint. It also establishes a General Teaching Council for Northern Ireland and replicates some of the key reforms in the School Standards and Framework Bill 1998: base line assessments, school development plans. Finally, the 1998 Order will change the funding arrangements for voluntary grammar and grant-maintained integrated schools, by transferring the responsibility for funding from the Department to ELBs.

INTERNATIONAL OBLIGATIONS

1.46 Article 26(1) of the United Nations Universal Declaration of Human Rights states:

> "Everyone has the right to education. Education shall be free, at least in the elementary and fundamental stages. Elementary education shall be compulsory."

The United Kingdom is a signatory to a number of other international instruments which recognise the right to education as a fundamental human right. The two most significant of these are (i) the United Nations Convention on the Rights of the Child and (ii) the European Convention on Human Rights.

United Nations Convention on the Rights of the Child

1.47 The UNCRC was adopted by the UN General Assembly on 20 November 1989 and came into force on 2 September 1990. The United Kingdom is a signatory to the charter (subject to a number of reservations). Article 28 of the UNCRC states:

> "State parties shall recognize the right of the child to education, and with a view to achieving this right progressively and on the basis of equal opportunity, they shall, in particular:
>
> (a) make primary education compulsory and available free to all;
>
> (b) encourage the development of different forms of secondary education, including general and vocational education, make them available and accessible to every child, and take appropriate measures such as the introduction of free education and offering financial assistance in case of need."

1.48 The UNCRC also enunciates a number of principles in relation to the treatment of children generally. One of the most significant Articles in the educational context is Article 12. This gives children who are capable of forming their own views, the right "to express their views freely in all matters affecting the child, the views of the child being given due weight in accordance with the age and maturity of the child". States are also required to provide the child with "the opportunity to be heard in any judicial and administrative proceedings affecting the child, either directly or through a representative or an appropriate body, in a manner consistent with the procedural rules of international law". This is potentially important in decisions relating to a child's education. However, it will be seen throughout the book that, in education law in many instances, national legislation equates children's rights with parents' rights and does not give the child an independent right to be heard.

1.49 The UNCRC has a number of limitations. First, many of the rights are drafted in very broad terms. For this reason, the Convention like many other international documents relating to children is seen to contain a statement of aspirations rather than a list of specific rights.[130] Secondly, the enforcement mechanisms are limited. In particular, there is no means by which an aggrieved individual can lodge a complaint against their government for failure to abide by the principles of the Convention. Instead, the UNCRC is enforced through a system of monitoring first by a specialist UN panel to which the state is required to report. The United Kingdom reported in 1994.[131] The report has been criticised as being too descriptive, providing only vague and superficial information about the United Kingdom's compliance with the Convention.[132] However, the government's information was supplemented by critical submissions made by non-governmental agencies concerned with children's rights. As a result, the UN Committee found a number of instances where national provision did not match the standard set out in the UNCRC.[133] In education, the Committee made general comments about failure to involve children in decision-making in schools.[134] Particular reference was made to the failure to give children an independent right to be heard in relation to expulsion decisions.[135] However, in spite of the Committee's comments in these regards, the law has not been changed to ensure compliance with the Convention. The United Kingdom reported again in 2000. Save the Children and the Children's Law Centre have issued a report which highlights various ongoing breaches of the UNCRC in the education system.[136] Possible breaches of the UNCRC are highlighted in relevant sections throughout the book.

1.50 In spite of its limitations, the UNCRC is an important document to those concerned with education law. Not only has it raised awareness of children's rights, but it also provides a base standard by which existing national provision might be measured. It is therefore significant for those who wish to campaign for policy changes in the field of children's rights. Secondly, as an international treaty, the UNCRC might be relevant in cases where the legislation is ambiguous in certain respects. It is a long-standing

---

[130] See generally, Fortin, *Children's Rights and the Developing Law* (1998), Chapter 1.
[131] *The UN Convention on the Rights of the Child: The UK's First Report to the UN Committee on the Rights of the Child* (1994), HMSO.
[132] See Fortin, *Children's Rights and the Developing Law* (1998), p.45.
[133] *Concluding Observations of the Committee of the Rights of the Child: United Kingdom of Great Britain and Northern Ireland*, CRC/C/15/Add 34 Centre for Human Rights, Geneva, January 1995. For a an analysis of the process of investigation, see, Kilkelly, 'The UN Committee on the Rights of the Child - an evaluation in the light of recent UK experience' (1996) 8 CFLQ 105.
[134] *Ibid* at para. 32.
[135] *Ibid*.
[136] See T. Geraghty, *Getting it Right?* (Save the Children and the Children's Law Centre, 1999)

principle of statutory interpretation that legislation would be construed in a way that is consistent with international obligations since it might be assumed that Parliament would not legislate so as to breach its promises in an international treaty.[137] In the longer term, its significance may increase in Northern Ireland as a result of the Northern Ireland Act 1998. In particular, the Northern Ireland Human Rights Commission will be seeking to ensure that legislation issued by the Assembly is compatible with the human rights standards for children set down in the UNCRC.[138] Moreover, the actions of the Minister for Education and the Department will be required to be compatible with the United Kingdom's international obligations in this respect.[139]

European Convention on Human Rights

1.51 The United Kingdom ratified the European Convention for the Protection of Human Rights and Fundamental Freedoms ('the ECHR') in 1951. The ECHR gives individuals a series of rights (including a right not to be denied education) and enables them to complain to the European Court of Human Rights in Strasbourg if their rights are breached by the state in which they live. One of the most fundamental changes to the United Kingdom's education system this century – the abolition of corporal punishment – occurred as a direct result of a case taken to the European Court of Human Rights.[140] However, this one exception aside, the ECHR has not been at the vanguard of parental or children's rights in education. In none of the other major cases heard by the European Court of Human Rights on the right to education has a parent been successful in establishing a breach of education rights.[141] This arises first because the Convention rights are interpreted by the European Court of Human Rights in a practical and effective way rather than literally. Secondly, the majority of rights in the ECHR (including the right to education) are not absolute. They may be limited by the application of other ECHR rights and for other reasons by the contracting state provided that the interference has a legitimate aim and is considered to be necessary in a democratic society. In determining the latter, the European Court has taken account of such issues as the economic well-being of the country, the protection of health or morals and the prevention or disclosure of confidential information. Finally, the European Court of Human Rights gives contracting states "a margin of appreciation" in their compliance with Convention obligations. This means that the European Court is reluctant to substitute its own view of the merits of a case for that of the domestic authority, particularly when it is considering justifications for the interference with a right. In spite of these broad limitations to the application of the rights, it is widely acknowledged that the ECHR has the potential to exercise a significant influence on the content of education law in the United Kingdom and will be

---

[137] See, *Salomon v Commissioners of Customs and Excise* [1966] 3 All ER 871, at 875.
[138] Northern Ireland Act 1998, s. 69. See further para. 1.28.
[139] *Ibid* s.26. See further para. 1.26.
[140] *Campbell and Cosans v United Kingdom* (1982) EHRR 293.
[141] *The Belgian Linguistic Case* (1968) 1 EHRR 252, *The Dutch Sex Education Case* (1976) 1 EHRR 711 and *Valsamis v Greece* (1997) 24 EHRR 294.

of increased significance in the United Kingdom generally from October 2000 (see further para. 1.61).[142]

The right to education

1.52 Article 2 of the First Protocol of the Convention states:

> "No person shall be denied the right to education. In the exercise of any functions which it assumes in relation to education and teaching, the state shall respect the right of parents to ensure such education and teaching in conformity with their own religious and philosophical convictions."

When the Convention was being drafted, the substance of the right to education was the subject of much dispute. It was initially drafted as a positive right (i.e. "every person has the right to education"). However, the wording was changed following objections by those who considered that this would impose over burdensome requirements on contracting states.[143] In *The Belgian Linguistic* case the European Court of Human Rights considered that the right to education under Article 2 of the First Protocol encompassed two key elements: (i) the right of access to existing educational institutions and; (ii) the right to official recognition of studies.[144] The judgment also implies a third right, the right to an effective education.[145] However, the court stressed that the Convention did not require contracting parties "to establish at their own expense, or to subsidise, education of any particular type or level". Moreover, it emphasised that the right of access to education "by its very nature calls for regulation by the State, regulation which may vary in time and place according to the needs and resources of the community and of individuals."[146] On the basis of this, it has been observed that the funding and organisation of education is the state's decision and "the rights that individuals have in the state system are only those which the state, in its discretion, provides".[147] Essentially, the state must establish a satisfactory system of education and individuals then have a right of access to whatever education system the state has decided to provide. Thus in *The Belgian Linguistics Case* the Court found that Article 2 of the First Protocol did not give parents a right to have their child educated in a minority language. In a similar vein, the European Commission on Human Rights considered that the Convention did not give parents the right to have their child educated at a private school which catered specifically for dyslexic children.[148]

---

[142] See generally, A. Bradley, 'Scope for Review: The Convention Right to Education and the Human Rights Act 1998' [1999] EHRLR 395.
[143] Robertson and Merrills, *Human Rights in Europe* (1993) pp. 218-9.
[144] (1968) 1 EHRR 252.
[145] See Harris, O'Boyle and Warbrick, *Law of the European Convention on Human Rights* (1995) p. 543.
[146] (1968) 1 EHRR 252 at p. 281.
[147] Harris, O'Boyle and Warbrick, *Law of the European Convention on Human Rights* (1995) p.541.
[148] *Simpson v United Kingdom* (1989) 64 DR 188.

Parental rights in education

1.53 The second sentence of Article 2 of the First Protocol is concerned with parental rights. Its purpose is to ensure that parents retain some control over their child's education and thus prevent indoctrination by the state.[149] The scope of the second sentence was considered in the case of *Campbell and Cosans* v *UK* in which a parent objected to the use of corporal punishment. The Court defined the term "philosophical convictions" to mean "such convictions as are worthy of respect in a 'democratic society' and are not incompatible with human dignity".[150] The European Commission has been similarly cautious about what constitutes a philosophical opinion. For instance, in *W and DM* v *United Kingdom* the Commission did not consider that the parent's wish for their child to attend a single sex grammar school because of a fundamental objection to comprehensive education amounted to a philosophical conviction.[151] Moreover in a case taken against Germany, the Commission considered that the second sentence of the provision did not give parents the right to insist on their child being taught "elementary arithmetic" rather than "modern mathematics".[152]

1.54 In *Campbell and Cosans* v *United Kingdom*, the Court considered that the convictions must not conflict with the fundamental right of a child to education because the whole of Article 2 of the First Protocol was "dominated by its first sentence". Thus parental wishes are not absolute, a point illustrated in The *Dutch Sex Education* case where the Court rejected a claim by parents that a system of compulsory sex education infringed their rights provided that the information was presented in an "objective, critical and pluralistic manner".[153] Similarly, the European Commission on Human Rights considered that even if a parent's objection to his or her child being educated in a special school was based on a philosophical conviction, the educational interests of the child could override this.[154]

1.55 In determining whether there has been a breach of the second sentence of Article 2 of the First Protocol, the Court will give consideration as to whether the state's action is actually incompatible with the parents' convictions. Thus, in *Valsamis* v *Greece* the European Court of Human Rights considered that the contracting state had not been in breach of its obligations under Article 2 of the First Protocol or Article 9 when it required a pupil to participate in a school parade to celebrate Greece's National Day.[155] The child was a Jehovah's Witness and her parents objected to her participation on the grounds that their religion prohibited any conduct associated with war. The Court considered that there was nothing in the school's requirement that could offend her parents' convictions.

---

[149] *Ibid* p.544.
[150] (1982) EHRR 293.
[151] (1984) 37 DR 96.
[152] *X, Y and Z* v *Germany* (1982) 29 DR 224.
[153] *Kjelsden, Busk Masden and Pederson* v *Denmark* (1976) 1 EHRR 711.
[154] *PD* v *United Kingdom* (1989) 62 DR 292.
[155] (1997) 24 EHRR 294.

1.56 When Article 2 of the First Protocol was in the process of being drafted many contracting parties had concerns about its scope and entered reservations.[156] In the United Kingdom's case, the reservation states that "the principle affirmed in the second sentence of Article 2 is accepted by the United Kingdom only so far as it is compatible with the provision of efficient education and training, and the avoidance of unreasonable public expenditure". This phrase appears throughout national education law and operates to limit state provision to what is considered to be a reasonable use of resources. Many of the cases which have gone before the European Commission on Human Rights have been considered inadmissible because of the wide discretion given to the United Kingdom when it is determining how best to use education resources.[157]

Other relevant Convention rights

1.57 Article 6(1) of the ECHR relates to the right to a fair trial. It states that: "in the determination of his civil rights and obligations... Everyone is entitled to a fair and public hearing within a reasonable time by an independent and impartial tribunal established by law". This has been taken to include a requirement to give a reasoned decision; to allow the person a meaningful opportunity to state their case; and to give reasonable notice of the length and time of the hearing. It also means that the tribunal must be ready and willing to conduct a thorough examination of the facts at issue. The potential scope of Article 6(1) in education cases is limited by the fact that it only applies to "civil rights and obligations" and does not cover rights which might be characterised as public. Thus in *Simpson* v *United Kingdom* the Commission ruled that a decision to deny a child access to a particular form of education was a public law issue and one to which Article 6(1) did not apply.[158] The Commission stated that: "the right not to be denied elementary education falls, in the circumstances of the present case, squarely within the domain of public law, having no private law analogy and no repercussions on private rights and obligations."[159] This would by analogy also apply to school admissions decisions generally. However, the scope of Article 6(1) is somewhat grey and continually evolving. It remains possible that it might be considered to apply to other educational issues such as those relating to school discipline. Support for this might be drawn from the fact that Article 6(1) has been taken to apply to disciplinary decisions in an employment context.[160] Moreover, some issues in school admissions, discipline and special educational needs also give rise to private law actions (such as actions for negligence) and may therefore be considered to fall within the scope of Article 6(1).

1.58 Article 14 of the ECHR states that "The enjoyment of rights and freedoms set forth in this Convention shall be secured without discrimination on any ground such as sex, race, colour, language, religion, political or other

---

[156] Robertson and Merrills, *Human Rights in Europe*, (1993) p.219.
[157] See for instance, *Graeme* v *United Kingdom* (1990) 64 Dr 158 (parents wanted special needs child to attend a mainstream school) and *W and DM* v *United Kingdom* (1984) 37 DR 96 (parents wanted child to attend a single sex grammar school).
[158] (1989) 64 DR 188.
[159] *Ibid* para. 1
[160] See for instance *Albert and Le Compte* v *Belgium* (1983) 13 EHRR 415.

opinion, national or social origin, association with a national minority, property, birth or other status". The phrase "or other status" has been interpreted by the European Court of Human Rights to include sexual orientation, marital status and disability. An important point to note about Article 14 is that it is not free-standing. It only attaches to discrimination in the provision of other rights under the ECHR (such as the right not to be denied education). However, Article 14 is potentially of great significance in the sphere of education because it opens the possibility of cases on issues not covered by domestic equality legislation. In particular current legislation on disability and religion contains exemptions in the case of education. Moreover, although the Race Relations (NI) Order 1997 does apply to education, there is no specific protection in relation to language discrimination where the language is not connected to a specific racial group. There are a range of issues where Article 14 may be of significance. The obvious areas for allegations of discrimination are in relation to decisions regarding school finance and individual admissions. That said, in *The Belgian Linguistics Case,* the European Court of Human Rights interpreted Article 14 in such a way as to give states a wide discretion in relation to the provision of education. In particular, it stated that Article 14 does not "prohibit distinctions in treatment which are founded on an objective assessment of essentially different factual circumstances and which. . . strike a fair balance" between the interests of the Community and respect for ECHR rights and freedoms.[161] Given that in *The Belgian Linguistics Case* Article 2 of the First Protocol was interpreted as a right of access to existing schools, cases which allege discrimination in relation to individual school admissions rather than discrimination in the funding arrangements between schools of different categories may be more likely to meet with success. In *The Belgian Linguistics Case* itself, the European Court of Human Rights considered that Belgium did not have to fund schools in a minority language within a region but that it was in breach of Article 14 when read with Article 2 of the First Protocol when it refused to allow pupils to go to schools outside their own region to receive education in their preferred language.

1.59 There are several other provisions in the Convention which are of relevance in schools. The first is Article 3 which states that no one will be subjected to "torture or to inhuman or degrading treatment or punishment". This has been considered in a number of cases involving discipline in schools and is considered further at paragraph 7.43. Three other ECHR rights of significance are Article 8 (respect for privacy and family life), Article 9 (freedom of thought, conscience and religion) and Article 10 (freedom of expression). In most cases relating to schools, arguments involving these have been combined with arguments about the right to education in Article 2 of the First Protocol.[162]

---

[161] (1968) 1 EHRR 252 at p. 293.
[162] See for instance, *The Dutch Sex Education Case* (Article 8) and *Valsamis* v *Greece* (Article 9) discussed above.

Implications for Northern Ireland

1.60 Individuals may complain about breaches of Convention rights to the European Court of Human Rights. Applications have been made regularly from Northern Ireland where "lawyers seem well aware of its existence and are prepared to invoke it without hesitation".[163] Many of the cases have concerned issues arising from the 'troubles'. However, this has raised general awareness of the Convention with the result that there have been a significant number of cases on ordinary civil issues. In *X* v *United Kingdom* parents complained that a failure to provide 100 per cent funding for integrated schools amounted to a breach of Article 2 of the First Protocol.[164] Although the case was not admissible, it did serve to raise awareness of the human rights implications of the issue (which has since been resolved to a large degree).[165] Moreover, the ECHR has had an impact on the development of education law in the United Kingdom generally. The most notable illustration of this was the landmark case of *Campbell and Cosans* v *UK*, a Scottish case which resulted in the abolition of corporal punishment in state schools throughout the United Kingdom.[166]

Human Rights Act 1998

1.61 The influence of the Convention within Northern Ireland has undoubtedly increased as a result of the provisions of Northern Ireland Act 1998 discussed earlier in this chapter.[167] However, the United Kingdom Human Rights Act 1998 which came into force on 2 October 2000 should have an even greater impact. The Act, which extends to Northern Ireland, allows individuals to complain about breaches of certain Convention rights in the national courts.[168] Secondly, the Act requires legislation, whenever made, to be interpreted and applied in so far as possible in a way that is compatible with the Convention rights.[169] If a higher court finds a legislative provision to be incompatible with Convention rights, the court can make a declaration of incompatibility.[170] In such cases, the legislation will continue to be valid but a Minister may remove the incompatibility with a remedial order. Finally, the Act makes it unlawful for a public authority (including courts and tribunals) to act in a way that is incompatible with Convention rights.[171]

1.62 It is apparent that the Human Rights Act will have far-reaching implications on the law in the United Kingdom. Education law is no exception to this. From now on those wishing to challenge school-related decisions will undoubtedly subject the relevant provisions or actions of the

---

[163] Dickson, "Northern Ireland and the European Convention", Chapter 5 in Dickson (ed), *Human Rights and the European Convention* (1997) p.182.
[164] (1978) 14 DR 179.
[165] In 1990 the government made a statutory commitment to the development of integrated education. In 1993 it offered voluntary schools the option of funding for full capital costs.
[166] (1982) EHRR 293. See generally Chapter 7.
[167] See the discussion at paras. 1.28-1.30.
[168] Human Rights Act 1998, s.1.
[169] *Ibid* s.3.
[170] *Ibid* s.4.
[171] *Ibid* s.6.

education authority to close scrutiny as regards their compliance with the Convention rights. In this respect, it should be noted that the government has included in the new legislation its existing reservation to the second sentence of Article 2 of the First Protocol, thus restricting compliance to instances which are compatible with the provision of efficient education or the avoidance of unreasonable public expenditure.[172] Its reason for doing so was to ensure that a balance would be struck between "the convictions of parents and what is educationally sound and affordable".[173] However, as Harris points out "not all shortcomings in the education system are attributable to the inadequacy of resources".[174] In such instances, suspected breaches of the Convention will be able to be brought to a national court or tribunal with relative ease. For this reason, the significance of the Convention is considered throughout the book: existing case law is discussed at relevant points and potential breaches of the Convention are highlighted as they arise.

---

[172] *Ibid* Sch. 3.
[173] The Home Office, *Rights Brought Home: the Human Rights Bill*, (1997) Cm. 3782, para. 4.6.
[174] See 'The Three R's: Rights, Remedies and Regulation – the Legal Frontiers of Education in the 1990s (1998) XX1 1/2 *Liverpool Law Review* 7, at p. 40.

CHAPTER TWO

THE NORTHERN IRELAND SCHOOL SYSTEM

INTRODUCTION

2.01 This chapter describes the legal provisions which govern the organisation of the Northern Ireland school system. The first three sections (paras. 2.04-2.31) give a basic account of the key players: the main statutory organisations and categories of school. The statutory organisations have a relatively simple hierarchical structure with the Department at the top overseeing Education and Library Boards who, when the 1998 Order is fully implemented, will provide funding to all schools. Added to this scheme is the Council for Catholic Maintained Schools (CCMS) who manage Catholic primary and secondary schools. In contrast, the categorisation of individual schools appears much more complicated, perhaps because the terminology may be unfamiliar to those outside the education system. Essentially there are three key categories of school: (i) controlled schools, (ii) voluntary schools and (iii) grant-maintained integrated schools. Controlled schools are under the domain of ELBs. Voluntary schools are owned by trustees (who are normally the local churches). Grant-maintained integrated schools were introduced in 1990 to increase opportunities for integrated education. A knowledge of the specific categories of schools is important for those wishing to exercise any legal rights in this area. For instance it is important to know that the CCMS has no responsibility for Catholic grammar schools and therefore could not be joined as a defendant in proceedings against such a school. The first part of this chapter attempts to clarify these relationships through a description of the management of each type of school.

2.02 Paragraphs 2.32-2.62 of the chapter examine how the state ensures that there is appropriate school provision and that it is organised in such a way that it does not unlawfully discriminate. There are a number of different types of school in Northern Ireland. These attempt to meet the different needs of children in terms of their age (nursery, primary and secondary), ability (special needs and grammar) and parental preferences (integrated and Irish medium). ELBs are under a statutory obligation to ensure that there are sufficient schools in their area in terms of number, character and equipment to afford all pupils the opportunity for education. The educational requirements of the children of Northern Ireland do not remain stagnant. Educational provision must reflect both demographic and geographic changes in the population. In addition, the increased popularity of newer forms of education such as integrated schools can have an effect on the overall pattern of education in an area. ELBs are responsible for monitoring the sufficiency of provision in their area. All major changes to educational provision must be advanced by the ELB but are ultimately subject to Departmental approval. The legislation prescribes the procedures which must be followed when major changes are proposed. It does not, however, specify any particular substantive conditions for the establishment, funding or discontinuance of grant-aided schools. This is left to the discretion of the Department. Decisions regarding provision may be subject to legal challenge where the Department or the ELBs have acted illegally, unreasonably or unfairly or can be considered to have discriminated unlawfully - a possibility considered in paragraphs 2.76-2.80. In Great Britain changes to schools are repeatedly challenged particularly where the decision involves the closure of a school in the process of a rationalisation exercise. In Northern Ireland, the Department has also pursued a policy of rationalisation although it has declared a commitment to retain small schools to meet the needs of local communities. Instead, the provisions in relation to major changes in schools in Northern Ireland have been most contentious in relation to the establishment and funding of new schools. Integrated schools and Irish medium schools have been at the forefront of attempts to secure state funding for new or existing independent schools. Since 1989, there have been specific statutory procedures in force for the establishment of integrated schools. These are considered separately in Chapter 9. All other schools are subject to the statutory requirements of article 14 of the 1986 Order which are considered in paragraphs 2.40-2.54.

2.03 The final section of the chapter (paras. 2.63-2.80) examines the way in which the various educational players may be held accountable at law. In recent years there has been a steady increase in the litigation and other challenges to decisions involving schools. There is no simple explanation for this although two factors are undoubtedly significant. First, the thrust of legislation in the past 20 years has been on education rights. This, coupled with documents such as the Parents' Charter, has increased parents' expectations, awareness of their entitlement and willingness to complain. The second factor is the fact that legal aid is now available to children in their own right. This means that it is assessed on the child's income and not the parents', a factor which opens the gateway to law for many parents who could not otherwise afford to embark on litigation. At the outset, it should be stressed that litigation is not the only way in which decisions regarding schooling can be challenged. The final section of this chapter sets out some of the key alternatives: complaints to the Department, the Ombudsman/Commissioner for Complaints and education appeal tribunals. It concludes with a brief analysis of the judicial review procedure which has become the main mechanism through which decisions taken by schools are scrutinised in court.

ORGANISATIONS WITH A STATUTORY REMIT

2.04 Northern Ireland has a number of bodies which have a statutory remit in relation to education. The functions of three of these: (i) the Department of Education, (ii) ELBs and (iii) the CCMS are considered in this chapter.

Department of Education

2.05 Under the system of direct rule which was in place in Northern Ireland until 1999, the overall responsibility for the internal government of Northern Ireland rested with the Northern Ireland Office, headed by the Secretary of State for Northern Ireland. The Department of Education (DENI) was headed by a British minister. As a result of the implementation of the Northern Ireland Act 1998, the Department of Education (the Department) is headed by a locally-elected Minister for Education. Prior to 1999 DENI had responsibility for the whole range of education from nursery education to further and higher education as well as sport and recreation, the youth service, libraries and community relations. As a result of the reallocation of functions between departments under the new devolved arrangements, the Department no longer has statutory responsibilities in relation to further and higher education.[1]

2.06 The Department's general duty under article 3 of the Education Reform (NI) Order 1989 is "to promote the education of the people of Northern Ireland". This is so broad that it would be difficult to enforce specifically. However, the Department is also placed under a number of quite specific statutory obligations which are considered in the relevant chapters of the book. At a more general level the Department has the responsibility for ensuring the efficient operation of the education system in Northern Ireland. Article 3(1)(b) of the 1986 Order requires it to:

> "to secure the effective execution by boards and other bodies on which or persons on whom powers are conferred or duties imposed under the Education Order of the Department's policy in relation to the provision of the Education service."

The Department is the body which acts as an umbrella over all the other educational institutions. It has the role of ensuring that other bodies are carrying out their statutory functions and that educational provision is operating satisfactorily throughout Northern Ireland.

Education and Library Boards

2.07 Since the foundation of Northern Ireland as a separate political entity, educational services have been administered by regional education bodies. The 1921 Lynn Report recommended that there should be a system of devolved administration to local education committees who would have a majority of representation from the local authority as well as those interested in education.[2] The Lynn Committee rejected the idea that these units should be organised on a county level as was the case in England and Wales in view of the more limited travelling facilities as well as the level of interest in and experience in local affairs. Instead, it recommended that committees should be based on smaller local units such as county boroughs, and urban and rural districts. The government accepted the need for smaller administrative units but chose to use regional education committees which were not based on the existing local government structures. The Education Act 1923 provided for regional education committees to exercise the powers and duties of county education authorities.[3] This system continued to form the basis for educational administration in Northern Ireland until after the general review of local government undertaken in Northern Ireland 1970. This recommended a system based on not more than five area boards "of broadly comparable size and importance from the point of view of the population and financial resources".[4] The recommendations were given effect by the Education and

---

[1] The responsibility for Further and Higher Education has been transferred to a new Department, the Department of Further and Higher Education
[2] *Interim Report of the Departmental Committee on the Educational Services in Northern Ireland* (1921) Cmd. 6, paras. 96 and 97.
[3] S.2.
[4] Para. 49.

Libraries (NI) Order 1972, article 3. This was consolidated in the Education and Libraries (NI) Order 1986 which contains the current provisions for the establishment of the Education and Library Boards.

2.08 There are five Education and Library Boards (ELBs).[5] These are as follows: (i) Belfast Education and Library Board; (ii) South Eastern Education and Library Board; (iii) Southern Education and Library Board; (iv) Western Education and Library Board; and (v) North Eastern Education and Library Board. The Department has the power to amend the name or area of an ELB but this is subject to affirmative resolution.[6] The Draft Education (NI) Order 1997 proposed reducing the number of ELBs to four, the objective being to save costs which the government considered arose from duplication of posts. The Order met with great resistance locally and was not implemented. However, the issue may resurface as the Assembly attempts to keep educational expenditure within its budget.

Composition

2.09 The composition of the ELBs was established following the general review of local government in 1970. The review was primarily concerned with ensuring local democracy and fair representation of both sides of the community in all aspects of local government. For these purposes, the report recommended that the membership of ELBs should consist of "responsible and public-spirited persons, who on the one hand would owe their primary loyalty to the Boards and on the other hand, because they would be in a position to interpret the views of the main sectional interests, might be expected to induce a spirit of confidence, co-operation and goodwill among those interests".[7] The proposals were translated into legislation by the Education and Libraries (NI) Order 1972.

2.10 Each ELB is composed of the following people: members of the local district councils; persons representing the interests of transferors; representatives of the trustees of maintained schools; and persons deemed to be suitable by reason of their interest in the services for which the ELB is responsible.[8] This represents a clear attempt to ensure a balanced representation of the key organisations in the education field. Moreover, unlike Local Education Authorities in England and Wales, no political party can have overall control of an ELB. The legislation states that local council membership should be equal to two-fifths of the membership of the ELB.[9] The difference is significant since many of the Conservative-inspired education reforms of the 1980s were intended to reduce the influence of politically-motivated LEAs in England and Wales. Many of these reforms (e.g. grant-maintained schools and the common curriculum) were adopted in Northern Ireland in spite of the different administrative and political conditions pertaining.[10]

---

[5] Art. 3 of the 1986 Order.
[6] *Ibid* art. 3(3).
[7] *Review Body on Local Government in Northern Ireland* (1970) Cmd. 546, para. 49. This is commonly referred to as the 'McCrory' Report.
[8] Sch. 2, to the 1986 Order.
[9] *Ibid* Sch. 2, para.2(1)(a).
[10] See further, para.1.07.

Statutory functions

2.11 The general statutory duty of ELBs is set out in article 5 of the 1986 Order. This is as follows:

> "... to contribute towards the spiritual, moral, mental and physical development of the community by securing that efficient education [throughout the three stages of education: primary, secondary and further education] is available to meet the needs of its area."

More specifically, ELBs are under a duty to ensure that there are sufficient schools in their area.[11] Their other statutory responsibilities include the following: the establishment of controlled schools; the identification, assessment and statementing of children with special educational needs; transport, school meals and clothing grants; the employment of peripatetic and supply teachers; the employment of non-teaching staff in controlled and maintained schools; curriculum advice and support; the enforcement of school attendance; and the administration of admission, curriculum and exclusion appeals. When the 1998 Order is fully implemented, they will also have responsibility for distributing funding to all grant-aided schools including voluntary grammar and grant-maintained integrated schools.[12]

Council for Catholic Maintained Schools

2.12 The Council for Catholic Maintained Schools (CCMS) was established by the 1989 Order.[13] The CCMS describes itself as "a strategic organisation whose primary focus is to raise standards in Catholic maintained schools and to provide an upper tier of management for that system". The CCMS has responsibility for all Catholic primary and secondary schools as well as nursery and special schools. Its remit does not, however, extend to voluntary grammar schools. In addition to its statutory functions in relation to management, the CCMS employs all teachers in Catholic maintained schools.

2.13 Prior to 1990, there was no body with responsibility for overseeing activities in voluntary maintained schools. In effect, each school operated on an independent and autonomous basis, responsible to the ELBs on some issues and to the Department on others. The 1981 Astin Report had highlighted the need for an upper tier to oversee provision in the maintained sector.[14] The Catholic Church had also argued that there was a need for an umbrella organisation to co-ordinate activities in voluntary maintained schools, the majority of which were Catholic. In doing so, they were able to draw a contrast with controlled schools all of which are grouped under their local ELB. The government appears to have recognised the benefits of an organisation which would assist in the planning of provision in Catholic primary and secondary schools and gave the CCMS a statutory basis and remit as part of the wider educational reforms in the 1989 Order.

---

[11] Art. 6 of the 1986 Order.
[12] Education (NI) Order 1998.
[13] Art. 141 of the 1989 Order.
[14] *Report of the Working Party on the Management of Schools in Northern Ireland* (1981).

2.14 The CCMS is now well established and plays a key role in the educational structures in Northern Ireland. There is no equivalent body to represent the interests of the Protestant churches in controlled schools. The three main Protestant churches (the Church of Ireland, the Presbyterian Church and the Methodist Church) have established a voluntary organisation, The Transferors' Representatives Council, which represents the interests of these churches in the educational system. They have argued for statutory recognition and funding on the same basis as the CCMS. This has been resisted on the basis that controlled schools are essentially non-denominational in spite of the transferors' representation on the Board of Governors of such schools.

Composition of the CCMS

2.15 The CCMS is a large body composed of representatives of the Catholic Church, persons nominated by the Northern Ireland Bishops, persons appointed by the Department and parents and teachers. The precise composition of the CCMS is as follows: the Archbishop of Armagh or nominee; the Bishops of Clogher, Derry, Down and Connor, Dromore, Kilmore or their nominees; 14 persons appointed by the Archbishop and Bishops acting jointly; eight persons appointed by the Department after consultation with the Bishops; four parents who are member of Boards of Governors of Catholic maintained schools;[15] and four assistant teachers who are elected members of Boards of Governors of Catholic maintained schools.[16] The members of the CCMS who are drawn from elected parents and teachers on Boards of Governors must be chosen so as to represent as equitably as possible the interest of both primary and secondary schools and the interest of each of the diocesan areas.[17]

2.16 In practice the CCMS works through a number of diocesan education committees. These also have a statutory basis. There are five diocesan education committees, one for each of the following areas: Armagh; Clogher and Kilmore; Derry; Down and Connor; and Dromore. Each committee consists of the Bishop for the area; the trustees of Catholic maintained schools in the area; persons appointed by the Department after consultation with the Bishop; and parents and teachers.[18]

Statutory functions of the CCMS

2.17 The statutory functions of the CCMS are set out in article 142 of the 1989 Order. They are as follows: to advise the Department or an ELB on matters relating to Catholic maintained schools; to promote and co-ordinate, in consultation with the trustees of Catholic maintained schools, the effective provision of Catholic maintained schools; to promote the effective management and control by Boards of Governors; and, with the approval of the Department, to provide advice and information to trustees, Boards of Governors, principals and staff. The CCMS also has a number of specific

---

[15] Sch. 8, para.1(2) to the 1989 Order.
[16] *Ibid.*
[17] *Ibid* Sch. 8, para.1(3).
[18] *Ibid.*

statutory functions in areas such as admissions, discipline and the curriculum. These are discussed in the relevant chapters of the book.

2.18 In addition to its statutory functions, the Council has a number of other statutory remits. In particular, there are numerous occasions when the Department, ELBs or Boards of Governors must consult the CCMS before taking decisions about maintained schools or their pupils. These include: the preparation of schemes for financing maintained schools; the determination of admission and enrolment numbers; and the drafting of admissions criteria by Boards of Governors. Many of these were added after consultation on the draft Education Reform (NI) Order 1989. The CCMS produced a detailed set of recommendations which extended its right to be consulted on issues which might affect voluntary maintained schools.[19] Many of these were accepted by government and inserted into the legislation, further strengthening the role of the CCMS in the decision-making process in maintained schools.

CATEGORIES OF SCHOOL IN NORTHERN IRELAND

2.19 Northern Ireland has a unique mix of schools. An initial distinction can be drawn between grant-aided schools (those which receive public funding) and independent schools (those which are privately financed). However, it is the categorisation of grant-aided schools which is particularly distinctive. There are four main types of school: controlled; voluntary maintained; voluntary grammar and grant-maintained integrated. The two factors which distinguish these schools are the composition of the management board of the school and the level of public funding. Moreover, these two factors are related. The composition of the Board of Governors is directly related to the level of funding. It is also related to sources of funding. Voluntary grammar schools and grant-maintained integrated schools both have Departmental representation on the Board of Governors, which is linked to the fact that they are both funded directly by Department.[20]

Controlled

2.20 Controlled schools are managed by their local ELB through Boards of Governors.[21] The Boards of Governors of controlled primary and secondary schools usually contain representatives from the Protestant Churches (transferors), parents, teachers and nominees of the ELBs.[22]. The Boards of Governors of controlled grammar schools are composed of parents, teachers and the nominees of the ELB. Running costs are met in full under local management schemes administered by the ELB for the area. The full capital costs of controlled schools are also met by the local ELB. Controlled schools cannot have a particular religious denominational ethos but in practice are attended mainly by Protestant children. In 1998/99 there were 461 controlled primary schools (including three controlled integrated primary schools) and 76 controlled secondary schools (including one controlled integrated secondary

---

[19] *Response by the Council for Catholic Maintained Schools to the Proposal for a Draft Order in Council* (CCMS, 1989).
[20] Until the 1998 Order is implemented and transfers the responsibility to ELBs.
[21] Art. 10 of the 1986 Order.
[22] Sch. 4 to the 1986 Order substituted by art. 89 of the 1989 Order.

school). Of the 76 controlled secondary schools, 18 are controlled grammar schools and can select children on the basis of ability.

Voluntary maintained

2.21 Voluntary maintained schools are managed by Boards of Governors. Voluntary maintained schools may have a denominational ethos. Most of these schools are Catholic maintained schools falling under the auspices of the CCMS. The Board of Governors contains members nominated by the trustees of the school, together with representatives of parents, teachers and the ELB.[23] Full running costs are met in the same way as with controlled schools. Since 1993, voluntary maintained schools can opt for full capital funding in which case the Department has the right to nominate members on the Board of Governors.[24] If schools do not opt for this they can still receive 85 per cent or 65 per cent of their capital costs. Voluntary maintained schools include various primary, secondary, nursery and special schools. They do not include any grammar schools. In 1998/99 there were 440 maintained primary schools, of which all but 11 were Catholic maintained schools. There were 78 maintained secondary schools, only one of which was not a Catholic maintained school.

Voluntary grammar

2.22 Voluntary grammar schools are permitted to select their pupils on the basis of academic ability. Voluntary grammar schools are managed by Boards of Governors consisting of representatives of parents, teachers and the trustees of the school.[25] Where schools have an agreement with the Department or an ELB or both, some members are appointed by these bodies. Since 1993, voluntary grammar schools have been allowed to opt for full capital funding in which case Departmental representation on the Board of Governors increases. In other cases 65 per cent or 85 per cent of capital expenditure is derived from the Department which also meets the school's maintenance costs.[26] There are also two voluntary grammar schools which do not receive any assistance with capital costs and which consequently have complete autonomy over their management structures.[27] Voluntary grammar schools may have a particular denominational ethos. In 1998/99 there were 54 voluntary grammar schools (including 14 boys' schools, 15 girls' schools and 24 co-educational schools). 32 of the voluntary grammar schools are Catholic denominational schools.

Grant-maintained integrated

2.23 Integrated schools aim to achieve a reasonable balance of Roman Catholic and Protestant pupils.[28] There are two types of integrated schools: (i) controlled integrated schools and (ii) grant-maintained integrated schools

---

[23] Sch. 4 to the 1986 Order substituted by Sch. 3 to the 1993 Order.
[24] *Ibid.*
[25] Sch. 5 to the 1989 Order substituted by Sch. 2 of the 1993 Order.
[26] The Education (NI) Order 1998 contains provisions which when implemented will mean that voluntary grammar schools will receive their funding from the ELB.
[27] They are Royal Belfast Academical Institution and Campbell College.
[28] Art. 64 of the 1989 Order.

(GMI). The Board of Governors of a GMI school is composed of foundation governors, Departmental nominees, parents and teachers.[29] GMI schools are now funded directly by the Department.[30] Existing controlled and voluntary schools can apply for grant-maintained integrated status and it is also possible to establish a grant-maintained integrated school from scratch. In 1998/99 there were 26 GMI schools, 15 primary schools and 11 secondary schools.

Independent

2.24 Independent schools do not receive grant aid.[31] Instead parents pay fees to finance the school's activities. The basis of the relationship between parents and the school is contractual.[32] Much of the education legislation does not apply to these schools. Where particular provisions do apply, these are highlighted in the text. There are just over 20 independent schools in Northern Ireland.

FORMS OF EDUCATIONAL PROVISION

2.25 Schools in Northern Ireland are normally categorised according to their funding and management structure. However, schools can also be categorised according to the nature of the education provided. The following categories constitute the types of educational provision which are given some form of statutory recognition in the Education Orders.

Primary schools

2.26 This is a school which provides primary education. Primary education is defined as full-time education suitable to the requirements of junior pupils.[33] A junior pupil is a child who has not attained the age of 11 years and 6 months.

Secondary schools

2.27 This is a school which provides secondary education. Secondary education is defined as full-time education suitable to the needs of senior pupils.[34] A senior pupil is a child who has attained the age of 11 years and 6 months but is not yet aged 19. Secondary schools are classified into two further categories: (i) intermediate and (ii) grammar. Intermediate schools are defined as those which provide free education, that is are not allowed to charge pupils fees. However, in practice the key distinction between the two categories is that grammar schools are permitted to select pupils for admission on the basis of their academic ability. The term "intermediate" is never used to describe non-grammar schools which are generally referred to simply as "secondary" schools.

---

[29] Sch. 5 to the 1989 Order.
[30] The Education (NI) Order 1998 contains provisions which when implemented will mean that grant-maintained integrated schools will receive their funding from the ELB.
[31] Art. 2 of the 1986 Order.
[32] See *R v Fernhill Manor School, ex parte A* [1993]1 FLR 620.
[33] Art. 2 of the 1986 Order.
[34] *Ibid.*

Special schools

2.28 A special school is a school which has been recognised by the Department as being organised to make education provisions for pupils with special educational needs.[35] A child has special educational needs if he has a learning difficulty which calls for special educational provision to be made for him. In 1998/99 there were 47 special schools in Northern Ireland.

Nursery schools

2.29 A nursery school means a primary school which is used mainly for the purposes of providing education to children between the ages of two and five.[36]

Integrated schools

2.30 There are two types of integrated schools: (i) controlled and; (ii) grant-maintained. Integrated education is defined as the "education together at school of Protestant and Roman Catholic pupils."[37] Schools are not recognised as integrated schools unless they are likely to be attended by reasonable numbers of both Protestant and Roman Catholic pupils.

Irish medium schools

2.31 Northern Ireland has a number of schools in which children are taught through the medium of the Irish language (seven primary schools and one secondary school were grant-aided in 1998/99). The Education Orders refer to such schools as schools which are "Irish Speaking". Part III of the 1989 Order (which relates to the Northern Ireland curriculum) defines an Irish speaking school as one in which more than half of the subjects (other than Irish and English but including religious education) are taught in Irish.[38]

DUTY TO PROVIDE SUFFICIENT SCHOOLS

2.32 The Department is under a general duty to "promote the education of the people of Northern Ireland".[39] It is also under a duty to ensure that ELBs effectively execute their policy in relation to the education service.[40] The Department is not, however, under any specific duty to ensure that there are sufficient schools to ensure that all children have access to free education. This responsibility falls upon ELBs. Article 5 of the 1986 Order requires each ELB, so far as its powers extend, "to contribute towards the spiritual, moral, mental and physical development of the community" by securing that efficient education is available to meet the needs of its area. Article 6 of the 1986 Order places further obligations on ELBs in relation to primary and secondary education. It states that:

---

[35] Art. 3 of the 1996 Order.
[36] Art. 2 of the 1986 Order.
[37] Art. 64 of the 1989 Order.
[38] *Ibid* art. 35.
[39] *Ibid* art. 3(a).
[40] *Ibid* art. 3(b).

> "...each board shall secure that there are available in its area sufficient schools for providing primary and secondary education and the schools available for an area shall not be deemed to be sufficient unless they are sufficient in number, character and equipment to afford for all pupils opportunity for education offering such variety of instruction and training as may be desirable in view of their different ages, abilities and aptitudes, and of the different periods for which they may be expected to remain at school, including practical instruction and training appropriate to their respective needs. . ."

At first reading this would appear to place ELBs under a fairly specific duty to provide "sufficient" education. However, the provision has not been interpreted this way by the courts with the result that article 6 is of little assistance to individual parents wishing to secure a particular form of education for their child.

What is the position if an ELB fails to provide sufficient school places?

2.33   Although there have been occasions when ELBs have not been able to provide full-time school places for all children, this issue has not come before the courts in Northern Ireland. However, the equivalent provision in England and Wales was considered by the Court of Appeal in *Meade* v *Haringey LBC*.[41]   In that case a strike by school caretakers led to the closure of almost all the LEA's schools. However, the Court of Appeal considered that a failure to provide places did not necessarily result in a breach of the statutory duty. The Court stated:

> "Provided the grounds which they genuinely have for their action can be regarded as such a state of emergency, in other words, as just and reasonable excuse for the closure, the authority would not be in breach of duty."

Moreover, in *R* v *ILEA, ex parte Ali*, the applicant sought judicial review and attempted to claim damages for the local education authority's failure to provide his son with a place at a school.[42] The situation had arisen because of a shortage of teachers in the inner London area. Woolf LJ was of the opinion that a failure to comply with the standard set by the provision did not automatically give rise to a breach of the section where this had occurred through no fault of the education authority. Moreover, even if there had been a breach of the statute, he considered that a court should refuse to grant relief if the local authority was taking all reasonable steps to remedy the action. Finally, he dismissed the action for damages on the basis that the legislation was "intended to enure for the public in general and not intended to give the individual a right of action". The result is that there may be little for individual parents to rely on in domestic legislation if an ELB is not in a position to secure a school place for their child. An alternative means of redress might lie in a complaint about a breach of Article 2 of the First Protocol of the ECHR -

---

[41] [1979] 2 All ER 1016.
[42] [1990] COD 317.

the right not to be denied education.[43] It has been suggested that this may extend to situations where a system of universal provision is interrupted by a strike, mal-administration or a shortage of funds.[44]

What happens if parents are unhappy with the nature of the education provided?

2.34 The scope of the duty under article 6 of the 1986 Order was considered by the Northern Ireland courts in the case of *In re Cecil*.[45] The applicant, who lived on Rathlin Island, was the parent of two children. The ELB provided one Catholic maintained school on the island. The applicant withdrew his children from the school owing to an objection to the children being educated in a Catholic ethos. The ELB provided the children with tuition by a supply teacher in a mobile home. The parents wished for the arrangement to be given recognised controlled status. The ELB refused because they considered the arrangement to be financially unviable. Its argument was that there would only be six children at the school and when they left to go to secondary school, there would be no guarantee of other children taking their places. The parents argued that the ELB were in breach of its duty under article 6 by failing to provide schools which were "sufficient in character" to afford their children an opportunity for education. The High Court disagreed. Nicholson J considered that article 6 did not require an ELB to provide schools sufficient in their religious outlook to cater for pupils of differing religious beliefs or to provide sufficient non-denominational schools to cater for all pupils of differing religious beliefs. He considered that the religious ethos of a school could not make it unsuitable unless such ethos does not afford an opportunity for education for some of the pupils. He referred to articles 21 to 23 of the 1986 Order and concluded that the pupils could be withdrawn from religious instruction and that the school had to be arranged in such a way that it would be open to pupils of all denominations. Furthermore Nicholson J stressed that the duty is limiting to ensuring that the schools are sufficient in character "to afford opportunities for education". He concluded:

> "The character of the school, as such, does not have to be suitable for all pupils. The school may be too academic for some, too practical for others, too keen on sport or particular sports for others, too religious for others. But if it affords for all pupils opportunities for education other than for religious instruction it fulfils the criteria set out in Article 6 (1)."

This interpretation is supported by the fact that the word "sufficient" is used rather than "suitable". Moreover, article 6 goes on to specify that the variety of instruction should be such as is "desirable" in view of children's different age, abilities and aptitude. On this basis, article 6 could be interpreted in such a way as to limit the ELB's duty to providing primary and secondary schools (age) and secondary, grammar and special schools (ability and aptitude). The duty is effectively restricted to providing schools which are appropriate for the

---

[43] See para. 1.52.
[44] See A. Bradley, 'Scope for Review: The Convention Right to Education and the Human Rights Act 1998' [1999] EHRLR 395 at 403.
[45] Unreported decision of the High Court of Northern Ireland, 27 January 1989.

child's educational needs and not to providing the type of education which the parent wishes for their child.

2.35 The equivalent provision in England and Wales has also been interpreted restrictively. In *Secretary of State for Education and Science* v *Tameside Metropolitan Borough* the House of Lords stated that the English equivalent of article 6 left local authorities with a broad discretion to choose what in their judgment were the means best suited to their area for providing instruction.[46] In *Smith* v *LEA* parents complained that their local LEA was in breach of its statutory duty when it proposed to abolish a grammar school as part of its ongoing plans for a complete comprehensive system in its area.[47] The Court of Appeal considered that this did not entail a breach of the statutory duty to provide schools "sufficient in character". Lane LJ said:

> "'Character' in this context means the intangible attributes of a school. For example, the type of pupil: girls, boys or mixed; the type of instruction available: religious academic or practical; and so on. What it does not mean is the size or method of selection adopted in any particular institution. Provided the authority make available for children in their (sic) area a sufficient variety of educational opportunity in the various subjects which should properly be taught, it matters not whether the schools are small or large, or whether the bright pupils are taught in a separate school from the less bright or whether all pupils are taught in the same school under one roof."[48]

In *In re Cecil* counsel for the applicant tried to use the above dicta to argue that "character" included religious ethos. Nicholson J did not accept the relevance of this taken in isolation from the rest of the provision, stressing that it was only if the "character" had the effect of excluding the pupils in question from the opportunity of education that article 6 was breached.

2.36 The ECHR does not extend parental rights in this context to any great extent. Although Article 2 of the First Protocol states that no person shall be denied the right to education, this has been interpreted to mean a right of access to such institutions as exist rather than those which the individual or parents would choose.[49] Moreover, although states are required to respect the right of parents to ensure education in conformity with their religious and philosophical convictions, the United Kingdom has entered a reservation limiting this to what is compatible with the provision of efficient education and the avoidance of unreasonable public expenditure.[50] There are consequently very limited rights to complain about the nature of the education provided in the United Kingdom's school system unless there are quite specific instances where schools have breached the Convention.

---

[46] [1976] 3 All ER 665.
[47] [1978] 1 All ER 411.
[48] *Ibid* pp. 424-425.
[49] *The Belgian Linguistic Case* (1968) 1 EHRR 252.
[50] See generally paras. 1.52-1.57.

PROVISION OF EDUCATION OTHERWISE THAN AT SCHOOL

2.37 Under article 6(3) of the 1986 Order, where an ELB was satisfied that, "by reason of exceptional circumstances", a child was unable to attend a suitable school, the ELB had a power (not an obligation) to make such special arrangements as it considered suitable for the education of the child otherwise than at a school. Article 6(3) has been replaced by article 86 of the 1998 Order. This requires ELBs to make arrangements for the provision of suitable education at school or otherwise than at school for those children of compulsory school age who by reason of, illness, expulsion or suspension from school or otherwise, may not for any period receive suitable education unless such arrangements are made for them. In this context, as in most others, suitable education is defined as "efficient education suitable to his age, ability and aptitude and to any special educational needs he may have".[51]

2.38 At the outset, this provision must be distinguished from the parent's right to educate his or her child at home, that is, to secure education for the child "otherwise than at school". This arises under article 45 of the 1986 Order.[52] Instead, article 86(1) covers illness, exclusion and the other circumstances when an ELB will take responsibility for securing educational provision but does so outside of a formal school environment. There are various ways in which an ELB can arrange suitable provision. For instance, the ELB may deem it appropriate to provide some home tuition. One example of this arose on the facts of *In re Cecil* where the ELB was providing the applicant's children with tuition in a mobile classroom.[53] ELBs can also establish special schools called pupil referral units to provide education for children outside of mainstream schools.[54]

2.39 Article 86 of the 1998 Order is similar to section 19 of the Education Act 1996. This provision was considered in a series of English cases which ended up in the House of Lords. In *R v East Sussex County Council, ex parte Tandy*, the applicant, a 15 year old girl with a debilitative illness, had her home tuition reduced from five hours to three hours because of financial cuts made by the LEA.[55] The High Court considered that it was unlawful for the LEA to take financial considerations into account when determining her educational needs but this decision was overturned by the Court of Appeal. The House of Lords restored the decision of the High Court. It considered that financial considerations were irrelevant to the question of what constituted suitable education. In its view resources could only be taken into account where there was more than one way of providing suitable education, for example a choice between a pupil referral unit and home tuition.

---

[51] Art. 86(5) of the 1998 Order.
[52] Education at home is considered in detail at paras. 6.24-6.29.
[53] Unreported decision of the Northern Ireland High Court, 27 January 1989.
[54] Art. 86 (2) of the 1998 Order.
[55] [1998] ELR 80.

PROPOSALS FOR CHANGES TO SCHOOLS

2.40 Schools cannot close or make major changes to their character or size on their own initiative. Nor does any school have an automatic right to be afforded recognised grant-aided status. Instead all major initiatives which may have an impact on the overall provision of grant-aided education are subject to the approval of the Department. This is necessary to ensure that there is an appropriate balance of schools and that public funding for education is being used efficiently. Article 14 of the 1986 Order regulates the establishment, recognition, discontinuance and other major changes in grant-aided schools. In each of the following prescribed circumstances, the ELB must submit a proposal to the Department for approval. Major changes in one ELB (e.g. a school closure) may have an impact on provision in another ELB particularly if it relates to a school on the administrative border. The involvement of the Department ensures that decisions are taken on a Northern-Ireland wide basis rather than simply within the five ELBs.

2.41 The circumstances covered by article 14 are as follows:

(1) Establishing a controlled or voluntary school;

(2) Having an existing (non grant-aided) school recognised as a controlled or voluntary school;

(3) Discontinuing a school;

(4) Making significant changes in the character or size of a controlled school;

(5) Making other changes which would have a significant effect on another grant-aided school.

There is no specific category for amalgamations. Amalgamations (i.e. the merger of two or more schools) could be handled in one of two ways: as a significant change in character or size or as a discontinuance followed by an establishment of a new school. There is authority to suggest that the correct proposal is for a significant change of character.[56] However, in *R v Secretary of State, ex parte Russell* an LEA adopted the latter approach.[57] The court considered that unless the LEA was trying to deceive those reading the notices, the court would not intervene.

Procedural requirements

Who can propose changes?

2.42 In each of these cases a proposal must be submitted to the Department by the ELB.[58] In controlled schools the proposal is submitted directly from the ELB. In voluntary schools, the proposal may be made by a person other than an ELB. In such cases, that person must submit a proposal to the ELB who will then submit the proposal to the Department along with its views on the

---

[56] See *Bradbury v Enfield* [1967] 1 WLR 1311.
[57] Unreported, 28 June 1983.
[58] Art. 14(5) of the 1986 Order.

proposal.[59] In certain specified circumstances, the Department can require the ELB to submit a proposal for change. These are: proposals to establish a new controlled school; proposals that a controlled or voluntary school should be discontinued; and proposals that a significant change should be made in the character or size of a controlled or voluntary school.[60]

Consultation by ELB

2.43 Before it submits a proposal to the Department, the ELB must consult the trustees and managers of any school or schools which would, in its opinion, be affected by the proposal.[61] After it has submitted the proposal it must furnish the trustees and managers of such schools with enough particulars of the proposal as are sufficient to show the manner in which the school would be affected.[62] The ELB must also publish in one or more newspapers circulating in the area affected by the proposal a notice stating the nature of the proposal, that the proposal has been submitted to the Department, that a copy of the proposal can be inspected at a specified place and that objections can be made within two months of the date specified in the advertisement.[63] Finally the ELB must provide any person who requests it with a copy of the proposal on the payment of a reasonable charge.[64] It should be noted that there is no specific duty to consult the parents of children at the school nor the pupils themselves. However, in a number of English cases, courts considered that a parent whose child's school was being discontinued had a legitimate expectation to be consulted at an early stage and in particular before proposals were published.[65] The equivalent legislation in relation to discontinuances in England and Wales now provides for a more extensive consultation exercise pre-publication.[66]

2.44 A failure to comply with the statutory requirements in relation to the consultation procedures may be challenged by way of judicial review. It is clear that the consultation must be adequate. In *R v Brent London Borough Council, ex parte Gunning*, the court accepted the formulation of Sedley QC (as he then was) who proposed some basic principles for fair consultation:

> "First, the consultation must be at a time when proposals are still at a formative stage. Second, that the proposer must give sufficient reasons for any proposal to permit intelligent consideration and response. Third, . . . that adequate time must be given for consideration and response and finally, fourth that

---

[59] *Ibid* art. 14(2).
[60] *Ibid* art. 14(3).
[61] *Ibid* art. 14(5).
[62] *Ibid* art. 14(6)(a).
[63] *Ibid* art. 14(6)(b).
[64] *Ibid* art. 14(6)(c).
[65] See for instance, *R v London Borough of Sutton,* unreported decision of the English High Court (1986). However, the courts were also prepared to consider whether any unfairness had been rectified in the subsequent statutory consultation. See *R v Secretary of State for Education, ex parte Cumbria County Council* [1994] ELR 220.
[66] S. 35 of the Education Act 1996.

the product of the consultation must be conscientiously taken into account in finalising any statutory proposals."[67]

The statutory requirements cover most aspects of the first three points. There may, however, be instance where objectors consider that the decision-maker has already made its mind up and is not open to any points made in the consultation process. For instance, in an English case, *R* v *Buckinghamshire CC, ex parte Milton Keynes* the applicant alleged that there had been a failure to consider objections properly because the council had imposed a three line whip.[68] The court rejected this, concluding that there had been a meaningful consideration of the results of the consultation in spite of the whip.

Approval by the Department

2.45 The Department must consider any objections made within the time specified in the notice published in the newspaper.[69] It may then make any modifications that it considers necessary or expedient after consultation with the ELB or person making the proposal. In cases where the Department has directed the ELB to submit a proposal, the Department must consult with the trustees or managers of the school to which the proposal relates. The Department may then approve the proposal and must inform the ELB or person making the proposal accordingly. A proposal may not be implemented until it has been approved by the Department.[70]

Establishment of a new school

2.46 Article 15 of the 1986 Order specifies the steps which must be taken in relation to a proposal to establish a new school from scratch. It should be noted that there are no specified substantive criteria for the establishment of a new school. Approval is at the discretion of the Department and is not open to challenge unless the Department acts unlawfully, unreasonably or unfairly. The Department has its own guidelines which specify what it considers to be necessary before a new school is considered to be viable and these are amended from time to time.[71] Instead, the statutory provisions set out the extra procedures which must be followed when a proposal for establishment is being submitted. These focus on the submission of specifications and plans for school premises. Article 15(1) requires the ELB or person seeking to establish the school to submit specifications and plans for the school premises. The Department must be satisfied that these conform to the standard it requires or else approve them with exemptions. Once the proposal, specifications and plans have been approved, the ELB or person establishing the school must adhere to them.[72] If the proposal is to establish a voluntary school, the Department will not approve the proposal unless the school is to be

---

[67] [1985] 84 LGR 168.
[68] [1997] Admin LR 158.
[69] Art. 14(7) of the 1986 Order.
[70] *Ibid* art. 14(9).
[71] These focus on the projected pupil enrolments. See generally, *In re Scullion* (1995), unreported decision of the High Court of Northern Ireland.
[72] Art. 15(2) of the 1986 Order.

a maintained school or if it is to be a grammar school, the trustees or Board of Governors must enter into an agreement under Schedule 6 to the 1986 Order.[73]

Recognition as a grant-aided school

2.47 Some schools begin independently through private finance or fund-raising initiatives and then seek grant-aided status. This is the way in which many integrated and Irish medium schools began. Recognition is also covered by article 15 of the 1986 Order. However, there are no extra statutory provisions on the procedure for acquiring recognition of an existing school other than the procedures set out in article 14 of the 1986 Order. Once again the Department applies its own criteria in determining which schools are eligible for grant-aided funding. Where the Department approves a proposal for recognition it may grant that recognition upon such terms and subject to such conditions as it may determine.[74] Moreover, if the proposal is to recognise a voluntary school, the Department will not approve the proposal unless the school is to be a maintained school or if it is to be a grammar school, the trustees or Board of Governors must enter into an agreement under Schedule 6 to the 1986 Order.[75]

Discontinuance

2.48 Both controlled and voluntary schools may be discontinued following the procedures in article 14 of the 1986 Order. However, there are additional rules which apply when a voluntary school is discontinued.[76] These appear to be designed to ensure that the Department will be able to recoup some of the public expenditure which it may have spent on the school's premises.[77] The trustees of the voluntary school must give the Department and the ELB two years' notice of their intention to discontinue the school. The trustees must also get the Department's prior approval to issue a notice if the school premises were built or altered with the aid of a grant from the Department or financial assistance from the ELB. The trustees are not required to give two months' notice if the Department and the ELB agree to dispense with the notice. If during the period of notice the trustees of the school inform the Department that they are unable or unwilling to carry on the school until the expiry of the notice, the Department may give such directions as to the carrying on of the school and education of the children attending the school as it thinks expedient.[78] When a voluntary school is discontinued, the trustees are liable to repay some of the money which has been given to the school in the form of grants by the Department.[79]

---

[73] *Ibid* art. 15(3).
[74] *Ibid* art. 15(4).
[75] *Ibid* art. 15(3).
[76] *Ibid* art. 16.
[77] For a dispute as to the amount of money which might be recouped, see *In re Walsh*, unreported decision of the High Court of Northern Ireland, 8 May 2000.
[78] *Ibid* art. 16(3).
[79] *Ibid* art. 16(4).

Significant changes in the size or character of a school

2.49 Schools are obliged to seek approval of any significant changes in the school's character or size.[80] Such a change may have a knock-on effect on the general pattern of educational provision. What constitutes a significant change in the size or character of a school is not defined. The only statutory provision on this issue states that any dispute on the matter will be determined by the Department.[81]

Significant

2.50 The statute does not define what is meant by a "significant" change. The equivalent English legislation states that it "implies that there has been a substantial change in the function or size of the school".[82] This was also the dictionary definition cited in a Northern Ireland case, *R v DENI, ex parte Campbell College*.[83] In that case, the admission of 40 girls was considered to be significant. However, much weight was put on the fact that the girls were to be admitted to the sixth form which was in the opinion of the court the 'copy book' for the lower forms in the school.

Size

2.51 There is no statutory definition of what constitutes a significant change in size. An assumption can be made that size in this context refers to physical size and not pupil numbers since the latter are regulated by the Department under article 11 of the 1997 Order. The equivalent English legislation refers to "enlargements". However, it might be assumed from the use of the words "change in size" that in Northern Ireland reductions are also covered.

Character

2.52 There have also been a number of English cases on what constitutes a change of character. In *Bradbury v London Borough of Enfield* Lord Denning considered that a change from primary to secondary education or from single sex to co-educational would be a complete change in character.[84] So too would changes in the admissions system such as a change from secondary to grammar or even part selection on ability. Other possible changes which might constitute a change in character include a change in the age range of pupils admitted or the establishment or removal of boarding facilities.

2.53 The issue of what constitutes a change of character was considered by the Northern Ireland courts in the case of *R v DENI, ex parte the Governors of Campbell College*.[85] In that case, an all-boys school proposed to admit a small number of girls to its sixth form college. Initially it did not submit a proposal because it did not consider its action to amount to a significant

---

[80] *Ibid* arts. 14(1)(d) and 14(2)(d).
[81] Art. 14(10) of the 1986 Order.
[82] 1996 Act, s. 573(5).
[83] [1982] NI 123.
[84] [1967] 1 WLR 1311.
[85] [1982] NI 123.

change in the character of the school. However, on request from the Department, it submitted a proposal which failed to get the Department's approval. One of the grounds of the challenge was that the admission of a small number of girls did not constitute a significant change in the character of the school. The court disagreed, concluding that the admission of girls to a single sex school, the process of selection on the basis of aptitude and the fact that the admission affected the influential sixth form all meant that the Department could properly determine that the school's proposal amounted to a significant change in the character of the school. However, the Department was considered to have acted unlawfully when it considered the impact of the change on other schools when it made its determination about whether the school's proposal amounted to a significant change in character. There is now a separate head for proposals where there is likely to be a significant effect on other schools.

Changes which have a significant effect on another grant-aided school

2.54 This is not defined. However, any dispute on the matter will be determined by the Department.[86] This head was added after the *Campbell College* case considered above. Kelly J (as he then was) considered that there could be situations where a change did not amount to a change in character but nevertheless had an adverse impact on competitors. He gave the following examples: an upsurge in reputation through a new principal or outstanding examination results. These examples are unlikely to constitute grounds for the submission of a proposal. Instead, the provision might cover circumstances where the change in size or character is not in itself significant but is likely to affect other schools in the area. This provision may be appropriate if there is a move to a new site. This will not necessarily entail a change in size or character but might well have an effect on an existing school's catchment area.

DISCRIMINATION IN THE PROVISION OF SCHOOLS

2.55 When the Department and the ELBs are determining levels of school provision, they must be careful not to discriminate unlawfully in the allocation of that provision. Provisions on three potential forms of unlawful discrimination are considered in detail below. They are: (i) sex discrimination; (ii) religious discrimination; and (iii) race discrimination. In addition section 75 of the Northern Ireland Act 1998 requires the Department and ELBs to have regard to the need to provide equality of opportunity in a variety of respects when it is determining school provision.[87] This means that when the Department is determining its policy on school provision or making decisions regarding particular schools, it will have to have regard to the impact of those decisions on various categories of persons including boys and girls, Catholics and Protestants and those with disabilities and those without. The Department is not prevented from taking decisions which may have differential impact but should have reasons for proceeding with a particular policy/action notwithstanding the adverse impact.

---

[86] Art. 14(10) of the 1986 Order.
[87] See generally paras. 1.32-1.35.

2.56 There are a number of international obligations which are also of relevance in this context. Article 14 of the ECHR states that the enjoyment of the rights in the Convention (including the right to education) "shall be secured without discrimination on any ground such as sex, race, colour, language, religion, political or other opinion, national or social origin, association with a national minority, property, birth or other status."[88] This may well have significance in relation to decisions regarding school finance and provision. Similarly, Article 2(1) of the UNCRC states that:

> "State Parties shall respect and ensure the rights set forth in the present Convention to each child within their jurisdiction without discrimination of any kind, irrespective of the child's or his or her parent's or legal guardian's race, colour, sex, language, religion, political or other opinion, national ethnic or social origin, property, disability, birth or other status."

These international obligations are of increased significance following the implementation of the Northern Ireland Act 1998. For a start, the actions of ministers and Departments must not be incompatible with Convention rights such as Article 14 of the ECHR.[89] Secondly, the Secretary of State has the power to direct that ministers and Departments do not take action that is incompatible with international obligations such as those arising under the UNCRC.[90] More generally, the Northern Ireland Human Rights Commission is required to advise the Secretary of State and the Executive Committee of the Assembly of the legislative and other measures which ought to be taken to protect human rights.[91] The NIHRC's predecessor, SACHR, had a particular interest in education and consistently drew attention to potential imbalances within overall school provision. It might be anticipated that the new body will continue to highlight discrepancies in provision.

Sex discrimination

2.57 Article 25 of the Sex Discrimination (NI) Order 1976 makes it unlawful for ELBs when carrying out their statutory functions to do any act which constitutes sex discrimination. Article 25 applies to all functions except those which arise in relation to its direct management of a controlled school as this is covered by article 24 of the Order. In addition, the ELB is under a general duty to secure that its facilities for education and any ancillary benefits or services are provided without sex discrimination.[92] In the latter case, this general obligation can only be enforced through a complaint to the Department under article 101 of the 1986 Order.

2.58 The scope of the sex discrimination legislation in the context of the provision of schools has been considered in a number of English cases. These cases have been based on the equivalent of article 25 of the Sex Discrimination (NI) Order 1976. The statutory function on which they were based is the duty to provide sufficient schools (the equivalent of art. 6(1) of

---

[88] See para. 1.58.
[89] Northern Ireland Act 1998, s. 24.
[90] *Ibid* s. 26.
[91] *Ibid* s. 69(3).
[92] Art. 26.

the 1986 Education Order). In *R* v *Secretary of State for Education and Science, ex parte Keating* the LEA proposed to close down the only single sex boys school in Bath while leaving two single sex girls schools open.[93] The court considered that there was no obligation on the LEA to provide single sex schools but if it did, it must do so without treating one sex less favourable that the other. Taylor J said that the correct approach was to consider whether the loss of the option of single sex schooling was a loss which reasonable parents might consider resulted in unfavourable treatment. He concluded that the LEA's decision was discriminatory and quashed it. However, in *R* v *Northamptonshire CC, ex parte K*, the court considered that an LEA's actions had not amounted to sex discrimination when the school proposed for closure was not viable due to falling rolls.[94] In such cases, the LEA could not fulfill its statutory duty to provide "sufficient" schools by keeping such a school open.

Religious discrimination

2.59 There are no specific provisions in the Education Orders to ensure that educational provision is made without discrimination on the basis of religion. Moreover, education is expressly exempted from the Fair Employment and Treatment (NI) Order 1998. However, section 24 of the Northern Ireland Act 1998 states that a minister or department does not have the power to discriminate against a person or class of person on the grounds of religious belief or political opinion or to aid or incite another person to do so.[95] In addition, section 76 of the Northern Ireland Act 1998 (which replaced s. 19 of the Northern Ireland Constitution Act 1973) prohibits public bodies from discriminating on the grounds of religion. This applies to both the Department and ELBs in carrying out their statutory functions. Given that Northern Ireland's school system is effectively religiously segregated, an action might arise if a decision about educational provision could be shown to discriminate on the grounds of religion. The only case which has been taken in this regard (albeit under s.17 of the 1973 Act which applied to legislation) is *In re Daly*.[96] In that case, the Catholic bishops argued that the provisions of the 1989 Order relating to integrated schools gave those schools an unfair advantage and thus discriminated against those attending Catholic schools. The court did not find religious discrimination in relation to the new provisions for grant-maintained integrated schools because it considered that the implications of such schools, if any, affected both religious communities. However, it remains possible that an action could be taken under section 76 if a decision by the Department or an ELB could be shown to have an unfavourable impact on one section of the community. There is also the possibility that differential treatment might constitute a breach of Article 14 of the ECHR in respect of the right to education in Article 2 of the First Protocol.[97]

2.60 In practice, the segregated nature of Northern Ireland's education system is such that it is quite possible for disadvantage to arise in terms of educational provision and the Department and ELBs must be careful to ensure

---

[93] [1985] 84 LGR 469.
[94] [1994] ELR 397.
[95] See generally para. 1.25.
[96] Unreported judgment of the High Court of Northern Ireland, 5 October 1990.
[97] See para. 1.58.

that policies and legislation do not have a disproportionate and disadvantageous impact on any of the key categories of school. For instance, research commissioned by SACHR indicated that there were fewer grammar school places for children attending Catholic schools.[98] This meant that Catholic children attaining high grades in the transfer procedure test were being refused admission to Catholic grammar schools even though Protestant children with the same grade were securing places in the controlled or Protestant voluntary sector. The discrepancy did not result in a legal challenge. Instead, the Department were prepared to review the levels of provision and increased the number of places at Catholic grammar schools by raising admission numbers at existing schools and approving the establishment of new Catholic grammar schools.

Race discrimination

2.61 Article 19 of the Race Relations (NI) Order 1997 makes it unlawful for ELBs when carrying out their statutory functions to do any act which constitutes racial discrimination. Article 19 applies to all functions except those which arise in relation to its direct management of a controlled school as this is covered by article 18 of the Order. In addition, the ELB is under a general duty to secure that facilities for education provided by it and any ancillary benefits or services are provided without racial discrimination.[99] In the latter case, this general obligation can only be enforced through a complaint to the Department under article 101 of the 1986 Order.[100]

2.62 Northern Ireland has only recently introduced legislation prohibiting discrimination on the grounds of race and there are, as yet, no reported cases involving schools or school provision. There have, however, been a number of high profile cases in England and Wales. One of the most controversial of these cases was *R v Cleveland County Council, ex parte Commission for Racial Equality*, in which a court held that an LEA's decision to admit a child to a different school on the basis that the school allocated was attended by a majority of Asian children was not unlawful discrimination.[101] It is difficult to see similar cases arising in Northern Ireland because the numbers of people from ethnic minorities are comparatively small and are not concentrated in one geographic area. One exception to this may relate to children from the travelling community. The 1997 Order defines "racial grounds" to include the grounds of belonging to the Irish traveller community.[102] There is a designated school for travelling children in Belfast, St. Paul's, which appears from its enrolment numbers to have sufficient places to deal with everyone who applies to it. Disputes in this context might be more likely to involve the admission of individual children to schools rather than broader decisions about educational provision.[103]

---

[98] Cormack, Gallagher and Osborne, 'Religious Affiliation and Educational Attainment in Northern Ireland' Annex E in the *Sixteenth Report of the Standing Advisory Commission on Human Rights (1990-91)* (HMSO, 1991) 117-212.
[99] Art. 20 of the Race Relations (NI) Order 1997.
[100] *Ibid* art. 20(2)-(3).
[101] [1993]1 FCR 597.
[102] Art. 5 of the Race Relations (NI) Order 1997.
[103] See further para. 4.45.

ACCOUNTABILITY

Complaints to the Department under article 101 of the 1986 Order

2.63 Article 101 of the 1986 Order contains a procedure whereby individuals or bodies can complain to the Department about the unreasonable exercise of powers under the Education Orders.[104] The power to complain and the Department's powers to remedy the action complained of are both wide ranging yet appear to be used infrequently.

Who can complain?

2.64 The right to complain is given to any person or body.[105] The obvious people who might wish to complain include parents, schools, ELBs, the CCMS or interested pressure groups. However, the legislation does not require the person or body to show any form of *locus standi*, for instance that they are in some way affected by the exercise or lack of exercise of the power.

Who can be complained about?

2.65 The legislation is quite specific about the authorities who may be the subject of a complaint. These include: ELBs, the Boards of Governors or trustees of grant-aided schools, the CCMS and the NICCEA.[106] This list was extended by the 1989 Order. Prior to that complaints could only be made about an ELB or the trustees or managers of voluntary schools. It is particularly significant that a complaint can now be made about the actions of any Board of Governors given that so much statutory responsibility now rests with the Board of Governors of the school. It should be noted that the right to complain does not extend to the actions of individual school principals or teachers. However, there will be occasions when it may be appropriate to complain under article 101 about a Board of Governors' failure to ensure that a principal has effectively carried out his or her obligations under the Education Orders.

The substance of the complaint

2.66 The substance of a complaint under article 101 must be that the relevant authority has acted or is proposing to act unreasonably with respect to the exercise of any power conferred or any duty imposed under any provision of the Education Orders. There is only one part of the Education Orders which is specifically excluded from this and that relates to complaints about the curriculum which should be pursued under article 33 of the 1989 Order.[107] In all other cases, a complainant will need to identify the relevant power or duty under the Orders which he or she considers has been unreasonably exercised. It is submitted that an unreasonable 'exercise' should cover both decisions taken and failures to act. Support for this can be taken from article

---

[104] Art. 101 was substituted by art. 158 of the 1989 Order.
[105] Art. 101(4) of the 1986 Order.
[106] Art. 101(3) amended by Sch. 4 to the 1993 Order.
[107] Art.33(8) of the 1989 Order. See further para. 5.87.

101(2) which details the power of the Department to direct that powers and duties are either exercised/performed or not exercised or performed in order to remedy the complaint.

2.67 The main difficulty for a complainant will be in showing unreasonableness on the part of the education authority. 'Reasonableness' is not defined in the legislation but is likely to be regarded in its *'Wednesbury'* sense, that is that no reasonable education authority would have acted that way. That said, it is notable that the legislation expressly permits the Department to issue directions to remedy the complaint notwithstanding the fact that the Education Orders render the exercise of the power or duty contingent upon the opinion of the authority.[108] Thus, the Department can in this instance substitute its own decision on the merits of an issue for that of the education authority. This would imply a less stringent test of reasonableness than is applicable under the *'Wednesbury'* formulation [1948] 1KB 223.

The power to issue directions

2.68 If the Department is satisfied that there has been an unreasonable exercise of the power or duty, it shall give such directions as are expedient to remedy the complaint.[109] Directions can require a power to be exercised, exercised in a specified manner, not be exercised or not be exercised in a specified manner. Likewise directions can require a duty to be performed, performed in a specified manner or not be performed in a specified manner. Before issuing a direction the Department must consult with the relevant authority.

Enforcement

2.69 The education authorities are under a statutory obligation to comply with any directions and directions can be enforced through the courts by an order of *mandamus*.[110] Moreover, if the Department is satisfied that an authority has failed to comply with a direction, it can make an order appointing a person or persons to discharge all or specified functions of the authority in the name of the authority.[111] This is quite a drastic course of action and is consequently rarely, if ever, used.

Further complaints

2.70 There is no specified method of complaining about any decision taken by the Department under article 101. If complainants are dissatisfied with the Department's response to their complaint, their only recourse to legal action will be by way of judicial review. However, experience in Great Britain indicates an unwillingness on the part of the courts to intervene in this context. In *Bradbury* v *London Borough of Enfield* the court commented that the Secretary of State's failure to use the powers in the equivalent English legislation could not be reviewed by the court since the Secretary of State was responsible to Parliament and not to the court in this area.[112] It would appear

---

[108] Art. 101(5) of the 1986 Order.
[109] *Ibid* art. 101(5).
[110] *Ibid* art. 101(6).
[111] *Ibid*.
[112] [1967] 1 WLR 1311.

that the courts will be reluctant to substitute their decision for that of the education authority on the ground of unreasonableness. In *Secretary of State for Education and Science* v *Metropolitan Borough of Tameside* the House of Lords stated that the courts should not interfere where the Secretary of State had properly directed himself in law, had considered all relevant considerations and excluded irrelevant considerations.[113] There has, however, been at least one successful challenge to the Secretary of State's refusal to use the powers available. The case involved a direct breach of duty by an LEA who had failed to provide a child with dyslexia with the special educational provision he required.[114] The child's parents were able to successfully challenge the Secretary of State's refusal to uphold their complaint and take remedial action.

The relationship between article 101 and actions for judicial review

2.71 It has been noted that the right to complain under article 101 is rarely used. In spite of this, the existence of a right of complaint under article 101 may be significant if a complainant intends to challenge a decision by way of judicial review. This is because a court may refuse to entertain a review action if the complainant has not pursued his or her right of complaint under article 101. One example of this is the English case of *Watt* v *Kesteven County Council* where the Court of Appeal considered that a parent's challenge to the LEA's failure to provide his sons with places at a local church school should be pursued via the English equivalent of article 101.[115] Similarly, in *Meade* v *Haringey LBC* the Court of Appeal considered that complaints about an LEA's breach of its statutory obligations should normally be pursued via the administrative right of complaint. However, the Court considered that the existence of a right of complaint to the Secretary of State did not stop the courts from intervening where the action of the education authority; "flies in the face of the statute, by doing something which the statute expressly prohibits, or failing to do something which the statute expressly enjoins, or otherwise so conducts itself, by omission or commission, as to frustrate or hinder the policy or objects of the Act".[116]

2.72 There are no equivalent authorities in Northern Ireland to suggest that the courts will refuse to allow a judicial review action where there is a right to complain under article 101. In *In re Cecil*, the court specifically referred to the right of complaint under article 101 but did not require the applicant to pursue his right of complaint against the ELB via the Department.[117] No reason is given but the court may have been influenced by the fact that a challenge was also being made to the actions of the Department itself and that one of the contentions in the case was that there had been a breach of the Northern Ireland Constitution Act 1973. On the other hand, it might indicate an increased willingness on the part of the courts in this jurisdiction to allow challenges by way of judicial review in spite of the fact that the complainant has not exercised their right to complain under article 101.

---

[113] [1976] 3 All ER 665.
[114] *R* v *Secretary of State for Education, ex parte Chance* (unreported 1982).
[115] [1955] 1 All ER 473.
[116] [1979] 2 All ER 1016, at p.1024.
[117] Unreported decision of the High Court of Northern Ireland, 27 January 1989.

Ombudsman and Commissioner for Complaints

2.73 A person who considers that they have sustained an injustice as a result of maladministration on the part of one of the education authorities may have a right to complain to the Ombudsman or Commissioner for Complaints. In Northern Ireland both posts are held by the one individual although the jurisdiction to investigate is dealt with in two separate statutes. Complaints against the Department are within the jurisdiction of the Ombudsman.[118] Complaints about the conduct of an ELB or the CCMS must be made to the Commissioner for Complaints.[119] There is no right of complaint against the actions of a Board of Governors or a principal. The Ombudsman/Commissioner may investigate any action taken by or on behalf of the relevant bodies in the exercise of its administrative functions. However, an investigation will not be undertaken if the complainant has a right of appeal to a statutory tribunal or court of law unless, in the particular circumstances, it is not reasonable to expect him or her to resort to that remedy. The purpose of the investigation will be to determine whether the matter warrants investigation, is in substance true and discloses any mal-administration. The Ombudsman/Commissioner may try to effect a settlement between the parties. If that is not possible he or she can state what he or she considers would be a fair settlement. If a complaint is upheld, a person can apply to the county court for damages.

2.74 The Ombudsman/Commissioner for Complaints publishes an annual report in which he or she sets out the action taken in relation to complaints from the previous year. In practice, few complaints are made about the Department in relation to schools.[120] There are, however, regular complaints to the Commissioner for Complaints about the actions of ELBs and the CCMS. Most of these relate to appointments to schools and are therefore outside the scope of this book. However, there have been occasional complaints about admissions, home to school transport and special educational needs. A complaint to the Commissioner for Complaints is a fairly limited remedy: the process is unlikely to achieve the quick results most parents would wish and the powers of the Commissioner are restricted. That said, it does provide another means by which parents can bring pressure to bear on an educational authority with which it has cause for complaint.

Education appeal tribunals

2.75 Since 1989 a number of tribunals have been established to enable parents to challenge decisions about their child's schooling. Three of these (in relation to admissions, the curriculum and expulsions) were established under the 1989 Order and are organised by local ELBs. Their composition and functions are considered in further detail in the relevant chapters of the book. The fourth tribunal, the Special Educational Needs Tribunal (SENT) operates on a Northern Ireland-wide basis (see paras. 8.64-8.81). The SENT was

---

[118] Ombudsman (NI) Order 1996, art. 8.
[119] Commissioner for Complaints (NI) Order 1996, art. 7.
[120] However, see the 1993 Annual Report, where the Ombudsman investigated a complaint by a voluntary body about the Department's decision to fund only one body for the promotion of integrated education (at p.22).

established by the 1996 Order and began operating in 1997. In each case, the tribunals are intended to offer parents an accessible means of challenging decisions about their child's schooling without having to resort to litigation. To underline this, the High Court will not normally accept an application for judicial review of these issues if the matter has not been referred to the appropriate tribunal. The decisions of the tribunals are, however, subject to judicial review (there is also an appeal on a point of law to the High Court from certain decisions of the SENT).

Judicial review

2.76 The main court-based strategy for challenging education decisions is by way of an application for judicial review. This procedure allows individuals such as parents and others to challenge the decisions of public bodies in the exercise of their administrative powers. In order to be amenable to judicial review, the actions of the body in question must come within the sphere of public law.[121] This is not always an easy issue to determine. However, in the educational system, many of the decisions of the following bodies are subject to review: the Department, ELBs, appeal tribunals and Boards of Governors.[122] Moreover, in a recent Northern Ireland case, *In re Kean* a court also accepted an application about the decision of a school principal to suspend a pupil.[123]

Procedural requirements

2.77 Applicants who wish to make an application for judicial review must seek the leave of the court. The court will only grant leave if it considers that the applicant has an arguable case.[124] Secondly, there are time limits for the making of the application. An application must be made promptly or in any event within three months from the date when the grounds for application first arose unless the court considers that there is good reason for extending the period.[125] Determining when the grounds for application arose is not always straightforward. Normally it will be when the decision which was taken is notified to the applicant. However, there will be times when the relevant decision cannot be precisely pinpointed. For example, if a parent wished to complain about the legality of a school's admissions criterion, it might be considered that the grounds for complaint arose when the criteria were published rather than the date on which they were applied adversely to the applicant's child.[126]

---

[121] For an analysis of this in the context of Northern Ireland, see Maguire, 'The Procedure for Judicial Review in Northern Ireland', Appendix in Hadfield (ed) *Judicial Review: a thematic approach* (1995) pp. 373 - 376.
[122] The decisions of these bodies taken with the private law sphere (e.g. on employment related issues) are not justiciable.
[123] [1997] NIJB 109. See further, paras.7.58-7.59.
[124] Ord. 53 of the Rules of the Supreme Court (NI) 1980.
[125] *Ibid.*
[126] See further, Chapter 4.

Grounds for review

2.78 The grounds for review can be categorised in a number of way. Essentially a decision of a public body can be challenged if it is unlawful, unreasonable or unfair. A decision may be considered to be unlawful in a number of instances. The first is where it is *ultra vires*, that is outside the statutory powers of the body in question.[127] The second ground of challenge arises where the decision is unreasonable in the '*Wednesbury*' sense, that is so irrational that no reasonable body would have reached the same decision. This has been argued in a number of schools cases.[128] A decision will be considered to have been unfair if it has been taken without regard to the rules of natural justice. This might arise if there is bias in the decision-making process or the affected party has not been given sufficient opportunity to state their case. As regards the latter, the requirements of fairness vary with the particular circumstances. As a minimum the party should know the case against them and be given an opportunity to respond.[129] However, in some cases the rules of fairness may require that the person be given an oral hearing or an opportunity to examine witnesses.

Remedies

2.79 Judicial review has its own specific remedies. An applicant in judicial review can apply for one of the following remedies: an order of *mandamus;* an order of *certiorari*, an order of prohibition, a declaration and an injunction.[130] In education cases, it is common for an applicant to seek an order for an order of *certiorari* quashing the original decision followed by an order of *mandamus* requiring a particular course of action. Each of these remedies is, however, discretionary. This means that, notwithstanding the fact that there has been illegality or unfairness, the judge can decide not to award any remedy. This arises typically where no useful purpose would be served, for example where there has been procedural unfairness but the outcome of the decision would have been the same had the correct procedures been followed. For instance, in *In re Campbell College,* the court found that the Department had taken an irrelevant matter (i.e. the impact on other schools) into account when refusing to allow the school to undergo a change of character but concluded that the decision would have been the same in any event.[131] The court might also refuse to grant relief where there is an alternative remedy available to the applicant which they have not pursued. In *In re Gribbon's Application* which concerned a challenge to an admission decision, the court did not find in favour of the applicant but considered that even if it had, it would have refused relief because the applicant had a right to pursue her claim in the admissions appeal tribunal.[132]

---

[127] See *In re Lagan College,* unreported judgment of the Northern Ireland High Court, 1992.
[128] See *In re Moore* [1994] NIJB 111 (CA).
[129] See *In re Kean* [1997] NIJB 109.
[130] Judicature (NI) Act 1978, s. 18(1). The applicant can also conjoin an application for damages at the time of the application.
[131] [1982] NI 123.
[132] [1990] NI 15.

Significance in education law

2.80 Judicial review has played a major part in the development of education law in the United Kingdom.[133] The vast majority of the cases reported in the Education Law Reports are applications for judicial review. In England and Wales, the numbers of applications have increased threefold in recent years.[134] This has inevitably impacted on the law relating to schools. In England and Wales many of the successful cases have concerned school re-organisation. In contrast, cases taken by parents in relation to individual children have generally met with less success. While these cases may have done little to advance parental rights, they have worked "to promote procedural propriety in many respects and they have acted as a moderating and mediating influence over the exercise of discretion".[135] In Northern Ireland there have also been a considerable number of cases involving schools.[136] Landmark decisions include: *In re Cecil's Application,*[137] *In re EOC's Application (No 2)*[138] and *In re Daly.*[139] However, the area which has been most affected by judicial review in Northern Ireland has undoubtedly been admission to schools. Each year there are a series of applications concerning pupils' failure to get into the school of their parents' choice.[140] The legislation has recently been changed to clarify the law and so reduce the need for these applications.[141] However, it is likely that lawyers' attentions in the educational domain will move elsewhere and it might be anticipated that there will be a rise in the numbers of applications in other areas such special educational needs and discipline.

---

[133] For a description of the key cases involving schools, see Harris, 'Education and Judicial Review - An Overview' (1997) 5 *Education Public Law and the Individual* 24. Also further, Harris, 'Judicial Review and Education' in Buck (ed.) *Judicial Review and Social Welfare Law* (1998) 1.

[134] Bridges, Meszaros and Sunkin, *Judicial Review in Perspective* (1995) p.15.

[135] Meredith, 'Judicial Review and Education' in Hadfield (ed) *Judicial Review: A thematic approach* (1995) p.95.

[136] Applications in education increased from 1.3 per cent to 3.6 per cent of the total between 1987 and 1991. See, Hadfield and Weaver, 'Judicial Review in Perspective' (1995) 46/2 *Northern Ireland Legal Quarterly* 113, Table 1, at p. 118.

[137] Unreported judgment of the High Court of Northern Ireland, 27 January 1989.

[138] [1988] NI 278.

[139] Unreported judgment of the High Court of Northern Ireland, 5 October 1990.

[140] For an analysis of the decisions in these cases see, Lundy, 'Selection on Ability: Lessons from Northern Ireland' (1196) 8/1 *Education and the Law* 29.

[141] The Education (NI) Order 1997 has further regulated admissions criteria and the appeal tribunal process.

CHAPTER THREE

SCHOOL GOVERNMENT

INTRODUCTION

3.01 All grant-aided schools have a Board of Governors, a body of people who are responsible for the management of the school. School governors are unpaid volunteers who generally have some connection with the school or local community in which the school is situated. The informal nature of governing bodies, described by one commentator as a "benign lay influence",[1] was deemed to be suitable in the management structures which operated prior to 1990 since the role of the Board of Governors was mainly advisory and governors had little direct involvement in the management of the school. However, the Education Reform (NI) Order 1989 significantly enhanced the role of Boards of Governors by giving them new statutory responsibilities in relation to the curriculum, the publication of information, discipline and admissions. At the same time Boards of Governors in controlled and maintained schools were given responsibility for managing the school's budget through a policy known as Local Management of Schools (LMS).[2] The result of the additional statutory duties combined with financial control is that Boards of Governors now constitute a significant tier in the management structure of the school. As Harris has observed, the role of governing bodies has been transformed from "relatively distant oversight of the conduct of a school to active management".[3]

3.02 In Great Britain the reforms to the role of governors in the Education Act 1988 were preceded by key changes to the composition of governing bodies introduced under the Education (No. 2) Act 1986. Much of this reform was motivated by the Conservative government's desire to reduce political control in schools.[4] This influence derived mainly from the representation of elected local councillors on the LEAs, many of which were Labour controlled. The transfer of many important functions away from LEAs to individual schools is one manifestation of this policy of de-politicisization. At the same time, the composition of Boards of Governors was reformed with more emphasis being placed on the involvement of parents, teachers and the local business community rather than the nominees of the local education authority. Similar changes to the composition of Boards of Governors were implemented in Northern Ireland by virtue of the Education Reform (NI) Order 1989.

---

[1] See R. Deem, 'The Reform of School Governing Bodies', Chapter 9 in M. Flude and M. Hammer (eds), *The Education Reform Act 1988: its origins and implications* (1990), 153, at p. 154.
[2] The Boards of Governors of voluntary grammar schools already had responsibility for managing the grant they received directly from the Department. Grant-maintained integrated schools, created by the 1989 Order, were given financial autonomy from their inception.
[3] N. Harris, *The Law Relating To Schools* (1995) p.10.
[4] *Better Schools*, (1985) Cmnd. 9469, para.221.

However, the reforms in Northern Ireland operate in a different context as local politics has not had the same influence on the management of schools. Although local Education and Library Boards have politically-elected representatives serving on them, no one political party predominates.[5] Instead the main factor which is likely to influence the management and ethos of the school is the representation of the various church bodies who are the mainstay of governing bodies in state schools in Northern Ireland.

3.03 The reason why the churches play such a predominant role in Northern Ireland's schools is essentially historical and can be traced directly to legislative reform in the 1920s and 1930s, a process which is described at paragraph 1.07. The current position is that the majority of schools in Northern Ireland have a management body on which the local churches exercise considerable influence. In the two main categories of school (controlled and voluntary), the majority of appointments to the Boards of Governors are still held by the nominees of the original transferors or the trustees of the school.[6] The Protestant church bodies which transferred their schools to controlled status are known as "transferors" and their successors continue to have the right to nominate members to the school Boards which transferred.[7] Thus, in the controlled sector, the largest single group of governors are the transferors' representatives. In voluntary schools, it is the trustees of the school's capital assets. In each case, these appointments are generally made by the local churches.

3.04 Grant-maintained integrated (GMI) schools, a new category of school created by the 1989 Order, have Boards of Governors which are constituted in a different fashion. These have broken the tradition of church representation in that the largest group of governors on the Board are foundation governors who are normally the parents of pupils who originally worked to establish the school. Although GMI schools seek to ensure that Boards of Governors are representative of both of the major religious traditions, the rights of nomination to the Board do not vest in the local churches. On the other hand, in controlled integrated schools, the legislation attempts to strike a balance between both religions by providing equal nomination rights to the transferors' representatives and the trustees of Catholic-maintained schools. Thus, with few exceptions, Boards of Governors in Northern Ireland have a significant proportion of their membership drawn from the local clergy or from those whom they have chosen to represent them. It is largely through these guaranteed positions on the management committees of individual schools that the churches in Northern Ireland have been able to exercise a significant influence on the development of the education system and indeed the legal provisions which govern it.

3.05 The Education Reform (NI) Order 1989 devolved responsibility for decision-making in key areas from local ELBs to individual governing bodies.

---

[5] See paras. 1.07 and 2.09.
[6] Education Act (NI) 1923. For an account of this process see, Dunn, 'A short history of education in Northern Ireland 1920-1990, Annex B in the *Fifteenth Report of the Standing Advisory Commission on Human Rights (1989-90)* (1990).
[7] Education Act (NI) 1930 gave the previous managers of schools the right to nominate at least half of the membership of the management committees of transferred schools.

The intention underlying the reforms was to allow schools to determine their individual objectives and priorities, thus making them more responsive to the needs of their pupils. It was envisaged that the new system would be "better for the customers because decisions are pushed away from the centre nearer to the point of delivery of the service".[8] However, the reforms to the role of governing bodies have been criticised, not so much on the basis of the philosophy underlying an increase in governor power, but on their capacity to meet their intended objectives. The onus placed on Boards of Governors by the 1989 Order and subsequent legislation is significant. This is apparent from the responsibilities on governors described in the chapters in this book on admissions, the curriculum, discipline and special needs. In Great Britain, there is evidence to suggest that many governors are ill-equipped to carry out their statutory functions.[9] Likewise, in Northern Ireland it is clear that some governors do not have the knowledge, expertise or time to cope with the nature or extent of their obligations. This can lead to a situation where much of the decision-making which is by law the responsibility of the governors is in fact carried out by the school principal assisted by his or her senior management team. This is borne out by research commissioned by the Department.[10] This found that the governing body tended to play a passive role in the management of the school, being content to receive reports and approve decisions rather than take an active role in the decision-making process.[11] The research concluded that the reforms had not seen the transformation of governing bodies into pro-active managers. Instead responsibility fell increasingly to the school principal with the result that the overall management structure was akin to "one of a Chief Executive with a relatively weak Board of Directors".[12] For some, the result is a school system where principals dominate through their increased influence over poorly-informed governing bodies. Others believe that the governors' inability to carry out their assigned tasks has left principals with an intolerable burden. In either case, the 1989 reforms are clearly not meeting all of their objectives. Decisions are being taken at a local level but not in the way envisaged by the policy makers.

3.06 From a legal perspective, the transfer of many functions from ELBs to Boards of Governors has widened the potential legal liability of governors. It is clearly of significance that governors may not be participating fully in decisions for which they are ultimately legally responsible since an absence of involvement could in itself constitute a breach of a statutory obligation. Although there are no official statistics of the number of cases involving schools in Northern Ireland, it would appear that litigation in this area is on the increase. In particular, there has been a steady rise in the numbers of

---

[8] J. Caines, 'Improving Education through Management: The view from the DES', Chapter 2 in Simkins, Ellison and Garrett (eds), *Implementing Education Reform: The Early Lessons* (1992, Longmans).
[9] See R. Deem, 'The Reform of School Governing Bodies', Chapter 9 in M. Flude and M. Hammer (eds), *The Education Reform Act 1988: Its Origins and Implications* (1990) p. 153
[10] McKeown, Byrne and Barnett, *'An initial analysis of the impact of formula funding and local mangement of schools on the management of Northern Ireland schools: A schools' perspective'* (1996, University of Ulster).
[11] *Ibid* p. 154.
[12] *Ibid* p. 155.

actions by way of judicial review, most notably in Northern Ireland in relation to admissions decisions for which governors are responsible.[13] Although these cases often involve challenges to the decisions of education appeal tribunals, it is inevitably the conduct of the Board of Governors which falls to be scrutinised. The upward trend in litigation seems likely to continue, particularly in the area of expulsions and special needs provision. However, although governors might not welcome the adverse publicity associated with a legal dispute, provided the individual governors act with good faith, there is little for them to fear in terms of personal liability. This is especially true since 1996 when the Boards of Governors of all grant-aided schools were incorporated thus removing personal liability of individual governors (see para. 3.58). The reform was appropriate and timely. School governors give up considerable time to perform difficult and time-consuming tasks for no financial reward. If this effort were to be overshadowed by the threat of personal legal and financial liability for the work done, it would eventually become even more difficult to find people willing to volunteer their services in this way. In time this could undermine one of the key policy objectives of the 1989 Order which was to increase the accountability of schools and involvement at a local level.

COMPOSITION OF THE BOARD

3.07 The composition of a Board of Governors depends on the type of school in question. The Board of Governors in most schools will include the principal and at least one elected associate teacher and parent. However, the majority of the Board's membership is generally determined by two factors. The first of these relates to the original or current ownership of the school's capital assets. Those who once had (i.e. transferors and superseded managers in controlled schools) or continue to have (trustees in voluntary schools) control over the school's capital assets are able to nominate a significant proportion of the Board's members. In practice these appointments are determined by the main churches who consequently continue to exercise significant influence in state-funded schools. The second factor which shapes the membership of the Board is the current funding arrangement for the school in that the balance of membership is determined by the proportion of funding provided. An illustration of this is the fact that maintained schools which have entered into a 100 per cent capital funding agreement with the ELB have a higher proportion of ELB representation on the Board than maintained schools which receive only 85 per cent capital funding. The same is true in relation to Departmental representation on the Boards of Governors of voluntary grammar schools which have opted for full capital funding. To some extent the character of a Board of Governors is determined by means of a balancing act between the representatives of the various churches and the government agencies which provide the school's funding. As a general rule, when the proportion of public funding towards capital costs increases, the balance of membership on the Board tips towards the state. The membership of Boards of Governors in each of the varying types of Northern Ireland schools is set out in the Appendix.

---

[13] See Chapter 4.

METHOD OF APPOINTMENT

3.08 The responsibility for making appointments to a Board of Governors varies with the type of school. Appointments to controlled schools are managed by the ELB.[14] Appointments to maintained schools are administered by the Department. However, where a maintained school has opted for 100 per cent capital funding, the Department must consult the CCMS (if the school is a Catholic maintained school) or the Board of Governors (of other maintained schools) before it makes any appointment.[15] Appointments to voluntary grammar schools are also the responsibility of the Department. Before an appointment is made to a voluntary grammar school, the Department must consult the Board of Governors of the school and the ELB in whose area the school is situated.[16] The responsibility for appointments to grant-maintained integrated schools is divided between the Department and the Board of Governors itself.[17]

3.09 The method by which a person may be appointed to a Board of Governors can take one of four forms: (i) base nominations; (ii) nomination by the ELB or the Department; (iii) election by parents or associate teachers; (iv) co-option. The legal requirements for each are set out below.

Base nominations

3.10 The term 'base nomination' has no legal or official foundation. It is being used in this context to describe the set of appointments which form the core of most of Northern Ireland's schools. In most types of school, the largest single group of appointments to the Board of Governors are the nominees of the original transferors or the trustees of the school.[18] In controlled schools, these appointments have an historical basis and can be traced to the original ownership and control of schools prior to their move to state control in 1923 and onwards.[19] The mainly Protestant bodies which transferred their schools to the state are known as "transferors" or "superseded managers" and their successors continue to have the right to nominate members to the school Board.[20] In voluntary schools the trustees of the school's capital assets are also invariably members of the clergy of the various churches. In contrast in grant-maintained integrated schools, the base appointments will be determined by the foundation governors who are normally the people who have been instrumental in establishing the school.

3.11 There are a number of schools which do not have any 'base' governors. They are controlled grammar, special and nursery schools and

---

[14] Art. 10 of the 1986 Order.
[15] Sch.5 para. 1(2) to the 1986 Order substituted by Sch. 2 to the 1993 Order.
[16] *Ibid* Sch. 6 para. 1(2).
[17] Sch. 5 to the 1989 Order.
[18] Such appointments are not made in the following schools: controlled grammar, special schools, nursery schools and controlled integrated grammar schools.
[19] Education Act (NI) 1923. For an account of this process see, Dunn, *op cit.*
[20] The Education Act (NI) 1930 gave the previous managers of schools the right to nominate at least half of the membership of the management committees of transferred schools.

Category B voluntary grammar schools (i.e. grammar schools which do not receive any capital funding from the state).[21]

Persons or bodies with responsibility for appointment/nomination

3.12 The persons or bodies who have responsibility for appointing or nominating governors varies with the category of school.

(i) *Transferors:* This is defined to mean the trustees or other persons by whom the school was transferred either to an education authority under the Education Act (NI) 1923 or the Education Act (NI) 1947 or to the Department under the Education (NI) Orders 1972 or 1986.[22] This includes trustees appointed in the place of the original transferring trustees and the representatives and successors of such persons. In practice, it was most common for Protestant religious bodies to transfer schools in this way. These organisations have combined to form a body called the Transferor Representatives' Council whose objective is to maximise co-operation within the three transferor churches: the Church of Ireland, the Presbyterian Church and the Methodist Church. The Council is privately funded. It does not have a recognised legal status although it has campaigned for status similar to that of the CCMS.

(ii) *Superseded manager:* This means the persons who were formerly trustees or managers of any schools which have been superseded by schools under the management of ELBs and their successors in office.

(iii) *Nominating trustees*: In a voluntary school "trustees" means the person or persons in whom the premises of the school are vested.[23] In maintained schools the term "nominating trustees" refers to such persons as the scheme of management may provide.[24] The proportion of nominations which can be made by the nominating trustees depends on the level of capital funding received by the school. Since 1993 voluntary schools have been allowed to opt for full funding of capital costs (as opposed to 85%), in which case state (i.e. ELB or Departmental) appointments on the Board of Governors is increased. This means that religious organisations will not have an overall majority on Boards which have entered into full capital funding agreements with the Department. However, in practice, Departmental and ELB nominees are only appointed after consultation with existing governors so the churches' influence in most voluntary schools has been largely unaffected.

(iv) *Foundation governors*: Grant-maintained integrated schools have foundation governors. This refers to the persons appointed by the person

---

[21] In Northern Ireland there are two voluntary grammar schools which do not receive capital funding. They are Campbell College and Royal Belfast Academical Institution.
[22] Art. 2 of the 1986 Order. The term transferor also "refers" to where a school transferred to the Department has been transferred to an ELB under art. 17(6) of the 1986 Order.
[23] Art. 2 of the 1986 Order.
[24] Sch. 5 para. 7(1) to the 1986 Order as substituted by Sch. 2 to the 1993 Order.

who submitted the proposal to acquire grant-maintained integrated status. In subsequent appointments, it refers to those holding office as foundation governors.[25]

The procedure for nomination

3.13 The procedure for such appointments varies once again with the type of school involved. The statutory requirements which apply in each case are set out below. It will be seen that the statutory requirements are so technical and complicated as to leave considerable scope for errors in the appointment process. Nevertheless a failure to comply with the statutory requirements will not render a decision of the Board of Governors invalid.[26]

(i) *Controlled primary schools*: In a controlled primary school, at least four members are nominated by the transferors and superseded managers of the school. When an ELB proposes to appoint such persons, it must serve a notice on the transferors and superseded managers stating its intention and requesting that they make a nomination to the ELB within 21 days.[27] If the transferors and superseded managers fail to make an appointment in the required period, the ELB can appoint persons whom it considers suitable and who are, where possible, resident in the locality of the school. If it is not practicable for nominations to be made because the school is not transferred or does not supersede any other school, the ELB will appoint people whom it considers to be representative of transferors and superseded managers in the area of the ELB as a whole.[28] Where possible, the appointees should be resident in the locality of the school. People appointed by the ELB in either of these ways are considered to have been duly nominated by the transferors and superseded managers.

(ii) *Controlled intermediate (i.e. secondary) schools*: In controlled secondary schools at least four members of the Board are nominated by the Boards of Governors of contributory schools from amongst the members of those Boards who represent transferors and superseded managers.[29] For these purposes a contributory school is a controlled primary school from which a substantial number of pupils are likely to proceed to the controlled secondary school in question.[30] This is determined by the ELB in whose area the controlled secondary school is situated. Where the ELB proposes to appoint such persons, it must serve a notice on the Boards of Governors of contributory schools stating its intention and requesting that nominations are made within 21 days. If the Boards of Governors fail to make nominations, the ELB may appoint such persons as it considers to be representative of the transferors and superseded managers of contributory

---

[25] Sch. 5 para. 2(2) to the 1989 Order.
[26] Art. 13(1) of the 1986 Order.
[27] Sch. 4 para. 6(1)-(3) to the 1986 Order substituted by art. 89 of the 1989 Order.
[28] *Ibid* Sch. 4 para. 6(5).
[29] *Ibid* Sch. 4 para. 3(2)(A).
[30] Art. 2 of the 1986 Order.

schools.[31] Persons appointed in this way are deemed to have been duly nominated.

(iii) *Controlled integrated primary and secondary schools*: In controlled integrated primary and secondary schools, one seventh of the Board is nominated by the transferors and superseded managers of controlled schools in the area of the ELB and one seventh by the nominating trustees of Catholic maintained schools in the area of the ELB.[32] If the ELB is proposing to appoint such persons, it must serve notice on the nominating authorities stating its intention and requesting nominations within 21 days.[33] These appointments can be difficult. Although the transferors will normally nominate representatives of the Protestant churches, the Catholic church has declined to do so. This can leave the Board of Governors of the school religiously unbalanced, something which integrated schools strive to avoid. Since 1989 the situation can be remedied to some extent by the ELB which has the power to nominate any person whom it considers suitable if the nominating authorities fail to make a nomination within the required period.[34] However, appointments from the ELBs have not been without difficulty, particularly where those appointed were not sympathetic to the concept of mixed schooling.[35] In view of this, there is now a statutory obligation on ELBs to appoint only those who are "committed to the continuing viability of the school as a controlled integrated school".[36]

(iv) *Maintained schools*: In a maintained school, at least four (if the Board has entered into a 100% capital funding agreement with the Department) or six (if there is no such agreement) members of the Board of Governors are nominated by nominating trustees of the school.[37] The process of appointment is determined by a scheme produced by the Department.[38] If a school enters into a full capital funding agreement with the Department, the existing members nominated under these provisions cease to hold office and further nominations must be made by the nominating trustees.[39] Likewise, if a school terminates an agreement with the Department, the existing members appointed in this way cease to hold office and further nominations must be made by the nominating trustees. In either case, the new nominees will only hold office for the remainder of the original term

---

[31] Sch. 4 para. 6(1)-(3) to the 1986 Order substituted by art. 89 of the 1989 Order.
[32] Sch. 4 para. 5(1)(c)-(d) to the 1986 Order substituted by art. 89 of the 1989 Order.
[33] Sch. 4 para. 6 to the 1986 Order substituted by art. 89 of the 1989 Order.
[34] Sch. 4 para. 6(1) to the 1986 Order, substituted by art. 89 of the 1989 Order.
[35] See, Moffat, 'The Transformation Option', in Moffat (ed) *Education Together for a Change* (1993).
[36] Sch.4 para. 6(2)(a) to the 1986 Order, substituted by art. 89 of the 1989 Order.
[37] Sch. 5 paras. 2(2) and 3(2) to the 1986 Order substituted by Sch.2 to the 1993 Order.
[38] Art. 11(2) and Sch. 5, para. 2(1) to the 1986 Order.
[39] Sch. 5 para. 4(3) to the 1986 Order substituted by Sch. 2 to the 1993 Order.

of office of those who have ceased to hold office. There is nothing in the legislation to prevent the same people from continuing in the posts.

(v) *Voluntary grammar schools*: In a voluntary grammar school which receives capital funding from the state the base membership is appointed in the manner provided in the scheme of management. At least one of these members must at the time of appointment be a parent of a pupil attending the school. If the school enters into a full capital funding agreement with the Department, the members appointed under these provisions will cease to hold office and new appointments must be made in accordance with the provisions for full capital funding (the converse applies when a school terminates an agreement for full capital funding with the Department). In either case, the new nominees will only hold office for the remainder of the original term of those who have ceased to hold office.

(vi) *Grant-maintained integrated schools*: In a grant-maintained integrated school, three-eighths must be foundation governors. One third of these must at the time of appointment be parents of pupils attending the school.[40] Foundation governors are persons who were appointed when appointments were first made to the Board of Governors by the body or person who submitted the proposal for the establishment of the school. In subsequent appointments, new foundation governors are appointed by existing foundation governors. Integrated schools will normally try to ensure that the Board of Governors contains a balance of representation of the two main religious traditions. There is nothing in the legislation to prevent them from doing this. Moreover, it might be argued that the Boards of Governors must strive for this balance in order to comply with their statutory duty to ensure that the "management, control and ethos of the school are such as are likely to attract to the school reasonable numbers of Protestant and Roman Catholic pupils". If those responsible for making foundation appointments are unable or unwilling to do so, the Department can make whatever provision it thinks fit in order to fill the vacancies.

Nominations by the ELB or the Department

3.14 Most grant-aided schools have members who have been nominated by an ELB or the Department or by both.[41] The power to nominate members reflects the primary source of the funding. ELBs finance and are consequently represented on the Boards of Governors of controlled and maintained schools. The Department provides direct funding to voluntary grammar and grant-maintained integrated schools and consequently has the power to nominate a significant proportion of the representatives on to the Boards of such schools.

---

[40] Sch. 5 para. 2(1)(a) to the 1989 Order.
[41] The exception to this is Category B voluntary grammar schools who do not receive funding for capital costs from the state. The composition of their Board of Governors is not regulated by statute.

Although it is intended that these schools will eventually receive their grant via the ELB for their area the link with the Department is maintained through representation on the Board of Governors.[42] The exact proportion of representation is directly linked to the extent of funding provided. Schools which have opted for full capital funding have a higher proportion of state appointments than schools which have not. In such cases, no single group of governors has an outright majority of places on the Board.

3.15 In voluntary grammar schools, the balance of appointments between the ELB and the Department may vary. The precise division of appointments depends on whether or not the trustees of the school have entered into an agreement which gives one or more ELBs the power to appoint members to the Board of Governors.[43] In practice, this applies only in a small number of schools which were previously in the controlled sector and which have subsequently transferred to voluntary status. If the school has not entered into this sort of agreement, appointments in this category are all determined by the Department and the ELB will consequently be precluded from making appointments.[44]

3.16 When an ELB is appointing a nominee to any controlled integrated school, it is under a duty to choose persons who appear to it to be committed to the continuing viability of the school as a controlled school.[45] Apart from this, there are no statutory restrictions on the types of people who can be nominated by the ELB or the Department.

3.17 It should be pointed out that the role of the nominee once appointed is not to represent the interests of the Department or the ELB. The appointee is an independent governor and can take decisions which do not necessarily reflect the opinion or stance of the appointing authority. The issue has been considered by the courts in Great Britain on several occasions, usually arising in circumstances where the Board is voting on a proposed change of status for the school. The best known case is *Brunyate* v *ILEA* where a local education authority removed governors from office when they refused to support its policy of opposition to grant-maintained schools. The House of Lords stated:

> "... individual governors, so long as they hold office as such, have both the right and duty to exercise the function of their office independently in accordance with their judgment."[46]

It is difficult to envisage a similar situation arising in Northern Ireland. It could in theory occur where a school is considering a change to integrated status. Article 64 of the 1989 Order places the Department under a statutory duty to encourage the development of integrated education. However, on past experience it is clear that the Department will adopt a neutral approach when a school is taking decisions of this sort and is very unlikely to place pressure on its nominees to support any particular course of action. Nonetheless, when important decisions are being made about matters on which the ELB or

---

[42] Education (NI) Order 1998.
[43] Sch. 6 para. 2 to the 1986 Order substituted by Sch. 2 of the 1993 Order.
[44] Sch. 6 para. 4(4)(B)(ii) and Sch. 6 para. 5(2)(B)(i) to the 1986 Order substituted by Sch. 2 to the 1993 Order.
[45] Sch. 4 para. 5(4) to the 1986 Order substituted by art. 89 of the 1989 Order.
[46] *Brunyate* v *ILEA* [1989] 2 All ER 417, 420

Department may have an interest, nominees of the Department and ELB will benefit from a clear understanding about the nature of their role on the Board of Governors.

Elections

3.18 All Boards of Governors contain members elected by assistant teachers and parents.[47] All elections must be by secret ballot. In controlled schools the arrangements for the election will be made by the ELB.[48] In maintained schools, voluntary grammar schools and grant-maintained integrated schools, the arrangements for the ballot must be made by the Board of Governors.[49] In all cases election arrangements are subject to the approval of the Department.[50] The election procedure is not prescribed by statute. The only statutory requirement is that the ballot is secret. Complaints about irregularities in balloting procedures cannot be made by way of judicial review. In *R v Northampton CC, ex parte Gray* the English High Court said that the court could strike out the decision but not remedy it and that the appropriate remedy was a complaint to the Secretary of State under section 99 of the Education Act 1944.[51] On this basis, complaints about election procedures in Northern Ireland should be made to the Department under article 101 of the 1986 Order.

3.19 The assistant teacher must be elected by other assistant teachers in the school or schools represented by the Board. For these purposes the term assistant teacher does not include the principal or a temporary or part-time teacher.[52] This means that people falling into these categories cannot stand for election and cannot vote in the election. The assistant teacher must also be currently employed at the school and will cease to hold office when they are no longer employed by the school. The role of the assistant teacher is not prescribed in the legislation. In particular, they are not bound to represent the interests of the majority of the other teachers. Although, they are elected by the other teachers, it would seem from the case of *Brunyate* v *ILEA* discussed above that they can make independent decisions in the same way as other governors. If teachers are unhappy with the participation of the teacher governor, their remedy is to vote for someone else at the next election.

3.20 The elected parent representative must be a parent of a child attending the school and must be elected by the parents of pupils attending the school. A parent includes a guardian and every person who has actual custody of the child. Departmental guidance emphasises that each eligible parent is entitled to nominate candidates to vote and to stand for election.[53] Participation must not be restricted to one parent per family. The Department is also committed to "securing the maximum participation by parents in the management of

---

[47] This applies even in voluntary grammar schools which receive no capital funding from the state. In such cases the schools must have either one or two elected parents and assistant teachers, depending on the size of the full Board (Sch. 7 to the 1989 Order).
[48] Sch.4 para. 6(4) to the 1986 Order.
[49] Sch.5 para. 2(4) to the 1986 Order substituted by Sch. 2 to the 1993 Order.
[50] DENI Circular 1993/35 provides guidance as to the procedures to be followed.
[51] *The Times*, 10 June, 1986
[52] Sch.4 para. 7 to the 1986 Order.
[53] DENI Circular 1993/35.

schools".[54] Difficulties arise because the number of parents standing for election is often less than the number of vacancies on the Board. The government's intentions regarding parental involvement in schools are frequently not matched by a willingness on the part of parents to volunteer their services. In order to address this, in 1989 Boards were given the power in such cases to make up the required number of parent members through direct appointments by the voting members of the Board.[55] In doing this the Board is under a duty to appoint a person who is a parent of a registered child at the school where it is reasonably practicable to do so. A person appointed in this way will be treated as if he or she had been duly elected by parents of pupils at the school.

Co-options

3.21 In all grant-aided schools, the voting members of the Board of Governors may co-opt up to three extra members onto the Board.[56] When a Board of Governors is considering co-options, it must co-opt someone from the local business community if no member of the Board of Governors is a member of the local business community or if the Board considers it desirable to increase the number of members who are business people. Apart from this, the co-options are at the discretion of the Board. All Boards of Governors would benefit from financial or legal expertise. However, many Boards would have difficulty securing such appointments. The co-optees do not have voting rights so as to preserve the general balance of power between the various other appointments.

The principal

3.22 The principal of the school is a member of the Board of Governors. He or she is entitled to attend and take part in any meeting. He or she is not however entitled to vote on any question. In spite of this lack of voting power, the principal is usually the most influential person on the Board. Research has shown that few decisions actually go to a vote and instead most Boards of Governors tend to approve the recommendations of the principal.[57] If the principal is absent or unavailable, the Board may invite the vice-principal or person performing the duties of the principal to attend any meeting of the Board.[58] That person may take part in the meeting but may not vote on any question.

ELIGIBILITY FOR APPOINTMENT

3.23 There is only one general restriction on eligibility for appointment to the Board of Governors of a school. That is that a person cannot hold office on more than three Boards of Governors without the approval of the

---

[54] DENI, *Proposals for Reform* (1988) p.7.
[55] Art. 13 (3A-D) of the 1986 Order substituted by art. 121 of the 1989 Order.
[56] Art. 122 of the 1989 Order.
[57] McKeown, Byrne and Barnett, '*An Initial Analysis of the Impact of Formula Funding and Local Management of Schools on the Management of Northern Ireland Schools*' (1996, University of Ulster), para. 2A.1.1.
[58] Art. 13(6) of the 1986 Order.

Department.[59] The limitation on membership applies to appointments by the Department, the ELBs and the election of parent members. An exception is generally made for other appointments. Other restrictions on the membership of the Board may be set out in the scheme of management. It is normal practice for the following persons to be disqualified from membership: those employed at the school (other than the elected assistant teacher); persons convicted of certain criminal offences within the previous five years and people adjudged bankrupt. In controlled schools, the legislation states that any question as to the right of any person to be, or to nominate a member of the Board of Governors shall be decided by the Department whose decision shall be final.[60] There is no equivalent provision for other schools. However, this is probably unnecessary given that such appointments are administered through the Department

DURATION AND TERMINATION OF APPOINTMENTS

3.24 Appointments are normally for a period of four years although a person can be repeatedly re-appointed to office. A member can resign at any time. There are specified circumstances in which an appointment will terminate prematurely. First, an assistant teacher who has been elected onto the Board must cease to be a member once they are no longer employed by the school.[61] On the other hand an elected parent member can continue to be a member of the Board even where they are no longer a parent of a child registered at the school.[62] Secondly, as described earlier in this chapter, the general members of the Board of a voluntary school will cease to hold office if there is a change in the capital funding arrangements for the school. The same people may however be re-appointed to the newly constituted committee. The scheme of management may also specify circumstances in which an appointment will end. This will normally include the power to terminate membership when a member has failed to attend a set number of meetings (usually three) unless the Board is satisfied that there was good cause for the absence. In *Brunyate* v *ILEA* the House of Lords made it clear that nominating authorities could not remove their nominees from office simply because they had not complied with the wishes of the authority.[63] Instead, governors could only be removed by their nominating authorities to the extent that it was necessary to prevent the policy of the legislation being frustrated. This might occur where the governors are negligent or deliberately obstructive in the exercise of their functions.

OPERATION OF THE BOARD

3.25 The operation of the Board of Governors in schools in Northern Ireland is regulated by a scheme of management which all schools must have. This is to be contrasted with the position in England and Wales where the operation of the Board of Governors is regulated by statute. The Education (School Government) Regulations 1989 prescribe the membership, procedure

---

[59] Art. 12 of the 1986 Order amended by art. 37 of the 1993 Order.
[60] Art. 10(4) of the 1986 Order.
[61] *Ibid* art. 13(4).
[62] Art. 13(5) of the 1986 Order.
[63] [1989] 2 All ER 417.

and voting rights in Boards of Governors in England and Wales. There is no specific reason for the less formal approach taken in Northern Ireland. However, it might be presumed that the size of the jurisdiction and the different management structures in place are such that there is perceived to be less need for formal legal regulation.

Scheme of management

3.26 Every grant-aided school is required to have a scheme of management.[64] This is a document which sets out how a school is to be managed. More particularly, it defines the membership and procedure of the Board of Governors. The responsibility for preparing the scheme of management varies according to the nature of the school. ELBs must prepare the scheme of management of controlled schools and maintained schools (other than Catholic maintained schools) in consultation with the Board of Governors, trustees or managers of the school.[65] The CCMS must prepare the scheme of management of Catholic maintained schools in consultation with the trustees or managers of the school and the ELB.[66] Boards of Governors have responsibility for preparing the scheme in voluntary schools and grant-maintained integrated schools.[67] In each case the persons or body responsible must take into account guidance given by the Department as to the provisions that it regards as suitable for inclusion in the scheme. The scheme of management must include provision for the membership and procedure of the Board of Governors and the exercise of statutory functions by the Board and principal. The scheme must also set out provisions requiring the Board of Governors to: prepare a disciplinary policy (art. 124 of the 1989 Order); produce an annual report (art.125 of the 1989 Order); hold an annual parents meeting (art.136 of the 1989 Order) and prepare a school development plan (art.13 of the 1998 Order).

3.27 The scheme must be submitted to the Department for approval.[68] The submission should contain information as to the results of any required consultations. The scheme does not come into effect until the Department has given its approval and the Department may approve with such modifications as it thinks fit after consulting the party who has submitted the scheme. If a scheme has not been submitted or the Department considers that the scheme submitted is not in accordance with its guidance, it may, after consultation, impose its own scheme of management. The scheme of management may be revised at any time but revisions are also subject to Departmental approval.

Meetings

3.28 The scheme of management will also specify the procedure to be followed at meetings. This will normally include the frequency of meetings: the order of business; the election of a chairman; the appointment of the secretary; declarations of interest; rules of debate and the minutes. The

---

[64] Art. 9A of the 1986 Order inserted by art. 123 of the 1989 Order.
[65] *Ibid* art. 9B(1) and (2).
[66] *Ibid* art. 9B (4)-(5).
[67] *Ibid* art. 9B(6).
[68] *Ibid* art. 9C and 9D.

proceedings of the Board of Governors will be valid even where there is an unfilled vacancy or where there has been a defect in the appointment, election or nomination of any member.[69] Moreover, if an election or nomination has not or cannot be effected, the Board of Governors will be regarded as fully constituted. Any provision which relates to the quorum for a meeting is not affected in either of these circumstances.

3.29 In normal circumstances all members of the Board are entitled to attend meetings. There is only one situation in which a member is required by statute to withdraw from a meeting. This is where a Board has joint responsibility for two schools and an issue is being discussed which is exclusive to one of the schools. In such circumstances, the principal of the other school is not entitled to attend or take part in any meeting.[70] However, the school's scheme of management may specify other circumstances in which members should withdraw from the meeting. This will normally exclude any person who has a direct interest, pecuniary or otherwise, in the issue being discussed. In Great Britain, the Education (School Government) Regulations 1989 prescribe the circumstances in which a governor may be required to withdraw from a meeting. Northern Ireland does not have equivalent legislation. However, the right of all governors to participate should be given careful consideration so as to avoid any allegations of bias in the decision-making processes.

3.30 In determining whether a decision might be invalidated on the basis of 'bias' the courts employ one of two tests: is there a real likelihood of bias or is it sufficient that a reasonable person would think that the decision-maker might be biased? In practice, the answer to both questions is usually the same. If there is considered to be a possible bias in the decision-making process, the decision of the Board of Governors could be challenged by way of judicial review. It is important for the Board to consider its composition carefully when taking decisions. An obvious example of bias would be where the elected teacher had a direct involvement in the issue being considered (e.g. they had been attacked by a pupil) and the Board of Governors is then considering whether the pupil should be expelled for the incident. However, generally speaking the two key forms of potential bias arise when a governor has a family connection or pecuniary interest in any issue being discussed. These are considered below.

Family connections

3.31 All of the schemes of management define family relationships to include the following: spouses and co-habitees; parents; grandparents; grandchildren; sons and daughters; brothers and sisters; first cousins; uncles and aunts; nephews and nieces and equivalent step-relationships. In practice, issues about family relationships may arise in two contexts. The first relates to employment matters within the school, including appointments, terms of employment, promotions, discipline, resignation and retirement. The second area where a family connection may be relevant is where the Board is considering disciplinary action against a pupil and the governor has a family

---

[69] Art. 13 of the 1986 Order.
[70] See, for instance, in relation to controlled schools, Sch. 4 para.1(2) to the 1986 Order.

connection to that pupil or to another pupil involved in the incident. For instance, it would be inappropriate for a governor to take part in a meeting discussing an expulsion if he or she was related to the pupil being discussed or related to another pupil who had been a victim of the pupil whose conduct were being considered.

Pecuniary interests

3.32 All of the schemes of management require a governor to withdraw from a meeting if he or she has any direct or indirect pecuniary interest in the issue being discussed. One obvious illustration of this is where the governors are considering entering into a commercial relationship with a company to which one of the governors is connected. However, in practice, the most common situation in which this is likely to arise is in discussions about the appointment and promotion of staff. In some situations, the possibility of bias will be apparent, for example where the discussion directly concerns the principal or teacher governor. However, it could also arise where a teacher governor may stand to benefit from the appointment of another member of staff. In *Noble* v *ILEA* the Court of Appeal found that the decision of a governing body to promote a teacher to deputy head was invalid because the teacher governor who had been at the interview was eligible for the post which the other teacher would vacate.[71] In view of this most schemes of management require the teacher governor to withdraw if the meeting is discussing the appointment, promotion, transfer, conduct, discipline, resignation or retirement of any member of staff holding a post senior to his or her own. They will also normally exclude the teacher or principal from discussions surrounding the appointment of a successor.

3.33 Secondly, the composition of the Board should be considered where the school is contemplating a change of status. There have been several cases in Great Britain focusing on what is meant by a direct pecuniary interest in the Education (School Government) Regulations 1989 in the context of proposals for a change of status.[72] In *Bostock* v *Kay* the Court of Appeal considered that teacher governors had a direct pecuniary interest in the outcome of proposals to change the status of the school to a City Technical College.[73] However in *R* v *Board of Governors of Small Heath School, ex parte Birmingham CC* the court considered that a direct interest did not arise where the proposal was to transfer to grant-maintained status as the financial position of the teachers would not alter in such circumstances.[74] This would presumably also be the case where a vote is taken to seek integrated status in Northern Ireland.

Voting rights

3.34 The voting members on the Board of Governors were identified in the tables earlier in the chapter (see post para. 3.07). The principal and co-optees are not voting members. There is only one situation specified by statute when certain members may not be entitled to vote. If the Board of Governors of a

---

[71] (1984) 83 LGR 291.
[72] Sch. 1 para. 2(4) to the 1986 Order.
[73] *The Times*, 20 April 1989.
[74] *The Times*, 14 August 1989.

voluntary grammar school holds capital assets, elected members (parents and associate teachers) are not entitled to vote on any matter relating to the acquisition, disposal or management of such assets without the permission of the other members of the Board.[75] In addition a governor will not be able to vote on an issue when he or she is required to withdraw from a meeting of the Board of Governors because of potential bias arising from family connections or pecuniary interests as described in the paragraphs 3.30-3.33. In practice, working relationships on Boards of Governors tend to be good with the result that few issues are ever put to a vote.[76]

Delegation of functions

3.35 It would be impracticable if every decision of a Board of Governors had to be taken at a meeting of the full Board. The Board is therefore permitted to delegate some of its duties to sub-committees which can include members who are not on the Board of Governors.[77] The scheme of management must specify which functions may be delegated and the membership and procedure of any sub-committees. It is common practice to have sub-committees for the following functions: finance; salaries; and appointments.[78] The Board can also delegate functions to the school principal. These must also be specified in the scheme of management. The scheme of management will specify which functions cannot be delegated either to a sub-committee or to the principal. These will usually include: drawing up admissions criteria; preparing the disciplinary policy; the co-option of governors; and the publication of information. In practice, however, it appears that many of these functions are not carried out by the full Board of Governors and are in fact left to the principal.[79] This is in spite of the fact that a failure to carry out specific statutory responsibilities could leave the decision open to challenge under article 101 of the 1986 Order or by way of judicial review.

Boards with joint responsibility for more than one school

3.36 A Board of Governors can have responsibility for more than one primary school (other than a nursery school).[80] This is likely to occur in small rural primary schools where it may be difficult or impractical to find sufficient members to serve on more than one Board. In controlled primary schools, the decision to group schools together in this way is taken by the ELB and is subject to approval by the Department.[81] In maintained primary schools the Board of Governors of each school must request that the schools are grouped together under one Board. In Catholic maintained schools the decision is taken by the CCMS.[82] In other maintained schools, the decision is taken by

---

[75] Sch. 6 para. 3(8) and Sch.7 para.2(6) to the 1986 Order.
[76] McKeown, Byrne and Barnett, *An Initial Analysis of the Impact of Formula Funding and Local Management of Schools on the Management of Northern Ireland's schools: A Schools' Perspective* (1996 University of Ulster), p.12.
[77] Art. 9A of the 1986 Order, inserted by art. 123 of the 1989 Order.
[78] See McKeown et al, *op cit*, p. 13.
[79] *Ibid* p.14.
[80] Sch. 4 para.1 and Sch. 5 para.1(2) to the 1986 Order.
[81] Art. 10(2) of the 1986 Order.
[82] Art. 11(3)(a) of the 1986 Order substituted by Sch. 2 to the 1993 Order.

the ELB.[83] In both cases, a decision to group primary schools under the management of one Board of Governors is subject to Departmental approval.

3.37 Where a Board of Governors has responsibility for more than one school, the principal of each school is normally entitled to attend meetings. However, where the matter being discussed relates exclusively to one school, the principal(s) of the other school(s) is (are) not entitled to attend or take part in the meeting.[84] Difficulties may arise in situations where an issue is being discussed which potentially affects both schools (e.g. a discussion over a merger or a prospective closure). Unless otherwise provided in the scheme of management, and subject to the rules about bias (see paras. 3.30 – 3.33), it would seem that in such circumstances both principals are entitled to attend and take part in discussions but not to vote.

3.38 Elected representatives (i.e. teachers and parents) are elected from a pool of people in both schools. Given that there is often only one assistant teacher elected onto the Board, one school will inevitably not have an assistant teacher on the Board. Both controlled and maintained primary schools have two elected parent members. Although it would seem appropriate, there is no stipulation that one should be elected from each of the schools which have been grouped together.

FUNCTIONS OF THE BOARD

3.39 Boards of Governors have a wide range of responsibilities. These will be looked at in individual chapters of the book. They include: admissions; discipline; attendance and the curriculum. However, there are three general management functions which will be considered in this chapter. The first two are the production of the annual report and the holding of an annual parents' meeting. Both functions were introduced in 1989 as part of the government's attempt to increase accountability to parents. The third general function is the production of the school development plan, a requirement introduced by the 1998 Order.

Annual report

3.40 As part of the drive to ensure increased accountability to parents, the 1989 Order placed Boards of Governors under a duty to produce an annual report.[85] This must contain certain prescribed information. This includes: the date, time, place and agenda of the next annual general meeting; the name and membership status of each member of the Board of Governors; the date on which individual member's terms of office come to an end; the name of the chairman and secretary; arrangements as to the next elections onto the Board; a financial statement; specified information about the school's performance of its obligations in relation to children with special educational needs; and the steps which have been taken by the Board to develop the school's links with the community and to promote Education for Mutual Understanding. Since 1998 schools have been under a requirement to include a general description of the arrangements made for the security of the pupils and staff at the school

---

[83] *Ibid* art. 11(3)(b).
[84] Sch. 4 para.1(2) and Sch. 5 paras.2(3) and 3(4) to the 1986 Order.
[85] Art. 125 of the 1989 Order.

and the school premises.[86] This requirement was introduced in England and Wales as one of a number of measures designed to alleviate public concern following the tragedy at Dunblane. It is also of significance to parents in Northern Ireland, since it is apparent that schools in this jurisdiction are not immune from violent intrusions.

3.41 The Board must take such steps as are reasonably practicable to secure that a copy of the report is given to the parents of all pupils registered at the school and all staff employed at the school and that copies are available for inspection at the school. If the report is to be considered at the annual meeting of parents, copies should be given to parents not less than two weeks before the meeting. This is designed to give parents a chance to read the report and to formulate a response should they wish to raise an issue at the meeting.

Annual parents' meeting

3.42 The Board of Governors is under a duty to hold a parents' meeting once a year.[87] The meeting is open to all parents of registered pupils. Other persons including assistant teachers may be invited by the Board to attend. The purpose of the meeting is to discuss the annual report and any other matters relating to the discharge of duties by the school, the ELB, the CCMS or the Department. The procedure for the meeting must be set down in the scheme of management. The elections of parent governors to the Board of Governors may also be conducted at the annual meeting. In practice, meetings tend to be very sparsely attended. Research commissioned by the Department concluded that the meeting held almost no attraction for parents and played only a "cosmetic role" in fostering school accountability to the parent body.[88]

School development plan

3.43 The scheme of management of each grant-aided school must provide for it to be the duty of the Board of Governors of the school to prepare, and from time to time revise, a school development plan.[89] This obligation was introduced as one of a number of measures designed by the Labour government in its efforts to raise standards in schools. The obligation to prepare the plan has been effective from 1 September 1999. In preparing the plan, the Board of Governors must consult the school principal and have regard to any guidance given by the Department, the ELB for its area and the CCMS (where the school is a Catholic maintained school).[90] The governors must also have regard to the findings of any inspection of the school under article 102 of the 1986 Order. Regulations to be issued under the 1998 Order will specify the matters to be dealt with in the plan; the period for which the plan is to have effect; the manner of publication; and the requirements in relation to revision.

---

[86] Art. 125(2)(a) of the 1989 Order, substituted by art. 15 of the 1998 Order.
[87] Art. 126 of the 1989 Order.
[88] McKeown et al, *op cit*, p.121.
[89] Art. 13(1) of the 1998 Order.
[90] *Ibid* art. 13(2)(a) and (b)(i).

GOVERNORS' RESPONSIBILITY FOR FINANCE

3.44 Each grant-aided school receives a proportion of the general schools budget from its ELB. The sum allocated to each school is referred to as the school's budget share.[91] The precise allocation is determined by a formula which takes into account factors such as numbers, ages of the children and the number of children with special educational needs.[92] Every ELB is required to prepare a scheme for the financing of grant-aided schools in its area. The scheme must include details of: each school's share of the general schools budget and, in the case of controlled and maintained schools, the provision for delegating the schools' budget share to each Board of Governors. The scheme is subject to the Department's approval.[93]

3.45 The rules governing Boards of Governors' obligations in relation to this finance are now contained in the 1998 Order. Controlled and maintained schools receive their finance from the ELB for the area. Currently voluntary grammar schools and grant maintained integrated schools receive their budget allocation directly from the Department. When the 1998 Order is fully implemented, these schools will receive their grants from their local ELB. However, the way in which this money is transferred from ELBs to Boards of Governors will differ between controlled and maintained schools on the one hand and voluntary grammar and GMI schools on the other. In controlled and maintained schools Boards of Governors receive their money through a scheme of financial delegation (in which ultimate control still rests with the ELB who may reclaim control if there are problems). In voluntary grammar schools and GMI schools the money will be paid as a grant by the ELB. If there are problems, finance can be withdrawn completely but the ELB cannot assume responsibility for the management of the school.

[N.B. *The analysis which follows is based on Part VII of the Education (NI) Order 1998 which is not in force at the time of writing.*[94]]

Controlled and maintained schools

3.46 The 1989 Order made a radical change to the financial arrangements in controlled and maintained schools through the implementation of a policy known as Local Management of Schools (LMS). Under LMS a budget to cover the school's annual running costs is delegated by the ELB to the Board of Governors of the school to spend as it sees fit. The rationale underlying LMS is that budgetary control allows Boards of Governors to be more flexible and responsive to the individual needs of their schools. Research indicates that schools believe that LMS has obtained its key objectives in that schools can determine their own priorities, target resources and control their staffing arrangements.[95] On the downside, LMS has meant an increased volume of

---

[91] *Ibid* art. 44.
[92] *Ibid* art. 50.
[93] *Ibid* arts.47-48.
[94] With the exception of art. 70(5), (6) and (8).
[95] McKeown et al, *op cit* p.147.

administration and schools have ongoing concerns about the level of funding.[96]

Financial delegation

3.47 Each financial scheme prepared by an ELB must include provision requiring the ELB to delegate the management of the school's budget share to the Board of Governors of controlled and maintained schools. If financial delegation is required in relation to such a school, the ELB must put the school's budget share at the disposal of the Board of Governors to be spent for the purposes of the school (unless the right of delegation has been suspended under article 55 of the 1998 Order discussed below). Any sums given to Boards of Governors may be given subject to conditions imposed by the ELB under the scheme.[97] Subject to this, the Board of Governors is entitled to spend the sum made available to it as it thinks fit for the purposes of the school.[98] The Board of Governors may delegate the power to spend the sums allocated to the principal of the school to such extent as is permitted by the scheme.[99] The members of the Board of Governors will not incur any personal liability in respect of anything done in good faith in the exercise or purported exercise of their powers in relation to the expenditure of the budget.

Suspension of delegation to schools

3.48 The right of financial delegation gives schools complete control over substantial sums of money. It is quite possible that not all Boards of Governors will be capable of managing that money effectively, a concern which is borne out by research which indicates that many schools feel that they have not received sufficient training to carry out their duties properly.[100] In view of this, the legislation gives ELBs the power to suspend the system of financial delegation to a school. An ELB can do this where it appears that the Board of Governors has been guilty of a substantial or persistent failure to comply with any requirements of the scheme or is not managing the appropriation or expenditure of the money in a satisfactory manner.[101] The ELB must give the Board of Governors one month's notice of the suspension. This notice shall specify the grounds for the suspension and the particulars of the alleged failure to comply with any requirements or conditions applicable under the scheme. A copy of the notice shall be sent to the principal, the Department and the CCMS if the school is a Catholic maintained school. The ELB may withdraw the notice at any time before the expiry of the period of notice and if it does so must notify the relevant parties accordingly. In exceptional cases, the ELB can suspend the right without giving one month's notice.[102] This is possible where the ELB considers it necessary by reason of gross incompetence or mismanagement on the part of the Board of Governors or some other emergency. In these cases, the ELB must give the Board of

---

[96] *Ibid* p.150.
[97] Art. 53 of the 1998 Order.
[98] *Ibid* art. 54(5)(a).
[99] *Ibid* art. 54(5)(b).
[100] McKeown et al, *op cit* p.152.
[101] Art. 55(1) of the 1998 Order.
[102] *Ibid* art. 55(4).

Governors, the Department and CCMS (where appropriate) written notification of its actions and the reasons for it.

3.49 Once a notice is issued the ELB is no longer under the obligation to put a sum of money at the disposal of the Board of Governors. The suspension effectively removes the school's right to manage its own finances. All suspensions must be reviewed at the beginning of the financial year.[103] The Board of Governors, principal and CCMS (where appropriate) must be given an opportunity to make representations on the suspension. The ELB must consider the representations and revoke the suspension if appropriate. A revocation will take effect from the beginning of the next financial year. The Board of Governors has a right to appeal to the Department against the imposition of the suspension or the ELB's refusal to revoke the suspension.[104] The Department will have regard to the gravity of the default and the likelihood of its continuance or recurrence and may allow or reject the appeal accordingly.

Special schools

3.50 The rules on financial delegation in special schools are different from other controlled and maintained schools. They are subject to regulation by the Department. The Department may issue regulations requiring or authorising schemes for special schools.[105] These regulations may include provision for the delegation of the school's budget share from the ELB to the Board of Governors.

3.51 Special schools which are not covered by a scheme for delegation will nevertheless receive a sum of money to be spent by the Board of Governors on such heads of expenditure as the ELB may specify or the Department directs.[106] The Board of Governors must comply with any reasonable conditions of the ELB when spending the money and may delegate to the principal its power to spend the sum.[107] The individual members of the Board of Governors are protected from personal liability for anything done in good faith for the purposes of the school.[108] The ELB may with one month's notice suspend the Board of Governors' right to have a sum given to it if there has been a substantial or persistent failure to comply with any conditions of the ELB or if the governors are not managing the money in a satisfactory manner.[109] The right to manage the money may be removed during the notice period if the ELB considers it necessary by reason of gross incompetence or mismanagement on the part of the Board of Governors or other emergency.[110]

---

[103] *Ibid* art. 56.
[104] *Ibid* art. 57.
[105] *Ibid* art. 59.
[106] *Ibid* art. 60(1).
[107] *Ibid* art. 60(2).
[108] *Ibid* art. 60(3).
[109] *Ibid* art. 60(6)-(8).
[110] *Ibid* art. 60 (9)-(11).

Voluntary grammar schools

3.52 ELBs make grants to voluntary grammar schools to cover the maintenance costs of the school apart from costs for premises and equipment.[111] These grants are subject to such conditions as the ELB may determine with the approval of the Department.[112] Subject to this, the Board of Governors may spend the sums received as it thinks fit for the purposes of the school and may delegate this power to the principal.[113] The members of the Board of Governors will not incur any personal liability in respect of anything done in good faith in the exercise or purported exercise of their powers in relation to the expenditure of the budget.[114]

Withdrawal of maintenance grants

3.53 The Department may give the Board of Governors a notice in writing that the duty to pay a maintenance grant will cease.[115] As a general rule, the Board of Governors must have at least two years' notice and the Department must consult with the Board of Governors and ELB before issuing a notice.[116] However, these obligations do not apply where the Department is satisfied that the school as currently constituted or conducted is unsuitable to continue as a voluntary grammar school on one of a number of specified grounds. These are: that the number of registered pupils at the school is too small for sufficient and suitable education to be provided at reasonable cost; that the Board of Governors has failed for a significant period of time to carry out its duties under Part III of the 1989 Order; or that the Board of Governors has been guilty of a substantial or persistent failure to comply or secure compliance with any other requirement or provision of the Education Orders or other statutory provision.[117] If the Department issues a notice on one of these grounds, it must state the grounds in the notice along with "full particulars" of the matters relevant to each ground.[118]

3.54 If any of the matters stated in the notice are irremediable, the notice will specify the date on which the ELB will no longer be under an obligation to pay maintenance grants. However, if the matters can be redeemed, the notice will state: that the ELB's duty will cease unless the matters are remedied; specify the measures which the Department considers are necessary to remedy the matters; and specify a time not less than three months from the date of the notice within which the Board of Governors must take the measures.[119] If the Board of Governors fails to take the measures within the specified time, the Department will issue a further notice within two months which will either extend the time or, after consulting the relevant ELB, give notice that the duty to pay a maintenance grant will cease on a specified

---

[111] The Board of Governors can also apply for grants for capital costs.
[112] Art. 61(4) of the 1998 Order.
[113] *Ibid* art. 61(6).
[114] *Ibid* art. 61(7).
[115] *Ibid* art. 62.
[116] *Ibid* art. 62(2).
[117] *Ibid* art. 62(3).
[118] *Ibid* art. 62(4).
[119] *Ibid* art. 62(6).

Grant-maintained integrated schools

3.55 Grant-maintained integrated schools have a large degree of autonomy over the management of school finances. However, when the Education (NI) Order 1998 is implemented fully, they will receive a grant to meet their running costs from the ELB for their area rather than the Department. There are no specific provisions as to the management of this finance other than the fact that the payment of grants subject to conditions as the ELB may determine with the approval of the Department.[122] Subject to this, the Board of Governors may spend the sums received as it thinks fit for the purposes of the school and may delegate this power to the principal.[123] The members of the Board of Governors will not incur any personal liability in respect of anything done in good faith in the exercise or purported exercise of their powers in relation to the expenditure of the budget.[124]

Withdrawal of maintenance grants

3.56 The Department may give the Board of Governors a notice in writing that the duty to pay a maintenance grant will cease.[125] As a general rule, the Board of Governors must have at least two years notice and the Department must consult with the Board of Governors, ELB and CCMS before issuing a notice.[126] However, these obligations do not apply where the Department is satisfied that the school, as currently constituted or conducted, is unsuitable to continue as a voluntary grammar school on one of a number of specified grounds. These are: that the number of registered pupils at the school is too small for sufficient and suitable education to be provided at reasonable cost; that the Board of Governors has failed for a significant period of time to carry out its duties under Part III of the 1989 Order; that the Board of Governors has been guilty of a substantial or persistent failure to comply or secure compliance with any other requirement or provision of the Education Orders or other statutory provision; or that the school is not attended by reasonable numbers of both Protestant and Roman Catholic pupils.[127] If the Department issues a notice on one of these grounds, it must state the grounds in the notice along with "full particulars" of the matters relevant to each ground.[128]

3.57 If any of the matters stated in the notice are irremediable, the notice will specify the date on which the ELB will no longer be under an obligation to pay maintenance grants. However, if the matters can be redeemed, the notice will state: that the ELB's duty will cease unless the matters are remedied; specify the measures which the Department considers are necessary

---

[120] *Ibid* art. 62(7).
[121] *Ibid* art. 62(8)-(10).
[122] *Ibid* art. 63(4).
[123] *Ibid* art. 63(6).
[124] *Ibid* art. 63(7).
[125] *Ibid* art. 63.
[126] *Ibid* art. 63(2).
[127] *Ibid* art. 63(3).
[128] *Ibid* art. 63(4).

to remedy the matters; and specify a time not less than three months from the date of the notice within which the Board of Governors must take the measures.[129] If the Board of Governors fails to take the measures within the specified time, the Department will issue a further notice within two months which will either extend the time or, after consulting the relevant ELB, give notice that the duty to pay maintenance grant will cease on a specified date.[130] The Department has the power to withdraw or vary any of the notices it issues.[131] It must give copies of all notices issued to the relevant ELB.

LEGAL STATUS

3.58 Until 1996, Boards of Governors did not have a recognised legal status. This meant that individual governors could be the subject of legal action. Article 40 of the Education (NI) Order 1996 states that all Boards of Governors constituted in accordance with Part III of the 1986 Order are constituted as a body corporate. The provision took effect from September 1 1996 and applies to all grant-aided schools other than grant-maintained integrated schools. Grant-maintained integrated schools automatically have corporate status from the date on which the proposal to become grant-maintained integrated is implemented.[132] A Board of Governors has an official name which is "The Board of Governors of ..." with the name of each school for which it has responsibility in alphabetical order.[133] The Board also has an official seal which must be authenticated by the chairman or some other member authorised by the Board and one other member. The primary effect of incorporation is that Boards of Governors form a single legal entity which is distinct from that of the individual members of the Board. In effect, this means that the Board can sue and be sued in its own name. On incorporation all property, rights and liabilities attributable to the Board of Governors before incorporation vest in the body corporate. Schedule 4 to the 1996 Order specifies the impact of incorporation on matters such as rights and liabilities under contracts of employment and data protection. The schedule also makes provision in the event of the dissolution of a Board of Governors and the division of property rights when a school ceases to be under the management of a Board which has responsibility for more than one school.

3.59 Membership of a Board of Governors is an onerous task not just because of the wide range of obligations involved but because many of the decisions taken are subject to challenge. The potential legal liability of the Board of Governors as a body corporate is significant. There are an increasing number of legal actions involving governors, particularly in the areas of school admissions and discipline. However, the potential liability of individual governors is not as marked. One commentator has observed that "governors need not fear if they act at all times reasonably, and with reasonable diligence. It would indeed be odd if it were not so".[134] Individual

---

[129] *Ibid* art. 63(6).
[130] *Ibid* art. 63(7).
[131] *Ibid* art. 63(8)-(10).
[132] Art. 72 of the 1989 Order.
[133] Art. 40(6) of the 1996 Order.
[134] Hyams, 'The potential liabilities of governors of education institutions' (1994) 6 *Education and the Law* 191, at 205.

governors should rarely be held personally liable for their actions. Quite clearly, few would volunteer their services if it were otherwise.

DISPUTES WITH EDUCATION AND LIBRARY BOARDS AND/OR THE DEPARTMENT

3.60 All grant-aided schools will co-operate with their local ELB in matters such as finance, special needs etc. Disputes are inevitable, particularly in voluntary schools where the relationship between the ELB and the school is less direct. If a dispute between an ELB and the trustees or managers of a voluntary school cannot be resolved between the parties, either party can refer the issue to the Department.[135] This is possible even where the exercise of the statutory power or duty which forms the basis of the dispute is contingent upon the opinion of either party. The Department's decision in such matters is final.

3.61 There is no specific statutory procedure for handling disputes between individual Boards of Governors and the Department. Disputes can arise in relation to matters such as funding or school admission numbers or changes in status. In such cases, the Department has the power to issue a direction if the Board of Governors is acting or proposing to act unreasonably with respect to any of its statutory functions. The direction can be enforced through the courts by an order of *mandamus*. Moreover, in exceptional circumstances, where the Board of Governors has failed to discharge its functions, the Department can appoint a person or persons to discharge the functions of the Board.[136] If the Board of Governors is unhappy with a decision of the Department, it may have recourse to an action for judicial review if the Department can be shown to have acted unreasonably, unfairly or unlawfully in the discharge of its functions.

---

[135] Art. 100 of the 1986 Order.
[136] *Ibid* art. 101(4).

CHAPTER FOUR

ADMISSIONS

INTRODUCTION

4.01 One of the key concerns of parents is that their child will be able to attend the school of their choice. This choice is influenced by a number of factors including the school's convenience to the home and existing family links as well as the school's academic standards. However, prior to 1990 admissions to grant-aided schools were administered by local education and library boards in a system which took limited account of the factors which motivated parents' desire for a particular school. Parents were asked to indicate which school they wished their child to attend but the ultimate decision was taken by the local ELB according to its general policy on school admissions. The Education Reform (NI) Order 1989 introduced the concept of 'open enrolment' to Northern Ireland by transferring responsibility for admissions to the Boards of Governors of individual schools and by allowing parents to express a statutory preference as to the school which they wished their child to attend. Boards of Governors were required to comply with parental preference provided that there were vacant places at the school. Article 44 of the 1986 Order expresses a general principle that pupils shall be educated in accordance with the wishes of their parents "so far as it is compatible with the provision of efficient instruction and the avoidance of unreasonable expenditure". It is the application of the proviso which means that in practice some children will not be able to have the education of their parent's choice. All grant-aided schools have fixed admission and enrolment numbers which are determined primarily by the school's physical capacity. Although Boards of Governors generally cannot refuse admission if they have vacant places, if a school is oversubscribed, the Board is required to apply pre-established criteria to determine which children will be admitted. This will inevitably mean that some children will be refused entry to popular schools.

4.02 The policy intention underlying open enrolment was to give parents more say in the choice of school for their child. The government's stated intention was that the legislation should give effect to the general principle that "admissions to all primary and secondary schools should normally be constrained only by the existing capacity of their accommodation".[1] The idea was that parents could vote with their feet by expressing a preference for a school and the school could only refuse to admit the child if it could not physically accommodate the numbers seeking admission. Thus, although the legislation does not give parents an absolute right to have their child educated at the school of their choice, their preference must be complied with unless all the available places at a school have been offered to children with a stronger claim on the basis of the published criteria. This approach can be contrasted with the system operating prior to 1990 which distributed children between

---

[1] *The Way Ahead* (DENI,1988), para. 3.1.

the various schools in the area and ensured to some extent that all schools had a sufficient proportion of the intake to secure their ongoing viability. In order to help parents make their selection, the 1989 Order also required schools and ELBs to provide specific information about the school, the admissions procedures and the school's performance measured on the basis of a number of criteria including attendance and examination performances.[2] In the case of secondary schools, information on the latter is published annually as 'league tables' which are intended to assist parents in selecting a school for their child.

4.03 In England and Wales, the operation of open enrolment has resulted in some schools closing due to falling rolls as parents exercise their preference and send their children to the schools which are perceived to be more successful. Critics have argued that this reduces rather than increases parental choice. Moreover, pressure for places in popular schools has meant that parents will go to considerable lengths to come within the admissions criteria for popular schools. One of the most common of these is a criterion which gives priority to children living within a certain catchment area. In some parts of England property prices have soared as parents rush to buy houses within the catchment area of successful schools. The pressure for places in good schools is such that some parents are willing to falsify the information given on application forms.[3] There has also been a rise in the popularity of church schools which are perceived to have better disciplinary and academic records than ordinary state schools. Church schools in England and Wales regularly resort to the use of criteria which overtly select pupils on the basis of their religion, distinguishing between candidates on matters such as the proportion of church attendances.[4] There have been a number of media reports which have highlighted a growing tendency for non-believing parents to embrace religion as they attempt to get their child into the local Catholic or Church of England school.[5] The religious option is perceived by some parents to be the only way of preventing their child from attending the local comprehensive school if they do not have sufficient money to send their child to a private school or object to private education on principle.

4.04 In Northern Ireland, open enrolment has operated somewhat differently as schools do not compete in the same way for pupils. The major difference here lies in the fact that open enrolment operates within a system which is segregated in a number of respects. First, although Northern Ireland has a large number of schools which are under the management and control of the local churches, schools do not use criteria which overtly select on the basis of religion. The reason for this is essentially practical. The system is such that most Catholic parents send their children to Catholic schools and most Protestant parents send their child to controlled schools or schools with a Protestant denominational ethos. There are sufficient numbers of both types of schools to ensure that these preferences can be accommodated. Moreover, it is widely recognised that there is no difference in the educational standards in church schools and others. Instead, in Northern Ireland, the most significant influence on the operation of open enrolment is the fact that Northern Ireland

---

[2] Art. 42 of the 1989 Order.
[3] See, L. Ward, 'The parents who cheat for their children', *The Independent*, 17 April 1997.
[4] M. Wroe, 'Middle class prays for children's education', *The Observer*, 18 February 1996.
[5] See A. Mc Elvoy, 'Blessed are the left-footers', *The Spectator*, 30 March 1996.

continues to maintain the grammar/secondary divide. It has been seen that attempts to introduce comprehensive schools in Northern Ireland have always met with failure.[6] Given the mark of achievement which ensues from selection on the basis of academic merit, many parents are keen that their child should attend grammar school. The consequence is that grammar schools are generally oversubscribed. Most grammar schools use the centrally organised transfer procedure tests (the successor of the old 11 plus) as the basis of selection. However, given the strength of parental desire for their children to attend grammar schools, it is perhaps not surprising that this has turned out to be one of the most litigious areas of education law.

4.05 The 1989 Order established a statutory appeal tribunal to which parents can appeal a refusal to admit. In spite of this, every summer since 1990 there have been a number of judicial review actions concerning the refusal to admit a child to the school of their parent's choice.[7] In the case of grammar schools, the judicial review actions exposed the difficulty which many schools ran into when they attempted to select pupils on the basis of ability using the results in the transfer procedure tests. In an attempt to clarify the use of the transfer procedure results, regulations were introduced which prescribed the criteria to be used in such circumstances.[8] These have effectively regulated the criteria for admission to grammar schools to performance in the transfer procedure tests. However, the judicial review actions also highlighted other weaknesses in the various systems employed to determine admissions with the result that the original provisions in the 1989 Order were replaced by the Education (NI) Order 1997 for admissions in the school year following June 1998. The new Order has re-structured the procedures for determining admissions and has further regulated the appeal process. It has also removed the statutory duty to comply with parental preference under article 36 of the 1989 Order and introduced a prohibition on schools from using the order of parental preference as one of their admissions criteria. One of the intentions underlying the reforms was to clarify the decision-making procedures and thus reduce the potential for challenges by way of judicial review. Nevertheless, the decisions of the Northern Ireland courts prior to the introduction of the 1997 Order continue to provide a valuable insight into the legal issues involved in the determination of school admissions.

4.06 In spite of these efforts, every year there is a fresh batch of admission appeals followed by judicial review applications. One consequence of this is that a number of schools are faced with bills for legal costs which they can scarcely afford. The judiciary appears to be conscious of this and has, somewhat unusually, expressed its concern about the proliferation of these actions. For instance in *In re Holmes* MacDermott LJ expressed a fear that "lawyers are capable of making even simple documents appear complex and confused".[9] If the challenges turn out to be unfounded, as has often been the

---

[6] See para. 1.11.
[7] For a discussion of the judicial review decisions, see, Lundy, 'Selection on ability: lessons from Northern Ireland' (1996) 8 *Education and the Law* 29.
[8] The Secondary Schools (Admission Criteria) Regulations (NI) 1995. These have since been replaced by the Secondary Schools (Admission Criteria) Regulations (NI) 1997.
[9] Unreported decision of the High Court of Northern Ireland, 27 September 1991.

case, much money can be wasted from the school's hard pressed resources on legal costs. One the strongest pleas for moderation was also made by MacDermott LJ in *In re Moore* where he said:

> "Each year the transfer procedures both delight and disappoint young children and their parents. Each year a number of appeals are brought by way of judicial review. It is important however to remember that such an application is not an appeal in the ordinary sense...Thus it must be remembered that disappointment is not itself a sound foundation for legal proceedings. Bringing vain proceedings does nothing but continue and increase existing anxiety and disappointment: it can be costly and frustrating. Legal advisers should bear this in mind when advising disappointed parents."[10]

4.07 In evaluating the success of the policy of open enrolment, the high level of litigation in relation to admissions decisions might be interpreted in one of two ways. First, it could be seen as an indication that parents are more willing to exercise their rights to the full, an important element of the open enrolment philosophy. On the other hand, the level of litigation is also an indication that many parents have not had their choices met under the system. The true picture could only be ascertained with a widespread survey of parents. That said, the reality is that most parents do get their child into the school of their choice. This is especially true for admission to primary schools. At secondary level the operation of the bi-partite system means that parental choice is severely constricted by legislation which determines entry with reference to the child's performance in the transfer procedure tests. However, even the much-prized Grade A does not guarantee entry into Northern Ireland's most popular schools. Moreover, parents wishing for a particular form of education such as integrated or Irish medium may find that their choices are restricted by the numbers of such schools available. In this respects, open enrolment may have had a limited impact in terms of increasing parental say in the choice of school for their child.

4.08 The whole system of determining admissions would be transformed if Northern Ireland was to abandon selection at secondary level. There are ongoing calls for the abolition of the grammar school system. The campaign was given a boost by the employment equality review undertaken by SACHR. This called for a major review into the selective system which would consider the arguments in favour of the retention of selection against "its contribution to educational inequality prior to school leaving age and its resulting hindrance of employment equality in later life".[11] The government response was not to abolish selection but to commission research on the impact of selection and to look favourably upon proposals by parents to end selection in their area.[12] Much will now depend on the attitude of the Assembly.[13]

---

[10] [1994] NIJB 111 (CA).
[11] SACHR, *Employment Equality: Building for the Future* (1997, The Stationery Office) Cm. 3684 pp.36-40.
[12] *Partnership for Equality* (1998, The Stationery Office) Cm. 3890 p.20.
[13] See further para. 1.20.

INFORMATION ON ADMISSIONS

4.09 The system of open enrolment is underpinned by a number of provisions which are intended to increase the amount of information available to parents about school admission procedures. Article 17 of the 1997 Order places ELBs and schools under a duty to supply parents with information which will assist them in making an informed choice of school for their child. ELBs are under a statutory duty to publish the following information: the arrangements for allowing parents to express their preference in relation to the school which they wish their child to attend; the arrangements for the admission to each grant-aided school in its area; and the arrangements for appealing admissions decisions.[14] The published details of the arrangements for each school must include particulars of the school's enrolment number; the school's admission number for that school year; the respective functions of the Board of Governors and principal in relations to admissions; and the criteria for admission to the school.[15] Article 17(3) of the 1997 Order states that Boards of Governors must publish such information as is required by regulations and such other information as it thinks fit. This can be done by the ELB on behalf of the Board of Governors. ELBs are also required to publish information on policy matters and other arrangements for primary and secondary schools in its area.[16]

4.10 In practice, each ELB will publish booklets describing the admission arrangements for each primary and secondary school in its area. These give details of the school's admission number as well as the number of applications in the previous year. This document is crucial to parents who wish to make an informed choice about their child's chance of admission to a particular school. If a school is generally undersubscribed, the child should have no difficulty gaining admission. If a school is regularly oversubscribed, then it is likely that admissions criteria will be used. Parents can study the criteria to assess their child's chance of success. One shortcoming is that the published information does not highlight any significant changes in the admissions criteria from the previous year. Nor does it draw attention to other changes in the area (e.g. the closure of a neighbouring school) which may result in a rise in admissions to the school. Such changes can have a considerable impact on the admissions patterns of a school from year to year. These might well affect a child's chance of getting admitted and consequently the parent's choice of school.

NORMAL AGE OF ADMISSION TO PRIMARY AND SECONDARY SCHOOLS

4.11 Article 46 of the 1986 Order defines the normal age of admission to both primary and secondary school. The age of admission mirrors compulsory school ages. Children who have not attained the relevant statutory age will only be admitted to schools in the circumstances prescribed below.

---

[14] Art. 17 of the 1997 Order.
[15] *Ibid* art.17(2).
[16] *Ibid* art. 17(4).

Primary schools

4.12 Children will not normally be admitted to primary school until they have attained the lower limit of compulsory school age.[17] The lower limit of compulsory school age is defined in relation to the date when the child is four years of age.[18] A child whose birthday falls on or between 1 September of one year and 1 July the following year, is deemed to have attained the compulsory school age on the 1 August of that following year. A child attaining the age of four in the period between 2 July and 31 August of one year is not deemed to be of compulsory school age until the 1 August in the following year. This means that these 'summer babies' will not normally start school until they are five. The parents of these children are not precluded from applying for admission before the child is of compulsory school age. However, if applications to a school exceed its admissions number, they will not be accepted.[19] Schools should indicate in their admissions criteria whether they are prepared to accept children under school age. However, primary schools are not obliged to admit underage pupils even if they have vacant places.

Secondary schools

4.13 Under article 46A of the 1986 Order the date on which a child will normally commence secondary education is related to the date on which he achieves the age of 11.[20]

The normal date of commencement of secondary education

4.14 Where a child attains the age of 11 years on a date occurring in the period beginning on 1 September in one year and ending on 1 July the following year, he or she will be able to start secondary education on or after the 1 August the following year. Where a child achieves the age of 11 on a date between the 2 July and 31 August the same year, he or she will normally start secondary school on or after the 1 August the following year. However, children born on or after 2 July may start secondary a year early in the circumstances described below.

Children seeking to transfer to secondary schools earlier or later than the normal date of commencement

4.15 The Education (NI) Order 1996 amended article 46A of the 1986 Order in relation to the procedures which must be followed when a child seeks admission to a secondary school earlier or later than is usual on the basis of the rules described above. Prior to 1997 the decision was taken by the Department. In order to speed up the process, the decision has now been transferred to the Board of Governors of the primary school which the child attends. A child will not be admitted to a secondary school a year earlier or later than is normal under the rules described above unless the Board of

---

[17] For further discussion of this see Chapter 6 on attendance.
[18] Art. 46 of the 1986 Order substituted by art. 156 of the 1989 Order.
[19] See para. 4.19.
[20] This was substituted by art. 156 of the 1989 Order which was subsequently amended by art. 31 of the 1996 Order.

Governors of the primary school at which he is a registered pupil is of the opinion that it is in the child's best interests to commence secondary education on that date and the parent of the child agrees.[21] The Board of Governors will take into account the advice of the principal of the primary school when determining what is in the child's best interest. If the child is not a registered pupil at a primary school, the ELB in whose area the child resides may direct that the child commences secondary education a year earlier or later.[22] Boards of Governors and ELBs must make their determination taking into account guidance issued by the Department.

LEGAL REGULATION OF THE NUMBERS OF PUPILS ATTENDING EACH GRANT-AIDED SCHOOL

4.16 Every grant-aided school has a fixed admissions number and enrolment number. The enrolment number refers to the overall number of pupils registered at the school. The admissions number is the number of pupils which the school can admit into its first year. Both are determined by the Department according to a fixed formula which is based on the school's area capacity. The admissions and enrolment numbers are crucial to each admissions decision. If a school is undersubscribed it must normally admit all children who apply for admission. Conversely, if a school is oversubscribed, it must apply admissions criteria to determine which children are to be admitted.

Enrolment numbers

4.17 Article 11 of the 1997 Order specifies the procedure for setting enrolment numbers. In determining the enrolment number, the Department must have regard to the accommodation which is available for use by pupils at the school and any directions as to school premises which have been made under article 8 of the 1986 Order. The Department may vary the enrolment number at any time. When it is making a determination or variation, it must consult the Board of Governors of the school, the ELB and where the school is a Catholic maintained school, the CCMS. Notice of any determination or variation must also be sent to these bodies. The Board of Governors may request a variation in which case it does not have to consult the ELB or CCMS.

Admissions numbers

4.18 Article 12 of the 1997 Order specifies the procedure to be followed in determining the annual admissions number for each school. In determining the admissions number, the Department will have regard to any requirements of a direction under article 18 of the 1986 Order in relation to the standard of school premises and the school's enrolment number. In addition, article 16 of the 1998 Order requires the Department to have regard to the limits on class sizes in key stage 1.[23] From 1 August 2000, the statutory limit on class sizes

---

[21] Art. 46A(2)-(3) of the 1986 Order. Guidance on such transfers is contained in DENI Circular 1996/24.
[22] Art. 46A(4) of the 1986 Order.
[23] Art. 12(2) of the 1997 Order has been amended by art. 16(7) of the 1998 Order to this effect.

in key stage 1 is 30.²⁴ The Board of Governors of a primary school must not permit the numbers of pupils in a class to exceed this limit although the ELB may make exceptions to this in prescribed circumstances.

4.19 The Board of Governors are required by statute to adhere to the admissions and enrolment numbers fixed by the Department. Article 10(2)(a) of the 1997 Order states that the Board of Governors must not admit to the school in any school year a number of children in the relevant age group which exceeds the school's admission number for that year. Article 19(2)(b) of the 1997 Order states that the Board of Governors must not cause or permit the number of registered pupils at the school to exceed the school's enrolment number at any time. When schools are calculating the number of children admitted or registered at the school, no account is taken of children admitted in compliance with a direction of an appeal tribunal, a direction under article 46 of the 1996 Order (expelled pupils), a school attendance order or a statement of special education needs in the year of that admission.²⁵ However, in all subsequent years, pupils admitted in this way are counted as part of the school's overall enrolment number. This means that a school which admits a large number of children who have successfully appealed an admission decision may in, subsequent years, have to admit fewer children to its first year so as to stay within its enrolment number.

4.20 Primary schools do have some leeway in respect of admissions numbers to allow for local variations from year to year. Departmental guidance states that primary schools can exceed their admission number by a fixed percentage provided that the school does not exceed its enrolment number. The permitted variations are determined with reference to the school's enrolment number. They are as follows:

Enrolment number	Permitted per cent increase in admissions number
0-42	50 per cent
43-70	30 per cent
71-140	20 per cent
141-350	10 per cent

Primary schools with an enrolment number of more than 350 may admit a maximum of five pupils in excess of the admissions number in any one year. In all cases, the school must not exceed its overall enrolment number.

4.21 The Department may vary the admissions number at any time.²⁶ Before it makes a variation or determination, the Department is required to consult the Board of Governors of the school, the ELB and where the school is a Catholic maintained school, the CCMS.²⁷ Notice of any variation or

---

[24] Class Sizes in Primary Schools Regulations (NI) 2000.
[25] Art. 10(3)-(4) of the 1997 Order.
[26] Art.12(3) of the 1997 Order.
[27] *Ibid* art.12(4), (6) and (7).

determination must also be sent to these bodies. The Board of Governors may request a variation in which case the Department does not consult with the ELB or CCMS.[28] Most schools are eager to have as many pupils as possible and will seek to have the numbers increased if they are oversubscribed. For its part, the Department has to be cautious about annual increases in admissions numbers since over time incremental additions can further the case for building extensions and increased capital expenditure. There is no specific sanction which can be applied to a school which exceeds its admission numbers. However, if a school admits children in excess of its number without the approval of the Department, funding for those children could be withheld. The Department might also issue a direction under article 101 requiring the school to comply with its admission number.

SIGNIFICANCE OF PARENTAL PREFERENCE

4.22 An ELB is under a duty to make arrangements for parents resident in its area to express a preference as to the school at which they wish their children to be educated and to give reasons for that preference.[29] Parents may apply for admission to a school which is not in their own ELB.[30] An expression of preference for a particular school is regarded as an application for admission to the school indicated by the parent to be their first choice. In a recent English case, it was determined that parents must be allowed to make an active choice; it is enough for the education authority to presume a certain choice of school until the parent expresses a different preference.[31] If the application to the first preference school is refused, the parent is taken to have applied for admission to the school which is the parents' second preference and so on taking each preference in order.[32] In practice, admissions are handled by the Board of Governors. However, where the school is oversubscribed, the ELB takes responsibility for distributing the excess applicants between the school of their second choice. This means that some undersubscribed schools or grammar schools who are admitting pupils with lower than average transfer procedure grades cannot finalise their admissions until they have received information about second choice applicants. This prolongs the admissions process in some schools and can leave parents in a state of uncertainty for quite some time particularly if their child's acceptance to a grammar school is conditional on the level of overspill from other more heavily subscribed grammar schools in the area.

4.23 Prior to 1997 Boards of Governors were under a statutory duty to comply with the preference expressed by parents unless compliance would "prejudice the provision of efficient education or the efficient use of resources".[33] The duty to comply with parental preference mirrored equivalent

---

[28] *Ibid* art.12(5).
[29] Art. 9 (1) of the 1997 Order.
[30] *Ibid* art. 9(3).
[31] *R v Rotherham MBC, ex parte Clark and others* [1998] ELR 152.
[32] Art.9(2) of the 1997 Order. This clarifies an argument which was advanced in *In re Moore* [1994] NIJB 111, judgment of the Northern Ireland Court of Appeal, i.e. that only the first choice could be a statutory preference.
[33] Art. 36(3) of the 1989 Order.

provision in England and Wales.[34] In *R v South Glamorgan Appeals Committee, ex parte Evans*, the application of the legislation was considered to involve a two-stage test.[35] First, could the school establish prejudice if the child was admitted? Secondly, could the parent's show that the child's interest in being admitted outweighed that prejudice? The task of balancing the duty to comply with parental preference and the school's claim of prejudice was not an easy one. Moreover, in Northern Ireland, the statutory emphasis on parental preference was frequently cited in court to argue that it was the predominant consideration in the determination of admissions.[36] Although this was not accepted by the courts, this particular statutory obligation has been removed by the 1997 Order and has not been replaced. In addition, schools are no longer permitted to use the order of parental preference as one of their admission criteria. Instead, the 1997 Order is more specific about the circumstances when a child can be refused admission and draws clear distinctions about the legitimate scope of refusals to admit. These are considered in the next section.

PROCEDURE FOR ADMISSION

4.24 Articles 13 and 14 of the 1997 set out the conditions of admission in all grant-aided schools apart from nursery schools, special schools, schools in hospitals and the preparatory departments of grammar schools. These rules draw a distinction between admissions to the first year of any school, admissions during the course of the first year and admissions in subsequent years. Article 13 of the 1997 Order applies to admissions to primary and secondary schools. Article 14 applies to grammar schools. The essence of the rules is the same in all cases. If a school is undersubscribed (i.e. has vacant places), it must admit all children who apply. If the school is oversubscribed (i.e. applications exceed the admissions number), it must use its published admissions criteria to determine admission.

4.25 The 1997 Order has regulated the procedure for determining admissions by drawing a distinction based on the time at which an application is made for admission to the school. The legislation distinguishes between three categories of application: (i) applications at the beginning of the school's first year; (ii) applications during the first year; and (iii) applications in subsequent years. The nature of the rules is such that schools have slightly more scope to refuse admission to children applying for entry at any time after the first year. In each of the following three categories the rules are defined with reference to children who are in the "relevant age group". This is defined by article 21(1)(g) of the 1997 Order to refer to the age group in which the majority of children below the upper limit of compulsory school age are normally admitted to school. Essentially this means children aged four or five entering Primary One in primary schools and children aged 11 or 12 entering Form One in secondary schools.

---

[34] This is now contained in the Education Act 1996, s. 411.
[35] Unreported, 10 May 1984.
[36] See for instance *In re Moore* [1994] NIJB 111 (CA).

Admission at the beginning of the first term of the first year

4.26 Articles 13(2) and 14(2) of the 1997 Order apply to children in the "relevant age group" entering the school at the beginning of the first term. These rules apply to the vast majority of children, that is those who enter primary school or transfer to secondary school in the normal way. Articles 13 and 14 both state that Boards of Governors are required to admit the child if the total number of applications does not exceed the admissions number of the school. In any other case, the Board of Governors must apply its published admissions criteria to select a number of children equal to the school's admission number and admit or refuse to admit accordingly. In addition, in grammar schools, the Board of Governors may refuse to admit a child if it is of the opinion that the admission would be detrimental to the educational interests of the child provided that it has obtained the approval of the Department to do so.[37] This latter provision allows a grammar school which is undersubscribed to refuse to admit a child who has not demonstrated grammar school ability in the transfer procedure test.

Admission during the course of the first year

4.27 Articles 13(3) and 14(4) of the 1997 Order apply to children in the "relevant age group" entering the school at any time after the start of the school year. These rules apply to children who enter the first year of a school sometime during the course of that year. In such cases admission will depend on whether there are vacant places at the school. A school is considered to have vacant places if at that time the enrolment number (N.B. not the admission number) of the school exceeds the number of pupils registered at the school.[38] If there are no vacant places, the Board of Governors must refuse admission. If there are vacant places, it must admit the child provided that the number of children applying at that time does not exceed the number of vacant places. If there are more children seeking admission than there are places, the Board of Governors must apply its published admissions criteria to select a number of children equal to the number of vacant places. In addition, even if there are vacant places, the Board of Governors of a grammar schools may refuse to admit a child where it is of the opinion that the academic ability of the children is not of a standard equivalent to that of the pupils with whom he would be taught at the school.[39] The legislation does not specify how this is to be measured but it might be assumed that it would be appropriate to refuse to admit a child with a Grade C in the transfer procedure test if all of the pupils previously admitted had obtained Grade A.

Admission at any time after the first year

4.28 Articles 13(4) and 14(6) apply to children who are not in the "relevant age group." This refers to children who seek admission at any time after the normal first year of entry. Admission will depend on whether there are vacant places at the school. A school is considered to have vacant places if at that time the enrolment number of the school exceeds the number of pupils

---

[37] Art. 14(3) of the 1997 Order.
[38] *Ibid* art.22(2).
[39] *Ibid* art.14(5).

registered at the school.[40] If there are no vacant places, the Board of Governors must refuse admission. If there are vacant places, it must admit the child provided that the number of children applying at that time does not exceed the number of vacant places. If there are more children seeking admission than there are places, the Board of Governors must apply its published admissions criteria to select a number of children equal to the number of vacant places. In addition, even if there are vacant places, the Board of Governors of all schools may refuse to admit a child if the admission of the child would "prejudice the efficient use of resources". This could arise, for instance, where, although the school has vacant places, the particular year to which the child seeks admission is full to capacity. In addition, even if there are vacant places, the Board of Governors of a grammar school may refuse to admit a child if the academic ability of the child is not of a standard equivalent to that of the pupils with whom he or she would be taught at the school.[41]

DUTY TO DRAW UP ADMISSIONS CRITERIA

4.29 Article 10 of the 1997 Order directs that a Board of Governors will not exceed its annual admissions number. If the school is over-subscribed, then admissions criteria must be used to determine which applicants will be accepted. Article 16 of the 1997 Order requires the Board of Governors of a grant-aided school to draw up the criteria to be applied in selecting pupils for admission to the school. In a controlled school the Board of Governors must take into account representations by the ELB. In a Catholic maintained school the Board must take into account representations by the CCMS. The Board of Governors may amend the criteria from time to time. However, when the criteria in respect of a particular school year have been published, no amendment can be made without the Department's approval.[42] The regulations which prescribe the content of the criteria apply to any amendments.[43]

4.30 The admissions criteria are crucial to a valid admissions policy. In drawing up admissions criteria, the Board of Governors must draft criteria which are clear and precise and must specify how the criteria are to be applied. This is not always an easy task as repeated judicial review actions have shown.[44] However, there are a number of comments which have been made in the course of these decisions which shed some light on what the courts perceive to be the correct approach to the interpretation of these criteria.

Wording of admissions criteria

4.31 In *In re Farren*, Kelly LJ stated that, if the application of the criteria is challenged, a court will not interpret the criteria to provide a reasonable and

---

[40] *Ibid* art.21(2).
[41] *Ibid* art.14(7)(a).
[42] Art.16(4) of the 1997 Order.
[43] In *In re Lagan College*, unreported judgment of the High Court of Northern Ireland (1992), it was argued on the applicant's behalf that the regulations only applied to criteria when they were first drafted. This was rejected by the court.
[44] For a discussion of the decisions of the Northern Ireland Courts between 1990 and 1995 see Lundy, 'Selection on Ability: Lessons from Northern Ireland' (1996) 8 *Education and the Law* 29.

tenable view but will attribute a literal interpretation to the criteria.[45] He considered that the words should be given an "ordinary and non-technical meaning" and that it would be "incorrect to add to them by way of gloss considerations in determining admission which are not expressly stated in or are implicit in the literal content".[46] The reason for this approach was that "it is the literal content of the criteria which the parents of applicant pupils absorb and on which they assess the chances of their children and pin their hopes".[47] In advocating a literal approach to the construction of admissions criteria, the courts' reasoning is persuasive. However, there will be times when Boards of Governors, appeal tribunals or courts will be faced with criteria whose wording is genuinely unclear. In this respect, the view of Girvan J in *In re Tucker* is worthy of note.[48] He stated that:

> "Having regard to the statutory imperative to give effect to parental wishes, the restrictions on the statutory imperative must in my view be strictly construed. It appears to me that if there is any ambiguity in the construction...that construction should be preferred which is in ease of parents and pupils."

The statutory preference referred to is not contained in the 1997 Order.[49] Nevertheless, the general rationale of interpreting the criteria in the way which they may have been understood by parents remains valid.

Manner of application of the criteria

4.32 The Board of Governors must also establish the manner in which the criteria will be applied. In this regard, in *In re Farren*, Kelly LJ stated that:

> "The statement of the criteria should make it clear how they will be applied and with what weight. This may well include a statement of the order of importance of the criteria, and what preference (if any) will be given to a particular matter in the consideration of a particular criterion."[50]

In *In re Farren* the school's criteria said that the criteria would be applied "in the order set down", a phrase which is commonly used to introduce the list of criteria. The school's first criterion was "Academic ability as indicated by a Category 1 or 2 grading in the transfer tests". In applying this, the Board of Governors had given priority to Grade 1. Hutton LCJ said that the phrase "in the order set down" meant that:

> "The criteria are to be applied in succession, one after the other, and the clear implication is that if a child satisfies one criterion the school authorities should move on to consider whether the child satisfies the next criterion, and not that the school authority should decide whether one child satisfies the criterion by a greater margin than another child."[51]

---

[45] *In re Farren* [1990] NIJB 72.
[46] *Op cit* at p.103.
[47] *Op cit* at p. 103.
[48] [1995] NI 14.
[49] See para. 4.23.
[50] *Op cit* at p. 100.
[51] *Op* cit at p. 91.

Similarly Kelly LJ said:

> "An affirmative answer to criterion 1 is sufficient to pass the child to criterion 2 for consideration under 2...Only the answer 'no' to a particular criterion will eliminate a child. This means that if a child can satisfy a particular criterion at all, to some degree, she will not be eliminated on that criterion because another child or children are considered to satisfy the criterion to a higher standard."[52]

In the subsequent case of *In re Moore* Carswell LJ said that the Court of Appeal's comments were not intended to lay down a general rule of construction for all types of criteria but were confined to the criteria in the case which it had considered.[53] While this is undoubtedly correct, it is worth bearing in mind that the wording of the criteria in the case of *In re Farren* is commonly employed by schools. Schools should therefore specify whether they wish a particular criterion to be a simple eliminator or whether they also wish to distinguish between different candidates who satisfy the criterion. If they intend to distinguish between candidates, they should draft two separate criteria.

Preambles

4.33 The final point on the construction of the criteria relates to the effect of preambles published with the criteria. The issue arose in the case of *In re Holmes* where the school's preamble stated that it would only admit pupils whom it considered suitable for the type of education offered in the school "i.e. pupils gaining Grade 1 and some pupils gaining Grade 2".[54] In distinguishing between the Grade 2s the school applied non-academic criteria (i.e. siblings at the school). Counsel argued that this use of non-academic factors was inconsistent with the preamble which he described as the "primary" criteria. MacDermott LJ posed the following question: "Are criteria to be found in the preamble?" He concluded that they were not. He agreed with counsel for the appeal tribunal that "a criterion is a factor which fulfills the task of either eliminating pupils or selecting pupils for admission" and considered that the wording in the school's preamble did not fall within this definition. However, it is clear that each case must be decided on its own facts. In *In re Patton* Kerr J considered that the preamble of a school's criteria did operate as an eliminator.[55] In this case an integrated school stated that its aim was to reflect the overall balance between the Roman Catholic and Protestant traditions. It then stated that details as to how this would be achieved were available from the school. Kerr J stated that:

> "... the statement of an aim can be a criterion if it is coupled... with an expression of intention to achieve that aim by a means which, though unspecified, involves the application of an eliminating or selecting procedure according to a characteristic

---

[52] *Op cit* at p.104.
[53] [1994] NIJB 99, judgment of the High Court in Northern Ireland.
[54] Unreported judgment of the High Court of Northern Ireland, 27 September 1991.
[55] Unreported judgment of the High Court of Northern Ireland, 30 September 1994.

possessed by an individual applicant viz. his or her religious affiliation."

Moreover, even in cases where the preamble cannot be construed as part of the selection criteria, if the school's actual criteria are vague, it might be argued that they should be interpreted in line with the preamble. This means that schools should at least ensure that the general statement of aspiration which usually precedes the criteria is actually consistent with what follows.

Unworkable criteria

4.34 The criteria employed must be workable, that is they must be capable of being applied in such a way that they distinguish between applicants. If criteria are unworkable, the Board of Governors has not complied with its statutory duty to draw up criteria "to be used" in selection. Nor has it complied with article 16(5) of the 1997 Order, that is to ensure that it can fill its places before the criteria are exhausted. Nevertheless, the courts appear to be disinclined to conclude that criteria are unworkable. In *In re Cunningham*, Girvan J stated:

> "What criteria mean and how they fall to be applied may in some cases tax the ingenuity of learned counsel and judges although at the end of the day, after much legal debate, the proper interpretation of the criteria can be arrived at. Merely to have difficulty construing a provision does not make the provision bad at law."[56]

SPECIFIC ADMISSIONS CRITERIA

4.35 While Boards of Governors have a wide discretion in selecting admissions criteria, they are not completely unfettered. First, the criteria must be reasonable in the *Wednesbury* sense.[57] However, schools are given a very wide discretion in this respect. An applicant who wished to challenge the criteria on this point would have to satisfy a court that the criteria were so unreasonable that no reasonable Board of Governors would have included them as part of its system of admissions. The argument has been unsuccessfully advanced in a number of cases. In *In re Moore* the High Court considered that a secondary school's decision to favour primary schools with which it had traditional links was not unreasonable in the *Wednesbury* sense and stressed that it was not the function of the court to adjudicate on the wisdom or fairness of the admissions policy of the school.[58] However, in a recent Northern Ireland case, the High Court considered that criteria which gave priority to those who had completed the school's pre-enrolment form were unreasonable in the *Wednesbury* sense.[59] Secondly, there are various pieces of legislation which restrict the type of criteria which might be applied. These are discussed below. Some of the criteria are general to all types of school. These are considered first. The discussion is then categorised into

---

[56] Unreported judgment of the High Court of Northern Ireland, 25 August 1995.
[57] See para. 2.78.
[58] [1994] NIJB 99.
[59] See *In re Fenton*, unreported decision of the High Court of Northern Ireland, September 2000.

Religion

4.36 Schools in Northern Ireland do not generally use criteria which select pupils for admission on the basis of their religion.[60] This would appear to be due to the fact that applications for admissions tend to reflect the religious divide therefore making such criteria unnecessary. In practice most Catholic parents will choose to send their children to Catholic schools and most Protestant parents will choose to send their children to controlled schools or schools with a Protestant ethos. That said, there are a small number of schools who do use direct references to the child's religion to determine admissions. For instance some published criteria give priority to "baptised Catholics" while others prioritise members of named Protestant churches. It is, however, somewhat unclear whether a school in Northern Ireland can lawfully include the child's religion as one of its admissions criteria or whether schools must consider all children on the same basis irrespective of their religion. There is nothing in the Education Orders or regulations made under them to prohibit religious discrimination of this kind. Moreover, in spite of recent extensions to the Fair Employment legislation, it still does not apply to education.

4.37 The only possible legal bar in domestic legislation arises under section 76 of the Northern Ireland Act 1998 (which replaces s. 19 of the Northern Ireland Constitution Act 1973). This prohibits government departments and agencies from discriminating on the grounds of religion. Both the Department and the ELBs are covered by this provision; Boards of Governors are not. It is questionable therefore whether section 76 has any bearing on school governors exercising their duty under article 16 of the 1997 Education Order to draw up admissions criteria. On the other hand, while it is clear that section 76 does not apply directly to Boards of Governors, it prohibits ELBs and the Department from "aiding" any discrimination. It might be argued that an ELB is "aiding" a Board of Governors to discriminate when it publishes the criteria or even more generally when it provides funding to maintain the school. Moreover, in controlled schools, ELBs have a majority on the Board of Governors and therefore have a significant degree of influence on the content of the criteria.

4.38 If one proceeds on the assumption that section 76 does apply to admissions criteria (and this is a fairly generous assumption), the question arises as to what might constitute unlawful religious discrimination in this context. Direct religious discrimination, that is, favouring Protestant applicants over Catholic applicants or vice versa might be covered by section 76.[61] However, schools in Northern Ireland generally do not employ such

---

[60] The exception to this is integrated schools. The admissions criteria in such schools are considered at paras. 9.37-9.38.

[61] There could be exceptions, e.g., if a school with a specific religious ethos had a foundation in statute.

criteria.[62] Instead, challenges to the validity of admissions criteria under the Northern Ireland Act 1998 are more likely to be based on criteria which it could be argued discriminate indirectly on the basis of religion. A criterion might be considered to be indirectly discriminatory if the proportion of Catholic (Protestant) children who can comply with the criterion is significantly less than the proportion of Protestant (Catholic) children. This could be argued when criteria are used which give preference to people with certain family connections to the school, who live in certain catchment areas or who have attended specific contributory schools. The major stumbling block to such challenges is that, based on the interpretation of its predecessor (s. 19 of the Northern Ireland Constitution Act 1973) it is unlikely that section 76 of the Northern Ireland Act 1998 will be interpreted to include indirect discrimination.[63]

4.39 One other possible basis for challenge to school admission criteria which discriminate on the basis of religion arises under Article 14 of the ECHR which, when read with Article 2 of the First Protocol of the ECHR, prohibits discrimination in access to education.[64] If a court were to conclude that schools could not lawfully discriminate in this way, many commonly used criteria would have to be reviewed. If, on the other hand, a court were to conclude that schools could select on the basis of religion, there might be high levels of parental dissatisfaction if schools were to choose to do this routinely. There is a small number of Catholic children who apply for admission to controlled or non-Catholic grammar schools.[65] If they were to be excluded directly or indirectly on the basis of their religion, their parents may well be aggrieved. On the other hand, since there is little traffic the other way, if the trend continues, the parents of non-Catholic children might view their children's educational opportunities in controlled or Protestant denominational schools as having been unfairly restricted. Thus, even if such issues never result in litigation, the Department may eventually face a difficult policy issue about whether schools should be able to select directly or indirectly on the basis of religion.

Gender

4.40 The Sex Discrimination (NI) Order 1976 applies to educational establishments. Article 25 of the Order prohibits ELBs from doing any act which constitutes sex discrimination when carrying out its functions under the Education Orders. The provision was used in a landmark case taken by the Equal Opportunities Commission for Northern Ireland and which resulted in a court declaration that the procedure which was previously used for awarding grammar school places discriminated against girls. In *In re EOC's Application*

---

[62] The major exception to this is integrated schools. If a court were to conclude that selection on the basis of religion was unlawful, an exception would have to be made for integrated schools so as to enable them to fulfil their statutory obligation to ensure a reasonable balance of Protestant and Catholic pupils.

[63] See paras. 1.36-1.37. It will be interesting to see if the interpretation of s. 76 will evolve in the light of judicial responses to s. 75 of the Northern Ireland Act 1998 (the equality duty).

[64] See para. 1.58.

[65] In 1997 the proportion of Catholic children in non-Catholic schools was 4.6% at primary level and 4.4 % at secondary level.

(No.2) the court considered that a system which awarded places to 27 per cent of boys and 27 per cent of girls rather than 27 per cent of all candidates irrespective of sex discriminated against girls.[66] The consequence of the system was that some boys were being offered fee-paying places even though they had obtained lower scores in the "11-plus" test than some girls who had been refused fee-paying places. One of the difficulties in the case lay in establishing who was responsible for the discrimination. Article 24 of the Order which refers to admissions places the obligation on the Board of Governors and ELB rather than on the Department who had devised and operated the discriminatory selection procedures. However, the court concluded that the Department had unlawfully instructed and procured the ELB to discriminate contrary to article 40 of the 1976 Order. It also considered that the ELBs were guilty of unlawful discrimination under article 25 of the Order when they adopted and acted upon the decision of the Department in relation to the selection procedures.

4.41 Since the onset of open enrolment, individual schools have much greater responsibility for admissions since they are under a duty to draw up the admissions criteria. The Sex Discrimination (NI) Order 1976 makes it unlawful for grant-aided schools to sexually discriminate against a person in the terms on which it offers to admit him or her as a pupil or to refuse or deliberately omit to accept an application for admission.[67] The provision in the legislation varies depending on whether the school is single-sex, turning co-educational or already co-educational.

Single sex schools

4.42 The prohibition on sex discrimination does not apply to the admission of pupils to any school which admits pupils of one sex only or which would be taken to admit pupils of one sex if one was to disregard pupils of the opposite sex whose admission is exceptional or whose numbers are comparatively small and whose admission is confined to particular courses of instruction or teaching classes.[68] The exception also applies to the admission of boarders to schools which are co-educational but admit boarders of one sex only.[69]

Single sex schools turning co-educational

4.43 Where a single sex school decides to become co-educational, the Board of Governors may apply for an order (known as a transitional exemption order) authorising discriminatory admissions during the transitional period specified in the order.[70] During such periods the Board of Governors may refuse or deliberately omit to accept an application for admission to the school on the ground of the sex of the applicant. The exception also applies to the period between the making of the application for the transitional exemption order and the determination of the application.

---

[66] [1988] NI 278.
[67] Art. 24(a)-(b) of the Sex Discrimination (NI) Order 1976.
[68] *Ibid* art. 27(1).
[69] *Ibid* art.27(2).
[70] *Ibid* art. 28.

Co-educational schools

4.44 Co-educational schools may not discriminate in their admissions policy on the grounds of sex. This means that schools cannot include criteria which are aimed at achieving a gender balance in the school. Schools should also be careful that criteria are not indirectly discriminatory. For instance, a secondary school should not give priority in its admissions criteria to children attending a single sex boys' primary school over a single sex girls' primary school. Co-educational secondary schools should generally be cautious about the use of single sex contributory primary schools as a criterion for admission as it may be difficult to ensure that no gender is disadvantaged by such a criterion. Likewise criteria which prioritise applicants with certain achievements such as sporting ability which might be considered to be gender-related and consequently have an indirectly discriminatory effect should be avoided.[71]

Race

4.45 The Race Relations (NI) Order 1997 makes it unlawful for an educational establishment to discriminate against a person in the terms on which it offers to admit him as a pupil.[72] The legislation prohibits direct and indirect discrimination as well as segregation.[73] One of the most renowned cases taken under the equivalent provisions in England and Wales was a schools case - *Mandla v Lee (Dowell)*.[74] In that case the House of Lords considered that a refusal to admit a Sikh child who was wearing a turban amounted to an act of unlawful discrimination on the grounds of race. In another English case, the Commission for Racial Equality were unsuccessful in seeking a declaration that a decision to move a white pupil from a predominantly Asian school was an act of discrimination.[75] The court considered that the duty to comply with parental preference was not overridden by the Race Relations Act 1976. The Race Relations (NI) Order 1997 has only been in place in Northern Ireland for a short time and it is difficult to envisage cases which might arise in this jurisdiction in the context of school admissions in relation to ethnic minorities. However, the Northern Ireland legislation specifies that the Irish travelling community are a racial group who enjoy the protection of the legislation. If an admission criterion specified a particular catchment area and the Board of Governors refused to admit the child because of their nomadic way of life, the child might be able to establish a case of unlawful discrimination.

Family connections

4.46 Schools often include criteria which give priority to children who have a family connection with the school. These generally take one of three forms: (i) siblings; (ii) ancestors; and (iii) teachers' children.

---

[71] Such criteria are probably precluded in any event by the restrictions against selection on ability or aptitude discussed at paras. 4-67 to 4-69.
[72] Art.18(1).
[73] Art. 3 of the Race Relations (NI) Order 1997.
[74] [1983] 1 All ER 1062.
[75] *R v Cleveland CC, ex parte Commission for Racial Equality* [1993] 1 FRC 597.

Siblings

4.47 Some schools give priority to children who have brothers and sisters at the school. Criteria of this sort have met with judicial approval.[76] There are practical reasons to justify this type of criterion, not least of which is parental convenience in taking children to school. However, it is worth noting that this type of criterion may put certain children at a disadvantage. These include the eldest child, only children and only sons and daughters when the application is to a single sex school. Some schools acknowledge this and give eldest children priority after those with brothers and sisters at the school. This puts them at an advantage compared to pupils who have older brothers and sisters who have attended a different school. Parents of children in this position should bear this in mind when applying to a school which is likely to be over-subscribed.

Ancestors

4.48 The question of criteria which include reference to ancestors having attended the school is more complicated. Departmental guidance does not preclude criteria of this sort. In spite of this, there is an argument that such criteria might be considered to be indirectly discriminatory on the grounds of religion. The difficulties in establishing that this is prohibited have been discussed earlier at paragraphs 4.36-4.39. However, it might be argued that a school which has a history of having a disproportionate number of pupils of one particular religion attending the school, as is the case in most Northern Ireland schools, might be considered to be indirectly discriminating against children with another religious affiliation if it includes this type of criterion.

Children of staff/governors of the school

4.49 Criteria which give priority to the children of staff and governors of the school are not prohibited at law. Although these criteria might be seen by some to be nepotistic, some schools consider that this type of preference as one of the few ways in which they can give staff a "family-friendly" perk.

Order of parental preference

4.50 Prior to 1997, many schools included criteria giving preference to students who had nominated the school as their first preference.[77] This meant that parents had to make a realistic assessment of their child's likelihood of meeting the other criteria of the school of their first choice. If the child did not meet the criteria, it was considered by the school of their second choice at which point the second school could well have been giving priority to children who had given it first priority. The same could then happen with the third preference with the result that the child did not get accepted by any of the preferred schools. In this sense the exercise of parental preference was a bit of a lottery. Article 16(8) of the 1997 Order now provides that a Board of

---

[76] See the judgment of Carswell J in *In re Gribbon* [1990] NI 15 at p.30 and the judgment of MacDermott LJ in *In re Holmes*, unreported decision of the Northern Ireland High Court, 27 September 1991.

[77] Grammar schools were not allowed to use the order of parental preference before performance in the transfer procedure tests.

Governors may not include the fact that the school was the first or only preference expressed by the parents of the child or was a higher preference than any other school or schools.[78] Although the previous position undoubtedly caused frustration in many cases where children did not manage to get into their first preference school, the removal of parental preference as a criterion has had a significant impact on the criteria used in many schools. It has particular significance for popular secondary schools which do not want to restrict their selection criteria to a specific catchment area. The order of parental preference was an easy way for such schools to determine admission and award places to those who had given it a vote of confidence by making it their first choice. From a more practical perspective, the removal of the emphasis on parental preference inevitably delays the admissions process as schools cannot finalise decisions until some of the more popular schools reject some of their first preference applicants and other schools are provided with details of their second and third preference applicants.

Catchment area

4.51 Most schools will include criteria which give priority to children living within its catchment area. This is practical. However, the catchment area should be clearly defined. This can be done with reference to particular areas or by setting a distance from the school. The decision on catchment area must not unreasonably exclude children coming from a particular area. However, Boards of Governors have a wide discretion in this respect. For instance, in the High Court's decision in *In re Moore,* Carswell LJ considered that a school could lawfully frame its criteria to perpetuate a "social pattern of intake".[79] In that case parents alleged that their area had been given reduced priority so that more affluent and academically able students would be admitted to the school. Carswell LJ stated that: "If a court were to reach the conclusion that they were opposed to the idea of public housing estate…it does not follow that they would have been acting contrary to the statutes or regulations by which they were bound". However, attention might also be paid to whether the catchment area indirectly discriminates on the grounds of religion. Further discussion of the possibility of this type of challenge is contained in paragraphs 4.36-4.39. Moreover, there is also an outside possibility that a court might consider criteria to be unreasonable if it could be shown, for instance, that a controlled school prioritised pupils living in an exclusively Protestant area which was at a greater distance from the school than a Catholic area which was not mentioned in the criteria. The easiest way to avoid this would be to define catchment area by distance from the school rather than specific geographical locations.

---

[78] In a recent Northern Ireland case the use of pre-enrolment forms was considered to be a form of expression of parental preference and therefore in breach of art. 16(8) of the 1997 Order; *In re Fenton,* unreported decision of the High Court of Northern Ireland, September 2000. See further para. 4.61.

[79] [1994] NIJB 99.

Contributory schools

4.52 Many secondary schools will give priority to children who have attended specified primary schools. These will normally be schools in its area with whom there has been a traditional intake. The issues which arise here are similar to those for catchment area which are considered above. In *In re Moore*, the Court of Appeal considered that the Board of Governors was justified in identifying certain primary schools with which it had traditional links.[80] This was acceptable even though one of the schools not given priority was in fact geographically closer. However, one difficulty with this type of criterion is that it might be considered to discriminate indirectly on the grounds of religion. This arises because Catholic secondary schools will normally give priority to Catholic primary schools and controlled secondary schools will normally give priority to children attending controlled primary schools. Given the fact that these schools are attended by a majority of one community, the proportion of children from one religion who could comply with such a criterion is likely to be significantly less than the proportion of children of the other religion. For instance a Catholic child who had attended a Catholic primary school might be able to establish discrimination if the secondary school to which he or she seeks admission gives priority to children from specified controlled schools and vice versa. Further discussion about the somewhat remote possibility of a successful challenge on this point is contained in paragraphs 4.36-4.39.

Residence in Northern Ireland

4-53 Article 16(4) of the 1997 Order requires all Boards of Governors to admit children resident in Northern Ireland before any child not resident may be selected for admission. Residence is not defined. In particular there is no qualifying period for residency. Once it is apparent that a child is living in Northern Ireland, they should be considered on an equal footing with all other children. The children who are most likely to be affected by this are children living in the border areas in the Republic of Ireland. Some of these children will have attended schools in Northern Ireland. The effect of the provisions is that children who are not resident in Northern Ireland will only be admitted to undersubscribed schools or schools which have private fee-paying arrangements. This does not appear to be prohibited by European legislation which only prohibits discrimination against non-nationals if they are resident in the Member State.[81]

Irish language

4.54 Irish medium schools may wish to use criteria which give priority to children who speak Irish, have attended an Irish immersion course or who come from homes in which Irish is spoken. There is nothing in the Education Orders which expressly prohibits this type of criterion. However, a possible basis of challenge arises from the fact that both primary and secondary schools

---

[80] [1994] NIJB 111.
[81] Art. 10(1) of Council Regulation no 1612/68.

are prohibited from selecting pupils on the basis of their ability or aptitude.[82] It might be argued that a criterion which prioritises children with Irish language skills (as opposed to children coming from families where Irish is spoken) amounts to selection on ability. The countervailing argument is that the phrase "ability and aptitude" should be interpreted to mean general intellectual ability given the specific context of Northern Ireland and in particular the segregated system at secondary level. Another possible basis for challenge may arise under Article 14 of the ECHR read with Article 2 of the First Protocol which prohibits discrimination on the basis of language in access to education.[83] If a court were to consider such criteria unlawful, there would be a case for legislative intervention which would permit this as a basis for selection to Irish medium schools.

Attendance/behavioural requirements

4.55 Some schools include criteria which give priority to children with good attendance or disciplinary records at primary school.[84] There are a number of difficulties with this. First, regulation 5 of the Secondary Schools (Admissions Criteria) Regulations (NI) 1997 precludes schools from selecting on ability or aptitude and there is an argument that attendance and behaviour is at least to some degree indicative of "ability" or "aptitude" for learning. More generally, it is unclear how schools can lawfully go about obtaining this information. Although there is nothing to prevent them from asking parents for it, it can only really be verified by the child's primary school principal. The problem with this is that regulation 5(c) of the 1997 Regulations suggests that only grammar schools can take into account the comments of primary school principals and, even then, that information can only be used for the purpose of assessing a child who wishes account to be taken of special circumstances which affected their performance in the transfer procedure test.

4.56 There are further specific problems with the criteria which take into account school attendance. For instance, prioritising children with good attendance records (without excepting those who have missed school through illness) might be seen as a form of discrimination against children with disabilities. Although the school access provisions of the Disability Discrimination Act 1995 do not apply in Northern Ireland, the statutory equality duty in section 75 of the Northern Ireland Act 1998 requires public authorities to have regard to the need to promote equality of opportunity between people with disabilities and people without.[85] More generally, it might be queried whether it is appropriate to distinguish primary school children in this way since non-attendance at primary school is more likely to be the fault of the parents than the child. To disadvantage children whose parents have not recognised the significance of good attendance at school might well have implications for the government's policy on New Targeting

---

[82] Primary Schools (Admission Criteria) Regulations (NI) 1997, reg. 5 and Secondary Schools (Admission Criteria) Regulations (NI) 1997, reg. 6.
[83] See para. 1.58.
[84] These can be distinguished from criteria which require parents to sign commitments to the school's ethos on discipline and attendance. These focus on future behaviour rather than past performance.
[85] Public authorities include the Department and the ELBs.

Social Need (TSN) given the accepted correlation between attendance and social deprivation.[86]

Selection down to the last available place

4.57 Article 16(5) of the 1997 Order requires Boards of Governors to ensure that they select children for admission before their criteria are exhausted. Boards of Governors are therefore under a statutory obligation to ensure that the criteria used will enable the schools to select pupils down to the last available place. Difficulties can arise when a Board of Governors has failed to exercise its duty under article 16(5) and is in a position where it has run out of criteria and cannot distinguish between remaining applicants. If a child were to be refused admission on some basis other than the published criteria, parents could automatically appeal to the admission appeals tribunal on the basis that the school had not applied its criteria properly. This would be established easily if the school had used some additional means of distinguishing between applicants. The difficulty facing a tribunal would be that it can only direct the school to admit the child if it considers that the child would have been admitted had the criteria been properly applied. On the one hand, parents can argue that the child has satisfied all the published criteria. On the other hand, in the absence of further criteria, it is arguable that the tribunal is not in a position to determine whether the school would have admitted the child given the school's legal obligation not to exceed its admissions number. There is an argument that the criteria in these instances are unworkable and that the tribunal cannot direct admission. The parent could challenge the legality of the criteria by way of judicial review but the court will not have the power to direct the school to admit the child.

4.58 One clear way of enabling Boards of Governors to choose candidates down to the very last applicant is to use home to school distances as a selector. This is the criterion recommended by the Department. There is no doubt that it can in some instances lead to fine distinctions being drawn, for instance between children who live in the same street. However, such criteria are objective, measurable and do at least have some rational justification since the school will be more convenient to those who live close by. That said, not all schools use this as their criterion of last resort. Three of the alternatives, (i) selection by lot, (ii) selection by date of birth and (iii) selection by time of application are considered below.

Selection by lot

4.59 Some schools include criteria which specify that remaining places will be drawn by lot. There is nothing in the legislation to prohibit this. However, Departmental guidance strongly advises schools not to select by lottery. Boards of Governors are under a statutory obligation to draw up criteria to be applied in selecting pupils for admission. It might be argued that the result of a drawing of lots, dependent as it is wholly on chance, is not a criterion in itself. The definitions of a "criterion" discussed earlier suggest that the criterion must itself act as a means of eliminating the individual applicant.

---

[86] See, e.g. the Department's Research Briefing, *Persistent School Absenteeism in Northern Ireland in 1992*, RB2/95 (DENI, 1992).

Moreover, it might be considered to be an unreasonable exercise of the statutory duty to leave a decision to chance rather than to use pre-formulated indicators which relate to the specific attributes of the individual applicants. The purpose of the criteria is to give parents an opportunity of pre-judging their child's chance of being admitted to the school. Selection by lot undermines this process.

Selection by date of birth

4.60 Some schools use the child's date of birth as their means of allocating the last available places. There is nothing in the legislation to prohibit them from doing this. The child's age is objective and easily measurable. On the other hand, all of the children being considered will be of compulsory school age and will have to be admitted somewhere. That said, if the criterion is restricted to the allocation of the last remaining places, it is unlikely that a court on judicial review would consider the criterion to be so unreasonable that no reasonable Board of Governors would have included it as one of its criteria.

Selection by date/time of application/ submission of pre-enrolment form

4.61 A number of schools use the date and/or time of the application or submission of a pre-enrolment form to distinguish between remaining candidates. Some schools have also used criteria of this sort as their primary criterion, a position which has been judged recently to be unreasonable by the Northern Ireland High Court.[87] There is nothing in the education legislation to explicitly prohibit criteria of this kind. One result of schools prioritising early applications is that certain popular schools witness lines of parents queuing to have their application form registered early. This can undermine the procedures to some extent by rushing parents into decisions rather than giving them time to consider the criteria and make informed choices. There are also problems where the criteria relate to pre-enrolment forms which pre-date the annual admissions process.[88] Although pre-enrolment forms do not tie parents to the school in question (a parent could pre-enrol his or her child at a number of schools), the use of such criteria can disadvantage children who have no previous connection to the school and are therefore not aware of the need for prior enrolment. As with the application forms, there is nothing in the legislation to prohibit it directly. Instead, there is an argument that by pre-enrolling children, parents are expressing a higher preference for that schools over any school in which they have not pre-enroled their child. Criteria of this sort are prohibited by article 16(8) of the 1997 Order. In *In re Fenton* the Northern Ireland High Court recently decided that such criteria were considered to be in breach of article 16(8).[89]

---

[87] *In re Fenton*, unreported decision of the High Court of Northern Ireland, September 2000.
[88] Such criteria are common in integrated schools who are able to use the pre-enrolment process to demonstrate their viability to the Department.
[89] Unreported decision of the High Court of Northern Ireland, September 2000.

RESTRICTIONS ON CRITERIA IN NURSERY SCHOOLS

4.62 Most primary schools have a nursery attached but many of the nursery schools are unable to admit all the children who will eventually gain admission to the primary school. Even so, some primary schools give preference to pupils who have attended their nursery school. The criteria for admission to the nursery school may therefore have ongoing consequences in the school admissions process. From September 1999 admission to nursery schools have been regulated by statute. The Pre-School Education in Schools (Admissions Criteria) Regulations (NI) 1998 set down the order of priority for admission to nursery places. Essentially these give priority to children from "socially disadvantaged circumstances" (i.e. children whose parents are in receipt of income support or income-based jobseeker's allowance) and children born in the summer who do not normally start school until they are five. Schools are required to admit children in the following order of priority: (i) children from socially-disadvantaged circumstances who will be aged four before 1 September in their final pre-school year (i.e. summer babies); (ii) children from socially-disadvantaged circumstances who will be aged three before 1 September in their final pre-school year; (iii) children aged four before 1 September in their final pre-school year; (iv) children aged three in their final school year. Schools are then required to apply the same priorities to children in their penultimate pre-school year. Nursery schools must give priority to children resident in Northern Ireland. However, they are no longer barred from selecting by reference to ability and aptitude or from using the results of any test or examination held by or on behalf of the Board of Governors.[90]

RESTRICTIONS ON CRITERIA IN PRIMARY SCHOOLS

4.63 Most parents will be happy for their child to attend the local primary school and most parents will have their choice of primary school accommodated. However, even at primary school level, certain schools have reputations for high levels of success in the transfer procedure tests and may consequently be over-subscribed. Admission to primary school is governed by the Primary Schools (Admissions Criteria) Regulations (NI) 1997. These require schools to establish criteria which include the order of priority in which pupils shall be admitted to the school where the number of applications exceeds the school's admissions number for any school year. The legality of certain forms of criteria is discussed below.

Ability and aptitude

4.64 Selection on the basis of academic ability at primary school level is not permitted. Regulation 5 of the Primary Schools (Admissions Criteria) Regulations (NI) 1997 prohibits the selection of children by reference to ability or aptitude or the performance in a test or examination held by or on behalf of the Board of Governors. Schools should not use other criteria which might be construed as an indirect attempt to select on the basis of ability, for example by deliberately defining their catchment area to target advantaged

---

[90] Pre-School Education in Schools (Admissions Criteria) (Amendment) Regulations (NI) 1999.

children. This issue was considered in the context of secondary schools by the Northern Ireland Court of Appeal in *In re Moore* and is discussed fully in paragraphs 4.67-4.68.

Age of the child

4.65 Regulation 4(d) of the Primary Schools (Admissions Criteria) Regulations (NI) 1997 directs that priority must be given to children who will have attained the compulsory school age at the time of their proposed admission over those who have not attained compulsory school age. Compulsory school age is defined in relation to the date when the child is four years of age.[91] A child whose birthday falls on or between 1 September of one year and 1 July the following year, is deemed to have attained the compulsory school age on the 1 August of that following year. A child attaining the age of four in the period between 2 July and 31 August of one year is not deemed to be of compulsory school age until the 1 August in the following year. This means that these 'summer babies' will not normally start school until they are five. The parents of these children are not precluded from applying for admission before the child is of compulsory school age. However, if applications to a school exceed its admissions number, they are unlikely to be accepted. If a parent of a child born in the summer months is keen for the child to start school when they are four, they would be advised to apply to a primary school which is unlikely to achieve its admissions number. Schools do not have to admit under age children but those which do must make this clear in their admissions criteria.

RESTRICTIONS ON CRITERIA IN SECONDARY SCHOOLS

4.66 Secondary schools are quite restricted in the criteria that they can use for admission. Most secondary schools rely on contributory primary schools and the catchment area. This is because they are subject to one specific statutory restriction: ability and aptitude.[92]

Ability and aptitude

4.67 The criteria for admission to a secondary school shall not include provision for the selection of pupils by reference to ability or aptitude or the performance in any test or examination held by or on the behalf of the Board of Governors.[93] Secondary schools should be careful that the criteria cannot be taken to indirectly select pupils on the basis of ability or aptitude. This issue was considered by the Court of Appeal in *In re Moore*.[94] In this case the school gave priority to students living in certain parishes and attending specified primary schools. Most of the schools given priority were in country areas. The schools given lower priority were situated close to local council estates in the town. Some of these schools were in fact geographically closer

---

[91] Art.46 of the 1986 Order substituted by art. 156 of the 1989 Order.
[92] Secondary Schools (Admissions Criteria) Regulations (NI) 1997, reg. 5(a).
[93] An exception is made for two secondary schools (Lagan College and St Patrick's Maghera) which are recognised by the Department for selection of some pupils by reference to ability or aptitude.
[94] [1994] NIJB 111.

to the school than the primary schools which were accorded priority in the admissions criteria. The applicants for judicial review were parents of children who had been refused admission because they did not live in the areas given priority in the school's criteria.

4.68 The argument put by the parents was that the adoption of the criteria was unlawful and unreasonable. In particular, it was alleged that the criteria were purposely framed to exclude children from a certain primary school and that this was motivated by a prejudice against children from urban housing estates in favour of those from rural areas and from a desire to maintain good academic standards by discouraging the admission of disadvantaged children unlikely to achieve academic success. The parents asserted that this was unlawful because it was indirectly taking account of ability and aptitude contrary to the statute. In this regard they called evidence that the school had a higher than average proportion of pupils with upper grades in the transfer procedure test. In response the school gave evidence that certain primary schools had been given priority on the basis of their traditional links with the school and that primary schools in the area of the newer housing estates simply did not have these traditional links. The High Court[95] considered that the criteria were not unlawful. In particular, the court did not find the allegation that the school was attempting to select pupils indirectly on ability proved on the evidence. The High Court's decision was appealed to the Court of Appeal which upheld the decision. The Court of Appeal did not directly address the issue of covert selection on ability. Instead, it observed that the onus was on those alleging bias to prove it and it was not sufficient for the appellants to raise a mere suspicion of bias in these cases. Nevertheless, it remains possible that in a different set of circumstances parents might be able to show bias in the catchment areas or contributory schools used for selection purposes.

4.69 Although the vast majority of secondary schools are not permitted to select on the basis of ability, exceptions can be made by the Department.[96] There are a small number of secondary schools which are "recognised" by the Department as schools which select part of their intake on ability. They are St Patrick's College, Maghera and Lagan College, Belfast. The issue of which secondary schools are recognised by the Department as selecting on ability was considered in *In re Lagan College*.[97] The school sought a declaration that a direction issued by the Department which sought to stop it from selecting some of its pupils on the basis of their ability was unlawful. The school has always presented itself as an 'all-ability' school and contended that this was recognised by the Department. However, the court considered that the fact that a school is an all-ability school does not necessarily mean that it selects pupils by reference to ability or aptitude. Moreover, it was also of the view that unless the Department was aware that the school was selecting by reference to ability, it could not have recognised the fact. On this basis, the school's application was refused. Lagan College has, however, since been permitted to select a proportion of its intake on ability.

---

[95] [1994] NIJB 99.
[96] Secondary Schools (Admissions Criteria) Regulations (NI) 1997, reg. 5(a)9(ii) and (iii).
[97] Unreported judgment of the High Court of Northern Ireland, (1992).

RESTRICTIONS ON CRITERIA IN GRAMMAR SCHOOLS

4.70 Northern Ireland has maintained the grammar/ secondary division in post-primary education. Approximately one third of the places available at secondary level are in grammar schools. The traditional method of selection for grammar school has always been a centrally organised aptitude test.[98] This is still referred to locally as the '11 plus' or 'qualifying' although it is now officially called the 'transfer procedure test'. Grammar schools are the only secondary schools in Northern Ireland which are permitted to select all their pupils on the basis of their ability and aptitude.[99] The Secondary Schools (Admissions Criteria) Regulations (NI) 1997 direct that secondary schools cannot include criteria which select on the basis of ability or aptitude except in the case of grammar schools or other schools recognised by the Department as schools which select on the basis of ability or aptitude. Most grammar schools use the results in the transfer procedure tests for these purposes.

Performance in the Transfer Procedure Test

4.71 The NICCEA organises an annual set of aptitude tests to enable grammar schools to select pupils on the basis of their academic ability. Children do not have to take these tests. However, if they wish to attend a grammar school, the child must normally sit the transfer procedure test. From the very beginning of open enrolment grammar schools ran into difficulty drawing up criteria which used the results of these tests as the basis for selection for admission. As a result of this the Secondary Schools (Admissions Criteria) Regulations (NI) 1990 set out how the results of the test were to be treated by grammar schools. Even so, many schools continued to experience difficulty in their attempts to distinguish between different applicants on the basis of ability. In particular it was difficult to distinguish pupils who had achieved Grade B in the transfer procedure test. The Secondary Schools (Admission Criteria) Regulations (NI) 1995 introduced a number of significant changes to the prescribed criteria to be used by schools which relied on the transfer procedure tests to distinguish between candidates on the basis of ability. In particular, the 1995 Regulations introduced a new system of classification of transfer procedure results. Grade A is awarded to the first 25 per cent of candidates, Grade B1 to the next five per cent, Grade B2 to the next five per cent, Grade C1 to the next five per cent , Grade C2 to the next five per cent and Grade D to the rest. The 1995 Regulations specify that priority is to be given to Grade A over all other grades, Grade B1 is to be given priority over Grades B2, C1, C2 and D etc. The statutory requirements are now contained in the Secondary Schools (Admissions Criteria) Regulations (NI) 1997. These provide that if a school relies on the transfer procedure tests pupils are to be admitted strictly on the basis of their performance in the test. Only after this is done can other criteria be used to distinguish between the remaining applicants who have the same test result. There are only two exceptions to these general rules about the results in the transfer procedure tests: (i) special circumstances and (ii) boarding pupils.

---

[98] See further, para. 1-11.
[99] St Patrick's College, Maghera and Lagan College are not grammar schools but are both permitted to select a proportion of their pupils on the basis of academic ability.

Special circumstances

4.72 Children who miss the main transfer procedure test through illness or other unforeseen factors can sit a supplementary test. Similarly, a child whose performance in the original transfer procedure test may have been affected through illness or other temporary problems can sit a supplementary test. If the parents decide that the child should not sit the supplementary test, the result of the original test stands unless there is good reason why the child has not taken the second test. If the child does elect to take the supplementary test, the result of the original test will be disregarded and the child will be considered by schools on the basis of his or her performance in the second test. However, in exceptional cases, where there is a long-term social, medical or other problem, the child will be considered by schools on the basis of both grades.

4.73 One of the most controversial aspects of the transfer procedure tests has been the regrading of children's results under the special circumstances exceptions usually contained in the admissions criteria. Regulation 4(a) of the Secondary School (Admissions Criteria) Regulations (NI) 1997 requires the Board of Governors to consider medical or other problems which may have affected a child's performance in the transfer tests if this is supported by documentary evidence of a medical or other appropriate nature. Schools who use the transfer procedure test results as a basis for admission must consider special circumstances. In *In re Trainor* Kerr J considered that the regulation imposed on Boards of Governors an obligation to include in their criteria a statement that admission dependent on grades achieved would be subject to consideration of medical or other problems which may have affected the candidate's performance.[100] In practice a Board of Governors will consider this evidence before it embarks on the general admissions process. Individual pupils are considered and the Board of Governors may allocate them whatever test classification it considers that the applicant would have received if it had not been for the special circumstances. The applicant is then treated as if they had achieved that mark in the first place.

4.74 The onus for determining whether to re-grade the applicant and which grade to award is on the Board of Governors of the individual school. It is important that decisions reached are consistent and reasonable and can be supported by documentary evidence. In view of this, the Department has issued guidance to Boards of Governors considering individual cases. This recommends that Boards of Governors should consider all aspects of the individual case and in particular the following: the grade actually obtained; the extent to which special circumstances are supported by documentary evidence; the nature of the evidence and the time-scale in which it was produced; whether the parents sought a supplementary test; comments from the primary school principal and information about the child's classroom performance; reports from educational psychologists provided by the parents; and any assessments by the ELB. It is also important that the Board gives appropriate consideration to any other matter drawn to its attention. The Board of Governors of an oversubscribed school has a difficult task when regrading applicants on the basis of special circumstances since upgrading one child will

---

[100] Unreported decision of the High Court of Northern Ireland, 28 August 1996.

usually have the effect of denying admission to a child who has obtained a better grade in the transfer test. This may well be widely known among parents and can generate sufficient dissatisfaction to lead to an appeal.

4.75 The application of special circumstances criteria have been considered by the Northern Ireland courts on numerous occasions. There are written decisions in four such cases: *In re Tucker, In re Cunningham, In re Trainor* and *In re Kerr*.[101] It should be stressed that in each of these cases, the criteria used were interpreted on their own individual wording. Nevertheless, there are several general principles which can be drawn from these cases. The first general point is that school's cannot impose a higher burden on applicants than that specified in the regulations. In *In re Trainor* the court considered that the school's criteria implied that the Board of Governors would only examine information about special circumstances where it was confirmed that various exceptional circumstances existed and where there were compelling reasons to conclude that the test results were unreliable. Kerr J accepted the argument that the criteria were not consistent with the regulations and quashed the decision of the Board of Governors.

4.76 Secondly, a school does not have to be specific about the special circumstances which it will consider. In *In re Cunningham* the court did not accept counsel's argument that criteria which were totally unspecific should be considered void for lack of certainty. Nevertheless, the court considered that in the event of a school applying an unreasonably restricted interpretation of special circumstances, an appeal tribunal might come to the conclusion that the criteria had not been correctly applied.

4.77 Thirdly, most schools define their criteria so as to place the onus on parents to produce the documentary evidence normally required to support an application for regrading. In such cases, the Board of Governors of the school to which the child seeks admission does not have to seek this itself. Moreover, if the decision is appealed to a tribunal, the tribunal must make its decision based on the evidence which was before the Board of Governors. In *In re Cunningham*, the court considered that parents cannot produce further evidence at tribunal as the tribunal is bound to consider only the evidence which was before the school's admission committee. In spite of this, in *In re Trainor* counsel was unsuccessful in his argument that the tribunal's decision should be quashed because the chairman had sought fresh evidence in the course of the hearing. The court declined relief because it considered that the material was background information only and had not played any relevant part in the tribunal's decision.

4.78 Fourthly, in *In re Cunningham*, Girvan J considered that a tribunal was wrong to have placed emphasis on a primary school principal's failure to fill in the special circumstances section of the transfer report form. The court considered that the principal's omission may have been due to the fact that he considered that there was enough information elsewhere to support the argument for special treatment or alternatively that he was trying to avoid the issue because he was unconvinced of the merits of the case. In either event,

---

[101] None of these decisions have been formally reported. The written decisions were given on the following dates: *Trainor*, 28 August 1998; *Cunningham*, 25 August 1995; *Tucker*, 25 August 1995; *Kerr*, 31 July 1996.

the omission was not a relevant consideration for the tribunal. Primary school principals should make some sort of assessment on the transfer form. Even though a Board of Governors or tribunal should not take an omission to do so into account, a failure to provide information may result in a claim for negligence if a child fails to have their grade raised due to a lack of evidence.

4.79 Finally, it is not enough for the parents to show only that there have been special circumstances. In *In re Kerr* it was stated that it must also be established on the documented evidence submitted in support of the criteria that the child would have been awarded a relevant higher grade. Thus, the Board of Governors must also be satisfied that the special circumstances have affected the child's performance and that this should be regraded. This can usually only be established with reference to other indicators of the child's academic ability such as their performance in mock tests.

Boarding pupils

4.80 A grammar school which operated a boarding school on 21 September 1990 may give preference to pupils who intend to board at the school without regard to the grades awarded in the transfer tests. However, this applies only so long as the number of pupils enrolled in the boarding department does not exceed the number enrolled on 21 September 1990 or 20 October 1998.[102] This is for some a way of getting into a popular grammar school with a below average result in the transfer tests. It might seem quite extreme but there is always a possibility that the boarding status could be changed at some stage post admission.

Tests held by or at the request of the Board of Governors

4.81 Grammar schools are not permitted to use the results of tests or examinations held by or on behalf of the Board of Governors of the school to select children for entry into the first year of the school.[103] The only exception to this relates to tests or examinations for individual children of a description determined by the Department. Such tests may be organised by the ELB at the request of the Board of Governors. Tests of this nature may be appropriate for children who have lived outside Northern Ireland and have not therefore had the opportunity to undertake the transfer procedure test.

4.82 The term "test" is not defined in the legislation. However, there is an argument that it would include the selection interviews used by a small number of grammar schools, particularly if the process scores children in a number of ability-related areas.

Primary school reports

4.83 Prior to 1996, reliance was often placed on reports by principals as to the pupil's general ability. However, these were widely considered to be too subjective. Once again schools ran into difficulty in their attempts to ensure

---

[102] Reg. 6 of the 1997 Regulations.
[103] Art. 16(6) of the 1997 Order.

parity between different schools.[104] The Secondary Schools (Admissions Criteria) Regulations (NI) 1997 prohibit schools from taking such information into account. No information of this sort is now contained on the transfer report form unless there have been special circumstances affecting performance in the transfer tests.

Key stage 2 assessments

4.84 Grammar schools must not refer to the outcome of any relevant assessment which may be conducted by the NICCEA under article 21(1)(b) of the 1989 Order in relation to a pupil at key stage 2.[105]

ADMISSION OF CHILDREN WITH DISABILITIES

4.85 The 1997 Order does not deal with the admission of children with physical or mental disabilities directly. Moreover, the education provisions of the Disability Discrimination Act 1995 do not apply to Northern Ireland.[106] There are, however, a number of relevant provisions scattered throughout the Education Orders. It has been seen that most schools are prohibited from selecting with reference to ability and aptitude. This would presumably cover both physical and intellectual ability. However, schools may refuse to admit a child at any time after the first year if the admission of the child would "prejudice the efficient use of resources".[107] This might be used by schools to object to the admission of disabled children. In practice, many schools retain a discretion to give priority to children with special circumstances in their admission criteria. Moreover, most children with significant disabilities will be statemented. In such cases, their admission to a school will depend on that school being named in their statement. This process is considered in detail in Chapter 8.

ADMISSIONS APPEAL TRIBUNAL

4.86 Every ELB is under a duty to make arrangements enabling the parents of a child to appeal against any decision made by or on behalf of a Board of Governors of a grant-aided school refusing the child admission to the school.[108] The only decisions which cannot be appealed in this way are decisions under: article 13(5) or 14(7) of the 1997 Order (admission prejudicial to provision of efficient education or efficient use of resources; article 14(3) (admission detrimental to educational interest of the child); and article 14(5) or (7)(a) (academic standards of grammar schools).[109] In such cases, dissatisfied parents could complain to the Department under article 101 of the 1986 Order.

---

[104] See for instance, *In re Holmes*, unreported decision of the High Court of Northern Ireland, 27 September 1991 and *In re McGurk* [1992] 11 NIJB 10.
[105] Reg. 5(b) of the Secondary Schools (Admissions Criteria) Regulations (NI) 1997.
[106] S. 29 of the 1995 Act requires a school to include information about admission and access in its annual reports. This provision does not apply in Northern Ireland (Disability Discrimination Act 1995, Sch. 8 para. 15).
[107] Art. 13(4) and 14(6) of the 1997 Order.
[108] Art.15(1) of the 1997 Order.
[109] *Ibid* art. 15(2).

Grounds of appeal

4.87 The grounds of the appeal must be that the school's criteria for admission were not applied or were not correctly applied in deciding to refuse the child admission to the school.[110] The actual substance of the criteria cannot be challenged in the appeal tribunal. This means that parents cannot argue that the criteria are unlawful, unreasonable or unworkable at the tribunal. In *In re Cunningham* Girvan J suggested that if the criteria were unlawful or unworkable, the tribunal should decline jurisdiction since it could not fulfill its statutory function to determine whether or not the criteria had been correctly applied.[111] In such cases, parents can either complain to the Department under article 101 of the 1986 Order that there has been an unreasonable exercise of statutory powers or take an action for judicial review.[112]

The composition of the appeal tribunal

4.88 The appeal tribunal is composed of three members who are appointed by the ELB from one of two panels: (i) persons appointed to act as chairmen and (ii) persons appointed to act as members.[113] Prior to 1998, tribunal members were drawn from one of three panels: (i) persons representing the interests of controlled schools in the area of the ELB; (ii) persons appearing to the ELB, after consultation with the CCMS and such other bodies as the ELB considers appropriate, to represent the interests of voluntary schools on the area of the board and persons appearing to the ELB to represent the interests of grant-maintained integrated schools in the area of the board; and (iii) persons who have experience in education, are acquainted with the educational arrangements in the area of the ELB, or are parents of registered pupils at a school. The fact that the tribunal now has a separate panel for chairmen is some recognition of the need to have the hearings conducted by people with a level of expertise in the procedures involved in such tribunals. Certain categories of people are precluded from sitting on an appeal tribunal. These include: employees of the ELB other than full-time teachers; those involved in the original decision to refuse to admit; teachers at the school to which admission was refused; teachers or a member of the Board of Governors of a primary school or preparatory department of a grammar school from which the child is transferring.[114]

Procedure for appeal and at hearing

4.89 An appeal must be made in writing to the ELB setting out the grounds on which it is made.[115] The tribunal must give the appellant the opportunity to make written representations and appear at the tribunal and make oral representations.[116] It must also give the Board of Governors the opportunity to make written representations and allow a representative of the Board of

---

[110] *Ibid* art.15(4).
[111] Unreported decision of the High Court of Northern Ireland, 25 August 1995.
[112] Both of these options are considered in further detail at paras. 2.63-2.80.
[113] School Admissions (Appeal Tribunals) Regulations (NI) 1998, Sch. 1 paras. 1-3.
[114] *Ibid* Sch. 1 paras. 4-7.
[115] *Ibid* Sch. 2 para. 1.
[116] *Ibid* Sch. 2 para. 3.

Governors to appear and make oral representations.[117] Appeals will generally be held in private. However, when the appeal involves the refusal of admission to a controlled school, a member of the ELB may attend as an observer.[118] The tribunal has the power to request the Board of Governors to supply the tribunal with information about admissions and proposed admissions to the school.[119]

4.90 In addition to the statutory requirements, the decision of the admissions appeal tribunal must comply with the principles of natural justice, that is the duty to be fair. Issues relating to this have been raised a number of times on judicial review. In *In re Holmes* it was argued (unsuccessfully) that a representative of the school should have been present at the hearing.[120] In *In re McGurk* it was argued that the chairperson should not have received legal advice in the course of the hearing which was not revealed to the applicant's representatives.[121] The court declined to grant relief on this point because it accepted that the applicant had not been disadvantaged. On the whole, the statutory procedures prescribed by the regulations are designed to ensure that applicants are given an adequate opportunity to state a case and respond to any arguments made against them.

Function of the appeal tribunal

4.91 The appeal tribunal must consider whether the school's criteria were applied or applied correctly. To do this, it must first construe the criteria. In *In re Farren* Kelly LJ stated:

> "... the tribunal in the discharge of its functions...should look at the wording of the criteria in deciding whether they have been applied or correctly applied. If what the school has done is contrary to the wording of the criteria, the school cannot avail itself of a defence before the tribunal that nevertheless the way they did apply them was tenable and reasonable."[122]

Having determined the appropriate meaning of the criteria, the tribunal must then consider whether the school applied the criteria correctly on the basis of the evidence before them. In *In re Tucker* Girvan J stressed that the statute requires the tribunal to look at the situation as it was before the school and not *de novo*.[123] If the tribunal concludes that the criteria were properly applied, the appeal will be dismissed. If the tribunal considers that the criteria were not correctly applied, it must then go on to consider whether the child would have been admitted to the school had the criteria been used properly. This is because the tribunal only has the power to direct that a child is admitted to a school if, on the correct application of the criteria, the child would have been admitted by the Board of Governors. Girvan J described the task of the tribunal as follows:

---

[117] *Ibid* Sch. 2 para. 4.
[118] *Ibid* Sch. 2 para. 6.
[119] *Ibid* Sch. 2 para. 7.
[120] Unreported decision of the High Court of Northern Ireland, 27 September 1991.
[121] [1992] 11 NIJB 10.
[122] [1990] NI 70 at p.111.
[123] [1995] NI 14.

> "The proper task which the tribunal should have posed was whether it was satisfied that the applicant would have been refused admission as opposed to whether she would have been refused admission in the view of the tribunal."

It follows from this that the tribunal cannot consider additional material which the school did not have an opportunity to consider (this is particularly likely to arise in special circumstances cases). In *In re Cunningham* Girvan J reiterated the approach he had taken in *In re Tucker* and concluded:

> "This focuses the tribunal's attention on the material which was before the school at the time when the school made its decision. Looking at additional material after the event cannot assist the tribunal in determining what the school would have done had it applied its criteria correctly at the time it made its decision."[124]

Powers of the appeal tribunal

4.92 A tribunal can do one of three things:

(1) It can dismiss the appeal if it believes that the admissions criteria were properly applied.

(2) It can dismiss the appeal if it believes that the admissions criteria were not properly applied but, if they had been, that the child would still not have been admitted to the school.

(3) It must allow the appeal if it appears that the admissions criteria were not properly applied and if they had been that the child would have been admitted to the school. In such a case the tribunal must issue a direction to the Board of Governors requiring it to admit the child to the school. The Board of Governors must comply with this direction. The fixed admissions numbers are not affected by such directions.

Tribunal's decision

4.93 In the event of a disagreement between the members of the tribunal, the decision will be by majority vote.[125] The decision and the grounds on which it was made must be communicated in writing to the appellant, the ELB and the Board of Governors.[126] Tribunals are required to state the grounds for the decision. In *In re Tucker* Girvan J interpreted "grounds" to mean the same as reasons, stressing how important these were to parents.[127] He did not, however, quash the decision for the failure to give reasons as the reasons had been given belatedly and had not prejudiced the applicant's ability to argue her case fully. Similarly, in *In re Trainor* Kerr J emphasised that a court would be slow to condemn a decision because of the inadequacy of reasons unless the subsequently proffered reasons amounted to an *ex post facto*

---

[124] *Ibid.*
[125] School Admissions (Appeal Tribunals) Regulations (NI) 1998, Sch. 28.
[126] *Ibid* para. 9.
[127] *Ibid.*

rationalisation.[128] On the facts, he considered that even though the original statement of reasons was deficient, they had been adequately explained by way of affidavit so as to cure the original deficiency.

Challenging the decision of the appeal tribunal

4.94 There is no specified means of appealing a decision of the admissions appeal tribunal. However, in Northern Ireland every year there are a series of applications for judicial review of the decisions of admissions appeal tribunals. The applicants are invariably children who have been refused admission to the school of their parent's choice. The action is usually taken on their behalf by their parents. The choice of applicant has important implications for legal aid. If the child alone is the applicant, legal aid will almost always be granted as it is determined with reference to the child's income. Counsel for the various ELBs have on several occasions argued that the child's parents should be made applicants. The point of this is that, if the application is unsuccessful, costs could be awarded against the parents. This would undoubtedly discourage many parents from taking actions. So far the point has not been accepted or fully considered by the courts on judicial review. In *In re Kerr* Girvan J declined to make a decision on this issue on the basis that it should have been raised earlier in the proceedings.[129] Nevertheless, he seemed somewhat sympathetically disposed to the argument. Moreover, a similar point was accepted by the English High Court in relation to the Special Education Needs Tribunal.[130]

4.95 The successful judicial review applications have been discussed earlier in the chapter. However, the most successful basis of challenge from an applicant's point of view is where the appeal tribunal has failed to interpret the criteria properly. This was the case in each of the following decisions: *In re Farren, In re McGurk and In re Patton* discussed earlier at paragraphs 4.31-4.34. In each of these cases, the decision turned on the correct interpretation of the published criteria. Guidance as to how criteria are considered by the courts is contained earlier at paragraph 4.32. The statutory function of the appeal tribunal is to see if the criteria were not applied or were not applied correctly. This requires the tribunal to construe the criteria. If it does so incorrectly and then employs the incorrect interpretation, the decision will be unlawful. In each of the successful cases, the court quashed the decision of the tribunal and issued an order of *mandamus* requiring the tribunal to reconsider the applicant's case in the light of its comments. The court in judicial review does not have the power to direct admission to the school. Only the tribunal has this power.

OTHER COMPLAINTS ABOUT ADMISSIONS

4.96 There are a number of issues which fall outside the jurisdiction of the admissions appeal tribunal but which nevertheless may give rise to parental dissatisfaction and complaints. In particular there is no appeal to the tribunal in cases where the child has been refused admission to a year group other than

---

[128] Unreported decision of the High Court of Northern Ireland, 28 August 1996.
[129] Unreported decision of the High Court of Northern Ireland, 31 July 1996.
[130] See *S v The Special Educational Needs Tribunal* [1995] 1 WLR 1627.

year 1 or 8 on the grounds that admission would be prejudicial to the efficient use of resources; or where a child has been refused admission to year 8 in a grammar school on the grounds that it would be detrimental to the educational interests of the child; or where a child has been refused admission to a grammar school any time after September of year 8 on the grounds that his or her academic ability is not of a standard equivalent to that of the pupils with whom he or she will be taught. In such cases, the parent may complain to the Department under article 101 of the 1986 Order. The Department's decision is subject to judicial review.

CHAPTER FIVE

THE CURRICULUM

INTRODUCTION

5.01 In this chapter the 'curriculum' refers to the substance of what is taught in schools, that is the knowledge, ideas and values conveyed in the educational process. The chapter outlines the legal provisions which regulate what is taught and the systems which are in place for enforcing those provisions and for challenging the type of education being provided. In the post-war educational reforms, introduced in Northern Ireland in 1947, no statutory provision was made in relation to the content of the curriculum which would be taught in state schools. The Education Act (NI) 1947 did draw a distinction at secondary level between schools which would provide an academic course of study (grammar schools) and those which would concentrate on practical, technical skills (secondary intermediate and technical schools). However, it did not go so far as to prescribe the content of the course of study at any stage of compulsory education. There was a widespread feeling that a nationally prescribed course of study would be undemocratic, a view expressed by one leading educationalist of the time who stated that "What we do not want is lessons laid down by law".[1] Thus, the substance of what was taught in schools in Northern Ireland was left largely to the discretion of individual schools guided by local education authorities and subject only to the practical (and not legal) constraint of meeting the requirements of external examining bodies. The only exception to this was in relation to religious education where legislation restricted the type of religious instruction which could be given in controlled schools.[2] This delegated model of curricular responsibility continued to operate right up until 1990.

5.02 In 1988 the government introduced legislation in England and Wales which prescribed the curriculum for children up to the age of 16.[3] The reform was motivated by the government's concern about the quality, content and lack of uniformity in the curriculum in state-funded schools.[4] The new National Curriculum prescribed areas of study, attainment targets and assessment arrangements for the four 'key stages' of study.[5] In England and Wales, the introduction of the National Curriculum met with great resistance from the teaching profession who considered it to be over prescriptive and too demanding in terms of the assessment arrangements. A year later almost

---

[1] H. Dent, *The New Education Bill* (1944) p. 30.
[2] Art. 21(2) of the 1986 Order prohibits controlled schools from providing denominational religious education.
[3] Education Act 1988. The provisions on the curriculum are now contained in the Education Act 1996, ss. 353-376.
[4] *The National Curriculum 5-16 - A Consultation Document* (London: DES/Welsh Office, 1987)
[5] Education Reform Act 1988, ss. 2-4.

identical proposals were made for Northern Ireland and were greeted with similar concern.[6] Teachers tried to argue that Northern Ireland already had sufficient safeguards in terms of the quality of the curriculum, pointing to a number of local initiatives which had been developed under the auspices of the Northern Ireland Curriculum Council.[7] However, attempts to argue that Northern Ireland should be treated differently from the rest of the United Kingdom on this issue were ultimately unsuccessful. The government acknowledged the progress which had been made in schools in Northern Ireland but insisted that it was still necessary to legislate to ensure equality of access to a broad and balanced curriculum. It stated that "voluntary participation in curriculum review and development would not achieve the aim of raising standards in all schools and improving educational opportunities consistently, or of ensuring that improvements occurred within a reasonable time scale".[8]

5.03 In fact, there was an argument that Northern Ireland's schools had a particular need for a common curriculum given the disparate nature of the educational structures in operation. Northern Ireland's schools are split between Catholic/ Protestant schools and grammar/ non-selective schools at secondary level. In addition, Northern Ireland has a very high proportion of single sex schools, thus adding a further level of segregation.[9] There was a considerable body of research which indicated significant differences in curricular structures and levels of attainment in the various categories of schools in Northern Ireland in the period prior to the introduction of the 1989 reforms.[10] The differences in the curricula employed by secondary and grammar schools were part of a deliberate educational philosophy. However, there were also disparities in relation to both gender and religious affiliation. In relation to gender, there was evidence that girls' schools were underachieving in science and technical subjects.[11] There was similar research which showed key differences in the curricula employed in Protestant and Catholic schools. Put simply, Protestant schools had more students studying science and technology while Catholic schools placed more emphasis on humanities.[12] Moreover Catholic school leavers had lower attainment levels than their Protestant peers, a fact which had knock-on effects in relation to levels of unemployment in the Catholic community.[13] The introduction of a common curriculum represented a step towards a closer alignment of the

---

[6] *The Way Forward* (Bangor: DENI, 1988).
[7] These included the 'Primary Schools Guidelines' and '11- 16 Programme'.
[8] DENI, *The Way Forward* (1988) para. 2.6.
[9] Over one third of secondary schools (76 out of 226) are single sex schools.
[10] See J. D'Arcy and A.E. Sutherland, "System Inequalities in Curriculum Provision and Educational Attainment in Northern Ireland", Annex C in the *Fifteenth Report of the Standing Advisory Commission on Human Rights (1990 - 1991)* (London: HMSO, 1990), 97 - 130.
[11] *Science and Arts Subject Choices* (Belfast, EOCNI, 1985).
[12] R. D.Osborne, A.M. Gallagher and R.J Cormack, "Review of Aspects of Education in Northern Ireland", Annex H in the *Fourteenth Report of the Standing Advisory Commission on Human Rights (1987- 1989)* (London: HMSO,1989), 123 - 160.
[13] R.D. Osborne and R.J.Cormack, "Gender and Religion as Issues in Education Training and Entry to Work", in Harbinson (ed) *Growing up in Northern Ireland* (Belfast: Stranmillis College, 1989).

provision made in the different categories of school, thus bridging some of the gaps engendered by Northern Ireland's segregated education system.

5.04 To a large extent, the Northern Ireland curriculum mirrors the National Curriculum applicable in England and Wales. The statutory framework is the same; children are divided into key stages, each of which has its own compulsory subjects, attainment targets and assessment requirements. However, although the structure is similar, the content of the Northern Ireland curriculum is distinctive from the National Curriculum in several respects. First, two of the curricular themes which Northern Ireland schools are required to follow across the areas of study are "Education for Mutual Understanding" (EMU) and "Cultural Heritage" (see paras. 5.10-5.14). Both are intended to promote cross-community understanding. A second issue which makes the Northern Ireland curriculum distinctive is the inclusion of the Irish Language (see paras. 5.34-5.39). Irish may be taught in all grant-aided schools as the required European Language provided that an alternative language is offered to pupils. In addition Northern Ireland has a small number of Irish Medium schools, that is schools where children are taught in Irish. Some of these receive state funding and the legal requirements of the curriculum reflect this. The final area of distinction, sex education, is most notable by the absence of regulation. In contrast to England and Wales, Northern Ireland does not have any specific provisions in this area. The implications of this are considered in paragraphs 5.27-5.32.

5.05 The content of the statutory curriculum has been the subject of continuous review nationally. This caused a lot of unrest among teachers who felt that they had to jump from change to change without having had time to assimilate the reforms. As a result the government declared a general moratorium on changes to the curriculum until the year 2001. However, since the Labour Party's election manifesto focused so heavily on education, reform in some shape or other was inevitable. This has focused not so much on the substance of what is taught in school, but on the more general quest for improved standards in education. In England and Wales the White Paper, *Excellence in Schools,* outlined major reforms in relation to standards and discipline in schools.[14] These have been introduced by the School Standards and Framework Act 1998. A number of these reforms have also been implemented in Northern Ireland by the Education (NI) Order 1998. Two are specifically intended to raise standards in the curriculum. The first is the forthcoming introduction of baseline assessment for all children in their first year of school.[15] This is intended to provide teachers with a consistent format to establish a pupil's stage of development on entry to school. Secondly, schools are required to set school performance targets which are intended to raise standards generally.[16] These proposals, coupled with other proposals such as school development plans and limitations on class sizes are part of a package of measures intended to tackle problems associated with underachievement.

---

[14] Cm 3681 (1997).
[15] Arts. 7-9 of the 1998 Order.
[16] See further para. 5.100.

5.06 It should be noted that the legislation draws a distinction between the secular and religious curriculum in schools. In the discussion which follows, references to the Northern Ireland curriculum should be taken to refer to the secular curriculum. Schools are under an additional but separate obligation to provide religious instruction for all registered pupils at the school.[17] This is considered further at paragraphs 5.46-5.55.

THE CURRICULUM IN GRANT-AIDED SCHOOLS

5.07 Part III of the Education Reform (NI) Order 1989 introduced a legally prescribed curriculum for children between the ages of 4 or 5 and 16. The government could have chosen to implement its plans for a nationally applicable curriculum informally through guidance and circulars. Instead it chose to place educational bodies under a series of quite specific legal obligations and to give the detailed content of the curriculum the force of law. The formalised legal approach appears to have been chosen primarily as an enforcement device. The government considered that voluntary participation would not raise standards consistently or quickly enough.[18] In view of this, it was considered to be "necessary to provide in law" for a basic curriculum. To support this, the Board of Governors of each school was placed under statutory duties to ensure that these requirements are met.

Statement of curricular policy

5.08 Article 10 of the 1989 Order requires the scheme of management of all grant-aided schools to require the Board of Governors to determine a curriculum policy for the school and to produce a written statement of that policy. The policy must be kept under review and the written policy kept up to date. When determining the policy, the Board of Governors must consider the range of the curriculum and the balance between, and coherence of, its different components. The policy must be compatible with the programmes of study of the contributory subjects; the syllabus of any course which forms part of the curriculum and which leads to an approved public examination; and the other statutory education provisions, particularly those relating to children with special educational needs. When making or reviewing the curriculum policy, Boards of Governors are under an obligation to take account of the findings of any inspection; to consider representations by the ELB or CCMS (if the school is a Catholic maintained school); and to consult the principal. The principal is under a statutory obligation to ensure that the curriculum is compatible with the policy contained in the written statement. For these purposes, article 10(5) of the 1989 Order specifies that the scheme of management of the school must provide for the principal to be allocated such functions as will, subject to the resources available, enable him or her to determine and organise the curriculum and secure that it is followed within the school.

---

[17] Art. 5(1)(a) of the 1989 Order.
[18] DENI, *The Way Forward* (1988) para. 2.6.

The requirement to ensure a "balanced and broadly based" curriculum

5.09 Article 4 of the of the 1989 Order places Boards of Governors and principals under a duty to ensure that the school offers a "balanced and broadly based" curriculum which:

> "a) promotes the spiritual, moral, cultural, intellectual and physical development of pupils at the school and thereby of society; and
>
> b) prepares such pupils for the opportunities, responsibilities and experiences of adult life."

This wide statement of obligation would be difficult to enforce on its own. However, it might be used to interpret the obligations placed on Boards of Governors and principals in relation to more specific aspects of the curriculum such as the provision of religious or sex education.

Educational themes

5.10 The introduction of a common school curriculum has provided a vehicle through which the government is able to attempt to foster the competences and attitudes which it considers appropriate for today's society. In particular, article 8 of the 1989 Order states that a curriculum will not be considered to comply with the above duty unless it promotes "wholly or mainly through the teaching of the compulsory subjects and religious education, the attainment of the objectives of a number of stated themes". The equivalent themes in England and Wales do not have a statutory footing. However, as in England and Wales, the themes in Northern Ireland include: Information Technology; Health Education; and in the third and fourth key stages, Economic Awareness and Careers Education. In Northern Ireland there are two further themes: (i) Education for Mutual Understanding (EMU) and (ii) Cultural Heritage. The intention of both these additional themes is to underpin the curriculum with knowledge and values aimed at encouraging greater tolerance and understanding between the two main religious traditions. The theme of Cultural Heritage is specifically intended to "lessen the ignorance which many feel contribute to the divisions in our society".[19] EMU has a similar goal.[20] As part of EMU, grants are available for activities which bring schools on each side of the community together for social, educational and sporting events. The Department had previously encouraged this through a circular entitled "The Improvement of Community Relations: the Contribution of Schools".[21] The Education Reform (NI) Order 1989 accorded statutory recognition to the importance of this type of activity for the future of peace in Northern Ireland.

---

[19] *Ibid* para. 2.13.
[20] For a description of the EMU programme, see, A. Robinson, "Education for Mutual Understanding" in *A Common Curriculum: The Case of Northern Ireland*, ed. L. Caul (Belfast: Stranmillis College, 1993), pp. 7-23.
[21] DENI Circular No. 1982/21.

5.11 The fact that the government feels the need to embed such matters in the school curriculum is itself recognition of the fact that they are not always being passed onto children at home. However, problems can arise if parents expressly disagree with the particular value being conveyed. In such instances there may be a clash between the public interest in having the child educated according to conventional moral norms and the parents' private interest in having the child educated in accordance with his or her wishes. The operation of EMU provides a case in point. In Northern Ireland the community divisions are such that some parents may forcefully object to their children being required to meet (never mind mingle) with 'the other side'. It is unclear whether parents have a right to object to their child participating in EMU activity. Under article 44 of the Education and Libraries (NI) Order 1986, education authorities must have regard to the general principle that children should be educated in accordance with the wishes of their parents. However, this duty applies only so far as this is compatible with the provision of "efficient instruction". Likewise, Article 2 of First Protocol of the ECHR gives parents the right to have their child educated in accordance with their religious and philosophical convictions. However philosophical convictions only include those convictions which are "worthy of respect in a democratic society".[22] It could be argued that there is a set of commonly agreed values which it is in the public interest to bestow upon children, irrespective of parental wishes on the subject. This is explicit in the UNCHR which states that education shall be directed to: "the promotion of understanding, tolerance and friendship among all nations, racial, ethnic or religious groups and the furtherance of the activities of the United Nations for the maintenance of peace".[23] It might be considered that EMU is an attempt to comply with this part of the Universal Declaration in a form which specifically recognises the peculiar context of Northern Ireland and in particular the entrenched community divisions.

The key stages

5.12 There are four key stages. These divide a child's school career until the age of 16 into four groupings which are then used as a base for the other requirements of the statutory curriculum. The boundaries of each stage are set out in article 5 of the 1989 Order which has been re-defined by article 34 of the 1996 Order.[24]

- Key stage 1 begins when a child attains compulsory school age and ends at the same time as the majority of children in the class complete four school years in that key stage. This generally covers children between the ages of four and eight.

- Key stage 2 begins in the school year after the first key stage and ends when the majority of the pupils in the class complete three years in that

---

[22] *Campbell and Cosans* v *United Kingdom* (1982) EHRR 293.
[23] Universal Declaration, Art. 26 (2). See further, Hodgson, "The International Human Right to Education and Education Concerning Human Rights", (1996) *The International Journal of Children's Rights* 237.
[24] Art. 5(6) of the 1989 Order as amended by art. 34 of the 1996 Order.

key stage. This generally includes children between the ages of nine and 11.
- Key stage 3 begins in the school year following key stage 2 and ends when the majority of pupils in the class complete three school years. This generally covers children between the ages of 12 and 14.
- Key stage 4 begins in the school year following key stage 3 and ends when the child ceases to be of compulsory school age. This covers children between the age of 15 and 16.

In each category the term "class" is defined to mean "the teaching group in which he is regularly taught that subject or, where there are two or more groups, such one of them as may be designated by the principal".[25] Key stages were not defined originally in relation to the progress of the child's classmates. The amendment was introduced as a means of accommodating a child who has not progressed through school at the normal rate.

Areas of study and the compulsory contributory subjects

5.13 Article 5(2) of the 1989 Order specifies that the curriculum in every grant-aided school must have six compulsory areas of study. These are: English; Mathematics; Science and Technology; the Environment and Society; Creative and Expressive studies; and Language Studies. All six are compulsory at each key stage except Language Studies. This is compulsory for all pupils at key stages 3 and 4 but is only compulsory at key stages 1 and 2 in Irish Medium schools. Each area of study has a list of subjects which are compulsory for each of the key stages. These are set out below in a table which is derived from Schedule 2 to the 1989 Order.[26]

COMPULSORY CONTRIBUTORY SUBJECTS

(1) Area of Study	(2) Compulsory contributory subjects in key stages 1 and 2	(3) Compulsory contributory subjects in key stage 3	(4) Compulsory contributory subjects in key stage 4
English	English	English	English
Mathematics	Mathematics	Mathematics	Mathematics
Science and Technology	Science Technology and Design	Science Technology and Design	Science Technology and Design
The Environment and Society	History Geography	History Geography	History or Geography
Creative and Expressive Studies	Art and Design Music Physical Education	Art and Design Music Physical Education	Art and Design or Music or Drama Physical Education
Language Studies	Irish (in Irish-Speaking schools only)	French or German or Italian or Spanish or Irish (in Irish-speaking schools only)	French or German or Italian or Spanish or Irish (in Irish-speaking schools only)

---

[25] *Ibid* art. 5(6A).
[26] This was substituted by Sch. 3 to the 1996 Order which has been amended by the Education Reform (Amendment) Order (NI) 1998.

5.14 Article 6 of the 1989 Order states that the curriculum in every grant-aided school shall require that each pupil at the school be taught within each area of study the contributory subjects which are compulsory for that pupil. Article 11(1)(b) of the 1989 Order requires a Board of Governors "to exercise its functions with a view to securing" and principals to secure that the listed contributory subjects are taught as required. When these provisions are read together, they would seem to place an obligation on Boards of Governors and principals to ensure that each child is taught in accordance with the Northern Ireland curriculum. The provisions might therefore be significant if an individual parent is dissatisfied with the education being provided for their child.

Programmes of study, attainment targets and assessment arrangements

5.15 One of the most controversial aspects of the statutory curriculum is the level of detail in its requirements. This occurs because the compulsory contributory subjects are underpinned by programmes of study, attainment targets and assessment arrangements.

5.16 *Programmes of study:* means the matters, skills and processes which are required to be taught to pupils of differing abilities and maturities during each key stage.[27]

5.17 *Attainment targets*: means the knowledge, skills and understanding which pupils of different abilities and maturities are expected to have by the end of each key stage.[28]

5.18 Article 5(4) of the 1989 Order states that the curriculum must include the specified attainment targets and programmes of study and must require that the content of the teaching of each contributory subject is consistent with those programmes of study and attainment targets. This would also fall within the obligation placed on Boards of Governors and principals by article 11(1)(b) of the 1989 Order. This means that parents could make a complaint about the school's failure to perform its statutory obligations if the child is not taught according to the precise programme of study for each contributory subject.

5.19 *Assessment arrangements*: These are the arrangements for assessing pupils at or near the end of each key stage for the purpose of ascertaining what they have achieved in relation to the attainment targets for that stage. In relation to subjects in key stage 4 which do not have attainment targets, it means the arrangements for assessing what the pupil has achieved.[29] The only compulsory contributory subjects which do not have to be assessed are those which fall within the area of Creative and Expressive Studies. The arrangements for assessing pupils have been one of the most controversial aspects of the curriculum reforms and their introduction has taken place on a rolling basis. From September 1996 pupils have been assessed at the end of key stages 1, 2 and 3 in English and Mathematics. Pupils at the end of key

---

[27] Art. 7(3)(b) of the 1989 Order.
[28] *Ibid* art. 7(3)(a).
[29] Art. 7(3)(c) as amended by art. 35(3) of the 1996 Order.

stage 3 are assessed in Science. The assessment arrangements for Irish in Irish medium schools are considered separately at paragraph 5.36.

5.20 The Department has the power to specify the programmes of study, attainment targets and assessment arrangements by order.[30] However, instead of publishing the full details in the order the Department may refer to a document published by The Stationery Office.[31] This is the procedure which is normally adopted. The information contained in the documents which describe the programmes, targets and assessment arrangements still has the force of law.

EXEMPTIONS FROM THE NORTHERN IRELAND CURRICULUM

5.21 The legal provisions relating to the Northern Ireland curriculum apply to all children attending grant-aided schools. The underlying philosophy of the common curriculum was to ensure equality of access to a balanced curriculum. This objective might have been seriously undermined if schools were given a broad discretion as to when the requirements could be set aside. Consequently, the legislation specifies the situations in which the requirements do not have to be met either in whole or in part. It will be seen that these are tightly drafted with the result that schools have very little scope when it comes to exempting individual pupils from the prescribed curriculum. This is not to say that all children of the same age should be receiving identical instruction. The curriculum does leave teachers with discretion as to what is taught and allows them to pitch materials at different levels in mixed ability groups. What it does not permit is for a child to be denied access to some aspect of the prescribed curriculum unless they fall within one of four exceptions. The first of these arises under article 15 of the 1989 Order which allows the Department to modify or disapply articles 5, 6 and 8 by regulations. This power has not been exercised. The 1989 Order also contains three specific exceptions which are considered below. There are no other exceptions in domestic legislation which allow a school to refrain from complying with the statutory requirements. The only other way in which an exception could arise is if a parent successfully argued that the content of the statutory curriculum was in contravention of his or her religious or philosophical convictions and therefore in breach of the second sentence of Article 2 of the First Protocol of the ECHR.[32] However, the European Court of Human Rights has shown itself to be reluctant to interfere with national programmes of study, particularly if they may have the effect of denying the child access to a suitable education and provided that the information is presented in an "objective, critical and pluralistic manner".[33]

Special educational needs

5.22 If a child has special educational needs which are the subject of a statement, his or her statement of special needs may include provision

---

[30] *Ibid* art. 7(1).
[31] *Ibid* art. 7(6).
[32] See paras. 1.53-1.56.
[33] *Kjelsden, Busk Masden and Pedersen* v *Denmark* (1976) EHRR 711.

applying articles 5, 6 and 8 of the 1989 Order with modifications or excluding the application of those provisions.[34] Such provision is common in statements of special educational needs as the requirements of the Northern Ireland curriculum are frequently inappropriate for a child with learning difficulties. Parents who are unhappy about the curriculum provided for their child can appeal against the content of the statement to the Special Educational Needs Tribunal under article 18 of the 1996 Order. It should be noted that this exception only applies to children with special educational needs which are the subject of a statement. There is estimated to be a further 18 per cent of all school children who are considered to have special needs but for whom no statement is maintained.[35] Problems may arise if these children are having difficulty coping with particular aspects of the curriculum since these children cannot be permanently exempted from any of the requirements of the Northern Ireland curriculum although temporary exceptions can be made in the circumstances described below.

Temporary individual exceptions

5.23 The principal of a school may direct that the statutory requirements will not apply or will apply with modifications in relation to a particular pupil if he or she considers that they are not appropriate for that pupil.[36] There are two types of direction which may be given: (i) a general direction and (ii) a special direction. A general direction may be given where circumstances are likely to change so that within six months it will be appropriate to apply the statutory requirements.[37] This would include situations where a student is suffering from a temporary condition affecting his learning. This might be the case if a pupil has arrived from a different educational system, has been in hospital, educated at home or excluded from school and needs time to adjust. Alternatively, it might be appropriate if a child is undergoing severe emotional problems. A special direction may be given where the pupil needs to be assessed by the ELB with a view to a statement of special educational needs being made or amended.[38]

5.24 If the principal considers a temporary individual exception to be appropriate, he or she must comply with a specific statutory procedure, the detail of which is clearly designed to ensure that such directions are used sparingly. A direction may not come into force less than one month after it is given unless the principal thinks it is essential. In no case is the duration of the direction to exceed six months although further directions can be made in restricted circumstances.[39] A direction must be in writing and will include information on the following: (i) the statutory requirements which will not apply or which will apply with modification; (ii) the date on which the direction comes into force and the period during which it will be in force; (iii) the reasons for the direction and an indication of whether it is a general or special direction; (iv) the differing provision which will be made for the

---

[34] Art. 16 of the 1989 Order.
[35] See further paras. 8.01-8.03.
[36] Education (Curriculum) (Temporary Exceptions) Regulations (NI) 1990, reg. 3(1)(a).
[37] *Ibid* reg.3(1)(b)(i).
[38] *Ibid* reg.3(1)(b)(ii).
[39] *Ibid* reg.4.

pupil's education during the period; and (v) the right of the parent to appeal.[40] A general direction must also include information on the manner in which the principal proposes to secure the full application of the curriculum after the period of the direction. A special direction must include a statement of the principal's opinion that the child has or probably has special needs and the reasons for it. The principal must keep a copy of the direction with the child's other school records and must send a copy within three days by first class post to: the chairman of the Board of Governors; the ELB in the case of a special direction; and the parent(s) of the pupil.[41] The principal has the power to both vary and revoke the direction. A parent can ask the principal to give a direction or revoke or vary a direction currently in force.[42] The request can be made orally or in writing but should state the reasons for which it is made.[43] The principal does not have to consider a request to vary or revoke a direction more than once during the period in which a particular direction is in force.[44] If the principal refuses the parent's request, he must give reasons for his decision and provide details of the parent's right to appeal.[45] This information must also be given to the Board of Governors.

5.25 The parent can appeal to the Board of Governors in one of three circumstances: (i) where the principal has given, revoked or varied a direction; (ii) where the principal has refused to give, revoke or vary a direction at the request of the parent; or (iii) where the principal has failed to respond to a request from a parent within two weeks.[46] The Board of Governors can confirm the principal's decision or can direct the principal to take such action as it considers appropriate in the circumstances.[47] The principal must comply with this direction. The Board of Governors is obliged to notify the appellant and principal of its decision in writing.[48]

Development work and experiments

5.26 The legislation provides an exception which allows schools to carry out development work and experiments in relation to the curriculum.[49] This could be used to allow a school to pilot a proposed change to the set curriculum. The rationale underlying the exception was that the common curriculum should not become a straight-jacket which would stifle innovation in curricular development in schools. However, the government was concerned that any freedom to experiment would not be misused by schools to avoid its responsibilities under the curriculum. The granting of exceptions is therefore carefully controlled. The exception can only be granted by a direction from the Department. This will specify any modifications to the

---

[40] *Ibid* reg.5.
[41] *Ibid* reg. 6.
[42] *Ibid* reg. 12(1).
[43] *Ibid* reg. 12(2).
[44] *Ibid* reg. 12(3).
[45] *Ibid* reg. 12(4).
[46] Art. 17(7) of the 1989 Order.
[47] *Ibid* art. 17(8).
[48] *Ibid* art. 17(9).
[49] *Ibid* art. 14.

provisions of articles 5, 6 and 8 of the 1989 Order.[50] The following bodies may apply for a direction: the Board of Governors of the school; the NICCEA with the agreement of the Board of Governors of the school; and the relevant ELB with the agreement of the Board of Governors.[51] If the application is made by the Board of Governors or the NICCEA, the Department will consult with the ELB.[52] The Department may require the body making the application to provide reports to the Department on specified matters.[53] In practice the exception has not been used widely by schools in Northern Ireland. It has been argued that it has untapped potential and in particular could be used by schools as a means of registering dissatisfaction with the common curriculum.[54]

SEX EDUCATION

5.27 One area of the curriculum which can be highly controversial is the provision of sex education. Some parents view sex education as an essentially private matter and one on which they would prefer to instruct their children themselves. Other parents may have strong religious beliefs and might consider the information provided by schools to conflict with their own moral values or tenets of their religion. In spite of the potential for conflict, there are no specific statutory provisions regulating sex education in Northern Ireland. In particular, schools are not under a direct legal obligation to provide sex education classes. Conversely, there is no legal provision which prohibits schools doing so and in practice most secondary schools do provide pupils with sex education. In fact, although schools are not under a direct obligation to provide sex education, it is arguable that a failure to provide some form of sex education would mean that the school's curriculum did not prepare its pupils for the "responsibilities and experiences of adult life" as is required under article 4 of the 1989 Order. Moreover, there are a number of subjects where issues relevant to sex education form part of the compulsory programme of study. For instance, schools are required to pursue the theme of health education throughout the curriculum and it seems obvious that this should include both the physical and emotional aspects of sexual activity.[55] Likewise, pupils study human reproductive systems in science at key stage 3. The result is that it would be unlikely that a child could leave secondary school without some knowledge of the basic facts pertaining to sex education.

Departmental guidance

5.28 DENI Circular 1987/45 provides guidance to schools on the provision of sex education. It states that sex education should be an important element in the curriculum of all schools and recommends that it "should be taught in a sensitive manner which is in harmony with the ethos of the school or college and in conformity with the moral and religious principles held by parents and

---

[50] *Ibid* art. 14(1).
[51] *Ibid* art. 14(3).
[52] *Ibid* art. 14(4).
[53] *Ibid* art. 14(6).
[54] See Tooley, 'Loopholes in the National Curriculum? The Genesis and Use of Sections 16 and 17 of the 1988 Education Reform Act' (1996) 8(4) *Education and the Law* 319.
[55] Art. 8 of the 1989 Order.

school management authorities".[56] The guidance states that all schools should have a written policy on sex education which is communicated to parents. However, a 1996 survey by the Health Promotion Agency for Northern Ireland found that the practice in many schools was not in accordance with the Department's recommendations.[57] For instance, only 50 per cent of secondary schools, 65 per cent of grammar schools and 15 per cent of primary schools had a sex education policy and half of these had not communicated this to the parents.[58] The survey also found wide variations in the approaches which schools took to sex education, both in relation to what was taught[59] and the subject in which it was taught.[60]

Parental rights

5.29   The provision of sex education is not usually a source of conflict with parents. In the Northern Ireland Health Promotion Agency survey only 2 per cent of parents said that they would withdraw their child from all sex education.[61] Instead, parents are more likely to be concerned at the inclusion of certain topics within the information provided. For instance 21 per cent of parents surveyed thought that homosexuality and lesbianism should not be taught in schools.[62] 13 per cent of parents felt similarly about abortion. In spite of these concerns, Departmental guidance states that reference to sensitive topics such as homosexuality and abortion should not be avoided since discussion of these matters is common in the media and elsewhere. The guidance is clear that "schools and colleges cannot ignore consideration of sexual practices which run counter to the moral standards of society in Northern Ireland".[63]

5.30   Parents do not have a specific statutory right to object to the provision of sex education generally or to any specific aspect of that education. Moreover, the Department's guidance does not address the issue directly except to say that "the counselling and advice available to individual pupils should complement and support the proper exercise of parental rights and responsibilities".[64] Article 44 of the 1986 Order may be of some relevance in this area since it requires the Department and ELBs to have regard to the general principle that pupils shall be educated in accordance with the wishes of their parents so far as this is compatible with the provision of efficient instruction and the avoidance of unreasonable expenditure. However, there is an argument that compliance with a parental request for withdrawal would be incompatible with the efficient education of the child in matters pertaining to

---

[56] *Ibid* para. 2.
[57] *Sex Education in Northern Ireland, Views from Parents and Schools* (1996) The Health Promotion Agency for Northern Ireland.
[58] *Ibid* p. 50.
[59] For instance, homosexuality was covered in only 56% of secondary schools (*Ibid* p. 53).
[60] Sex education appeared in a variety of subjects including science, religious education, personal and social development and health education. Only 12% of schools taught it as a subject in its own right. (*Ibid* p. 55).
[61] *Ibid* p. 35.
[62] *Ibid* p. 25.
[63] DENI Circular 1987/45, para. 8.
[64] *Ibid*, para. 10.

sexual development. Moreover, parents wishing to pursue an objection in the courts would not find much to assist them in the ECHR. In the case of *Kjeldsen, Busk Masden and Pedersen* the European Court of Human Rights found that the provision of compulsory sex education in Denmark did not contravene a parent's right to have their child educated in accordance with their own religious or philosophical beliefs under Article 2 of the First Protocol of the ECHR provided that the information was presented objectively, pluralistically and critically.[65]

Conflicts in relation to consent

5.31 In practice most schools in Northern Ireland will seek parental consent as a matter of course before giving a child sex education.[66] However, a request for consent can cause problems in two situations. The first is where the parents disagree between themselves about whether the child should have sex education. This might arise where the parents are estranged and disagree about the child's upbringing. In such instances one parent could seek a specific issue order under article 8 of the Children (NI) Order 1995. A court would have to decide what was in the child's best interests having regard to the welfare check list in article 3 of the 1995 Order. The second situation in which difficulties might arise is where the child wishes to receive sex education but the parents do not consent to them having it. In such instances, schools are faced with a conflict which may be difficult to reconcile. A child of sufficient understanding can apply for a specific issue order under article 8 of the Children (NI) Order 1995. Moreover, the 1995 Order specifies that, in any decision about the child, the child's best interests must be the paramount consideration. In determining this, the child has a right to have his or her views considered.[67]

5.32 It would be better for everyone if the law in Northern Ireland were to provide a clear statement of parental and children's rights in this area. In England and Wales schools are required to provide sex education but parents have an absolute right to withdraw their child from it. Although this leaves schools in no doubt as to their legal obligations, the legislation may be in conflict with the UNCRC which requires Member States to take the child's views into account in all matters pertaining to him or her.[68] The other way to achieve a high degree of certainty would be to make sex education compulsory for all by denying parents the right to withdraw their child. Some commentators have advocated this approach, arguing that a child has a fundamental right to accurate knowledge of the facts of sexual activity and that the issue is too important to be left in the hands of parents who may discharge the duty imperfectly or not at all.[69] A suggested compromise is that parents should only have a right to withdraw their child from sex education if this could be shown to be both in the best interests of the child and the public

---

[65] (1976) 1 EHRR 711. See paras. 1.53-1.56.
[66] In the 1996 survey 69% of schools gave parents the right to withdraw children from sex education classes.
[67] *Gillick* v *West Norfolk and Area Health Authority* [1986] 1 AC 112.
[68] Art. 12 of the UNCRC. See Chapter 1.
[69] Bainham, *Children Parents and the State* (1988) p. 186.

at large.[70] This latter formulation does shift the presumption towards the provision of education but it would undoubtedly be a difficult exercise to balance the various interests at stake in the face of stringent parental opposition.

Comparisons with Great Britain

5.33 The unregulated nature of sex education in Northern Ireland can be contrasted with the legal position in other parts of the United Kingdom. It has already been mentioned that in England and Wales sex education is compulsory in secondary schools although parents have an absolute right to withdraw their child from this type of instruction.[71] The substance of the education provided is also subject to statute. Schools are prohibited from covering anything other than the biological aspects of sex education in the ordinary part of the curriculum. Instead, sections 403-405 of the Education Act 1996 require governing bodies to secure that sex education is given in such a manner as to encourage pupils to "have due regard to moral considerations and the value of family life".[72] Moreover, section 2A of the Local Government Act 1986 prohibits local authorities from promoting the teaching in maintained schools of the acceptability of homosexuality as a "pretended family relationship".[73] The provision was introduced as a result of controversy surrounding the adoption of a book "*Jenny lives with Eric and Martin*" by the Inner London Education Authority. The provision was exceptionally controversial and the Labour Party gave a manifesto commitment to repeal it. A replacement provision which requires the Secretary of State to produce guidance on sex education which includes an objective that pupils "learn about the nature of marriage as the key building block of society and its importance for family life and for the bringing up of children" has had a turbulent passage in the House of Lords.[74] Northern Ireland does not have equivalent restrictions on the content of any sex education programme. The influence of the churches on the school system and the whole tenor of society in Northern Ireland is such that it is unlikely that a school or even an individual teacher would provide sex education which was anything other than suitably moral. It is almost inconceivable that schools would promote homosexuality or even sex outside marriage. It may be considered that there is no need for legislative intervention where practice uniformly reflects the position set out by statute in England and Wales.

IRISH LANGUAGE

5.34 The official language of Northern Ireland is English. However, Northern Ireland has a number of citizens who regard Irish as their first

---

[70] Furniss and Blair, 'Sex Wars: Conflict In, and Reform of, Sex Education in Maintained Secondary Schools' (1997) 19(2) *Journal of Social Welfare and Family Law*, 189, at p. 199.
[71] S. 2(1) of the Education Reform Act 1988 amended by s. 241 of the Education Act 1993
[72] For a discussion of the meaning of this provision see Poole, 'Sex Education, Morality and the Wednesbury Omnibus' [1988] *Local Government Review* 203
[73] See further, Macnair, 'Homosexuality in Schools - Section 28, Local Government Act 1988' (1989) (1) *Education and the Law* 35
[74] The Learning and Skills Bill, s. 403A.

language and English as their second.[75] Many of these people want their children to be taught in Irish and there are a number of Irish-speaking schools which facilitate this choice. Other parents, while happy for their children to be taught in English, want their children to learn Irish as a means of both preserving the language and their cultural identity. In practice, Northern Ireland's history is such that it is the Catholic population who particularly identify with the Irish language. As a result, most Catholic secondary schools in Northern Ireland offer pupils the opportunity to learn Irish. In view of this, the Irish language has a distinctive place in the Northern Ireland curriculum.[76] The provisions which relate to the Irish language vary depending on whether the language is being taught in a school which uses English as the medium for teaching or is an Irish medium school.

Irish in English medium schools

5.35 The Northern Ireland curriculum makes specific provision for the teaching of Irish in grant-aided schools. Irish language does not have to be taught at primary school level although it may be offered as an addition to the curriculum once the other statutory requirements have been complied with. Students at key stages 3 and 4 are required to undertake Language Studies. Irish may be taught as an alternative to French, German, Italian or Spanish to fulfil this requirement.[77] Under the original proposals Irish was not part of this list. It was inserted following the proposal's consultation period as a result of representations by the Catholic church and Irish language pressure groups. This means that pupils can study Irish instead of any other European language provided by their school. However, schools are under no obligation to offer Irish as one of the language choices. If they do offer Irish, they must offer an alternative European language as well. In contrast the National Curriculum applicable in Great Britain provides a much wider choice of modern European Languages including Dutch and Modern Greek (but not Irish in spite of the large emigrant population).[78] It also permits pupils to study one of a number of other non-European languages (including Japanese, Urdu, Hindi) provided at least one of the foundational European languages is offered by the school.

Irish in Irish medium schools

5.36 A school is considered to be an Irish-speaking school if religious education and more than one half of the compulsory contributory subjects

---

[75] In the 1991 Census, 79,012 people indicated that they could speak, read and write in Irish. A further 45,332 can speak Irish. (*Northern Ireland Census: Irish Language Report*), HMSO, 1990/1991, Table 1.) See generally, '*The UK Government's Approach to the Irish Language in Light of the European Charter for Regional or Minority Languages*' (Belfast: CAJ, 1992), 4 -7 and 26 - 31.

[76] No provision is made for Ulster-Scots. This might change in the light of the Belfast Agreement which promotes the "importance of respect, understanding and tolerance in relation to linguistic diversity, including in Northern Ireland ... Ulster-Scots."(p. 19)

[77] Education Reform (NI) Order 1989, Sch. 2, substituted by the Education (NI) Order 1996, Sch. 3.

[78] The government has recently announced an intention to include Irish in the list of European languages which can be taught in England and Wales.

(other than English and Irish) are taught wholly or partly in Irish.[79] The legal position in relation to the curriculum in Irish medium schools which are grant-aided is prescribed as part of the Northern Ireland curriculum. In Irish-speaking primary schools, Irish is compulsory at key stages 1 and 2 and is assessed accordingly.[80] Irish-speaking primary schools are excepted from the normal requirement to teach English in the first, second and third years of the first key stage.[81] English remains a compulsory subject in relation to pupils in the fourth year of the first key stage and in the whole of the second key stage. The legal position for primary schools appears to represent a balance which enables children to settle into the use of Irish in the early stages of their development but which does not completely deprive them of the opportunity to be taught the main language of the society in which they live. The position of Irish in Irish-speaking secondary schools has recently been consolidated in legislation. The Education Reform (Amendment) Order (NI) 1998 adds Irish in Irish-speaking schools to the Language Studies Area of Study at key stages 3 and 4. The programme to be followed is detailed in an Order which has been effective in Irish speaking schools from 1 August 1998.[82]

Right to Irish language education

5.37 Parents do not have a statutory right to have their child educated in the medium of the Irish language. Moreover, such a right cannot be derived from the international human rights documents to which the United Kingdom is a signatory. In *The Belgian Linguistics Case*, the European Court of Human Rights found that the ECHR did not give parents the right to choose the language in which their child would be educated.[83] The most specific international document in this area is the Council of Europe's Charter for Regional or Minority Languages. The United Kingdom agreed to sign this Charter as part of the Belfast Agreement, although it has not yet been ratified. Article 44 of the Education and Libraries (NI) Order 1986 requires the Department and ELBs to ensure that pupils are educated in accordance with the wishes of their parents provided that this is compatible with the provision of efficient instruction and the avoidance of unreasonable public expenditure. This means that parents can request that their child be educated in the medium of the Irish language but the government does not have to fund Irish medium schools unless it is satisfied that the education being provided is of satisfactory quality and that there are sufficient numbers attending the school to justify its long-term funding.[84]

---

[79] Art. 35(2) of the Education Reform (NI) Order 1989.
[80] Education Reform (NI) Order 1989, Sch. 2, substituted by the Education (NI) Order 1996, Sch. 3 and amended by the Education Reform (Amendment) (NI) Order 1998. Students who have studied Irish in an Irish-speaking school at key stages 1 and 2 must follow the programme of study set down in the Curriculum (Programme of Study and Attainment Targets in Irish in Irish-speaking Schools at Key stages 3 and 4) Order (NI) 1998.
[81] Education Reform (NI) Order 1989, Sch. 2, substituted by the Education (NI) Order 1996, Sch. 3. Curriculum (English in Irish-speaking Schools) (Exceptions) Regulations (NI) 1996.
[82] The Curriculum (Programme of Study and Attainment Targets in Irish in Irish-speaking Schools at Key stages 3 and 4) Order (NI) 1998. See DENI Circular 1998/13.
[83] (1968) 1EHRR 282.
[84] See further para. 2.47.

5.38 Education in the Irish language has received a boost as a result of the Belfast Agreement. The agreement states that the government will "where appropriate and where people so desire it" take resolute action to promote the Irish language.[85] More specifically in relation to education, the government agreed to place a statutory duty on the Department to encourage and facilitate the development of Irish medium education. This is contained in article 89 of the Education (NI) Order 1998. In a recent case, *In Re Martin's Application*, the High Court considered that article 89 did not override other obligations in the Education Order and in particular article 52 of the 1986 Order which relates to assistance with home to school transport.[86] The Department has also been given the power to pay grants to any body appearing to have as its objective the encouragement or promotion of Irish medium education. These obligations are similar to those currently in force in relation to integrated schools. Before the Assembly was suspended, Martin McGuinness announced that funding would be provided to Comhairle Na Gaelscholaiochta and that it would have a trust fund of half a million pounds each year for the next two years to promote Irish language education. In practice, whether or not there is an increase in the number of children being educated in Irish medium schools depends mainly on the viability criteria which the Department sets for new schools. However, the Minister for Education also gave the go-ahead for a review of these criteria. Thus the statutory duty has already had more than a symbolic significance for the development of Irish medium schools.

Comparison with Great Britain

5.39 The position of Irish-speaking schools is broadly similar to that of Welsh-speaking schools in Wales. Both have their respective languages recognised as core subjects.[87] However, the position of Irish-speaking schools goes one step further by removing the requirement to study English in the first three years. This was an exception which was sought by the Irish-speaking community who consider it important that children are taught exclusively in Irish in the early stages of their development, particularly given that pupils are living in an English-speaking environment. It might be assumed that a similar exception was not sought in Wales because there is already a high level of bi-lingualism which is not apparent in Northern Ireland. In contrast, the position of Welsh in English-speaking schools is completely different from that of Irish in Northern Ireland's schools. Welsh is taught in all schools in Wales.[88] This explicitly recognises the accepted cultural significance of the language to the whole community. In contrast, the study of Irish is generally optional in Northern Ireland schools. It is difficult to imagine it otherwise given that Protestants in Northern Ireland do not normally speak Irish. Most do not

---

[85] P. 19.
[86] Unreported decision of the High Court of Northern Ireland, 8 May 2000, see para. 10.08.
[87] Welsh is a core subject in Welsh-speaking schools and a foundational subject in other schools in Wales (Education Act 1996, s. 354(1) (b) and 2(d) respectively).
[88] Education Act 1996, s. 354(2)(d) and s. 354(5). However, the attainment targets and programmes of study do not apply in non-Welsh-speaking schools at key stage 4 (Education (National Curriculum) (Attainment Targets and Programmes of Study in Welsh) Order 1995 (SI 1995 No 69).

identify with it culturally and some regard it with hostility.[89] In this context, it is difficult to envisage a situation where Irish is given the recognition afforded to Welsh.

DISCRIMINATION IN THE CURRICULUM

5.40 Northern Ireland has legislation which deals with discrimination on the grounds of sex, race and disability respectively. The import of these in the field of education is considered separately below. In addition, there are a number of new provisions arising out of the Northern Ireland Act 1998 which deal with discrimination in a more general way (see paras 1.31-1.37). These may have some bearing on the Department and the ELBs when carrying out their functions in relation to the curriculum. Likewise, Article 14 of the ECHR when read with Article 2 of the First Protocol prohibits discrimination in access to education.[90] Although the state is given a large degree of leeway in determination of what is a suitable curriculum, it would undoubtedly be difficult for it to justify differential access to the nationally agreed curriculum based on one of the categories covered by Article 14.

Sex

5.41 Article 24 of the Sex Discrimination (NI) Order 1976 makes it unlawful for an ELB or Board of Governors to discriminate against a girl (or a boy) who is a pupil in the way it affords her access to any of the benefits, facilities or services, or by refusing or deliberately omitting to afford her access to them. This means that co-educational schools must offer pupils of both sexes equal access to all courses and facilities provided as part of the curriculum. Direct discrimination does not appear to be the key problem in this area. Research conducted by the Equal Opportunities Commission in Northern Ireland has highlighted the hidden gender differences in the curriculum.[91] Much of this stems from the high level of single sex education in Northern Ireland rather than discrimination within individual institutions. The common requirements of the Northern Ireland curriculum should in theory redress any imbalance by ensuring that girls' schools devote as much time to sport and science as boys' schools. However, it would appear that differences remain both in the way resources are deployed in schools and in the attitudes of pupils and their parents. For instance recent research indicates that girls in single sex schools are less likely to study science at A level than boys or girls in co-educational schools.[92] On the other hand, research also indicates that there is now no clear pattern of difference in levels of attainment between boys and girls at GCSE and A level.[93]

---

[89] See Crozier (ed), *Cultural Traditions in Northern Ireland* (1989, QUB, Institute of Irish Studies) report of Education Group, p. 64.
[90] See para. 1.58.
[91] *Common Curriculum - Equal Curriculum?* (EOCNI, 1992).
[92] *Girls and A Level Science 1985.1995* (EOCNI, 1996)
[93] *Girls, Boys and Exam Results, a Northern Ireland Perspective* (EOCNI, 1996)

Race

5.42 Northern Ireland has had legislation prohibiting discrimination on the grounds of race since 1997. Article 20 of the Race Relations (NI) Order 1997 places a general obligation on educational bodies to secure that educational facilities are provided without racial discrimination and article 19 makes it unlawful for ELBs or the CCMS to do any act which constitutes racial discrimination while performing their functions under the Education Orders. More specifically, article 18 makes it unlawful for educational establishments to discriminate against pupils in the way in which it affords them access to benefits, facilities or services, or by refusing or deliberately omitting to afford them access to them. There are no reported decisions on the issue of race discrimination in the curriculum. However, an issue might arise if, for instance, a school were to prohibit a pupil from taking part in sporting activities because he or she refused to wear the normal sports kit for some reason connected with their race.[94] It could also occur if a school used a textbook which included pejorative racial stereotypes. This might arise in Northern Ireland in relation to members of the Irish Travelling community who are specifically protected by the legislation.[95]

Disability

5.43 The Disability Discrimination Act 1995 extends to Northern Ireland. However, the education provisions do not.[96] Those advocating the rights of disabled people were disappointed that education was not made integral to the anti-discrimination legislation. However the government chose to deal with the issue within the education statutes. Thus, in Northern Ireland, the legal provisions in relation to access to the curriculum for children with disabilities derive mainly from the provisions of the 1996 Order which deal with children with special educational needs.

5.44 The legal provisions for children with special educational needs are considered in detail in Chapter 8. However, two provisions are particularly relevant in relation to access to the curriculum. Article 8 of the 1996 Order requires the Board of Governors of a mainstream school to ensure that these children (whether statemented or not) engage in the activities of the school together with children who do not have special education needs so far as this is reasonably practicable and compatible with the child receiving the education that they need, the efficient education of the other children and the efficient use of resources. In addition schools are required to ensure that the child receives the full curriculum except in so far as a statement says otherwise or where there is a temporary exception.[97] It is possible that a pupil who is denied access to a part of the curriculum on the basis of a disability may have grounds for complaint that there has been a breach of Article 14 of

---

[94] See *Mandla v Lee (Dowell)* [1983] 1 All ER 1062.
[95] Art. 5(3) of the Race Relations (NI) Order 1997.
[96] S. 29 places a duty on Boards of Governors to include information about access in its annual report. This duty does not, however, apply in Northern Ireland.
[97] See paras. 5.21-5.25.

the ECHR, combined with Article 2 of the First Protocol (the right not to be denied education).[98]

POLITICAL/CULTURAL ISSUES

5.45 In England and Wales, principals, Boards of Governors and LEAs are obliged to prohibit the pursuit of partisan political activities by any registered junior pupils and to prohibit the promotion of partisan views in the teaching of any subject in the school. Schools are also required to take reasonably practicable steps to secure balanced treatment of political issues where they arise in school or extra-curricular activity.[99] This provision was introduced in 1986 by the Conservatives who alleged that Labour-controlled LEAs were pursuing political agendas in their schools.[100] These concerns did not extend to Northern Ireland and there is no equivalent restriction in this jurisdiction. Nevertheless, if a teacher were to take a party political line in class, parents might complain that their child was not receiving a "balanced" curriculum as is required by article 4 of the 1989 Order.[101] That said, there may well be occasions when certain activities endorsed by the state curriculum raise political or cultural issues on which parents have strongly held views. One obvious area where this might arise is in cross-community contact schemes under Education for Mutual Understanding. A staunchly loyalist parent may not want their child to engage in Irish dancing and a staunchly nationalist parent may not want their child to learn about the cultural heritage of the Orange Order. Article 44 of the 1986 Order requires the Department and ELBs to ensure that education is in accordance with parental wishes in so far as this is compatible with efficient education and the efficient use of resources. Moreover, a further legal basis for objection may arise under Article 2 of the First Protocol of the ECHR, that is that education should be in accordance with a parent's religious or philosophical convictions.[102] In such cases, a court way consider that the child's overriding right to a suitable education outweighs the parent's objections.[103] Nevertheless, schools would be advised to handle these issues with sensitivity, informing parents in advance of any activity to which objections might be anticipated.

RELIGIOUS EDUCATION IN THE CURRICULUM

5.46 There are a number of different approaches which a state can adopt when it comes to the issue of religious education in state schools. Some countries adopt a wholly secular approach to state education.[104] The United States is one such country. This strict separation of church and state has its

---

[98] See further para. 1.58.
[99] Education Act 1996, ss. 406-407.
[100] Particular concern was voiced about "peace studies". S. 44 of the Education (No. 2) Act 1986.
[101] This could be the subject of a complaint to the Curriculum Appeal Tribunal. See paras. 5.87-5.94.
[102] See paras. 1.53-1.57.
[103] See for instance, *Kjelsden, Busk Masden and Pedersen* v *Denmark* (1976) 1 EHRR 711.
[104] This is the position in France. This has given rise to difficulties in relation to Muslim pupils wearing the chador. See, Bell, 'Religious Observance in Secular Schools: a French Solution' (1990) 2 (3) *Education and the Law* 121.

roots in the first amendment to the United States constitution which forbids government from enacting laws "respecting an establishment of religion, or prohibiting the free exercise thereof".[105] However, the ban on religion in schools is not uncontentious. There have been a series of high profile cases in which the US Supreme Court has had to balance its citizens right to freedom of religion with the prohibition on the establishment of religion in the context of state education.[106] The United Kingdom takes the opposite approach, by first requiring all publicly funded schools to provide religious instruction and secondly by stipulating that the religious instruction provided must be of a Christian character. In England and Wales the religious education requirements stem from the Education Act 1944 when, in the midst of major re-organisation, many religious schools transferred control to the state but argued successfully for the maintenance of religious education.[107] For once, Northern Ireland's legislation had come in advance of that of its neighbouring jurisdiction. Similar requirements had come into force in Northern Ireland 14 years previously albeit for different reasons.

5.47 Northern Ireland's schools have not always been under an obligation to provide religious instruction. In fact, the Education Act (NI) 1923 prohibited the teaching of religion in state run schools (i.e. provided and transferred schools) during school hours.[108] The intention underlying this was to keep the state system secular. The difficulty was that voluntary schools (the majority of which were Catholic in ethos) were able to provide denominational religion if they wished. This differentiation was a source of disquiet to the Protestant churches in Northern Ireland when it became apparent that it was predominantly Protestant children who were attending state schools.[109] The Education Act (NI) 1930 addressed this by allowing state schools to provide Bible instruction provided that not less than 10 per cent of the parents requested it. Religious education became the norm in the state controlled sector with the result that the Education and Libraries (NI) Order 1972 required all schools to provide collective worship and religious education but restricted controlled schools to non-denominational Christian instruction. This continues to be the model for the teaching of religion in grant-aided schools today. Current legislation requires grant-aided schools to do two things: (i) have a daily period of collective worship and (ii) provide religious education to pupils.

Collective worship

5.48 Each grant-aided school must gave a daily period of collective worship in an assembly or assemblies.[110] Voluntary schools are not under any restriction as to the nature of the collective worship. However, in controlled schools, the worship must not be distinctive of any particular religious

---

[105] See Choper, 'The Religion Clauses of the First Amendment: Reconciling the Conflict' (1980) Vol.41, *University of Pittsburg Law Review* 673.
[106] See further, Smith, 'Relations between Church and State in The United States, with Special Attention to the Schooling of Children' (1987) 35 *American Journal of Comparative Law* 1.
[107] See, Hamilton, *Family, Law and Religion* pp. 241-247.
[108] Ss. 26-28.
[109] See Atkenson, *Education and Enmity*, Chapter 4 'The Protestant Church Attack' 1923-25.
[110] Art. 21(1) of the 1986 Order.

denomination.[111] The legislation in Northern Ireland does not specify that the worship must be Christian although such a requirement might be inferred from the general context of article 21 of the 1986 Order and in particular the preceding references to religious education. In contrast, the equivalent legislation in Great Britain requires that the collective worship be "wholly or mainly of a broadly Christian character".[112] It would appear that this does allow some non-Christian elements in the collective worship.[113] Nevertheless, the provision has also been controversial in some English schools where a high proportion of the pupils are of other faiths and object to the emphasis on Christianity.[114]

Religious education

5.49 The curriculum of all grant-aided schools (other than nursery schools) must include provision for the religious education for all registered pupils.[115] The Board of Governors and principal of the school are under an obligation to secure that this is complied with.[116] Article 25 of the 1996 Order extends this obligation to special schools. Schools are required to follow the core syllabus for religion which was prepared by the main church bodies in Northern Ireland.[117] This is of a Christian nature but is not distinctive of any particular denomination. Schools are not tied exclusively to this but can include additional matters, skills or processes in that teaching. However, in a controlled school (other than a controlled integrated school) the religious education provided must always be non-denominational.[118] It must be based on the "Holy Scriptures according to some authoritative version or versions thereof" but must not include instruction "as to any tenet distinctive of any particular religious denomination".[119] An exception is made for controlled integrated schools who may provide denominational religious instruction for their pupils. Similarly, voluntary schools are free to provide religious instruction which reflects the beliefs of a particular religious denomination. Ministers of religion and others may be granted reasonable access at convenient times to give religious education whether distinctive of a particular denomination or not provided that the parents do not object.[120]

Parental rights

5.50 Parents may request that their child be wholly or partly excused from attendance at religious instruction or collective worship or both.[121] This request must be complied with and the parent is not required to provide

---

[111] *Ibid* art. 21(2).
[112] Education Reform Act 1988, s. 7(1).
[113] *R v Secretary of State for Education, ex parte R and D* [1994] ELR 495.
[114] See Hamilton and Watt, 'A Discriminating Education - Collective Worship in Schools' (1996) 8/1 *Child and Family Law Quarterly* 28-40.
[115] Art. 5(1) of the 1989 Order.
[116] *Ibid* art. 11(1)(a).
[117] Art. 13 of the 1989 Order.
[118] Art. 21(2) of the 1986 Order.
[119] *Ibid*. This provision can be traced directly back to the Education Act (NI) 1930, s. 4(5).
[120] Art. 21(7) of the 1986 Order.
[121] *Ibid* art. 21(5).

reasons. Although the legal position seems clear, problems might arise in a number of instances. First, although it may be a relatively straightforward matter for a child to be withdrawn from time-tabled religious education classes, issues impinging on religion can arise spontaneously in other classes such as English, history or science. It would be difficult to anticipate these and impractical to make alternative arrangements for a child each time. However, a literal and indeed pragmatic interpretation of the legislation would favour schools by implying that the parental right of withdrawal relates to classes devoted exclusively to religion. The second circumstance in which disputes might arise is where the child's parents disagree as to whether the child should receive religious instruction. The legislation gives schools no direction on this issue with the result that it may have to be resolved by the parents in court. In an English case, *Re T and M*, the boys concerned attended a Church of England school.[122] The children's mother who had converted to Islam exercised her right of withdrawal. The child's father (with whom they lived) applied for a prohibited steps order to prevent the mother removing the child from religious education. The court applying the welfare principles concluded that removing the children from religious education would be disruptive for them. The judge did, however, stress that he was not judging between Christianity and Islam and that the mother could provide the children with Islamic instruction if she wished.

5.51   Children who have been withdrawn by their parents from religious instruction are given further protection under the 1986 Order. Article 21(4) provides that religious instruction must be arranged in such a way that the school is open to children of all religious denominations and that no pupil is excluded from any other advantages that the school offers.[123] This provision was considered to be significant in the case of *In re Cecil*.[124] The applicant who lived on Rathlin Island did not want his children to attend the only state funded school on the island which was a Catholic maintained school. He argued that his children would inevitably be exposed to the Catholic ethos if they attended the school even if they were to be withdrawn from religion classes. However, the court considered that the effect of article 21(4) of the 1986 Order was to ensure that his children would not be prejudiced if attending the school. This is in spite of the fact that the Catholic Church considers that religion is an integral part of the life of a Catholic school and is not confined to religion classes.[125]

Children's rights

5.52   In domestic legislation the right to determine whether a child should receive religious education is vested in the child's parents. Problems may arise where the child and parent hold different views on the issue, for example the child does not wish to attend and the parent will not withdraw them or *vice versa*. As the legislation stands, if the parent and child hold conflicting views on the matter, the parent's views prevail. Thus a parent can both insist on a

---

[122] [1995] ELR 1.
[123] Art. 21(4).
[124] Unreported decision of the High Court of Northern Ireland, 27 January 1989.
[125] See further *In re Daly* unreported judgment of the High Court of Northern Ireland, 5 October 1990.

child receiving religious education and can withdraw them from such classes as he or she wishes.

5.53 The parents' absolute right of withdrawal would appear to be in conflict with the UNCRC which requires its signatories to take account of the views of the child in all matters affecting them.[126] However, while Article 14 of the UNCRC respects the child's freedom of thought, conscience and religion, it also enshrines the parents' right "to provide direction to the child in the exercise of his or her right in a manner consistent with the evolving capacities of the child". Likewise, Article 2 of the First Protocol of the ECHR specifically enshrines the right of parents to have their child educated in accordance with their religious and philosophical convictions.[127] The child may have a separate and individual right to freedom of conscience under Article 9 of the ECHR but, as yet, the potential conflict between the two Articles has not been resolved by the European Court of Human Rights.

Teachers' rights

5.54 Teachers in controlled schools may be required by the ELB to conduct or attend collective worship and to provide non-denominational religious instruction.[128] A teacher can ask the Board of Governors to be wholly or partly excused from this on the grounds of conscience.[129] This exemption can be traced to the 1930 legislation which first allowed religious instruction in what are now controlled schools.[130] If a teacher wishes to rely on the exemption, he or she must make a statutory declaration to this effect. This declaration will be sent to the ELB. The individual concerned must be excused and whilst he or she is excused he or she must not suffer any detriment in terms of emoluments, promotion or any other advantage because of his or her failure to participate in the collective worship or religious instruction in the school. Schools which do not have sufficient teachers to conduct collective worship or to provide religious instruction can ask the ELB to advertise for and appoint a teacher to carry out these duties.[131] However, the statute does not provide any protection for teachers in controlled schools who are not appointed because of their stated unwillingness to participate in activities of a religious nature.[132] Moreover, there is no legislative provision in relation to teachers in voluntary schools who may therefore be asked to provide religious instruction and do not have a statutory right to object on the grounds of conscience.

Comparison with England and Wales

5.55 The provisions on religious education in Northern Ireland are very similar to those in England and Wales in that all schools are required to

---

[126] Art. 12.
[127] See paras. 1.53 to 1.57.
[128] Art. 22(1) of the 1986 Order.
[129] *Ibid* art. 22(2).
[130] Education Act 1930, s. 4(3).
[131] Art. 22(4) of the 1986 Order.
[132] This protection was contained in s.5 of the Education Act 1930.

provide religious education and daily collective worship.[133] However, Northern Ireland does not have any bodies equivalent to the Standing Advisory Councils on Religious Education (SACREs). Each LEA must have a SACRE whose membership includes representatives of the Church of England as well as the other principal religious traditions in the area. The SACREs agree the core syllabus for their area and consider applications from schools which want exemption from the requirements in relation to Christian worship. In Northern Ireland, the core curriculum for religious education was agreed by the four main churches. Moreover, because of the relatively small number of non-Christian residents, there is no provision for schools to be granted exception from the collective worship provisions. However, the major difference between the two jurisdictions lies not so much in the content of the legislation as in the response to the equivalent provision. In England and Wales the religious education provisions have proved controversial. Particular criticisms have surrounded the emphasis on Christianity when many schools have a majority of pupils who are non-Christians.[134] In contrast, in Northern Ireland, schools and parents are generally supportive of the importance of an integral Christian education. This can be explained to some extent by the fact that Northern Ireland is not an ethnically diverse society.[135] However, it is also a further indication of the status of the churches in Northern Ireland society. Northern Ireland has an extremely large number of people affiliated to the main Christian traditions and it is unsurprising that the community is generally supportive of integral religious education.[136]

CHARGING FOR THE CURRICULUM

5.56 Article 28 of the UNCRC requires State Parties to provide children with free education. Education cannot be regarded as free if parents are required to pay for essential aspects of that education. In practice, a line is drawn between activities which form a necessary part of the child's education and other 'optional' activities which although desirable, the state is not under an obligation to finance. Thus, as part of their general management functions, Boards of Governors in Northern Ireland are entitled to charge pupils for certain items or services. There are, however, restrictions as to the activities for which they can charge. These are contained in articles 128-137 of the 1989 Order. These provisions are possibly the most technical in the Education Orders. However, DENI Circular 1991/21 provides useful guidance to schools on the implementation of these rules. The major principle underlying the rules is that activities organised wholly or mainly during normal teaching time should be made available to pupils regardless of the parents' ability or willingness to meet the cost. An important distinction is drawn between

---

[133] The provisions for England and Wales are contained in Chapter III of Part IV of the Education Act 1996.

[134] See, C. Hamilton and B. Watt, 'A Discriminating Education - Collective Worship in Schools', *Child and Family Law Quarterly* 8/1 (1996), 28-40.

[135] In the 1991 census the Northern Ireland population was 1, 577, 836. The largest non-Christian religious tradition was Mohammedan with 972 believers. There were 742 people who registered as Hindu and 255 as Buddhists (*Northern Ireland Census 1991: Religion Report* (Belfast, HMSO: 1991) p. xvi.

[136] *Ibid*. In the 1991 Census, 81.3% of the population of Northern Ireland registered themselves as Roman Catholic, Presbyterian, Church of Ireland or Methodist.

grammar schools which do not receive capital funding from the state and all other grant-aided schools. The former have considerably more discretion in determining the charges which can be levied on parents for education and other services provided for their children.

Charging and remission policies

5.57 ELBs and Boards of Governors are required to have an agreed policy on the charges which they propose to make on parents.[137] The ELB policy must specify the circumstances in which it proposes to charge for services and the circumstances in which it proposes to remit charges. The ELB policy will cover services provided by the ELB. The ELB can require Boards of Governors to remit these charges to the ELB. This means that the policies of individual schools are determined initially by the charging policy of the ELB in whose area it is situated. The school's policy is the responsibility of the Board of Governors. It must specify three things: (i) the circumstances in which it proposes to make charges; (ii) the circumstances in which it proposes to remit any charges; and (iii) the circumstances in which the Board of Governors proposes to meet any charge which is payable to the ELB in accordance with the ELB's policy on optional extras.[138] ELBs and Boards of Governors are prohibited from making any charge which is not specified in the charging policy.[139]

Grant-aided schools (other than category B voluntary grammar schools)

5.58 The rules contained in articles 128 to 131 of the 1989 Order apply to all grant-aided schools other than voluntary grammar schools which have not entered into a capital funding agreement with the Department. This means that the following rules apply to all primary and secondary schools along with controlled grammar schools and voluntary grammar schools which have entered into a funding agreement with the Department. However, in addition to these rules, the rules on charges in all grammar schools are slightly different and are considered separately at paragraphs 5.71-5.74.

5.59 Article 128 of the 1989 Order specifies the aspects of the curriculum for which these categories of grant-aided schools are not permitted to charge its pupils. The legislation does not, however, provide a specified list of "optional extras" for which schools are allowed to charge. The power to charge is defined negatively. Article 130 of the 1989 Order permits schools to make charges in respect of the educational provision or transport which is not expressly prohibited by article 128. The rules are considered in their individual categories as outlined below.

---

[137] Voluntary grammar schools which have not entered into an agreement with the Department are not required to produce a policy on charges under art. 131 of the 1989 Order.
[138] *Ibid.*
[139] *Ibid.* art. 131(2).

Admission to the school

5.60 Schools covered by articles 128-131 of the 1989 Order may not charge pupils any fee for admission.[140] The only schools which can charge for admission are voluntary schools which have not entered into an agreement with the Department. In addition, all grammar schools may charge pupils falling into exceptional categories (usually students from abroad) an admission charge.[141]

Education and tuition

5.61 Schools covered by articles 128-31 of the 1989 Order may not charge pupils for education provided during school hours other than individual music tuition in playing any musical instrument.[142] Each school must specify its school hours in its prospectus. This does not include the break in the middle of the day for lunch. There are also special rules in relation to education provided partly during and partly outside school hours. Article 129 of the 1989 Order draws a distinction between educational activities where 50 per cent or more of the time falls during school hours and educational activities where more than 50 per cent of the time is outside school hours. For these purposes, time spent travelling to or from the place where the activity takes place is counted as being during school hours if it is spent on travel during school hours. If 50 per cent or more of the time occupied on the activity together with any connected travelling time takes place during school hours, then the activity is treated as being provided wholly during school hours and no charge can be made on parents. In all other cases it is treated as being provided outside of school hours.

5.62 Schools can charge for any education which is provided outside school hours provided that it is not being given to meet the school's obligations in relation to article 11(1)(a) and (b) of the 1989 Order; the duty to provide religious education and the contributory subjects of the Northern Ireland curriculum. The only charge which schools can make for education which is given wholly or mainly in school hours is in relation to individual tuition in playing a musical instrument. Even in this situation, if the tuition is provided to prepare the pupil for an approved public examination then no charge can be made.[143] According to Departmental guidance, this is only likely to arise in relation to tuition for A level music.[144] It should be noted that the exception only applies to individual tuition in music and does not extend to individual tuition in singing.

Examinations

5.63 The Department specifies a list of approved public examinations. Schools may not provide education for examinations which are not on the approved list. Schools to which this paragraph applies may not charge pupils for any entry fees or education required as part of a syllabus for an approved

---

[140] Art. 128(1) of the 1989 Order.
[141] See para. 5.74.
[142] Art. 128(2) of the 1989 Order.
[143] *Ibid* art. 128(2).
[144] Circular 1991/21, para. 31.

public examination for which the pupil is being prepared at the school.[145] Pupils are regarded as having been prepared by the school if any part of the education was provided at the school with a view to preparing him or her for the examination.[146] Schools may charge a pupil the entry fee for an approved public examination if they have not prepared the pupil for that examination. Departmental guidance suggests that schools can charge pupils for entry in an examination where the pupil is re-sitting an examination but has received no additional preparation since the previous examination entry.[147] Although schools are not allowed to prepare pupils for non-approved public examinations they may enter the pupil in such an examination and make a charge for the entry fee.

Education provided in accordance with the requirements of statute

5.64 Schools may not charge pupils for education provided in pursuance of the duty imposed by article 11(1)(a) or (b) of the 1989 Order.[148] This refers to the duty to provide religious education and to each of the contributory subjects which form part of the Northern Ireland curriculum. This prohibition on charging is separate from the rules on charging for education outside school hours. Therefore, if schools provide education outside of school hours in order to fulfil their statutory obligations, they may not charge for that education.

Materials, books, instruments or equipment

5.65 Schools may not charge for materials, books, instruments or equipment for use in connection with education at the school for which no charge can be made or for approved pupil examinations for which the pupil has been prepared at the school.[149] Departmental guidance suggests that this does not prevent a school from inviting parents to provide children with certain items of equipment such as pens and pencils and sports equipment.[150] However, these must be considered to be voluntary contributions and if parents are unwilling or unable to provide necessary equipment, the school must provide it and not charge the parents for it. Schools can, however, charge for material if the parent indicates in advance that he or she wishes to keep the finished product.[151] This might be the case in an art or design class or in Home Economics where there is a finished product to eat or wear. Schools can also ask parents to make voluntary contributions to the cost of the expenses in which case the rules described in paragraph 5.76 must be observed.

Transport

5.66 Schools may not charge for transport which is incidental to the education being provided or is provided to enable the student to meet any examination requirement for any syllabus of an approved public examination

---

[145] Art. 128(4)(a) of the 1989 Order.
[146] *Ibid* art. 128(11).
[147] Circular 1991/21, para. 34.
[148] Art. 128(4)(b) of the 1989 Order.
[149] *Ibid* Art. 128(6).
[150] Circular 1991/21, para. 20.
[151] Art. 173(3) of the 1989 Order.

for which he is prepared at the school.[152] Transport is considered to be incidental to the education being provided if it is provided for the purpose of carrying pupils to or from any part of the school premises. This would occur where a school has buildings or sports facilities on more than one site. Transport is also considered to be incidental to the education if the purpose is to carry pupils to any place outside the school premises in which education is provided in accordance with an arrangement made by the school or ELB. This would occur where pupils are taken to another school for part of their instruction or to a public sports facility.[153]

5.67 Schools may charge for transport which is not provided during school hours, is not connected to the statutory education requirements and is not provided to enable the pupil to meet an examination requirement. This could cover the costs of transport to sports matches outside school hours. The rules on charging for transport in connection with education are entirely separate from the provisions requiring ELBs to make provision for home to school transport under article 52 of the 1986 Order and considered in Chapter 10.

Residential trips[154]

5.68 Residential trips are defined by article 128(10) of the 1989 Order to mean trips which are arranged by or on behalf of the Board of Governors of a school and which require pupils to spend one or more nights away from their usual overnight accommodation. Residential trips can be a source of contention between schools and parents because of the relatively high levels of expenditure involved. As a result of this, there are very detailed restrictions on the circumstances in which a school can charge for costs incurred on such trips. Once again the legislation draws a distinction between education during school hours and education outside of school hours. The thrust of the rules is that schools may charge for residential trips when the time occupied on such trips amounts to more than 50 per cent of the time which would otherwise have fallen during normal school hours. If the time spent on the trip occupies 50 per cent or more of normal school hours, then it is deemed to fall within school hours and no charge can be made.[155] There are however, detailed provisions for determining which school sessions are taken up by the trip. A school trip is treated as occupying a school session if the time spent on the trip occupies 50 per cent or more of the time allowed for that session at the school.[156] If the number of sessions taken up by the trip is equal to or greater than 50 per cent of the number of half days spent on the trip, the education is treated as being provided in school hours.[157] In all other cases, it is deemed to fall outside school hours (in which case charges can be made). A half day is defined to mean any period of 12 hours ending with noon or midnight on any

---

[152] *Ibid* art. 128(7).
[153] *Ibid* art. 128(8).
[154] *Ibid* arts. 128(9), 129(3)-(6) and 131(3).
[155] *Ibid* art. 129(3).
[156] *Ibid* art. 129(6).
[157] *Ibid* art. 129(3).

day.[158] However, where 50 per cent or more of a half day is spent on a residential trip, the whole of the half day is treated as being spent on the trip.[159]

5.69 The provisions on educational trips are convoluted and exceptionally difficult to follow. Departmental guidance provides useful illustrations to assist schools in determining when they can charge for educational trips.[160] For example, a term time trip from noon on Wednesday to 9pm on Sunday would take up nine half-days, five of which would be school sessions. Five ninths is more than 50 per cent so the trip would be treated as education during school hours and no charge could be made. However a trip from noon on Thursday to 9 pm on Sunday would take up seven half-days or three school sessions. Three sevenths is less than 50 per cent so the trip would be treated as education outside school hours and a charge could be made.

5.70 One final point about residential trips is that the Board of Governors must remit all charges to the parents who are in receipt of income support, family credit and income-related jobseeker's allowance if the education provided on the trip is education for which no charge can be made under article 128 of the 1989 Order. This applies to trips where the educational activities organised are of the kind which must be provided free of charge. This would be the case where the trip is organised as part of one of the contributory subjects under the Northern Ireland curriculum.

Grammar schools

5.71 The legislation draws a distinction between grammar schools which have entered into a capital funding agreement with the Department under Schedule 6 to the 1986 Order (Category A schools) and those which have not (Category B schools). There are now only two Category B schools in Northern Ireland: Campbell College and Royal Belfast Academical Institution. These have considerably more discretion to charge pupils than any other grant-aided schools since they receive less state funding.

Category A

5.72 The rules in articles 128 to 131 of the 1989 Order which apply to all other grant-aided schools apply to Category A schools. In addition, these schools may in certain circumstances make a charge for the cost of meeting the expenditure incurred in providing or altering school premises or in providing equipment in connection with these purposes.[161] Schools which receive 85 per cent funding of capital costs may charge pupils but this is subject to a statutory limit which is currently £80.[162] Schools which receive 100 per cent funding of capital costs cannot charge pupils a capital fee without the permission of the Department.

---

[158] *Ibid* art. 129(4).
[159] *Ibid* art. 129(5).
[160] Circular 1991/21, para. 16 and subsequent tables.
[161] Art. 132 of the 1989 Order.
[162] Grammar Schools (Charges) Regulations (NI) 1992 as amended by the Grammar Schools (Charges)(Amendment) Regulations (NI) 1995.

Category B

5.73 The provisions of articles 128 to 131 do not apply to Category B schools. Boards of Governors may not make a charge in respect of the entry of a registered pupil for any approved public examination for which the pupil has been prepared at the school. Apart from this, the Board of Governors may make charges of such amounts as it may determine in respect of any registered pupil for the purpose of meeting expenditure required to carry on the school.[163] Such charges are however restricted by regulations. Category B schools may not charge pupils for the purposes of meeting any expenditure which is met or likely to be met under a grant under article 60 of the 1989 Order (which covers non-capital running expenses).[164] Moreover, the amount of any charge shall not be more than the amount of any corresponding charge made for an excepted pupil (see below).[165]

Excepted pupils in grammar schools

5.74 The statutory restrictions on charging do not apply to certain pupils attending grammar schools.[166] These are: pupils who are not resident in Northern Ireland; pupils whose parents are not nationals of an EU Member State;[167] pupils in the preparatory department; and fee-paying pupils who were admitted to the grammar school before the rules on charging came into effect (April 2 1992) (unless the ELB for the area directs that the pupil is no longer to be treated as an excepted pupil). In each of these cases the restrictions on charging are covered in regulations.[168]

Boarding schools

5.75 Parents must normally pay for board and lodging provided by the Board of Governors of all grant-aided schools.[169] An ELB will, however, meet such costs if it considers that the pupil requires board and lodging in view of his or her age, ability, aptitude and any special educational needs which he or she may have. Moreover, in other cases, if the ELB is satisfied that the payment of the full charges would cause hardship to the parent of any pupil, the ELB must remit such part of the charges as the ELB considers necessary to avoid that hardship. The ELB must remit all of the charges if that is the only way in which hardship is to be avoided.

Voluntary contributions

5.76 Schools are not prohibited from asking for voluntary contributions for the benefit of the school or any school activities.[170] However, such requests or invitations to contribute must make it clear that there is no obligation to make

---

[163] Art. 133 of the 1989 Order.
[164] Reg. 4 of the Grammar Schools (Charges) Regulations (NI) 1992.
[165] *Ibid* reg. 4(4).
[166] Art. 127 of the 1989 Order.
[167] Art. 127(6) defines this to mean the same as in the Community treaties but does not include those from the Channel Islands and Isle of Man.
[168] Reg. 5 of the Grammar Schools (Charges) Regulations (NI) 1992.
[169] Art. 135 of the 1989 Order.
[170] *Ibid* art. 137(1).

any contribution and that pupils will not be treated differently according to whether or not their parents made any contribution.[171] Most schools will have children from a variety of backgrounds and must be sensitive to the fact that some parents may not be in a position to assist. Departmental guidance states that the amount requested may be calculated to cover all or part of the cost and may, if desired, include the cost of subsidising pupils from low income families or the cost of travel for accompanying teachers.[172] There is, however, no limit on the amount of the voluntary contribution. Nor is there any restriction on the purpose for which such contributions might be sought subject only to the expenditure being reasonably required for the purposes of the school.

PROVISION OF INFORMATION ON INDIVIDUAL PUPIL'S ACHIEVEMENT

5.77 One of the cornerstone principles of the 1989 reforms was that parents should be permitted to have greater involvement in their child's education. The legislation gave parents statutory rights to be informed about their child's educational progress. Article 31(2)(iii) of the 1989 Order gave the Department the power to issue regulations prescribing the information which must be given about the educational achievements of pupils. The current rules are contained in the Education (Individual Pupil's Achievements) (Information) Regulations (NI) 1998. These apply to all pupils in grant-aided schools apart from children who have not yet reached compulsory school age.[173] Principals are under a statutory duty to provide information about the educational achievements of all pupils who have attained compulsory school age. The information falls into the following three categories.

(i) Annual school reports

5.78 These must be provided at the end of each school year which is not the final year in a key stage or a year in which the pupil is in sixth form.[174] The report must include brief particulars of the pupil's achievements in any subject or activity which forms part of the curriculum. If it includes reference to attainment, the report must specify that this has not been assessed in accordance with the statutory arrangements. The annual report must also include the results of any public examination for which the pupil has been prepared for by the school that year.[175] The information must be supplied by post not later than 30 June each year.[176] Examination results which come out after that date must be supplied as soon as is reasonably practicable.[177]

---

[171] *Ibid* art. 137(2).
[172] Circular 1991/21, para. 63.
[173] Education (Individual Pupil's Achievements) (Information) Regulations (NI) 1998, reg. 5(2).
[174] *Ibid* reg. (7)(1)(d).
[175] *Ibid* reg. 7(2).
[176] *Ibid* reg. 8(1). This provision does not apply to a pupil in the final year of the second key stage.
[177] *Ibid* reg. 8(2).

(ii) Reports at end of each key stage and in sixth form

5.79 Principals must provide information on the performance of each pupil at the end of each key stage and each year of sixth form. The precise information to be provided varies at each stage.[178] For pupils in the final year of key stages 1 or 3, this includes: the summary results of any assessment of the pupil in that year; comparative information about the performance of other pupils in the same school; results of examinations; exemptions from the statutory requirements; and particulars of achievements in any other subject or activity which forms part of the curriculum. If the pupil is in the final year of key stage 2, the information consists of the results of any assessment of the pupil in that year and in each attainment target of each such subject; comparative information about the performance of other pupils in the same school; the results of examinations; and particulars of achievements in any other subject or activity which forms part of the curriculum. If the pupil is in the final year of key stage 4 or is in the sixth form, the information consists of details of the pupil's performance in public examinations and brief particulars of his achievements in any other subject or activity which forms part of the curriculum. The information must be supplied by post not later than 30 June each year.[179] Examination results which come out after that date must be supplied as soon as is reasonably practicable.[180] In addition, parents may at any stage request that the principal provide them with information on their child's level of attainment in each target of the compulsory contributory subject for which the child has been assessed.[181] The principal must supply this information within 15 school days.[182]

(iii) Records of achievement

5.80 Principals must provide a summative record of achievement at each of the significant transitory stages of a pupil's education: the final year of the second key stage; the final year of the fourth key stage; and in the case of those who stay on in sixth form, the year in which they cease to be a pupil".[183] Thus, all pupils receive at least two records of achievement: one on leaving primary school and the other at the age of 16. Those who stay on at school (for instance to do A levels) receive an update of their year 12 record. The content of the record of achievement will include: performance in compulsory contributory subjects; examination results; school achievements; societies, clubs and positions of responsibility. The precise information to be supplied at each stage is specified in the Schedules to the 1998 Regulations.[184]

---

[178] The requirements are specified in the Schedules to the 1998 Regulations. Sch. 1 covers the final years in key stages 1, 2 and 3. Pupils in the final year of key stage 2 will have their information provided in the form set out in Sch. 5 or a form to the like effect. Sch. 2 covers key stage 4. Sch. 3 covers pupils in the sixth form.
[179] *Ibid* reg. 8(1).
[180] *Ibid* reg. 8(2).
[181] *Ibid* reg. 9(1).
[182] *Ibid* reg. 9(2).
[183] *Ibid* reg. 6(3)-(4).
[184] *Ibid* reg. 10. Pupils in the final year of the second key stage receive the information set out in Sch. 4. Paras. 1-3 of Sch. 4 shall be provided in the form specified in Sch. 5 or a form to

5.81 The record of achievement must be sent (by post or otherwise) to the parent of a child who has ceased to be a pupil of the school at the end of key stage 2 by post not later than 30 June that year.[185] The records of achievement at the end of key stage 4 and sixth form must be made available to the pupil not later than 30 June. They must also be given to the pupil if the pupil so requests and in any case not later than 30 September.[186] If examination results come out after these dates, the principal will send this to the pupil as soon as is reasonably practicable.[187] It should be noted that there is no specific statutory duty to provide this information to the parents of pupils who are over the age of 16.

PUPIL RECORDS

Formative records of progress and achievement

5.82 Under the Education (Pupil Records) Regulations (NI) 1998, Boards of Governors are under an obligation to make arrangements for keeping formative records of progress on all pupils. A formative record of progress and achievement is defined as a formal record of a pupil's academic achievements, his or her other skills, talents and achievements and his or her educational progress".[188] The Board of Governors is also required to make arrangements for the disclosure and supply of copies of the record to "entitled persons". These are defined to be the pupil's parent where the pupil is in primary school and the pupil or the pupil's parent where the child is in secondary school. If a child is in a special school, the parent is entitled to see the record where the child is aged under 11; the pupil or the parent may see the record where the pupil is aged 11 or over.[189] In addition, any school to which the child seeks admission may request to see the record at any time other than at the end of the second key stage (the normal transfer from primary to secondary school).[190] The request must be complied with within 15 school days of the first school day following the day on which the request was received.[191]

5.83 People who are entitled to obtain records of progress and achievement may submit a notice in writing to the effect that he or she regards the record of

---

the like effect. Pupils in the final year of key stage 4 receive the information set out in Sch. 6. This must be provided in the form specified in Sch. 8 or a form to the like effect. Pupils who are in the sixth form and in a year in which he or she ceases to be a pupil at the school receive the information set out in Sch. 7 provided in the form set out in Sch. 8 or a form to the like effect.

[185] *Ibid* reg. 11(1).
[186] *Ibid* reg. 11(2).
[187] *Ibid* reg. 11(3).
[188] Education (Pupil Records) Regulations (NI) 1998, reg. 3.
[189] *Ibid* reg. 3.
[190] *Ibid* reg. 6(3). Where a pupil is transferring schools at the end of the second key stage, the school must transfer the information prescribed in Sch. 1 to the Regulations (in the form prescribed in Sch. 2), not later than 30 June of that school year. The principal of the other school may also request in writing a transfer of the pupil's formative record of progress and achievement (reg. 6(1)(d)).
[191] *Ibid* reg. 6(2).

progress as inaccurate.[192] "Inaccurate" is defined as inaccurate or misleading as to any matter of fact.[193] If the holder of the record is satisfied that the record is inaccurate, the record is amended by the removal or correction of the part which is regarded as inaccurate or if the holder of the record is not satisfied that the record is inaccurate, the notice is appended to the record and subsequently treated as forming part of it.[194]

Other records

5.84 Boards of Governors are also required to make arrangements for disclosure and transfer of any other educational records. This includes "teacher's records" which are defined as any record kept at the school by a teacher other than a record kept and intended to be kept solely for that teacher's own use.[195] A copy must be supplied to the parent of the pupil, the pupil where he is aged 16 or over and the principal of any school in respect of which the pupil is being considered for admission. The Board of Governors must also make arrangements for the correction of such records as if they form part of the pupil's formative record of progress and achievement.

Complaints

5.85 Boards of Governors must make arrangements enabling the parent, pupil or school to which the pupil seeks admission to appeal to the Board of Governors against any decision refusing disclosure or transfer or the supply of a copy of any of the above records or any decision refusing amendment in cases where the arrangements made by the Board of Governors provide for those decisions to be taken by a teacher at the school.[196] If the decisions are taken by the Board of Governors itself, there is no such right of appeal. If a parent wishes to challenge the decision of the Board of Governors whether on appeal or otherwise, it might be possible to complain to the Department under article 101 of the 1986 Order.[197] A further possibility is an action for negligence. This might arise where the information is inaccurate and the pupil loses out (e.g. does not gain admission to a school of their choice) because of the information contained in the record. A further more drastic action could be an action for damages for defamation.

Exceptions

5.86 There are a number of major exceptions to the rules regarding disclosure of pupils records. First, information will not be disclosed if: (i) it originates from a person other than a teacher at the school, an employee of the ELB, the pupil or his or her parent; (ii) reveals or enables to be deduced the identity of a person (other than the pupil or a person mentioned in (i) as the source of the information or as a person to whom the information relates or of any other person; (iii) the disclosure would in the opinion of the holder of the

---

[192] *Ibid* reg. 6(1)(1)(c).
[193] *Ibid* reg. 6(4).
[194] *Ibid* reg. 6(1)(c).
[195] *Ibid* reg. 7(3).
[196] *Ibid* reg. 8.
[197] See further paras. 2.63 to 2.72.

information be likely to cause serious harm to the physical or mental health or emotional condition of the pupil to whom the information relates or of any other person; (iv) in the opinion of the holder of the information it is relevant to the question whether the pupil to which it related is or has been the subject of or may be at risk of any harm. Secondly, schools are not required to disclose any reference given by a teacher in respect of a pupil in response to a request from potential employers of the pupil, the Universities Central Admissions Service or any other national body in the United Kingdom or Republic of Ireland concerned with student admission, an institution of further education, a college of education or any other educational or training institution.[198] Finally there are a number of exceptions in relation to: (i) educational records which are data for the purposes of the Data Protection Act 1998; (ii) statements of special educational needs; (iii) reports for the purposes of proceedings to which the Magistrates' Courts (Children and Young Persons) Rules (NI) Order 1969 apply; information about the pupil's home circumstances and religious denomination; the results of an individual pupil's assessment; and records made before 1 September 1990.

THE CURRICULUM COMPLAINTS TRIBUNAL

5.87 The introduction of the Northern Ireland curriculum was intended to ensure greater consistency in the education provided in grant-aided schools. State inspections are the primary means for ensuring that schools adhere to the statutory requirements of the Northern Ireland curriculum. However, the provisions may also be enforced by individuals such as parents through the statutory curriculum complaints procedure. Article 33 of the 1989 Order requires ELBs to establish a tribunal which will consider complaints about the actions or omissions of ELBs or Boards of Governors in matters relating to the curriculum. DENI Circular 1993/1 provides guidance on the remit of the tribunal and the procedures involved in making a complaint. There are no available statistics on the number of complaints made to these tribunals. However, it would appear that parents use the procedure extremely infrequently (if at all). This is somewhat surprising given the general trend for parents to challenge decisions about their child's education and the fact that the tribunal's remit is quite wide-ranging. The lack of complaints is probably an indication of the fact that most parents are happy with the curriculum provided by their child's school or are able to resolve their grievance internally. However, it is also possible that parents who have ongoing complaints are unaware of the existence of the tribunal.

Who can complain?

5.88 Article 33 of the 1989 Order does not specify who can make a complaint. Article 33(4) defines the complainant as the person by whom or body by which the complaint was made. The people who are most likely to use the procedure are parents who are dissatisfied with the provision being made for their child. However, there is nothing to prohibit a child or a teacher or an interested educational body from making a complaint. Moreover, the

---

[198] Education (Pupil Records) Regulations (NI) 1998, reg. 10.

legislation does not appear to prohibit a Board of Governors from complaining about the actions of an ELB and vice versa.

Who can be complained about?

5.89 Article 33 refers specifically to the actions of ELBs and Boards of Governors. Article 33(4) defines the respondent as the ELB or Board of Governors in respect of which the complaint was made. There is therefore no specific means of complaining about the actions of individual teachers although this is probably in practice the source of most parental dissatisfaction. However, it could be argued that a Board of Governors which has failed to ensure that individual teachers comply with the requirements of the Northern Ireland curriculum has itself failed to comply with its statutory duty under article 11(1) of the 1989 Order which requires it to secure that the statutory requirements are complied with.

What are the grounds for complaint?

5.90 The grounds for complaint are that: the ELB or the Board of Governors has failed to discharge a duty or has acted or is proposing to act unreasonably with respect to the exercise of any power or duty under Part III of the 1989 Order; articles 147-149 of the 1989 Order; any statutory provision relating to the curriculum; and any statutory provision in relation to collective worship.[199] These are considered separately below.

(i) Part III of the 1989 Order

This covers articles 4-35. The matters included in these provisions are as follows: the implementation of the Northern Ireland curriculum; the determination of a curriculum policy; the provisions in relation to religious education; temporary exceptions; the provision of information; the keeping of educational records; and the provision of curriculum advice by ELBs. The matters covered by Part III of the 1989 Order are very wide-ranging. For instance, parents might complain that the curriculum was not "balanced and broadly based" (as required by art. 4 of the 1989 Order) if a teacher were to adopt a highly politicised or prejudiced approach to any subject taught. One area of complaint peculiar to Northern Ireland might arise in the preparation given for the transfer procedure tests. Not all children sit these tests and a parent might have a legitimate complaint if the teacher was neglecting the general curriculum in favour of practice aptitude tests.

(ii) Articles 147 - 149 of the 1989 Order

These provisions relate to the provision of training of teachers and Boards of Governors by ELBs.

(iii) Any other statutory provisions relating to the curriculum for grant-aided schools

This is a 'catchall' clause which allows some scope for argument on other provisions in the Education Orders provided that they relate in some way to

---

[199] This was inserted by art. 47 of the 1993 Order

what is taught in grant-aided schools. For instance, it would be possible to complain to the curriculum complaints tribunal about the operation of charging policies under articles 128-138 in so far as these relate to the curriculum in grant-aided schools.

(iv) Provisions relating to collective worship in grant-aided schools

This was added by article 47 of the 1993 Order. At the same time religious education came within the remit of the curriculum complaints tribunal. Prior to this, complaints about religious education were made to the Department. The Department would consider complaints about religious education provided that the complaint was made by at least 20 per cent of the parents of the pupils registered at the school.[200]

(v) Article 46A of the 1986 Order

This was added by Schedule 5 to the 1996 Order. Article 46A of the 1986 Order relates to the date of commencement of secondary education and in particular the circumstances in which a child may be transferred to secondary school earlier or later than is usual.[201] Article 33(2) of the 1989 Order provides that an ELB or Board of Governors will not be taken to have acted unreasonably in this respect if it has complied with or is proposing to comply with guidance issued by the Department under article 46A of the 1986 Order.[202]

5.91 The tribunal's remit does not extend to nursery schools or to nursery classes in primary schools except in so far as the provisions of articles 29-32 of the 1989 Order apply to nursery schools.[203] Moreover, a complaint cannot be made to the curriculum complaints tribunal about curricular provision contained in a child's statement of special educational needs. The appropriate venue for this type of challenge is the special educational needs tribunal.[204] However, if a child with special educational needs does not have a statement, complaints could still be made to the curriculum complaints tribunal if the Board of Governors or ELB has failed to discharge its statutory functions with respect to that child.

Composition of the tribunal

5.92 The members of the curriculum complaints tribunal are appointed by the ELB. The tribunal is composed of three members, one drawn from each of the following three panels: (i) persons representing the interests of controlled schools; (ii) persons representing the interests of maintained schools, voluntary schools and grant maintained integrated schools; and (iii) persons with experience in education who are acquainted with the educational arrangements in the ELB or are the parents of pupils registered at a grant-aided school.[205] A person will be disqualified from membership if they are (or

---

[200] Art. 23(2) of the 1986 Order.
[201] It was inserted by art. 31 of the 1996 Order
[202] This was inserted by Sch. 5 to the 1996 Order
[203] Art. 35(6) of the 1989 Order amended by Sch. 4 to the 1993 Order
[204] See paras. 8.64 to 8.84.
[205] Curriculum (Complaints Tribunal) Regulations (NI) 1992, Sch. 1

were at the time when the circumstances giving rise to the complaint first arose): a member of the Board of Governors against whom the complaint is being made; an officer of the ELB against whom the complaint is being made (this does not exclude teachers employed in other schools by the ELB); a person employed to work in the school; a parent of a registered pupil at the school; or an officer or employee of the Department. The members of the tribunal elect one person to act as the chairperson.

Procedure for a complaint

5.93 The complaint must be in writing and must specify the grounds of the complaint.[206] The appeal is heard in private except where the ELB specifies otherwise. Both the complainant and the respondent must be given the opportunity to make written representations; to attend with a representative; and to make oral representations. The chairman of the tribunal will determine the order of oral representations. All other procedural matters are determined by the ELB.

Decision of the tribunal

5.94 The tribunal will consider whether the ELB or Board of Governors has failed to discharge its duties or has acted or proposes to act unreasonably with respect to a power or duty. Departmental guidance suggests that:

> "Consideration of a complaint will need to be directed towards establishing whether a board or Board of Governors is carrying out its statutory functions reasonably and within the law and meeting its obligations so far as is practicable; or whether this is not the case, and some remedial action is required."[207]

In the event of a disagreement between the members of the panel, the matter will be decided by a simple majority of vote cast.[208] The tribunal will send a notice of its decision and of the reasons for the decision to the complainant and to the ELB or Board of Governors against whom the complaint was made. If the tribunal upholds the complaint in whole or part and considers that any matter should be remedied, the notice may require the respondent to take certain steps within a specified time to remedy the matter. If the respondent fails to comply with the requirements stated in the notice, the tribunal may refer the matter to the Department. The Department will consult the tribunal, the complainant and the respondent and may give a direction under article 101 of the 1986 Order if it considers that this is expedient in order to remedy the matter.[209] The Department will not consider a complaint about the curriculum under article 101(4) of the 1986 Order unless a complaint has been determined by the complaints tribunal.

---

[206] *Ibid* Sch. 2
[207] DENI Circular 1993/1, para. 21
[208] Curriculum (Complaints Tribunal) Regulations (NI) 1992, Sch. 2, para. 6.
[209] See further paras. 2.63 to 2.72.

INSPECTIONS

5.95 The power of inspection is contained in article 102 of the 1986 Order which gives the Department the power to inspect all schools (including independent schools). The power of inspection was extended in 1989 to include a general duty to promote educational standards.[210] The 1996 Order introduced further amendments by involving lay persons (i.e. those not working directly in education) in the inspection process. Article 33 of the 1996 Order has substituted new articles 102 and 102A in the 1986 Order. In this instance, the legislation deals mainly with the procedural aspects of the inspection process. Further guidance on the nature of inspections is contained in guidance issued by the Education and Training Inspectorate.[211]

Inspectors

5.96 All schools are required to be open to inspection at all reasonable times.[212] Inspections are carried out by officers appointed by the Department. The inspectors' duty is to "promote the highest standards of education and of professional practice among teachers".[213] This is done through monitoring, inspecting and reporting on the standard of education being provided and the standards of professional practice among teachers. Inspectors are also required to monitor, inspect and report on the nature, scope and effect of the advisory and support services provided by ELBs. It should be noted that the remit of inspectors does not extend to religious education in the curriculum of the school unless the Board of Governors gives its agreement for it to be inspected.[214]

5.97 Inspectors may be "accompanied and assisted" by lay persons drawn from a panel appointed by the Department.[215] The lay inspectors are intended to provide "an additional, impartial perspective" on the work of the school and process of inspection.[216] They must not have significant personal experience in the management of an educational institution and the provision of education. They may however be involved in educational management in a voluntary capacity or as a member of a Board of Governors or manager of the institution. The lay person may not be involved in the inspection of a particular school if he or she has at any time had any connection with: the school; a person employed at the school; a person on the Board of Governors of the school; or the proprietor of the school if that connection is of the kind which might reasonably be taken to raise doubts about his or her ability to act impartially in relation to that establishment.[217]

---

[210] Art. 30 of the 1989 Order.
[211] ETI, *The Inspection Process in Schools* (DENI, 1998).
[212] Art. 102(1) of the 1986 Order.
[213] *Ibid* art. 102(5).
[214] *Ibid* art. 102(7).
[215] *Ibid* art. 102A.
[216] *The Inspection Process in Schools* (DENI, 1998), p. 7.
[217] Art. 102A(4) of the 1986 Order.

The inspection report

5.98 Inspectors will produce a report on the quality of education at the school. They may advise the Department on any aspect of the curriculum which the Department may refer them to or on which they think advice is appropriate.[218] Inspectors themselves do not have the power to give directions for change. However, the Department may give directions under article 101 of the 1986 Order for the purpose of remedying any matter referred to in the report of an inspector.[219] The school must comply or the direction can be enforced in a court through an order of mandamus. The Department also has the power to make an order appointing a person or persons to discharge any or all of the functions of a Board of Governors if the Board of Governors has failed to discharge those functions itself.[220]

Recommendation to appoint additional governors

5.99 The 1998 Order has added further force to the inspection report. Article 14 allows the Department to appoint additional governors to the Board of Governors if an inspection report states that a school is failing to give its pupils an acceptable standard of education and that failure is due (in whole or in part) to the management of the school by the Board of Governors. If the inspection report recommends that additional governors should be appointed, the Department may appoint as many additional voting governors as it thinks fit.[221] The additional governors will hold and vacate office in accordance with their terms of appointment.[222] The Department may specify that one of the new governors should chair the Board of Governors.[223] Before making additional appointments, the Department must consult the trustees of the school, the ELB and the CCMS if it is a Catholic maintained school.[224] To date no school in Northern Ireland has been considered to have such poor education to justify emergency measures of this sort. However, the equivalent powers in England and Wales have been used frequently in so-called 'failing' schools.[225]

TARGET SETTING

5.100 The 1998 Order introduced a series of reforms which were intended to promote the raising of standards in schools. One of these reforms, which relates directly to the delivery of the curriculum is an obligation to set annual targets for student performance. In the House of Commons, it was stated that this would "inform and provide an impetus for all involved".[226] Boards of Governors are required, in consultation with the principal, to set targets for the

---

[218] *Ibid* art. 102B.
[219] *Ibid* art. 102(8).
[220] *Ibid* art. 101(4)-(5).
[221] Art. 14(1) of the 1998 Order.
[222] *Ibid* art. 14(5).
[223] *Ibid* art. 14 (2).
[224] *Ibid* art. 14(4).
[225] The most publicised instance was Manton Junior School in Yorkshire which had severe discipline problems.
[226] House of Commons Standing Committee on Delegated Legislation, 2 July 1998, *per* T. Worthington.

overall performance of the pupils at the school. This duty applies in all grant-aided schools apart from nursery schools, schools attended wholly by pupils in the first three years of compulsory education; and special schools.[227] In primary schools, the targets must include the following measures of performance: (i) the proportion of pupils which should be achieving the second and third level of attainment (or above) of the Northern Ireland curriculum in English (Irish in Irish-speaking schools) and in mathematics at the end of key stage 1; and (ii) the proportion of pupils which should be achieving the fourth and fifth level of attainment (or above) of the Northern Ireland curriculum in English (Irish in Irish-speaking schools) and in mathematics at the end of key stage 2.[228] In secondary schools, the targets must include the proportion of pupils which should be achieving the fifth and sixth level of attainment (or above) of the Northern Ireland curriculum in English and in mathematics at the end of key stage 3.[229] In secondary schools, the relevant measures of performance also include performance in public examinations. The targets differ in secondary and grammar schools.[230]

REDRESS FOR POOR QUALITY EDUCATION

5.101 Parents who consider that their child's education is of an unacceptable standard have a number of options. In the first instance, they would be advised to raise the issue with the child's teacher, principal or the Board of Governors. If they are not satisfied with the response, they can complain to the curriculum appeal tribunal if they consider that the school is not meeting its statutory responsibilities in relation to the curriculum.[231] Finally, if they consider that their child's educational progress has suffered they may be able to take an action for negligence. Although there are no reported cases on this issue, the prospect of a successful action has increased following the House of Lords' decision in *X* v *Bedfordshire County Council*.[232] In that case the Lords accepted that an ELB might be vicariously liable for the failure of its employees to identify and provide suitable education for a child with special educational needs.[233] However, the impact of *X* v *Bedfordshire CC* has not been restricted to special needs cases. The House of Lords' decision has prompted a number of actions involving pupils in 'failing' schools whose examination results are below what would be expected for a child of similar intelligence.[234] Establishing liability in such cases may be difficult. Nor will it be easy to determine the damage suffered and the level of contributory negligence. Therefore the outcomes of these actions are awaited with interest. Moreover, it should be noted that, prior to the 1997 general election, the Labour Party had stated that if such actions were successful they would be prepared to introduce legislation granting teachers immunity from liability. That said, in a recent House of Lords' case, Lord Clyde was of the firm

---

[227] Education (Target-Setting in Schools) Regulations (NI) 1998, regs. 3 and 4.
[228] *Ibid* Sch. 1.
[229] *Ibid* Sch. 2, paras. 1 and 2.
[230] *Ibid* Sch. 2, paras. 3 and 4.
[231] See generally, *The Parents' Charter for Northern Ireland* (DENI, 1992) p. 17.
[232] [1995] 3 All ER 353.
[233] This is considered in detail in Chapter 8.
[234] See O'Sullivan, 'D? E? Get me a lawyer', *The Independent* 20 May 1997.

opinion that teachers owe a general duty of care to the children they teach and that liability could be established if they were negligent.[235] He stated:

> "If a teacher carelessly teaches the wrong syllabus for an external examination, and provable financial loss follows, why should there be no financial liability? Denial of the existence of a cause of action is seldom, if ever, the appropriate response to fear of its abuse. Rather, the courts, with their enhanced powers of case-management must seek to evolve means of weeding out obviously hopeless claims as expeditiously as is consistent with the court having a sufficiently full factual picture of all the circumstances of the case..."

However, he went on to stress:

> "This is not to open the door to claims based on poor quality teaching. It is one thing for the law to provide a remedy in damages when there is manifest incompetence or negligence comprising specific, identifiable mistakes. It would be an altogether different matter to countenance claims of a more general nature, to the effect that the child did not receive an adequate education at the school, or that a particular teacher failed to teach properly. Proof of under-performance by a child is not by itself evidence of negligent teaching."

---

[235] *Phelps* v *London Borough of Hillingdon, Anderton* v *Clyde CC, In re G (A Minor), Jarvis* v *Hamshire CC*, unreported decision of the House of Lords, 27 July 2000.

CHAPTER SIX

SECURING EDUCATION: SCHOOL ATTENDANCE OR OTHERWISE

INTRODUCTION

6.01 The United Nations Universal Declaration on Human Rights requires its members not only to provide free elementary education but also to make it compulsory.[1] The United Nations Convention on the Rights of the Child contains similar provision but goes a step further and requires parties to the Convention to take measures to encourage regular attendance at schools.[2] Education, unlike other aspects of the Convention, is not just a right but an obligation. The right to receive an education is based upon the widely accepted view that a child needs to be educated in order to develop his or her full potential.[3] The obligation to educate is based on the assumption that this is not universally accepted. Children generally do not have sufficient maturity to understand the future benefit that they will derive from education. Parents, on the other hand, normally want their child to receive a good education. However, the fact that education is "compulsorily administered indicates that its intrinsic value is not immediately apparent to all citizens".[4] Most countries take legal steps to ensure that children attend school. There has been a system of compulsory education since 1892.[5] The system is enforced by placing parents under a legal duty to ensure that their child receives a suitable education.[6] Compliance with this duty takes one of two forms: (i) sending the child to school; or (ii) arranging his or her education at home.

6.02 Not all parents wish to send their child to school but prefer instead to arrange for them to be educated at home. Article 26(3) of the United Nations Declaration on Human Rights states that "parents have a prior right to choose the kind of education that shall be given to their children". This might be construed to include the right of parents to educate their child at home. However, other international obligations are less positive in relation to the right to educate children at home. For instance, although Article 2 of the First Protocol of the ECHR requires Member States to ensure that education is in accordance with parents' religious and philosophical convictions, the European Commission considers that this does not prevent a state from insisting on compulsory schooling or on requiring parents to comply with

---

[1] Art. 26(1).
[2] Art. 28(1)(e).
[3] For a discussion of the rationale underlying compulsory education, see Grenville, 'Compulsory School Attendance and the Child's Wishes' (1988) *Journal of Social Welfare Law* 4, at p. 15
[4] Finch, *Education as Social Policy*, (1984) p. 89
[5] Irish Education Act 1892, s. 1 required parents to have their child educated between the ages of 6 and 14.
[6] Art. 45 of the 1986 Order.

procedures designed to assess whether home schooling is satisfactory.[7] Although the international documents are less than clear on this issue, the law in Northern Ireland does provide parents with the option of educating their child at home. This arises through the inclusion of the words "regular school attendance *or otherwise*" in article 4(1) of the 1986 Order. However, even if parents assume this responsibility, the state's obligation to the children does not come to an end. Just as for children who attend schools, the state maintains some degree of responsibility for ensuring that the child who is educated at home is receiving a suitable education. The extent of this regulation is considered at paragraphs 6.24-6.29.

6.03 Most parents fulfil their duty to educate their child by sending them to a recognised school. However, non-attendance at school has been an ongoing problem for education authorities. In recent years it has received increased attention, not because levels of non-attendance are rising but because truancy is becoming associated with the wider social ills of under-achievement, delinquency and crime.[8] The Department conducted research into persistent absenteeism in Northern Ireland in 1992.[9] One of the key findings was that unauthorised absenteeism had decreased significantly in Northern Ireland from previous surveys in 1977 and 1982.[10] However, the research also indicated that, in the majority of cases, parents were aware that their child was missing school, a finding which has obvious implications for the way in which compulsory education is enforced. Prior to 1996, the key method of dealing with persistent absenteeism was for ELBs to bring a criminal prosecution against the parents. If parents are deliberately keeping their child from school, it is appropriate for legal action to be directed at the parents. However, criminal sanctions, although available, are not always effective. Imprisoning parents or fining them if they are not well off will do little to assist the child. Moreover, it seems unfair to punish parents when the child is refusing to attend school in spite of the parents' best efforts to make them attend. It can be difficult for parents to physically force a child into the school premises and even if they do make sure that the child arrives at school, parents have no means of ensuring that they stay. In such circumstances, legal action directed at parents seems meaningless.

6.04 The area became part of the wider review of child law which resulted in the Children (NI) Order 1995.[11] This introduced a new device for dealing with absenteeism, the education supervision order (ESO), which places an emphasis on partnership with the family rather than punishment of the parents when a child fails to attend school. The new order came into force in Northern Ireland in November 1996. The ESO was intended to become the main tool to be used by ELBs in their attempts to secure the school attendance of persistent absentees. However, in practice it would appear that ESOs are

---

[7] See *H v United Kingdom* (1984) 37 DR 105.

[8] For a review of some of the research, see Brown, 'Truancy, Delinquency and the Leeds Adjournment System', (1990) 2 *Education and the Law* 47.

[9] DENI Research Briefing, *Persistent School Absenteeism in Northern Ireland in 1992*, RB2/95 (1992, DENI).

[10] Absenteeism had decreased from 7.8% in 1977 to 6.1% in 1982 to 3% in 1992. *Ibid*. Table 1 and Figure 1.

[11] *Child Care Review* (1985).

being used infrequently (see para. 6.30). This has also been the case in England and Wales where truancy is an increasing problem. The issue is considered to be so fundamental in England that the issue was reviewed by the Social Exclusion Unit (SEU) which was charged by the Labour Government to "make a step change in the scale of truancy and exclusions".[12] The SEU made a number of recommendations including: target-setting in schools, changes to the curriculum, and the introduction of Parenting Orders. Similar strategies are also being considered in Northern Ireland.[13]

REGISTRATION AND THE MONITORING OF ATTENDANCE

6.05 A necessary part of the enforcement of compulsory education is an effective means of monitoring school attendance. The proprietor of a school is under a duty to ensure that a register is kept with respect to all persons of compulsory school age who are pupils at the school.[14] The proprietor is defined as the person responsible for the management of the school. In a grant-aided school this would be the Board of Governors. The Education (Registration and Attendance of Pupils) Regulations (NI) 1974 set out the information which must be registered. Schools are required to keep two registers: (i) a general register; and (ii) an attendance register.

General register

6.06 The general register must contain a list of the names of pupils in alphabetical order.[15] It must also contain the following information: sex; religious denomination; name and address of parent; date of birth; date of admission or readmission to the school; the class in which the pupil is enrolled on first admission; the classes in which the pupil is subsequently enrolled and the date of each enrolment; the number of attendances made in each school year; the date on which the child ceased to be a pupil at the school; the destination of the child on leaving the school; and in the case of a school which offers boarding arrangements, a statement as to whether the child is a day pupil or a boarder. The information contained in the register is important for monitoring school attendance. For this reason there are special rules which apply when a child is being placed on the register for the first time or when the child is being withdrawn from a register. When a child is being registered at school for the first time, a copy of the child's birth certificate should be produced.[16] A child can only be withdrawn from the register in specified circumstances: transfer to another school; departure from Northern Ireland; expulsion; death; and leaving school having completed compulsory education.[17] When a child is being withdrawn from a school at which he is registered, the parent must first let the principal know that it his intention to

---

[12] *Truancy and School Exclusion Report* (SEU, 1998).
[13] *Promoting and Sustaining Good Behaviour* (DENI, 1998) p. 26.
[14] Art. 48 of the 1986 Order.
[15] Education (Registration and Attendance of Pupils) Regulations (NI) 1974, reg. 4.
[16] Reg. 5.
[17] DENI Circular 1994/15. Similar provisions in Great Britain have caused difficulty when parents have withdrawn a child so as to educate him or her at home. See para. 6.25.

withdraw the child from the school.[18] The principal will then give the parent a Certificate of Attendance and delete the child's name from the general register. If the parent wishes to register the child at another school he must give the Certificate of Attendance to the principal of the other school. The principal must not register a child until he or she has received the Certificate of Attendance supplied by the former school.[19] These rules do not apply to a child who has withdrawn from a primary school and is admitted to a secondary school as part of the ordinary transfer procedure.

Attendance register

6.07 The proprietor of a school is required to keep an attendance register.[20] This must record the presence or absence of all registered pupils on each school day. Departmental guidance specifies how attendance is to be recorded.[21] Since 1994 secondary schools have been required to record both morning and afternoon absences. Family holidays and other parentally-condoned absences are all categorised as unjustified absences along with truancy and false allegations of illness. On a related but slightly different point, it is worth noting that a late arrival can legally be classified as a failure to attend. In *Hinchley* v *Rankin* it was held that a school could validly record that a child who arrived at school after the attendance register had closed was absent for that day.[22]

Monitoring of the registers

6.08 The school is required to make returns on both the general and attendance registers to the Department and ELB.[23] Inspectors of the Department and/or the ELB are entitled to inspect the registers and to make extracts from them.[24] When a child lives in one ELB area and attends a school in another ELB area, the ELB in which the child is a registered pupil is required to supply the ELB in which the child resides with information regarding the child's attendance at school.[25] This is important because the responsibility for ensuring that a child is receiving a suitable education rests with the ELB in which the child resides.

Publication of attendance statistics

6.09 Boards of Governors of grant-aided schools must publish attendance rates as part of their annual reports. Regulation 10(g) of the Education (School Information and Prospectuses) Regulations (NI) 1993 requires Boards of Governors to provide information on "the total number of days attended by pupils at the school in the school year to which the annual report relates".

---

[18] Education (Registration and Attendance of Pupils) Regulations (NI) 1974, reg. 6(1).
[19] *Ibid* reg. 6(3).
[20] *Ibid* reg. 7.
[21] DENI Circular 1994/15. Absences are recorded through a computer system known as CLASS in secondary schools and CLASP in larger primary schools.
[22] [1961] 1 All ER 692.
[23] Education (Registration and Attendance of Pupils) Regulations (NI) 1974, reg. 9.
[24] *Ibid* reg. 8.
[25] *Ibid* reg. 18.

This must be expressed as a percentage of the total number of days of attendance by those pupils in that school year. The provision is designed to supply parents with information which will facilitate them when selecting a school for their child. The presumption is that schools with high rates of absenteeism will be less attractive to parents. This places pressure on schools to attempt to demonstrate high levels of attendance. It has been suggested that in England and Wales schools may be over generous in determining which absences are authorised (e.g. sicknesses) because they are under pressure to keep unauthorised absences low.[26] This onus on schools might be questioned on the basis that schools have no legal duty or statutory powers which can assist them in tackling truancy. In fact, high percentages of absenteeism may just be an indication of the levels of social deprivation in the school's catchment area. The research published by the Department in 1992 indicates a strong correlation between persistent absenteeism and social disadvantage.[27]

PARENTAL DUTY TO SECURE THE CHILD'S EDUCATION

6.10 Parents are under a statutory duty to secure education for their child. Article 45(1) of the 1986 Order states that "the parent of every child of compulsory school age shall cause him to receive efficient full-time education suitable to his age, ability and aptitude and to any special educational needs he may have, either by regular school attendance or otherwise". Full-time education is not defined. Likewise there is no explanation of what is meant by "efficient" and "suitable". Parents can comply with the statutory duty in article 45 in one of two ways. The first (and most common method in practice) is to send their child regularly to a recognised school. The second is to make arrangements for their child's education outside of school. These options are considered below. However, the extent of the duty can only be understood with a fuller explanation of what is meant by the terms "parent" and "compulsory school age".

Definition of parent

6.11 For these purposes, the term "parent" includes any person who is not the parent of the child but who has parental responsibility for him or who has care of him.[28] This includes both parents where they were married at the time of the child's birth or subsequently (irrespective of a later separation); step-parents where they have care of the child; an unmarried mother; an unmarried father where there is a parental responsibility order, or a formal agreement with the mother; any person who has been granted a residence order, appointed a guardian, or has an emergency protection order or adoption order made in their favour; and the local Health and Social Services Trust which has a care order in force in respect to the child. It is therefore quite common for more than one person to have parental responsibility for the child at one time.

---

[26] Whitney, 'Enforcing School Attendance: Thoughts on a Flawed Framework' (1998) *ELAS Bulletin* p. 7.
[27] *Ib:·l* para. 14 and Figure 4.
[28] Art. 2 of the 1986 Order. This was substituted by art. 128 of the Children (NI) Order 1995.

Compulsory school age

6.12 A child is of compulsory school age between the ages of four or five and 16.[29] The onus of proving the age of the child is on the parent where the person bringing proceedings is unable after applying reasonable diligence to obtain evidence as to the child's age.[30] Children reaching the age of four on or between September 1 and July 1 the following year are deemed to be of compulsory school age on 1 August of that following year and must normally start school that September.[31] However, children born on or between 2 July and 31 August in the same year are not deemed to be of compulsory school age until August 1 the following year. In effect this means that 'summer babies' are not required to start school until they are five years old.[32] These children are the exception. In Northern Ireland most children are four when they start school. In contrast, in England and Wales most children start school when they are five years old. SACHR recommended that the age limit in Northern Ireland should be raised to five on the basis that that most children are too young to benefit from the formal curriculum before the age of five.[33] Their recommendation was rejected by the government who did not consider that it was substantiated on educational grounds.[34]

6.13 Special rules apply where a person has attained the age of 16.[35] A child whose sixteenth birthday falls on or between September 1 to 1 July of the following year continues to be of compulsory school age until 30 June of that following year. A child whose birthday falls between 2 July and 31 August is deemed to be of compulsory school age until 30 June the following year. These rules can result in some 16 year old pupils being made to stay on at school nearly a year after their sixteenth birthday. This has been criticised by the Northern Ireland Working Party on School Discipline which considered that the apparent unfairness of such a situation could generate a threat to discipline.[36] However, the alternative - allowing children who wish to do so to leave a year early - would mean that their total period of compulsory education would be cut from 12 to 11 years. There have been a number of proposals to deal with disaffected older pupils (including reducing the school leaving age to 14 and/or introducing a more vocationally-based curriculum). These are considered further at paragraphs 6.30-6.32.

---

[29] Art. 46(1) of the 1986 Order. This was substituted by art. 156 of the 1989 Order.
[30] Art. 47 of the 1986 Order.
[31] *Ibid* art. 46(2).
[32] Schools may admit these children a year earlier if they have vacant places. See further, para. 4.12
[33] *Employment Equality: Building for the Future* (1997, The Stationery Office) Cm 3684, p. 35. The recommendation arose in the context of a consideration of inequalities in nursery education provision. SACHR recommend that all children should have access to nursery education at four.
[34] *Partnership for Equality* (1998, The Stationery Office) Cm 3890, para. 3.4, p. 19.
[35] Art. 46(2) of the 1986 Order.
[36] DENI *Discipline in Schools in Northern Ireland*, para. 3.7.

REGULAR ATTENDANCE AT SCHOOL

6.14 Once a child is registered at a school, the parent is under a duty to secure his regular attendance at that school.[37] Regular attendance is not defined in the legislation. Moreover, ELBs do not have a set number of absences which they consider to justify intervention. Much depends on the circumstances of the case including the level of attendance at the school which the child attends. In the Department's research into school attendance, pupils were considered to be persistent absentees if they were absent for 14 or more days in a 12 week period (just under 25% of the total days).[38] Likewise, ELBs would normally be concerned if absences amounted to over 20 per cent of the total school days. The only statutory indication of poor attendance is given in the provisions which apply to children of no fixed abode: these require such children to attend school for at least 100 days in any 12 month period.[39] In *Crump v Gilmore*, the court concluded that a failure to attend on 12 days out of a possible 114 was a failure to attend regularly.[40] This would indicate that absences of over 10 per cent of total school days constitute irregular attendance. However, it would still be open to a court to conclude that absences of less than this amount to a failure to attend regularly.

Defences to non-attendance at school under the Education Orders

6.15 The reason why a child has failed to attend school is important. This is because not all absences are considered to be unjustified. However, the legislation is quite specific about the reasons which are deemed acceptable. A child who is registered at a school as a day pupil will not be deemed to have failed to attend school regularly if his absence is caused by one of the circumstances listed in Schedule 13, paragraph 3 to the 1986 Order. There are no other specific statutory defences to the parent's failure to secure the child's regular attendance at school. In particular, the following do not provide a defence: the fact that the child has been expelled; or that the child was on a family holiday. Moreover, it is no longer an excuse to say that a child is needed for work at home at certain times of the year.[41] The recognised defences are as follows.

Sickness

6.16 Sickness is not defined.[42] However, it has been established that the sickness must be that of the child and not another family member.[43] Moreover, it is implicit that the sickness is of sufficient severity to justify the

---

[37] Sch. 13, para. 3(1) to the 1986 Order.
[38] *Ibid* para. 2.
[39] Sch. 13, para. 3(6) to the 1986 Order.
[40] (1969) 68 LGR 56.
[41] The Irish Education Act 1923 made it an excuse if the child was needed in "necessary operations of husbandry and the ingathering of crops, or giving assistance to the fisheries". (s.1(2)(b)).
[42] Sch. 13, para. 3(2)(a) to the 1986 Order.
[43] *Jenkins v Howells* [1949] KB 218, at p. 220.

length of the absence. It can be difficult for schools to determine whether sickness is genuine. The school may ask the child to produce medical evidence to verify the reason for their absence. However, this can cause the parents difficulty if their general practitioner refuses to provide a certificate as the general practitioner is under no legal obligation to do so. Similarly, doctors should not supply the school directly with such information as this would be a breach of confidence.[44] Where a child is absent due to sickness, the ELB may require that the child is examined by a doctor either in his or her own home or elsewhere. If the parent unreasonably prevents the ELB from doing this, he or she will be guilty of a criminal offence.[45]

Unavoidable cause

6.17 Parents will have a defence if their child's non-attendance is a result of an unavoidable cause other than sickness.[46] What constitutes unavoidable cause is not specified in the legislation. In *Jenkins v Howells* it was stated that the cause must affect the child directly and suggested that it would normally be something in the nature of an emergency.[47] The court considered that a child's home being destroyed by fire might constitute unavoidable cause for a day or two but that family duties such as looking after a sick relative would not. However, in *Rogers v Essex County Council* the House of Lords suggested *obiter* that the parent of a child who had temporarily missed school because of some crisis such as the illness of the parent who accompanied them to school could put forward the defence of unavoidable cause.[48] The judgments can be reconciled if the House of Lords' comments are restricted to short periods of absence during which alternative arrangements are made to accompany the child to school. In *Jenkins v Howells* the Court of Appeal appeared to be influenced by the fact that a wider interpretation of "unavoidable cause" could justify a child missing out on their education as a result of the long-term illness of a family member. Other matters which might constitute unavoidable cause include situations where there is a bereavement in the immediate family or where a child cannot get to school because of severe weather conditions or because there is civil unrest in the area. It does not include family holidays. In fact some schools have been so disrupted by children's absences on holiday that they have campaigned for parents who take their child on holiday during the school term to be fined.

Transport difficulties

6.18 A parent will have a defence to his or her child's failure to attend school regularly where the school at which the child is registered is not within walking distance of the child's home; and the ELB is obliged to provide the child with transport; and no suitable arrangements have been made by the ELB for either transport, boarding accommodation or enabling the child to become a registered pupil at a school nearer his or her home. Walking

---

[44] See further, Grenville, 'Sickness and Compulsory School Attendance' (1989) (1) *Education and the Law*, 113.
[45] Sch. 13, para. 3(5) to the 1986 Order.
[46] *Ibid* Sch. 13, para. (3)(2)(a).
[47] [1949] KB 218.
[48] *Rogers v Essex CC* [1986] 3 All ER 321, at 326.

distances are set at two miles for a child at primary school and three miles for other children.[49] The distances are measured by the nearest available route.[50] In *Rogers* v *Essex CC* the House of Lords determined that the nearest available route is the route along which the child could walk to school with reasonable safety when accompanied by an adult.[51] A route does not therefore fail to qualify as available because of dangers which would arise if the child was unaccompanied. This means that parents can be expected to walk distances of up to 60 miles a week accompanying their child to and from school. It is, however, still arguable that a route would not be available if is was dangerous for both a parent and a child (e.g. because of the danger of sectarian attacks).

6.19 ELBs are under a statutory duty to make transport arrangements where they consider it to be "necessary" to facilitate the child's attendance at school.[52] In *George* v *Devon CC*[53] the House of Lords considered that it would be unreasonable for a local education authority not to provide free transport if this would mean that the parents were not under a legal obligation to secure their child's attendance at school. All ELBs make transport arrangements for children living outside statutory walking distances unless they consider that there is a suitable school closer to the child's home. Further detail on the nature of the ELB's obligation in relation to the provision of free school transport is provided in Chapter 10. The fact that the defences to non-attendance are linked to the provision of school transport is problematic. It would be simpler if the defence was worded to say that parents would not be liable where the ELB is under an obligation to provide assistance with transport and no assistance has been provided. The detail of the conditions of entitlement (e.g. the walking distances) could then be brought together in the one provision – the current article 52 of the 1986 Order.

Absence due to work experience

6.20 A child will not be considered to have failed to attend school during any period in which he is on work experience under article 63(2) of the 1986 Order.[54] Periods when the child is missing school to take part in a public performance may be considered to be absence due to work experience for these purposes.

Children of no fixed abode

6.21 Special rules apply to the children of people who are of no fixed abode.[55] The first major difference in the rules is that the provisions relating to transport difficulties do not apply. Instead, if a child is of no fixed abode, a parent will not be guilty of a criminal offence if he proves that he is engaged in a trade or business of such a nature as to require him to travel from place to place and that the child has attended the school as regularly as the parent's

---

[49] Sch. 13, para. 3 (6) to the 1986 Order. See generally Chapter 10.
[50] Sch. 13, para. 3(2) to the 1986 Order substituted by art. 23 of the Education (NI) Order 1997.
[51] [1986] 3 All ER 321.
[52] Art. 52 of the 1986 Order.
[53] [1988] 3 All ER 1002.
[54] *Ibid* Sch. 13, para. 3(2)(c).
[55] *Ibid* Sch. 13, para. 3(3).

trade or business permitted. The trades or businesses to which this applies may include travelling people and circus workers. However, in the case of a child who has attained the age of six, the child must have attended the school at least 100 days during the 12 month period ending with the date on which the proceedings were instituted.

Boarders

6.22 A child who is a boarder will not be deemed to have failed to attend regularly only if he is absent by reason of sickness or other unavoidable cause.[56] The exception in relation to travelling distance is inappropriate for such pupils given that they are living on the school premises.

Defences to non-attendance under the European Convention on Human Rights

6.23 Parents will from time to time withdraw their child from school because they are in dispute with the school or with the education authorities. This occurred in the case of *Campbell and Cosans* v *United Kingdom* over the issue of corporal punishment in schools.[57] Under Article 2 to the First Protocol of the ECHR parents have a right to have their child educated in conformity with their religious or philosophical convictions. Article 2 of the First Protocol does not give parents the right to object to compulsory education itself.[58] However, it might be relevant where attendance interferes with religious observances, for example Jewish parents may wish their child to be at home before sunset on the Sabbath. In Great Britain, absences due to religious observance constitute a separate statutory excuse.[59] Northern Ireland does not have an equivalent provision. However, the mode of recording of attendance acknowledges such absences by placing them in a special category.[60] The position in relation to non-attendances in protest at a particular educational policy or school decision is less clear. The substance of the protest will be important as only those views which can be considered to be "philosophical" convictions will be protected. On this basis, parents could face legal action for failing to send their child to school because of an objection to the school allocated for their child [61] or in protest at a Board of Governors' failure to expel a disruptive pupil.[62]

---

[56] *Ibid* Sch. 13, para. 3(4).
[57] See para. 1.53.
[58] *H* v *UK* (1984) 37 DR 105. See generally paras. 1.53-1.57.
[59] Education Act 1944, s. 39(2)(b).
[60] See DENI Circular 1994/15.
[61] See *W and DM* v *United Kingdom* (1984) 37 DR 96 where it was considered that Article 2 of the First Protocol of the ECHR did not give parents the right to object to comprehensive education.
[62] In Northern Ireland, a number of parents have been prosecuted after failing to send their child to school in protest. The nature of the protests has varied but has included dissatisfaction with the school allocated for the child or disagreement over a decision to discipline the child.

EDUCATION AT HOME

6.24 Article 45 of the 1986 Order places a duty on parents to secure their child's education by "regular school attendance or otherwise." The inclusion of the "or otherwise" leaves open the possibility that a parent might educate his or her child either at home or in a school setting which does not have official recognition. The organisation which advises parents on home education - Education Otherwise - has taken its name from the statutory phrase.[63] Some parents opt to educate their child outside of mainstream schooling at the outset of their child's education. There are various reasons for this including: dissatisfaction with the existing state system; the desire for a specific religious environment; and geographical isolation. Others may decide to pursue home education after their child has been attending a state school. This can arise either compulsorily (because the child has been expelled) or voluntarily (because the parents are dissatisfied with the school allocated for the child).

6.25 Parents might also wish to withdraw their child after having registered him or her at a school because they are unhappy with the education being provided. This latter situation may cause problems because there appears to be no formal manner in which a child can be de-registered from school in this way. Regulation 6 of the Registration and Attendance of Pupils Regulations (NI) 1974, requires parents to inform the school principal when they intend to de-register their child. However, the reasons for de-registering given in Departmental guidance are as follows: transfer to another school in Northern Ireland; departure from Northern Ireland; expulsion; death; and leaving school at the end of compulsory education.[64] There is no mention of de-registering so as to provide education otherwise than at school. As long as the child is registered, the school continues to be under an obligation to educate the child and the parent is under an obligation to secure their attendance at school. Similar provisions in Great Britain have given rise to legal action when a local education authority insisted that the child stay on at school until home education was satisfactorily established.[65] The court considered that parents should be given time to set up arrangements for home education. The position in England and Wales has since been clarified by a provision which now allows parents to de-register the child on the specific ground that the child is receiving education otherwise than at school.[66]

Suitable education "otherwise" than at school

6.26 If parents opt to educate a child at home, they must still satisfy the ELB that the child is receiving "efficient full-time education suitable to his age, ability and aptitude and to any special educational needs he may have". Parents do not have to prove that the education that their child is receiving is equivalent to or as good as that which they would receive at school.[67] The

---

[63] Education Otherwise can be contacted at the following address: PO Box 7420, London N9 9SG.
[64] See DENI Circular 1994/15.
[65] *R v Gwent County Council, ex parte Perry* [1985] 129 Sol. J 737.
[66] Education (Pupil Registration) Regulations (NI) 1995, reg. 9(1)(c).
[67] *Bevan v Shears* [1911] 2 KB 936.

onus is simply to show that it is "suitable". Questions inevitably arise as to what constitutes a "suitable" education. Parents do not have to show that the course of instruction complies with the Northern Ireland curriculum as its requirements are specific to grant-aided schools. In fact, parents may have chosen to educate their child at home because of dissatisfaction with the prescribed curriculum in schools. In spite of this, the content of the Northern Ireland curriculum is undoubtedly an indicator of what might be considered to be a "suitable" education. In *Bevan* v *Shears* the court considered that the standard of education accepted by schools for a child of the same age was a "useful guide" in determining whether a child was receiving an efficient education.[68] The older the child is the more difficult it will be to show that the child is receiving a suitable education. Once the child has attained the normal age for secondary education, the child's needs becomes more specialised and it may be difficult for these to be met at home if resources are limited.

6.27 A different issue arises where parents wish to teach their child according to a particular philosophy or educational style. At this point the provisions of article 44 of the 1986 Order may be relevant. This requires the Department and ELB in the exercise of their powers and duties to have regard to the general principle that "so far as is compatible with the provision of efficient instruction and training and the avoidance of unreasonable public expenditure, pupils shall be educated in accordance with the wishes of their parents". This general statutory principle would provide some support to the case of a parent who wishes his or her child to be educated in a particular way.[69] Likewise, a similar argument might be mounted under Article 2 of the First Protocol of the ECHR if the education provided in grant-aided schools contravenes a parent's religious and philosophical convictions. While there is clearly some flexibility in the determination of what amounts to a suitable education, it is submitted that this flexibility is more likely to apply to the use of different types of teaching methods (e.g. self-directed (autonomous) as opposed to teacher-led (transmissive) learning) rather than to the content of the actual curriculum. Courts are unlikely to be persuaded that a course of study which focuses on what is generally considered to be an unbalanced set of beliefs provides a child with "efficient" or "suitable" instruction.[70]

Procedure for establishing suitability

6.28 The legislation does not specify the procedure which must be followed in determining whether the child is receiving a suitable education. However, the ELB cannot assume that a failure to register at school is in itself a failure to provide a suitable education. Under Schedule 13 paragraph 1(1) steps can only be taken to enforce attendance at school "where it appears" to the ELB that the education is not suitable. This implies that the ELB should take preliminary steps to find out whether or not the child is receiving suitable education outside school. In *Phillips* v *Brown* the court considered that education authorities should be able to ask parents for information in order to

---

[68] *Ibid* at p. 941, *per* Bankes J.
[69] See further Petrie, 'Education at Home and the Law' (1993) 5(3) *Education and the Law* pp. 140.
[70] See for instance the attitude of the English' courts to Scientology in *Re B and G* [1985] FLR 493.

establish whether the child was being educated.[71] Parents are not, however, under a legal obligation to reply. Nor is there any statutory provision which allows the ELB to inspect the child's home. Parents who wish to satisfy an ELB that they are providing a suitable education would obviously be advised to comply with any request for information or to inspect the child's home. The onus of proof is on the parent and the obvious way of proving that education is suitable is to let ELB officials see what is actually happening. Moreover, there is English case authority to suggest that education authorities may in exceptional cases require an inspection of the child's home.[72] Moreover, in *H v United Kingdom* the European Commission on Human Rights considered that the state had the right to carry out assessments to ensure that a child was receiving an appropriate home education.[73]

6.29 If the ELB has doubts about the suitability of the child's education, it must investigate fairly the education being provided. In *R v Gwent CC, ex parte Perry*, the Court of Appeal stated that the education authority must give the parent a proper opportunity to satisfy it of the suitability of the child's education.[74] In particular, the court considered that the education authority should let the parent know of the particular issues causing concern so that the parent has an opportunity of both making representations and of taking measures to deal with the areas of concern. If a parent is successful in satisfying the ELB that the child is receiving a satisfactory education, then the parent is required to continue to satisfy the ELB of the suitability of the education at intervals of not less than 12 months.[75]

FAILURE TO COMPLY WITH THE PARENTAL DUTY TO SECURE EDUCATION

6.30 There are various options open to an ELB when a parent fails to comply with his or her duty to secure the child's education. These depend initially on whether or not the child is registered at a school. If the child is not registered at a school, the first stage will normally be the serving of an attendance order. This is an order requiring the parent to register the child at the school named in the order. If the parent does not comply with an attendance order or if a child who is already registered at a school does not attend school regularly, the matter can be pursued in the courts in one of three ways. First, the ELB can institute criminal proceedings in the magistrates' court. Secondly, it can seek an education supervision order (ESO). Finally, in extreme cases, the local social services authority can seek a care order. Since November 1996 the emphasis is supposed to have been placed on education supervision orders as the most appropriate way to deal with persistent absenteeism. However, the evidence shows that ESOs have been used infrequently since their introduction.[76] The Northern Ireland Children Order

---

[71] Unreported (1980). Cited in Petrie, *op cit* p. 142.
[72] *R v Surrey Quarter Sessions Appeals, ex parte Tweedie* [1963] LGR 464.
[73] (1984) 37 DR 105.
[74] *R v Gwent County Council, ex parte Perry* [1985] 129 Sol. J. 737.
[75] Education (Registration and Attendance of Pupils) Regulations (NI) 1974, reg. 14.
[76] Between November 1996 and December 1997 there were just 14 applications, 12 of which were successful. *The Children Order Advisory Committee: First Annual Report* (1998) p. 45.

Advisory Committee has stated its intention to seek information about possible causes for the small number of applications to the courts for ESOs.[77] One possible limitation is that the means of enforcing these orders is limited.[78] Moreover, in England and Wales it appears that ESOs have not had the impact which was envisaged largely because most LEAs do not have the resources to give cases the large amount of time which it takes to make and implement an ESO.[79] It is likely that ELBs in Northern Ireland harbour similar concerns.

6.31   There is considerable disagreement as to the best way to deal with non-attendance. It has been suggested that more effective coercion (possibly through larger fines for the parent's breach of home/school agreements) would be the most effective way of ensuring that children attend school.[80] Other commentators consider that the law has a limited role to play in this area and that successful implementation of the policy must have an education-based focus (i.e. give children the education they desire and they will turn up).[81] That said, there would be little point having a compulsory school age without some sort of legal sanctions to assist in its implementation. Once the state has settled on the principle that any activity should be mandatory it needs to find an effective system of enforcing it. However, in terms of school attendance, the reality is that much depends not just on the parent's desire to send the child to school but also the child's desire to go. Most would accept that there is little that can be done for the disaffected 16 years old. The reality is that most mechanisms are fairly ineffective in the face of deliberate intransigence on the part of either parents or children. Instead enforcement might best be targeted at the cases where it serves most purpose. There is general agreement that the law has some role to play in protecting the right to education of younger children whose parents are apathetic about their attendance at school.

6.32   It might be possible for the law to draw a distinction between young children and children who have reached a sufficient level of maturity to take responsibility for their own decisions on this issue. For instance, it has been suggested that children from the age of 13 should be placed under an independent duty to attend school.[82] Their parents would have a defence to their non attendance if they had done everything in their power to get them to attend school. The child would either then be subject to welfare-based sanctions (such as ESOs) or, more radically, nothing at all. This latter approach has recently been suggested by Ofsted who have proposed that the school leaving age should be reduced to 14. It is clearly open to question whether there is any point in forcing these children to attend school against their wishes. At best they will not gain anything useful from their attendance in body but not in mind and at worst they might be disruptive and have an

---

[77] *Ibid* p. 38.
[78] For criticism, see Brown, Berg and Hullin, 'Truancy, Delinquency and the Leeds Adjournment System' (1990) *Education and the Law* 2(2) 47 and Whitney, 'Enforcing School Attendance: Thoughts on a Flawed Framework' (1998) *ELAS Bulletin No.19* p. 7.
[79] Whitney *ibid*.
[80] Haward, 'Head to Head Confrontation' (1998) *ELAS Bulletin No. 20* p. 5.
[81] For a discussion of this, see Harris, 'Supervision of Truants: Whose Role?' [1989] *Fam Law* 404.
[82] Grenville, 'Compulsory School Attendance and the Child's Wishes' (1988) *Journal of Social Welfare Law* 4, at pp. 18-20.

adverse impact on the education of the children who do wish to learn. On the other hand, school attendance does keep such children off the street and there is a chance that they may learn something useful. More generally, the existence of enforcement mechanisms, however ineffective, does send out a symbolic message about the significance of education generally. Thus it has been argued that on this issue: "the child's right of recipience should prevail over his autonomy interest...it is through the process of education that the child acquires the capacity to exercise meaningful independence".[83]

ATTENDANCE ORDERS

6.33 An attendance order is an order requiring the parent to cause the child to become a registered pupil at the school named in the order.[84] The making of an attendance order will normally be the first step in a ELB's strategy for dealing with children who are not registered at school. Attendance orders are not a court-based measure. They are a 'warning shot' designed to let the parents know that the child's education is not suitable and that the ELB intends to take steps to remedy this if the parent does not. If an ELB considers that a parent may not be performing his or her duty in relation to securing their child's education, the ELB will serve a notice on the parent requiring him or her to satisfy the ELB that the child is receiving "suitable" education.[85] Suitable education means efficient, full-time education suitable to his age, ability and aptitude and to any special educational needs which he may have. The parent must have at least 14 days to respond to the notice. If the parent does not respond or the response does not satisfy the ELB, the ELB will serve an attendance order if it is of the opinion that it is expedient that the child should attend school.[86] If an attendance order has been issued, the Board of Governors of the school named in the order must admit the child to the school. This requirement does not, however, affect its power to suspend or expel any pupil.

Choice of school

6.34 Before serving the order on the parent the ELB must serve a notice informing the parent of its intention to make the order; specifying the school which the ELB intends to name in the order and, if it thinks fit, one or more other schools which it regards as suitable alternatives.[87] The notice must also state what will happen if the parent accepts one of the schools named in the notice and how he or she can apply to have a different school specified. If the parent selects a school specified by the ELB in the notice, that school will be the school named in the order. If the parent wishes his or her child to attend a different school, they have 14 days to apply for the child to be admitted to a different school and to notify the ELB accordingly. If the child is offered a place at the school of the parent's choice, then that school will be named in the attendance order. Although the procedure appears to be straightforward, problems can arise if the parent names an inappropriate school or the school is

---

[83] Bainham, *Children, Parents and the State* (1988) p. 168.
[84] Art. 45 and Sch. 14 to the 1986 Order substituted by art. 27 of the 1996 Order.
[85] Sch. 13, para. 1(1) to the 1986 Order.
[86] *Ibid* Sch. 13, para. 1(2).
[87] *Ibid* Sch. 13, para. 1A(2).

unwilling to accept the child or the parent does not undertake all the necessary steps for registration.[88]

SUMMARY OF PROCEDURE FOR ISSUING ATTENDANCE ORDER ON THE PARENTS OF A NON-STATEMENTED CHILD

ELB: Notice requesting proof of suitable education
↓
14 days
↓
(Parent can attempt to prove suitable education)
↓
ELB: Notice of intention to serve order
↓
14 days
↓
(Parent can apply to school not proposed)
↓
ELB: Attendance Order

Duration of the order

6.35 The order will normally apply so long as the child is of compulsory school age.[89] However, if a child is attending a school which does not provide education up to compulsory school age, the order will expire when the child reaches the age at which he would normally leave that school. A parent may apply at any time for the child to be admitted to a school not named in the order. If the child is offered a place at the school of the parent's choice, then the parent can require the ELB to change the school named in the order. A parent cannot apply for admission to an independent school unless, in the opinion of the ELB, the school provides suitable education.

6.36 A parent can apply to the ELB at any time for the order to be revoked on the grounds that arrangements have been made for the child to receive suitable education otherwise than at school.[90] The ELB will comply with the request unless it is of the opinion that no satisfactory arrangements have been made for the education of the child otherwise than at school. A parent who is unhappy with the ELB's failure to revoke the order may refer the matter to the Department who can give such direction determining the question as it thinks fit.[91]

---

[88] Whitney, 'Enforcing School Attendance: Thoughts on a Flawed Framework' (1998) *ELAS Bulletin* p. 7.
[89] Sch. 13, para. 1(3) to the 1986 Order.
[90] *Ibid* Sch. 13, para. 2(2).
[91] *Ibid* Sch. 13, para. 2(4).

Children with statements of special educational need

6.37 Special rules apply in relation to attendance orders in respect of a child for whom the ELB maintains a statement.[92] These rules ensure that the school named in the attendance order is the school named in the statement. The normal procedures for consulting the parent about the school to be named in the order do not apply. In cases where a statement is maintained, the school specified in the statement will be the school named in the attendance order. Where the statement does not specify a school, the ELB will amend the statement so that it specifies a school and that school will be named in the attendance order. Where a school attendance order is in force and the school specified in the order differs from the school specified in the statement, the ELB will amend the order so that it names the school specified in the statement. If a school is specified in the statement, parents cannot ask for the attendance order to be revoked on the grounds that arrangements have been made to educate the child otherwise than at school. If a school has not been specified in the statement, the parents can ask the ELB for such a revocation and can refer the matter to the Department if dissatisfied with the ELB's refusal.

CRIMINAL PROSECUTION

6.38 An ELB may decide that the only way to secure the child's education is to prosecute the parents.[93] Such prosecutions have been quite common in the past. However, since November 1996, the emphasis is intended to be on education supervision orders (ESOs) which are considered below. That said, criminal prosecution remains an option and can be sought instead of or in addition to an ESO. A parent will be guilty of a criminal offence in two circumstances. The first is where he or she fails to comply with a school attendance order. The second is where a child who is a registered pupil at a school fails to attend regularly at that school. In the latter case, the parent can raise one of the defences set out in Schedule 13, paragraph 3 to the 1986 Order which are discussed above (i.e. sickness, unavoidable cause, transport difficulties). Moreover, in all cases, it is a defence to show that the child is receiving a suitable education, for instance where the parent has made arrangements to have the child educated at home.

6.39 The offence is an offence of strict liability. This means that the prosecution do not have to prove that the parents intended to prevent their child from receiving an education. Nor is it a defence for the parents to show that as soon as they became aware of the absences, they took all reasonable steps to ensure that the child attended school.[94] The absolute nature of this offence has been criticised. It has been suggested that parents should have a defence where the parent has done everything in his or her power to make sure that the child has attended school since: "there is no reason why the parent of

---

[92] *Ibid* Sch. 13, para. 1B.
[93] *Ibid* Sch. 13, para. 4.
[94] *Crump* v *Gilmore* [1969] 68 LGR 56.

a child who does not attend school should be placed in a less favourable position than the parent of one who steals or commits an act of violence".[95]

6.40 The parent of the child will be required to give the court any information which he or she has in relation to the date and place of registration of the birth of the child. If the parent refuses or is unable to give the information, the child will be presumed to have been of compulsory school age at any time material to the offence. The Family Proceedings Court may direct the ELB to apply for an ESO unless the ELB, having consulted the appropriate authority, decides that the child's welfare will be satisfactorily guarded even though no education supervision order is made. In such cases the ELB will inform the court of its reason for the decision within eight weeks of the direction.

Sentencing

6.41 Criminal prosecution may appear to be quite a drastic course of action for failure to secure a child's education. However, prior to the introduction of the ESO it was the only court-based remedy (bar a Care Order) which an ELB could pursue. Although courts had the option to impose a custodial sentence, they were understandably reluctant to do so. A parent in custody is much less likely to be able to secure a child's attendance at school than a parent living in the same house. For this reason, the offence can no longer incur a sentence of imprisonment.[96] Instead parents may be fined for a failure to secure attendance. A parent convicted of an offence is liable to a fine not exceeding level 3 on the standard scale. The difficulty with this is that financial penalties may have an impact on the well-being of the whole family, particularly if resources are limited. This seems unfair if the parent is doing his or her best to get the child to go to school. Moreover, the scale of the fine is unlikely to make much difference if the parent is withholding the child as some sort of protest. In such situations the ESO would seem to be a more appropriate option and to facilitate this, a court considering a criminal prosecution may now direct an ELB to apply for an ESO.[97]

EDUCATION SUPERVISION ORDERS (ESOS)

6.42 Education supervision orders were proposed during the Child Care Review as a less draconian measure for tackling truancy than a care order, that is an order placing the child in social services care.[98] Prior to 1996 care orders were the alternative legal option for dealing with persistent absenteeism apart from criminal prosecution.[99] Although they were rarely used in Northern Ireland for these purposes, it was in theory possible for children in otherwise good family circumstances to be removed from their homes if they were continually playing truant or if they were kept from school by their parents in

---

[95] Grenville, 'Compulsory School Attendance and the Child's Wishes' (1988) *Journal of Social Welfare Law* 4, at p. 18.
[96] Children (NI) Order 1995, Sch. 10.
[97] Sch. 13, para. 6 to the 1986 Order substituted by art. 131 of the Children (NI) Order 1995.
[98] *Review of Child Care Law*, para. 12.22.
[99] The other option was a training school order.

protest about a particular educational policy.[100] The ESO is a mid-way measure designed to be used where non-school attendance appears to be the only problem in the child's life. Where absenteeism is part of a wider set of problems within the family a care order may be appropriate.

6.43 It should be noted that the legal provisions on both ESOs and care orders are contained in the Children (NI) Order 1995 and not in the Education Orders. As a result of this, they are both subject to the general provisions of the Children (NI) Order 1995 and in particular, the welfare checklist set out in article 3 of the 1995 Order. This is considered further in paragraphs 6.54-6.57.

Procedure for application

6.44 Applications for ESOs are made to the Family Proceedings Court. Any ELB may apply to the court for an education supervision order. However, proceedings will normally be instigated by the ELB in whose area the child resides or in which the child's school is situated. The application may arise in a number of circumstances. First, the ELB may apply for an ESO on its own initiative.[101] Secondly, it must consider whether it is appropriate to apply for an ESO when it is considering a criminal prosecution for failure to secure a child's education.[102] Thirdly, it may apply for an ESO if it appears to the ELB that a child in its area is being cared for by a person who is "habitually wandering from place to place"[103] Finally, a court dealing with a criminal prosecution in this area may direct the ELB to apply for an ESO.[104] When an ELB is proposing to apply for an ESO it must consult the local authority in whose area the child lives.[105] An ESO may not be made in relation to any child who is the subject of a care order. In such cases, the local authority has responsibility for securing the child's education.

Grounds

6.45 A court can make an ESO if it is satisfied that the child is of compulsory school age and is not being properly educated.[106] A child will not be considered to be receiving a proper education unless he is receiving full-time education suitable to his age, ability and aptitude and to any special educational needs that he may have. The onus of proof is on the parent to show that the child is receiving a suitable education. It is presumed that a child who is the subject of an attendance order which has not been complied with or who is a registered pupil at a school which he is not attending is not being properly educated. When deciding whether to make an order, the paramount consideration will be the welfare of the child. The court must also consider the general criteria set out in article 3 of the Children (NI) Order (these are discussed at paras. 6.54-6.57 below) In *Essex County Council v B*

---

[100] See *Re DJMS (a minor)* [1977] 3 All ER 582 where the father kept his son from school because he objected to comprehensive education.
[101] Art. 55 (1) of the 1995 Order.
[102] Sch. 13, para. 4(1) to the 1986 Order substituted by art. 130 of the Children (NI) Order 1995.
[103] Sch. 13, para. 5(1) to the 1986 Order.
[104] Sch. 4, para. 6 to the 1986 Order substituted by art. 131 of the Children (NI) Order 1995.
[105] Art. 55(7) of the 1995 Order.
[106] *Ibid* art. 55(2)-(3).

the High Court overturned a decision by the Family Proceedings Court on the basis that it had not given proper consideration to these factors.[107]

6.46 An ESO will not always be the appropriate course of action in the case of non-attendance. In particular, it would be impractical to undertake the effort to get an ESO when the child is a disaffected pupil in year 12. Instead it has been suggested that ESOs are appropriate where "education is the major focus of problems, when voluntary ways of working have broken down but there is still a realistic chance of improving the child's performance before they leave school".[108]

Effect of an ESO

6.47 The effect of an ESO is that responsibility for securing the child's education is removed from the parents and transferred to the ELB named in the order.[109] This will normally be the ELB is whose area the child resides but may be the ELB is whose area the child's school is situated provided both ELBs agree to this.[110] An attendance order which was made prior to the ESO will cease to have effect once the ESO is in force. Similarly, an ELB can no longer issue an attendance order during the operation of an ESO. These are logical consequences of the fact that the parent is no longer under a legal obligation to ensure that the child attends school. Moreover, while the ESO remains in force, certain statutory provisions which give parents rights in education cease to have effect. These are: (i) article 44 of the 1986 Order, the principle that a child should be educated in accordance with the wishes of his or her parents; (ii) article 36 of the 1989 Order, the duty to comply with a parental preference as to the choice of school; and (iii) article 37 of the 1989 Order, the parents' right to appeal a decision to refuse admission.

6.48 When an ESO is made, an education supervisor will be appointed for the child. It is the duty of the supervisor to advise, assist and befriend the child and his parents. The supervisor is also under a duty to give directions to the child and his parents for the purpose of securing that the child is properly educated. Directions might require parents to get up and accompany the child to school; to visit the school; or to sign and check the child's homework. The supervisor could direct the child to meet with him or her on certain specified occasions or to sign in and out of classes. Before giving directions the supervisor should attempt to ascertain the wishes and feelings of the child and his parents and should give these due consideration. The supervisor may direct the child to attend a particular school or tuition unit. He or she cannot, however, force the child to attend school. This point was emphasised in *Essex County Council* v *B* where Douglas Brown J pointed out that "there is no question under an education supervision order of force being used. There is no question of this girl physically being taken to school and physically being made to stay there".[111]

---

[107] [1993] 1 FLR 866.
[108] Field, *The Children (NI) Order 1995* (BELB).
[109] Sch. 4 to the 1995 Order.
[110] *Ibid* art. 55(6).
[111] [1993] 1 FLR 866 at p. 878.

6.49 Educational supervisors may require pupils or parents to provide them with certain information.[112] He or she can require the child to keep them informed of any change of address and to allow them to visit him or her wherever he is living. This would only seem appropriate for an older child, particularly one who has a habit of absconding from home. The parent must, if asked, inform the ESO of the child's address (if known to him or her) and, if he or she is living with the child, must allow the supervisor reasonable contact.

Enforcement

6.50 If the ESO's directions are not complied with, it is the duty of the supervisor to consider what further steps should be taken.[113] The reason for non-compliance is important. In particular, an ESO will need to establish whether the fact of non-compliance rests with the parent or the pupil. If a parent persistently fails to comply with a direction, he or she will be guilty of a criminal offence.[114] Parents will have a defence if they can show that they took all reasonable steps to comply; or that the direction was unreasonable. On similar lines, there is a defence if it was not reasonably practicable to comply with both a direction under an ESO and a requirement of a supervision order, probation order or an order under section 74(1)(c) of the Children and Young Persons Act 1968 (i.e. the power of a court to make a supervision order on a finding of guilt).[115] A person who is found guilty of an offence will be liable on conviction to a fine not exceeding level 3 on the standard scale. For the first time in this area a distinction is drawn between non-compliance by the parents and non-compliance by the pupil. This has given recognition to the fact that parents are not always able to force their children to go to school. Paragraph 9 of Schedule 4 to the Children (NI) Order 1995 states that if a child persistently fails to comply with any direction under the ESO, the ELB will notify the appropriate authority. This might seem to be a relatively insignificant comeback to the child, but is actually an indication of the fact that the education supervisor considers that the child is beyond his or her help and that the possibility of seeking a care order should be considered. The education supervisor's ultimate weapon somewhat paradoxically is an application to discharge the ESO under Schedule 4, paragraph 7(1)(c). At this stage, if the court is concerned that the child's educational needs are not being met, it may direct the social services authority in whose area the child lives to investigate the circumstances of the child. Once again, this means that it is more likely that a care order will be sought.

Duration

6.51 An ESO will initially have effect for one year beginning on the date on which it was made.[116] However, this may be extended provided that the application to extend is made at least three months prior to the date of expiry.

---

[112] Sch. 4 para. 6 to the 1995 Order.
[113] *Ibid* Sch. 4, paras. 7-8.
[114] *Ibid* Sch. 4, para. 8.
[115] *Ibid* Sch. 4, para. 4.
[116] Sch. 4 paras. 5-7 to the 1995 Order.

Further extensions may be sought but no one extension period may exceed three years. The ESO will cease to have effect when the child reaches compulsory school age; the child is made the subject of a care order; or the court discharges the ESO. The court may discharge the order on the application of the child, the parent or the ELB. In all cases the court will have regard to the principles set out in article 3 of the Children (NI) Order 1995 and discussed at paragraphs 6.54-6.57 below. The reasons for discharge are essentially twofold; either that the ESO has been successful or unsuccessful. If it has been successful, (i.e. the child is now receiving a suitable education) no further intervention is necessary. If, on the other hand, the discharge is sought because the ESO has failed to secure the child's education, the court might direct the social services authority to investigate the child's circumstances.[117]

CARE ORDERS

6.52 A care order is an order which will transfer the child's care from the parents to the local Health and Social Services Trust.[118] This may mean that the child will be taken from the family home and looked after in a children's home or foster care. Applications can only be made by the local Health and Social Services Trust. It is quite a drastic course of action which is rarely used in education cases as it is reserved for cases where the child is in danger of suffering significant harm. Prior to 1996, a care order could be made on education grounds alone. In fact, it was the only alternative open to the court for severe cases of absenteeism. The ESO is intended to become the norm in most of these cases. However, there are still occasions when a care order may be necessary. The first is where the child's absenteeism is part of the wider set of problems with the family. The second is where the efforts made under the ESO have failed to secure the child's education. The third is where the ELB has taken all steps which it might have taken had an ESO been issued to no avail. In *In re O (a minor)* the court considered that it was not necessary for the local authority to seek an ESO first if it was clear that the ESO would have no effect.[119] Each case must be considered on its own facts since the informal requests of an education welfare officer cannot be comparable to directions under an ESO because the former have no legal force and cannot, for instance, result in criminal prosecution for non-compliance. On the other hand, it is clear that an authority can apply for a care order without an ESO having been issued, otherwise the legislation would have made an ESO a pre-requisite to an application for a care order on education grounds.

Grounds for making a care order

6.53 There are two threshold criteria which must be met before a court can make a care order.[120] The first is that the child is suffering or is likely to suffer significant harm. "Harm" means ill-treatment or the impairment of health or development. "Development" means physical, intellectual, emotional, social or behavioural development.[121] When the court is considering whether the

---

[117] *Ibid* Sch. 4 para. 7(2).
[118] *Ibid* art. 50.
[119] *In re O (a minor)* [1992] WLR 912.
[120] Art. 50(1) of the 1995 Order.
[121] *Ibid* art. 2.

harm is or would be significant in relation to the child's health or development, it will consider what would be reasonably expected of a similar child.[122] In *In re O* the court considered that if a child was missing their education, it was not difficult to draw the conclusion that if they had gone to school they would have improved their intellectual and social development. The court said that in this context a "similar child" means a child of equivalent social and intellectual development who has gone to school and not just an average child who may or may not be at school.[123] On this test it was quite clear that the child's development had been impaired. The second condition which must be satisfied is that the risk of harm is attributable to the care not being what it would be reasonable to expect a parent to give or the fact that the child is beyond the parent's control. A child might be considered to be outside of parental control where the child refuses to go to school and they are not in a position to make them go. Parents would not be considered to be giving reasonable care if they are indifferent to the child's absence or are actually keeping the child from school as a form of protest. In *In Re DJMS (a minor)*, an English case decided prior to the Children Act 1989, a court made a care order in relation to a child whose parents kept him from school because they objected to comprehensive education.[124] Lord Denning was clear what was best for the child's welfare, stating:

> "Everybody knows that a child ought to be properly educated. It is utterly unreasonable for the parents to keep him back from school because of their implacable opposition to a comprehensive school system…He should be at home and go to school as all the other children do. But if the parents will not do this, then it seems to me that the only sensible alternative is for a care order to be made." [125]

In *In re O* the court considered that if a child who is living at home is not going to school and is suffering harm, it follows that the child is beyond the parents' control or that they are not giving the child the care it would be reasonable to expect a parent to give. On this basis, it would seem to be quite easy to establish that the threshold criteria for a care order have been met in any case where the child is not receiving an education. However, the court must also consider the general welfare criteria set out in article 3 of the Children (NI) Order 1995. These are discussed below.

GENERAL PRINCIPLES TO BE CONSIDERED WHEN MAKING EDUCATION SUPERVISION ORDER AND CARE ORDERS

6.54 When a court is determining any question with respect to a child's upbringing, the child's welfare will be the paramount consideration.[126] The parents' wishes may be a factor but the overriding concern is the child's interest. Moreover, in determining whether to make an order and what order to

---

[122] *Ibid* art. 50(3).
[123] *Op cit* at p. 917.
[124] [1977] 3 All ER 582.
[125] *Ibid* p. 590.
[126] Art. 3(1) of the 1995 Order.

make, the court will have particular regard to the welfare criteria set out in article 3(3) of the Children (NI) Order 1995 and the principle of non-intervention in article 3(5). These apply to all decisions made under the Children Order but will be considered here in the particular context of measures designed to remedy a child's non-attendance at school. There are a range of orders which a court can make, including child assessment orders and supervision orders. However, the two orders which are most likely to be made in this context are an ESO or a care order, both of which are discussed above.

The welfare criteria

6.55 When a court is considering whether to make, vary or discharge an order, it will have particular regard to certain factors specified in article 3(3) of the Children (NI) Order 1995. A failure to have regard to these criteria can result in a decision being overturned. The criteria are as follows:

(1) *The child's wishes and feelings.* These must be considered in the light of the child's age and understanding. The more mature the child, the more weight should be attached to their wishes and feelings. The reasons given by the child as to why they are not attending school are important if the court is to find an appropriate solution. The court may also have regard to the child's own choice of school particularly if non-attendance is motivated by a dislike of the school at which he or she is registered. However, the fact that the child does not want an order to be made is not an overriding factor. In *Essex County Council v B* the court stressed that the child does not have a veto on an order being made.[127]

(2) *Physical, emotional and educational needs.* The latter will be of most significance in this context. On the basis of the court's approach in *In re O*, it could be concluded that a child who is not attending school is quite clearly not having his or her educational needs met.[128]

(3) *The likely effect of any change in his circumstances.* In *Essex County Council v B* the court considered the most significant change in circumstances to result from an ESO to be the child's return to mainstream education.[129] This criterion will also be of significance if the court proposes to issue a care order which may result in the child being removed from the family home. However, there may be other factors which go against the making of an order, such as the knowledge that the child has secured a place in a school which they are happy to attend.

(4) *His age, sex, background and other characteristics.* The age of the child might be considered to be relevant to the issue of an order. For instance, a court might be more inclined to intervene where the child is at a particularly important stage of his school life, for example beginning primary one or about to take their GCSEs. On the other hand, a court might be disinclined to intervene if the pupil is aged 16 and coming towards the end of their school life.

---

[127] [1993] 1 FLR 866.
[128] [1992] WLR 912.
[129] *Op cit.*

(5) *Any harm which he has suffered or is at risk of suffering.* In most contexts, if there are no other factors present, the child's non-attendance at school will be considered to put him or her at risk of suffering an impairment to his intellectual development unless other arrangements have been made for his or her education.

(6) *How capable of meeting his needs are his parents or any other person in relation to whom the court considers the question to be relevant.* This will be of key importance where the parents claim that they can provide a suitable education at home. If this is not the case, and the child is not attending school, the court will consider whether the parents are able to secure the child's attendance at school. Presumably, in cases of wilful truancy, the court should consider also whether the local authority will be any better at securing the child's attendance at school.

(7) *The range of powers available to the court.* In this respect the court is more likely to favour the less drastic ESO rather than a care order. However, as has been seen, a care order can still be made instead of an ESO where everything that might have been done under an ESO has been done with no positive improvement in attendance. Other powers include a supervision order.

6.56 It should be noted that parental wishes are not a specified factor to be taken into account. However, the court is not precluded from taking them into account. Moreover, a consideration of parental wishes will inevitably arise in the context of other factors such as the child's characteristics and parental capabilities.

Principle of non-intervention

6.57 Article 3(5) of the Children (NI) Order 1995 directs that a court will not make an order unless it considers that "doing so would be better for the child than making no order at all". This is referred to as the principle of non-intervention. Thus, if an order is likely to make no difference to the child's education, the court should not make either an ESO or a care order. However, on the facts of *Essex County Council* v *B* the court concluded that it was better to make an ESO than no order because "no order would let things drift on, possibly, until...she ceases to be eligible for full-time education".[130] A different approach might be taken in the case of a child who deliberately absconds from school after having been safely delivered there. It could be argued that in these circumstances the local Health and Social Services Trust is in no better position to secure the child's education than his or her parents.

---

[130] [1993] 1 FLR 866 at p. 878.

CHAPTER SEVEN

DISCIPLINE

INTRODUCTION

7.01 Discipline is necessary both for the effective functioning of a school and for the pupils' personal development. To a lay person, the notion of discipline in schools is often synonymous with the imposition of punishment. In the educational context the term is interpreted in its broadest sense and is considered to refer to the general good order of the school.[1] There are a number of measures which schools can take to promote orderliness. These are not limited to punishments for bad behaviour. However, positive approaches such as reward systems are unlikely to result in legal challenge. The focus of this chapter is consequently upon disciplinary measures which are intended to punish, discourage or deter as it is the exercise of this type of discipline which may result in a legal dispute. For teachers, a key issue will be what they may lawfully do to assert control and discourage poor behaviour without exposing themselves to either criminal or civil liability. Parents, while realising that it is in their child's best interests for the school to have an effective disciplinary policy, will wish to ensure that their child is not subjected to disciplinary measures which they believe to be unjustified or to usurp their authority as parents. Given the potential for conflict, it is inevitable that the imposition of disciplinary sanctions will occasionally result in disputes between parents and the school. The objective of this chapter is to outline when that conflict may have legal consequences and what those consequences may be.

7.02 The law relating to discipline in schools has not developed systematically. While it has its foundations in a series of judgments on the use of corporal punishment given by the courts in and around the turn of the century, it now encompasses provisions from the Education Orders as well as child law, criminal law, tort and international human rights. Given its varied sources, it is perhaps not surprising that the law in this area has witnessed rapid change in the past decade. Two areas in particular have been transformed. The first relates to the use of corporal punishment in schools. The change in this instance was brought about as a result of an application to the European Court of Human Rights. In *Campbell and Cosans* v *UK*, the Court found that the use of corporal punishment on pupils against the will of their parents amounted to a breach of Article 2 of the First Protocol of the European Convention on Human Rights.[2] This requires Members States to ensure that education is in conformity with parents' religious and philosophical convictions. The United Kingdom had argued that such a

---

[1] See for instance, *The Report of the Working Party on Discipline in Schools in Northern Ireland* DENI (1990), para. 1.2.
[2] *Campbell and Cosans* v *UK* (1982) EHRR 293. For a discussion of the implications of this judgment see, Lonbay, 'Rights in Education under the European Convention on Human Rights' (1983) *Modern Law Review* p. 345.

decision would necessitate the establishment of a dual system of schools, one category using corporal punishment and the other refraining from it. The court considered that the government could offer individual parents the opportunity to exempt their child from corporal punishment. Ultimately, the government decided to completely abolish corporal punishment in all grant-aided schools.[3]

7.03 The second key change has been in the area of exclusions from school. Prior to 1985 the grounds and procedures for exclusions were very much at the discretion of the individual school. In 1985 regulations were introduced which limited the periods during which a pupil could be suspended and provided for consultations to be made before an expulsion.[4] However, there were continued legal challenges concerning the failure of schools to provide pupils and their parents with a fair hearing prior to the decision to exclude.[5] In 1994 parents were given a right to appeal to a local tribunal against a decision to expel.[6] In 1995 further changes were introduced, the most notable of which is a prohibition on the use of indefinite exclusions.[7] The result is that, while the reason for excluding a pupil still lies at the discretion of the school, the procedures which must be invoked when giving effect to the decision are now subject to specific legal requirements.

7.04 The response to the changes in the area of school discipline has been mixed. At one level it is undoubtedly the case that parental rights in this area have been significantly enhanced. The key area of conflict between teachers and parents (corporal punishment) has been resolved. Moreover, parents now have a designated means of challenging the ultimate disciplinary measure, the decision to expel. However, the effect of the changes have been criticised by teachers who believe that their basic authority has been undermined and that the growing level of indiscipline in schools is the result. Studies suggests that there are increasing levels of disruptive and aggressive behaviour in schools.[8] The previous response to this type of extreme misbehaviour would have been an expulsion. However, schools are no longer in a position to refuse to re-admit difficult children if directed to do so by an appeal tribunal. The difficulties are compounded by the fact that teachers are uncertain as to the precise scope of their other disciplinary powers and are under the perception that each decision to discipline is now shadowed by the potential threat of legal action.[9]

---

[3] This was accomplished by the Education (Corporal Punishment) (NI) Order 1987.
[4] Schools (Suspension and Expulsion of Pupils) Regulations (NI) 1985.
[5] See, for instance, *R v Board of Governors of London Oratory ex parte Regis*, *The Times*, 17 February 1988.
[6] Education and Libraries (NI) Order 1986, art. 49 substituted by the Education and Libraries (NI) Order 1993, art. 39.
[7] Schools (Suspension and Expulsion of Pupils) Regulations (NI) 1995.
[8] The Elton Committee (*Discipline in Schools* HMSO (1989)) was asked to report on this issue as a result of concern about levels of indiscipline in schools in England and Wales. It found that teachers considered persistent disruption to be more of a problem than violent behaviour. However, local studies have highlighted an increasing trend in the number of assaults on teachers and fellow pupils. See for instance The Ulster Teacher's Union, *Survey on Indiscipline* (1987).
[9] DENI, *Report of the Working Party on Discipline in Schools*, (1990).

7.05 There have been recent changes to the legislation on discipline arising out of recommendations made as part of the 1998 School Improvement Programme. One of the reports which was part of this initiative specifically addresses the issue of schools' disciplinary strategy.[10] Although the focus of the report was on ways of promoting good behaviour (e.g. raising literacy standards, support for the weakest schools etc), there were a number of recommendations for legislative change in relation to disciplinary measures. These have been implemented in Northern Ireland in the Education (NI) Order 1998. This places additional responsibilities on the Board of Governors for determining the school's disciplinary policy and clarifies the situations in which teachers can detain pupils or use physical force to restrain them (see para. 7.34) The 1998 Order also contains new provisions on pupil referral units and the education of children with behavioural difficulties (see para. 7.71). The reforms mirror similar provisions introduced in England and Wales by the Education Act 1997, one of the last pieces of legislation introduced by the Conservative government.[11] The reforms will go some way to addressing teachers' concerns but, as will be seen, there are still areas where there is considerable doubt about the legitimacy of certain types of punishment.

GENERAL LEGAL PRINCIPLES

7.06 The power of a teacher to impose discipline is not specified in statute. Instead its legal basis must be gleaned from a series of judgments by the national and international courts (in the latter case the European Court of Human Rights). These establish a series of general principles which are relevant to all decisions to impose discipline.

The legal basis of a teacher's authority

7.07 Teachers (including principals) do have legal authority to impose disciplinary measures on pupils whose behaviour has not been of an acceptable standard. In *Mansell v Griffin* the court considered that this authority could be presumed from "the fact of a parent sending a child to school".[12] This was affirmed in *R v Newport Salop Justices, ex parte Wright* where the court stated that:

> "... any parent who sends a child to school is presumed to give to the teacher authority to make reasonable regulations and to administer to the child reasonable [corporal] punishment for breach of those regulations."[13]

The existence of some sort of authority to discipline is also implicit in the existing statutory provisions in relation to school discipline. These require schools to produce a disciplinary policy and to restrict the use of certain forms of discipline such as corporal punishment. However, the precise basis and consequently the scope of teachers' authority in this area is unclear. It was initially considered that a teacher's authority derived from the principle of *in*

---

[10] *Promoting and Sustaining Good Behaviour: A Discipline Strategy for Schools* (DENI, 1998)
[11] For a discussion of the legislation see, Monk, 'School Exclusions and the Education Act 1997' (1997) 9/4 *Education and the Law* 304.
[12] [1908] 1 KB 160 at p.169.
[13] [1929] 2 KB 416 at p. 428.

loco parentis. This would mean that while the child is in the teacher's care, the teacher stands in the place of the parent and can do anything which the parent would authorise. In *Cleary* v *Booth* Collins J referred to the authority "delegated" by the parent to the teacher.[14] However, this principle originated from cases prior to the introduction of compulsory education and arguably makes more sense in that context. It is now thought that the *in loco parentis* principle does not fully explain the extent of the teacher's authority and that a teacher can lawfully impose punishments which the parent has not in fact authorised.[15] The cases which have been taken under the ECHR indicate that a teacher's authority to impose discipline is limited only to the extent that the use of discipline would contravene a parent's religious and philosophical convictions or breach other provisions of the Convention.[16] Moreover, article 6 of the Children (NI) Order 1995 states that a person who does not have responsibility for a child but who has the care of the child may do what is reasonable in all the circumstances of the case for the purposes of safeguarding or promoting the child's welfare. This would extend to teachers and might provide some basis for authority. However, there is no specific statute giving teachers the power to exercise discipline. This absence of a clear legal authority was highlighted by the Elton Report.[17] The report concluded that "the accumulation of case law is probably sufficient to inhibit litigation by parents opposed to particular actions such as putting a child in detention". However, the Elton Committee was not certain whether the legal basis of a teacher's authority was "beyond challenge". It recommended that legislation should state the precise scope of the teacher's power to impose disciplinary measures on pupils.

The reasonableness of the punishment

7.08 Although the precise scope of a teacher's authority to impose discipline remains uncertain, it is clear that it extends only to the use of 'reasonable' punishments.[18] The classic statement of 'reasonableness' in this context is set out in *Mansell* v *Griffin* by Phillimore J. He said that the teacher who has imposed discipline should be able to say:

> "The punishment which I administered was moderate; it was not dictated by any bad motive, and it was such as is usual in the school and such as the parent of the child might expect if it did wrong."[19]

Two factors will be particularly relevant to the reasonableness of any decision to impose discipline. The first relates to the manner in which the punishment is administered. It has been stated that punishment must not be inflicted "for the gratification of passion or rage" and must not be protracted.[20] Instead it

---

[14] *Op cit* at p. 469.
[15] See further Crook 'In Loco Parentis. Time for a Reappraisal?' [1989] *Family Law* 447.
[16] See for instance *Campbell and Cosans* v *UK* (1982) EHHR 293 and generally paras. 1.51-1.57.
[17] *Discipline in Schools* HMSO (1989) at pp. 83-84.
[18] See, for instance, *R* v *Newport Salop Justices* [1929] 2 KB 416.
[19] [1908] KB 160, at p. 168.
[20] *R* v *Hopley* [1860] 2 F&F 202.

should involve a controlled, if not entirely cool response to the misbehaviour.[21] The second aspect of reasonableness is the nature of the punishment itself. National authority places emphasis on the fact that the punishment must be "moderate" and not "excessive".[22] Moreover, there is authority to suggest that the punishment must be proportionate to the misbehaviour.[23] Finally, Article 3 of the ECHR is also relevant in this context. It states that a person has a right not to be subjected to "torture, inhuman or degrading treatment or punishment". This has been used to challenge the punishments applied in several English schools.[24] Similarly, the UNCRC specifies that state parties shall take appropriate measures to ensure that school discipline is administered in a manner consistent with the child's human dignity and in conformity with the rest of the Convention.[25]

7.09 The authority of a teacher to impose reasonable discipline should not be confused with the duty on public bodies to act reasonably. This is known as the *Wednesbury* principle.[26] It is incumbent upon public bodies (such as Boards of Governors and ELBs) to act reasonably when taking disciplinary decisions. In this context a decision would only be considered to be unreasonable if no other public body acting with due regard to its responsibilities would have reached the same decision. In the context of school discipline, the public law duty to act reasonably has most significance in relation to decisions to exclude pupils from school. This is considered further at paragraph 7.51 below.

The significance of parental wishes

7.10 An important aspect of discipline is the parental support for the system of discipline imposed. The area which was the biggest source of conflict - corporal punishment - has now been settled. However, there may be other instances where a parent objects either to the prohibition of a certain type of conduct or to the use of a particular form of punishment. In both instances, the general position is that schools have a large degree of control over the content of their disciplinary policies and parents have little right to object to the substance of these policies. In the first type of situation, where the parent approves of the conduct which the school has prohibited, the school may still punish the child for failure to comply with the school's rules. In *R v Newport Salop Justices, ex parte Wright* a court considered that a school was justified in punishing a pupil for smoking outside school even though he had his father's permission to do so.[27] Similarly, a parental objection to the use of a particular form of discipline does not in itself preclude the school from using

---

[21] *R v Taylor, The Times*, 28 December 1983 where a teacher who threw a book at a pupil was found guilty of assault occasioning actual bodily harm.
[22] *R v Hopley, op cit.*
[23] See *R v Governors of St Gregory's RC Aided High School, ex parte M, The Times*, 27 January 1994. Art. 5 of the 1998 Order specifically requires schools to consider whether detention is a proportionate punishment when determining whether the punishment is reasonable.
[24] See the cases cited at para. 7.40 *post*.
[25] Art. 28(2).
[26] It has its foundation in the case of *Associated Provincial Picture Houses Ltd v Wednesbury Corporation* [1948] 1 KB 223.
[27] [1929] 2 KB 416.

it. National legislation does not give parents the right to object to any aspect of school discipline. Article 2 of the First Protocol of the ECHR requires Member States to "respect the rights of parents to ensure that education is in conformity with their own religious and philosophical convictions".[28] In *Campbell and Cosans* this was considered to uphold a parent's objection to corporal punishment.[29] It could therefore in theory also extend to other aspects of discipline provided that the parent can put forward a cogent argument that the punishment contravenes a particular religious or philosophical belief. Religious or political convictions were described by the court as being those "that are worthy of respect in a democratic society and are not incompatible with human dignity".[30] However, in spite of this broad definition, it is difficult to envisage a form of punishment commonly used by schools which could be considered to contravene any particular philosophical conviction. It is more likely that a school rule (e.g. about dress or participation in sport) might interfere with a religious conviction. In such cases parents should immediately inform the school about their objection; a school will not be considered to have failed to respect parental wishes if these were never drawn to their attention.[31]

7.11 The converse situation (where a parent approves or assents to a particular form of punishment) will not necessarily prevent the exercise of discipline from being unlawful. It has been suggested that parents may still give teachers the authority to carry out corporal punishment.[32] However, even if permission is given by parents, the action will still be unlawful if it goes beyond the realms of reasonable discipline. In *R v Hopley* a teacher wrote to a pupil's father asking for his permission to chastise him severely.[33] The father assented. The boy died as a result of the beating and the teacher was found guilty of manslaughter. The court stated that the father could not authorise an excessive punishment of this nature. The import of this is that schools cannot rely on parental consent to protect them from liability for conduct which would otherwise be unlawful. However, the reality in such situations is that legal action is less likely to arise given that most disputes occur as a result of parental dissatisfaction.

THE SCHOOL'S STATEMENT ON DISCIPLINE

7.12 Article 3 of the 1998 Order requires that the scheme of management of each grant-aided school shall require the Board of Governors to ensure that policies designed to promote good behaviour and discipline on the part of pupils are pursued at the school.[34] The Board of Governors is required, after consulting the principal to make, and from time to time review, a written statement of general principles to which the principal is to have regard when

---

[28] See generally paras. 1.51-1.57.
[29] (1982) EHRR 293.
[30] *Campbell and Cosans v UK*, *op cit* at para. 36.
[31] See *App. No.9146/80* 8.
[32] See Smith and Hogan, *Criminal Law* (1992) at p. 411. This issue must be reconsidered in the light of the European Court of Human Rights' decision A on the use of corporal punishment by parents.
[33] (1860) 2 F&F 202.
[34] Art. 3(1) of the 1998 Order.

determining disciplinary measures.[35] This is a new duty. Under the 1989 Order the Board of Governors was not required to produce such a statement, although, if it did, the principal was required to comply with it.[36] If the Board considers that any particular measure should be determined by the principal, it must notify him or her of those measures or matters and give such guidance as it considers appropriate.[37]

7.13 The principal must determine the standard of behaviour which is to be regarded as acceptable at the school (in so far as this has not been determined by the Board of Governors). The principal must prepare a statement of disciplinary measures, taking into account the statement of principles and any other guidance given by the Board of Governors.[38] These measures may include the making of rules and provision for enforcing them. In determining the measures to be included in the scheme, the principal must have regard to the following objectives: the promotion of self-discipline and proper respect for authority; encouraging good behaviour and respect for others on the part of pupils; securing that the standard of behaviour is acceptable; and otherwise regulating the conduct of pupils.[39]

7.14 It is important that the disciplinary policy is recognised and supported by parents at the school. In view of this, the principal must ensure that the statement on discipline is given free of charge to the parents of all pupils registered at the school.[40] It must also be kept for inspection at the school. There is however no specific obligation to bring the policy to the attention of pupils or staff. This can be contrasted with the provision in England and Wales which requires principals to take steps to bring the measures to the attention of all pupils and parents and persons employed at the school at least once a year.[41]

7.15 The statement of disciplinary policy is an important document. It should set out clearly what the school considers to be unacceptable behaviour and what consequences will result if a pupil's actions do not meet the required standard of conduct. If the rules are fair, publicised and consistently applied, disputes will be less likely to arise. The Northern Ireland Working Party on Discipline in Schools recommended the following:

- A clear school policy on discipline, established by the principal and the teachers, which is understood and accepted by both pupils and their parents.
- The establishment of a clear disciplinary procedure applied by all teachers, with a system of referral to a higher authority.

---

[35] *Ibid* art. 3(2).
[36] Art. 124 of the 1989 Order.
[37] Art. 3 (2)(b) of the 1998 Order.
[38] *Ibid* art. 3(3).
[39] *Ibid* art. 3(3)(a).
[40] *Ibid* art. 3(3)(c).
[41] Education Act 1997, s. 154(7)(a).

- The fair and consistent application of school rules, fully understood by teachers, pupils and parents alike, with the penalties for any breach of the rules known to all.[42]

The legislation now requires schools to meet these general objectives in most respects. However, there are some instances where it might be argued that the legislation does not go far enough. For instance in England and Wales the equivalent provision requires governing bodies to consult with parents when making or revising the statement of principles.[43] In neither jurisdiction is there a requirement to consult with pupils. The Elton Report recommended that pupils should actively participate in shaping the school's disciplinary policy so as to "foster a sense of collective commitment to it".[44] The failure to involve pupils by law has been criticised as another instance where education fails to recognise the views of children as separate from the rights and interests of their parents.[45] The failure to take pupils' views into account in determining disciplinary measures is also another instance where education law falls short of Article 12 of the UNCRC.

ACTIONS GIVING RISE TO DISCIPLINARY MEASURES

7.16 Most schools have a set of rules which are intended to define the boundaries of acceptable behaviour on the part of pupils. These rules form the backbone of a school's disciplinary policy. However, the school should not only clearly identify the standard of behaviour which it expects and what consequences flow from a failure to meet the required standard, but it should also have an agreed procedure as to how misbehaviour is to be identified and investigated.

DETERMINING WHAT IS UNACCEPTABLE BEHAVIOUR

7.17 Each school will define what it considers to be acceptable behaviour on the part of its pupils. There will be considerable variation on what is considered acceptable from school to school. However, most schools will consider the following actions to be unacceptable: foul language; poor punctuality; theft; disruption in class; failure to comply with requests or homework requirements; bullying; violence towards pupils or staff; breaching dress codes; graffiti or damage to school property; and use of drugs, alcohol or weapons on school premises. As a general rule, a school is free to determine what it considers to be inappropriate behaviour. Some schools inevitably will have stricter disciplinary regimes than others, a fact which the courts appear to be willing to take into account.[46] However, there are two possible exceptions to this wide discretion which require particular consideration.

---

[42] *Op cit.*
[43] Education Act 1997, s. 154(3)(b).
[44] *Op cit* n. 8, recommendation 76.
[45] See Monk, 'School Exclusions and the Education Act 1997' (1997) 9/4 *Education and the Law* 277, at 279.
[46] See *R v Governors of St Gregory's RC Aided High School, ex parte M, The Times*, 27 January 1994.

Rules on appearance

7.18 Schools will often specify that pupils wear a particular uniform and have other rules for general matters of appearance. Some schools go a step further and require pupils to purchase a uniform from a particular supplier, a practice which has been criticised by the General Consumer Council for Northern Ireland.[47] However, it would not be unlawful for a school to discipline a pupil who fails to comply with such a requirement Instead, school rules on uniform and appearance are only likely to be successfully challenged where the rules can be considered to be discriminatory on the grounds of sex or race.

7.19 In terms of sex discrimination, disputes might arise in co-educational schools if boys are not allowed to wear earrings or have long hair or if girls are not permitted to wear trousers. In a 1954 case a mother was successfully prosecuted for failing to secure her child's education after her daughter was expelled from school for wearing trousers.[48] However, not only do such practices generate feelings of unfairness, they are probably unlawful under the Sex Discrimination (NI) Order 1976. Article 24 of the Order makes it unlawful for schools to discriminate against a pupil in the terms on which it offers to admit him/her to the establishment; in the way it affords access to any benefits, facilities or services; or by subjecting him or her to any detriment. The provision is possibly wide enough to found a case where schools have different dress codes applying for boys and girls although there are as yet no reported cases on this point. In one English case, boys who were excluded from school for wearing earrings threatened legal action and the school withdrew the exclusions.[49] However, the attitude of the courts in reported employment cases on this issue is that different rules concerning appearance are not discriminatory provided they enforce a common principle of smartness or conventionality.[50]

7.20 Northern Ireland introduced legislation which prohibits race discrimination relatively recently. The provisions of the Race Relations (NI) Order 1997 extend to schools. In one case under existing legislation in Great Britain, a headmaster's refusal to permit a Sikh pupil to wear a turban was considered to amount to discrimination on the grounds of race.[51] The same might apply to women wearing jewellery, head scarves or trousers in conformity with race or religious norms unless the rule can be considered to be justified on other grounds such as health and safety. Challenges of this nature could probably also be made under Article 9 of the ECHR which protects freedom of religion. Moreover, it has also been suggested that Article 10 of the ECHR which protects freedom of expression might prohibit a principal from suspending a pupil who is wearing something to make a particular ideological point provided that this does not interfere with the rights of other pupils.[52] In an American case, the United States Supreme Court

---

[47] *School Uniforms,* General Consumer Council for Northern Ireland (1992) pp. 14.
[48] *Spears v Warrington Corporation* [1954] 1 QB 61.
[49] Reported in the *The Times* (9 January 1993).
[50] See *Smith v Safeway* [1996] IRLR 456.
[51] *Mandla v Lee (Dowell)* [1983] 1 All ER 1062.
[52] See, Lonbay *op cit* n. 2 at p. 347

considered that pupils' right to free speech under the First Amendment to the American Constitution meant that their school could not prohibit them from wearing black armbands in protest at the Vietnam war.[53] In Northern Ireland pupils wearing political emblems on their uniforms might be able to advance a similar argument under the ECHR (provided again that it does not interfere with the rights of other pupils).

Punishment for behaviour occurring out of school

7.21   An issue may arise when the action giving rise to the decision to discipline occurs outside of the school boundaries. It is clear that schools can punish pupils for conduct out of school.[54] In *Cleary* v *Booth* the court stated that the teacher's authority "must to some extent include an authority over the child while he is outside the four walls".[55] The court considered that each case may be a question of fact. However, it would seem reasonable to require that there should be some connection between the behaviour and the child's attendance at the school. This might be established by the fact that the misbehaviour concerned other pupils at the school.[56] Alternatively a sufficient link might be established due to the fact that the offending behaviour took place while the pupil was wearing a school uniform or was on the school bus.[57] The position in relation to behaviour which does not have such a direct connection to the school has not been considered by the courts. This might arise, for example, where the pupil commits a crime which in itself has nothing to do with the school such as a car theft or drugs offence. Schools might well consider that it is appropriate to discipline (or even expel) pupils for incidents such as these which tend to bring the school's name into disrepute. The broad nature of the approach of the court in *Cleary* v *Booth* suggests that the teacher's authority to discipline would extend to such cases. Collins J considered that the purpose of discipline was to provide moral education and that "there is not much opportunity for a boy to exhibit his moral conduct while in school under the eye of the master".[58] However, if schools wish to be able to discipline (e.g. expel) pupils for actions taken outside the school, this should be specifically set out in the school's disciplinary policy.

INVESTIGATING AN INCIDENT OF MISBEHAVIOUR

7.22   Parents will be more likely to object to the use of discipline if they believe that their child has been punished for something which he or she did not do. If a school intends to impose discipline for misbehaviour, it should

---

[53] *Tinker* v *Des Moines Independent Community School District* (1960) 393 US 503.
[54] *R* v *Newport Salop Justices, ex parte Wright* [1929] KB 416. See also *R* v *London Borough of Newham* (unreported, LEXIS CO/3130/94) where the court rejected the submission that the principal had no authority to discipline for conduct outside the school premises.
[55] [1929] 2 KB 416 at p. 469.
[56] This occurred in *R* v *London Borough of Newham, ex parte X, The Times*, 15 November 1994, where a pupil pulled a fellow pupil's trousers down.
[57] See Chapter 10 for further discussion of disciplinary measures for misbehaviour on school buses.
[58] [1929] 2 KB 416 at p. 469.

have good grounds for believing that the pupil has actually behaved in the way alleged. In most cases, this will be apparent. However, if something has occurred and the school is unclear as to who the culprit is, it should investigate the incident properly. The pupil should also be given an opportunity to refute any allegations made against him or her before disciplinary measures are imposed. A failure to comply with these basic procedures could be considered to be a breach of natural justice. This is particularly likely if a Board of Governors takes a decision to exclude a pupil. In *R v Board of Governors of London Oratory, ex parte Regis* the court compared the decision to expel to a decision to send a student down from university and concluded that the ordinary rules of fairness applied in such cases.[59]

7.23 In *R v Roman Catholic Schools, ex parte S* the court set out three principles for determining whether a pupil has had a fair opportunity to exculpate themselves.[60] They are that:

> " (1) Those conducting an enquiry must decide what critical issues of fact they should resolve and what enquiries could reasonably be made to resolve those issues.
>
> (2) They must give careful and even-handed consideration to all the available evidence in relation to those issues.
>
> (3) Those conducting an enquiry do not need on every occasion carry out searching enquiries involving the calling of bodies of oral evidence."[61]

The first two principles hold true in all investigations. However, it is inevitable that the level of enquiry will vary depending on three things: (i) the severity of the behaviour; (ii) the level of doubt about the accused's involvement; and (iii) the punishment which might be imposed. Clearly, a full scale investigation would be inappropriate for a minor incident, for example if a pupil had spoken in the library when he or she was meant to be quiet. However, if there has been a serious incident; and it is unclear who the culprit is; and the likely punishment will be an exclusion, then the investigation must be undertaken with the utmost care. In such cases, a proper investigation would normally involve interviews with the alleged culprit, the victim (if there is one) and any witnesses. In effect, the investigator should do two things: investigate thoroughly and give the pupil concerned a chance to respond to the allegations.

7.24 In *R v Camden LBC, ex parte H* the Court of Appeal set aside a decision by a Board of Governors to reinstate two pupils on the basis that the Board had made insufficient inquiries before it reached its decision.[62] The case was somewhat unusual in that the judicial review was initiated by the father of a pupil who had been injured in the incident which had led to the expulsion. When the Board of Governors determined not to expel the pupils, it was influenced by the fact that the boys had not intended to injure the other child. However, the Court of Appeal considered that the governors had made

---

[59] *The Times*, 17 February 1988.
[60] [1998] ELR 304.
[61] *Ibid* at p. 312.
[62] *The Times*, 15 August 1996.

insufficient inquiries in this respect. In particular, they had made no attempt to find out what the pupils had said during police investigations. The Court of Appeal concluded that the investigation lacked balance.

7.25 The alleged culprit should also have an opportunity to respond to allegations. In the Northern Ireland case of *In re Kean*, which concerned a decision to suspend a pupil, the court considered that "basic fairness would have required that the applicant should have been given an opportunity to consider the case against her by, for example the statements of the others pupils".[63] Similarly, in *R v Board of Governors of London Oratory, ex parte Regis* McCullough J considered that the requirements of fairness were such that the pupil facing expulsion should know the nature of the accusation against him and have an opportunity to answer it.[64] A pupil will not be able to exculpate him or herself unless he or she knows why they are being accused and the substance of the accusation. It is particularly important that all the evidence is placed before the pupil when the source of incriminating evidence is another pupil who was involved in the incident. In *R v Dunraven School, ex parte B* the Board of Governors and expulsion appeal tribunal did not give the pupil or his parents access to statements made by another pupil who was involved in the incident which incriminated the applicant.[65] The English Court of Appeal concluded that the Board of Governors who considered the decision to exclude could not fairly take account of statements made by the other pupil which had not been disclosed to the applicant. Sedley LJ stated that:

> "Where what is being said has taken at least two different and arguably inconsistent forms, fairness will ordinarily require enough disclosure to reveal the inconsistency...A second, related, principle is that it is unfair for the decision maker to have access to damaging material to which the person at risk - here the pupil through his parent - has no access".[66]

7.26 In general terms the standard of proof applicable is the balance of probabilities. This means that the person investigating must be satisfied that it is more likely than not that the pupil was involved in an incident of misbehaviour. This is the standard which an exclusion appeal tribunal will use when determining whether it is satisfied that a pupil has committed a serious breach of discipline. However, in cases where a school is investigating an incident which involves a criminal act, it may be increasingly difficult to establish that the pupil was more likely than not to have been involved. In *R v Dunraven School, ex parte R* Brooke LJ quoted with approval the House of Lords' approach in *Re H (Minors) (Sexual Abuse: Standard of Proof)*[67] where the correct approach to be adopted for determining allegations of criminality in a civil case was described as follows:

> "...this does not mean that where a serious allegation is in issue the standard of proof is higher. It means only that the inherent probability or improbability of an event is itself a matter to be

---

[63] [1997] NIJB 109.
[64] *The Times*, 17 February 1988.
[65] [2000] ELR 156.
[66] *Ibid* at p. 190.
[67] [1996] AC 563.

taken into account when weighing the probabilities and deciding whether, on balance, the event occurred. The more improbable the event, the stronger must be the evidence that it did occur before, on the balance of probability, its occurrence will be established."[68]

7.26 One final point about investigations of behaviour which might amount to a criminal offence is that the person doing the investigating is not considered to be a person "charged with the duty of investigating offences" under the Police and Criminal Evidence (NI) Order 1989 (PACE). This issue arose in an English case, *DPP v G*, in which a teacher was charged with assault on a pupil.[69] The incident was investigated initially by the head teacher. If the teacher had been considered to have fallen within the definition in PACE, he would have had to comply with the Code of Practice issued under the legislation. The court considered that the head teacher's role in investigating incidents in school did not fall with the ambit of PACE. This was reiterated in *R v Dunraven School ex parte B*.[70] However, the Court of Appeal considered that PACE and its Codes did serve as a touchstone of fair procedures outside the criminal justice system. In particular, it considered that if a principal investigating an alleged criminal incident secured an admission from a pupil through conduct tantamount to oppression, then it would be unfair to rely on that admission in exclusion proceedings.

Searches

7.28 There are times when the investigation of an incident of indiscipline will entail a search of pupils or their belongings. Those conducting the search should always get the consent of the pupil before a search. If a pupil is physically searched without his or her consent, the person conducting the search could be prosecuted for assault and sued for damages for trespass to the person. A teacher might be able to raise a defence under article 4 of the 1998 Order if the reason underlying the search was to prevent the pupil committing an offence or causing personal injury or damage to property.[71] This might be appropriate in cases where the school believes that the pupil is carrying a weapon or an illegal substance. Similarly, consent should be obtained for searches to property otherwise an action could be taken for trespass to property (assuming that some damage is caused). If the pupil refuses to give his or her consent to a search, schools will have to resort to other disciplinary sanctions (such as suspensions). If the school believes that the pupil is in possession of something which is illegal or dangerous or which has been used to commit a crime, it should inform the police.

Listening to "accomplices"

7.29 It is frequently the case that an incident of misbehaviour in a school may involve more than one pupil. In such cases, those investigating the incident may interview the alleged perpetrators individually. This can result

---

[68] Quoted at [2000] ELR 156 at p. 204
[69] *The Times*, 24 November 1997.
[70] [2000] ELR 156.
[71] See further, para. 7.34.

in a situation where the key evidence implicating a pupil is derived from another pupil involved in the misbehaviour - an accomplice. The difficulties of 'accomplice evidence' are well documented in criminal law. In *R v Dunraven School ex parte B* the English Court of Appeal considered some of the issues relevant to accomplice evidence.[72] In particular, it emphasised that the pupil should know what the other pupil has said if those statements implicate him or her in the incident (see para. 7.25). One difficulty with that is that a school may wish to keep the source of the information secret for fear of reprisals on the informant. In such cases the Court of Appeal considered that those investigating should ask two questions: (i) could the identity of the informant be concealed? (ii) if it could not, they had to consider whether to go ahead without reliance on the informant's evidence or to drop the case.[73] What they could not do was rely on the evidence without revealing it to the pupil implicated by it.

Problems with identification

7.30 There may be times when the perpetrator of an act of indiscipline is not immediately known. If the incident has been witnessed, the perpetrator may have to be identified by a member of staff or another pupil. Identifications of this kind must be handled carefully. In an English case, *R v Roman Catholic Schools, ex parte S* a court quashed the decision of a Board of Governors and appeal committee not to re-instate an excluded applicant because it considered that they had failed to make such enquiries as to the circumstances of identification as fairness demanded.[74] The court considered that:

> "...it was of importance that those conducting the inquiry should remind themselves of the dangers of identification evidence and the need for safeguards to avoid such dangers...Such safeguards normally require an account of the initial description given by the witness of the culprit before the identification took place, an account of the process of identification and the steps taken to avoid any identification being tainted by suggestion."

The court did not think that those investigating should have regard to *R v Turnbull* (the key authority on identification evidence in criminal cases).[75] However, it was important for them to be aware of the dangers of identification cases. In *Turnbull* the court considered that the following factors were particularly relevant to identification: the conditions under which and the length of time for which the observation took place; whether the person was known to the witness or if there was any particular reason they might be expected to remember them; and how soon after the event the identification was made. Clearly there are dangers in identification evidence. These might be magnified in a school where all the pupils are of a similar age and wearing the same uniform. In *R v Roman Catholic Schools ex parte S*, the court expressed a hope that its decision would not impose an unreasonable burden

---

[72] [2000] ELR 156.
[73] *Ibid* at p. 192.
[74] [1998] ELR 304.
[75] [1977] QB 244.

Block punishments

7.31 Inevitably there will be situations in which it is impossible to determine which pupil was responsible for a particular action (e.g. graffiti). One response to this is to impose a block punishment; punish the entire class because the true culprit fails to own up. The Elton Report discouraged the use of such measures, stating that "punishing the innocent with the guilty is always seen as unfair by pupils and their sense of grievance damages the school's atmosphere".[76] It is also consequently more likely to give rise to dispute and a dispute which the teacher may not be able to withstand. In one English case, the judge said:

> "Punishment should not be indiscriminate. A blanket punishment such as detention of a whole class must only be used as a last resort, otherwise people who are quite innocent may be detained incorrectly or unlawfully."[77]

If a teacher decides to detain a whole class, an aspect of the lawfulness of the detention will be reasonableness.[78] An aspect of the reasonableness will be whether it was appropriate to apply the punishment to the whole class for the actions of one or two pupils. In such cases, it is arguable that the detention cannot be construed as being intended to punish the original misbehaviour but instead is being applied to punish the other pupils for their failure to identify the wrongdoer. Given the pressure on school children not to tell tales on their classmates, such punishments may well be considered to be unreasonable.

PARTICULAR FORMS OF DISCIPLINE

7.32 There are many forms of discipline which do not have legal consequences; for example the setting of extra work or the removal of privileges. However, there are certain forms of punishment which may expose a teacher to civil and/or criminal liability. These are: corporal punishment; detention; confiscation of property; degrading treatment; and isolation. Each of these is considered separately below. It should be borne in mind that the general principles about the reasonableness of the punishment discussed at paragraphs 7.08-7.09 above apply in each case.

Corporal punishment

7.33 In 1987 corporal punishment was effectively abolished in all grant-aided schools and in relation to any pupil whose education is funded at any other school by an ELB.[79] Corporal punishment is defined to include any

---

[76] *Discipline in Schools* HMSO (1989) para. 59
[77] *Terrington v Lancashire CC*, 26 June 1986, cited in Harris, *The Law Relating to Schools*, (1995) p. 324
[78] See para. 7.08.
[79] The change in the law followed the decision of the European Court of Human Rights in *Campbell and Cosans v UK* [1982] 4 EHRR 293. Education (Corporal Punishment) (NI) Order 1987. See further, para. 7.02.

conduct which would be classified as battery. Battery has been defined as "the actual infliction of unwanted force on another person".[80] This includes all forms of undesired physical contact. The contact does not have to be direct; throwing a book at someone, or grabbing something from them could amount to battery. Moreover, the contact does not have to be aggressive or violent; an unwanted hug could constitute a battery. However, battery is not considered to include normal everyday contact such as tapping someone's arm to get their attention.[81] Nor would it in normal circumstances cover the situation where a teacher puts his or her arm round the shoulders of distressed children in order to comfort them.

7.34 If a teacher or other member of staff inflicts battery on a pupil, he or she can be sued for damages in a civil action. Article 49A of the 1986 Order states that such punishment cannot be justified on the ground that it was done in pursuance of a right exercisable by the member of staff by virtue of his position as such.[82] In effect, this means that if a teacher has carried out an act of corporal punishment and is subsequently sued for damages, he or she cannot argue that they had authority to inflict the punishment by virtue of their authority as a teacher. Moreover, article 49(1A) of the 1986 Order now states that, where, in any proceedings, it is shown that corporal punishment has been given to a pupil by or on the authority of a member of the staff, giving the punishment cannot be justified if the punishment was inhuman or degrading.[83] In determining whether the punishment is inhuman or degrading regard shall be had to all the circumstances of the case, including the reasons for giving it, how soon after the event it was given, its nature, the manner and circumstances in which it was given, the persons involved and its physical and mental effects. This amendment is clearly intended to bring the United Kingdom practice into line with Article 3 of the ECHR.

7.35 The use of corporal punishment in schools is not a specific criminal offence. However, a teacher who inflicts corporal punishment on a child may be charged with one of a number of general criminal offences including assault, battery and occasioning actual bodily harm. Self-defence is a defence to such a charge. However, it should be remembered that a teacher does not have to have physical contact with a pupil to be guilty of a criminal offence. An assault occurs where there is an act which causes another person to apprehend the infliction of a battery.[84] This could occur where a teacher pretends that he is going to hit a pupil but does not actually carry the attack out. Threatening words alone do not normally constitute an assault but they may operate to establish the basis for assault. This could happen where a teacher chases a pupil threatening to 'break their neck'. Verbal threats accompanied by aggressive gestures can amount to a criminal offence.

---

[80] *Collins v Willcock* [1984] 1 WLR 1172.
[81] *Ibid.*
[82] Smith and Hogan, *Criminal Law* (1992) at p. 411 suggest that parents could still give teachers authority to use corporal punishment.
[83] Inserted by art. 32 of the 1996 Order.
[84] *Fagan v Metropolitan Police Commissioner* [1969] 1 QB 439.

Power of member of staff to restrain pupils

7.36 One of the difficulties teachers have faced since the abolition of corporal punishment is knowing when it is lawful for them to have any physical contact with a child. This is particularly problematic when they are trying to stop him or her from doing something which will harm themselves or others. Article 49A of the 1986 Order permitted physical contact for reasons that included "averting an immediate danger of personal injury or damage to the property of any person ..." The 1998 Order has attempted to further clarify the circumstances when a member of staff at a school can lawfully restrain a pupil. Article 4 of the 1998 Order provides that a member of staff at a grant-aided school may use, in relation to any pupil at the school, such force as is reasonable in the circumstances for the purpose of preventing the pupil from doing (or continuing to do) any of the following:

(1) Committing an offence. This includes anything which would be an offence but for the operation of the presumption that children of a certain age are incapable of committing an offence;

(2) Causing personal injury to, or damage to the property of any person (including the pupil himself); or

(3) Engaging in any behaviour prejudicial to the maintenance of good order and discipline at the school or among any of its pupils, whether that behaviour occurs during a teaching session or otherwise.[85]

It is apparent that this would cover a member of staff who intervenes to prevent a child hurting another person or themselves or damaging property. However, one issue which faces teachers and which is not covered directly by the legislation is the absconding child; the pupil who attempts to leave the school in the middle of the school day. The situation poses a dilemma for teachers since they may not want to physically restrain the child but recognise that the child is in the school's care during school hours and the school may be liable for compensation should the child be injured outside the school during that time. Although not specifically addressed by the legislation, it is arguable that the provision gives a member of staff the power to restrain on the basis that the absconding child may injure themselves or that the act of defiance is "prejudicial to the maintenance of good order and discipline in the school". However, while it is obvious that no primary school should let a child leave during school hours, the issue of what force is reasonable becomes more problematic when a school is dealing with an older child since the likelihood of the pupil coming to harm outside the school premises diminishes.

7.37 A member of staff is defined as any teacher who works at the school and any other person who, with the authority of the principal, has lawful control or charge of the pupils at the school.[86] The power to restrain applies while the member of staff is on the premises of the school or elsewhere provided that he or she has lawful control or charge of the pupil concerned.[87]

---

[85] Art. 4(1) of the 1998 Order.
[86] *Ibid* art. 4(4).
[87] *Ibid*.

The member of staff's power to restrain does not authorise them to commit any act which would amount to corporal punishment under article 49A of the 1986 Order. However, the defence does not preclude them from relying on any other defence, for example self-defence.[88]

Detention

7.38 A common form of punishment is to require a pupil to do detention, that is, to stay in school outside normal hours. Prior to 1998 there was no specific statutory provision on the use of detention. However, it was clear that detaining a child without parental consent could amount to false imprisonment which is both a criminal offence and can be the basis for a claim for damages.[89] Some schools were wary of using detention as a punishment for fear of the potential legal consequences. The government was conscious of teachers' concerns and article 5 of the 1998 Order now regulates the circumstances when a pupil under the age of 18 may be required to spend time in detention. This provides that a detention will not be unlawful by virtue of the lack of parental consent provided certain conditions are satisfied. These are both procedural and substantive.

Procedural requirements

7.39 First, the principal of the school must have previously determined that detention was one of the disciplinary measures employed by the school.[90] This must have been made known within the school and steps must have been taken for this to be brought to the attention of the parents of all pupils.[91] Secondly, the detention must be imposed by the principal or another teacher specifically or generally authorised to do so.[92] Finally, the pupil's parents must have been given at least 24 hours' notice in writing that the detention was due to take place.[93] This last condition should prevent the type of situation which schools would wish to avoid, that is, where a child is kept back, misses the bus home and has to walk a long distance or through areas considered to be unsafe. A further protection against this - a requirement to consider whether alternative travel arrangements reasonably can be made - is considered below. Schools might be liable for damages in negligence if a child was to be injured in these circumstances.

The requirement to be reasonable

7.40 The detention must be reasonable in all the circumstances.[94] In deciding whether it is reasonable, the principal must take into account a number of factors. The first is whether the detention constitutes a proportionate punishment in the circumstances. Secondly, regard must be had to any special circumstances which are known to the person imposing the

---

[88] *Ibid* art. 4(3).
[89] There is authority to the effect that a parent may falsely imprison his or her own child. See *R v Rahman* [1985] 81 Cr App R 340.
[90] Art. 5(3) of the 1998 Order.
[91] *Ibid* art. 5(3)(a).
[92] *Ibid* art. 5(3)(b).
[93] *Ibid* art. 5(3)(d).
[94] *Ibid* art. 5(3)(c).

detention including: the pupil's age; any special educational needs; any religious requirements affecting him or her; and where arrangements have to be made for travel, whether suitable alternative arrangements can reasonably be made by his parent. These considerations are not exhaustive. The factors in relation to reasonableness discussed earlier in this chapter may also be relevant. Moreover, schools would be advised to avoid the use of mass detentions as it is uncertain whether these can be considered to be lawful.[95]

Pupils aged 18 and over

7.41 The requirements in article 5 of the 1998 Order only apply to pupils who have not attained the age of 18.[96] Article 5 hinges on the issue of parental consent which is not appropriate when the pupil has attained what is generally perceived to be the age of adulthood. In such circumstances the school would need to have the pupil's consent to undergo detention if it wishes to avoid an action for false imprisonment. If the pupil refuses to give that consent, the school may wish to consider further disciplinary measures (e.g. suspension) for failure to comply with the approved punishment.

Confiscation

7.42 A teacher may take property from a child if he or she considers it to be inappropriate or dangerous for the child to have it in his or her possession while at school. However, the property should be returned to the pupil when the school day is over. If the property confiscated is, in the teacher's opinion, inappropriate for the pupil the teacher should give the child's parent an opportunity to collect the confiscated item. If the property is illegal, for example a weapon or drugs, the police should be informed. If a teacher keeps a pupil's property for his or her (or the school's) use he or she may be guilty of the criminal offence of theft.[97] If he or she destroys the property without lawful authority he or she may be guilty of the criminal offence of criminal damage and could be sued for damages for trespass to property.

Degrading punishments

7.43 Schools may use certain forms of punishment which are designed to make an example of a pupil who has behaved in a certain way. The classic, if somewhat outdated example, is the child who stands in a corner wearing a hat with a big 'D' on it.[98] Other illustrations would be requiring a child who has forgotten his or her PE kit to participate in his or her underwear or making a spectacle of a child at assembly in front of the whole school. The Elton Committee recommended the avoidance of such punishments commenting that "Humiliating young people in front of their friends by, for example, public ridicule makes good relationships impossible".[99] Punishments designed to achieve this effect are not expressly excluded by national legislation. However, in *Mansell* v *Griffin* it was suggested that a teacher who kept a child

---

[95] See the discussion at para. 7.29.
[96] *Ibid* art. 5(2)(b).
[97] Theft Act (NI) 1969, s. 1.
[98] In December 1998 there were number of reports in the media about a teacher who had written "prat" on a child's forehead.
[99] *Ibid* n. 8 at para. 60.

standing for an hour "subjecting him thus to fatigue and to the derision of all his class-mates" might be liable for an action for trespass to the person.[100] Moreover, Article 3 of the European Convention on Human Rights precludes treatment which is "degrading". The comments of the European Court of Human Rights on the meaning of this phrase in an educational context have been confined to the use of corporal punishment. However, the court has also given some general indications as to the circumstances in which a punishment might be considered to be degrading. In *Tyrer* v *UK* the court stated that the humiliation and debasement involved must attain a particular level of severity over and above the usual element of humiliation involved in any kind of punishment.[101] It has to be determined with regard to all the circumstances of the case but with particular regard to the nature and context of the punishment itself and the manner and method of its execution. In the *Tyrer* case the court considered that beating a 15 year old boy with a birch amounted to degrading treatment. An important factor in determining this was the delay between the sentence and administration of the punishment. The court considered that the following factors did not prevent the punishment from being degrading: the absence of publicity (the court considered that the victim might be humiliated in his own eyes); the fact that the victim did not suffer long-lasting effects; and the fact that the birching was chosen by the applicant as an alternative to detention. In *Warwick* v *UK* the court considered that an important factor was whether the person administering the punishment was a stranger.[102] In *Y* v *UK* the physical effects of the punishment were deemed to be severe enough to render the punishment degrading.[103] This would suggest that significant mental effects might also be sufficient to render a punishment degrading. However, it should be noted that a complaint under Article 3 of the Convention will be admissible normally only where punishment has actually been imposed; the proposed infliction of a punishment is unlikely to be considered to be sufficiently degrading.[104]

Isolation

7.44 A common form of punishment for disruptive children is to isolate them or require them to take 'time out'. This involves removing the pupil from the classroom for a specified period. Such punishments are lawful. However, the pupil should not be put in a locked room as this could amount to false imprisonment. Moreover, a pupil who has been excluded should be properly supervised during the period of isolation. Schools might be considered to be in breach of their duty of care if a pupil who has been left unsupervised during school hours is injured. Moreover, the way in which the child is "isolated" should be carefully considered so that it does not amount to "degrading" treatment.[105]

---

[100] [1908] 1 KB 160 at p.167.
[101] *Tyrer* v *UK* (1992) 17 EHRR 1.
[102] *Warwick* v *UK* (1986) 60 DR 5.
[103] *Y* v *UK* (1992) 17 EHRR 238.
[104] *App. No. 9119/80.*
[105] See para. 7.40.

EXCLUSIONS

7.45 The ultimate disciplinary sanction for most schools is the exclusion of the pupil from the school either temporarily (by a suspension) or permanently (by an expulsion). In England and Wales the rising levels of exclusion gave such cause for concern that the issue became one of the key focuses of the Social Exclusion Unit (SEU) set up by the Labour government in 1997. The SEU published a report on truancy and exclusions which found that there were rising numbers of exclusions and a disproportionate number amongst children in care and children from Afro-Caribbean backgrounds.[106] The report also acknowledged a clear link between exclusion and youth offending. The report made a number of recommendations for change which include the setting of targets to reduce the numbers of exclusions.

7.46 The issue of school exclusions has not been as high profile or as controversial in Northern Ireland. The issue did, however, form part of the discipline report of the School Improvement Programme.[107] Research commissioned by the Department showed that in Northern Ireland in 1996/97 there were 2631 suspensions and 76 expulsions from school.[108] The level of expulsion was not considered to be excessive although concerns have been expressed about the length of time expelled pupils spend out of school.[109] In contrast, the level of suspensions was considered to be an object of concern, particularly because suspension has been used for relatively moderate misbehaviours such as smoking and not wearing the school uniform. As a result, the Department is proposing to issue guidance to promote a common reporting system for suspensions and to encourage a more consistent and appropriate use of suspension as a sanction for severely disruptive behaviour.[110]

The scheme for suspension and expulsion

7.47 Schools are required to follow the procedures in the Scheme for Suspension and Expulsion. ELBs produce a scheme for controlled schools.[111] The CCMS produces the scheme for Catholic maintained schools and Boards of Governors prepare the scheme in other schools. The schemes specify the procedures which should be followed in the decision-making process. It is worth reiterating the fact that the principles of natural justice apply to these cases. Many aspects of the duty to be fair are expressly incorporated into school disciplinary schemes by the Schools (Suspension and Expulsion of Pupils) Regulations (NI) 1995 which specify the procedure which must be included in the disciplinary scheme of all grant-aided schools.

---

[106] *Truancy and School Exclusion*, The Social Exclusion Unit, The Cabinet Office 1997.
[107] *Promoting and Sustaining Good Behaviour: A Discipline Strategy for Schools* (DENI, 1998), p. 13.
[108] Kilpatrick, Barr and Wylie, *The 1996/97 Northern Ireland Suspension and Expulsion Study*, DENI Research Report No. 13, 1999.
[109] *Promoting and Sustaining Good Behaviour: A Discipline Strategy for Schools* (DENI, 1998), p. 13.
[110] *Ibid* p.14.
[111] Art. 49 of the 1986 Order substituted by art. 39 of the 1993 Order.

7.48 The 1995 Regulations confer rights on the "parent of a pupil". However, regulation 2 states that "any reference to the parent of a pupil shall include, in the case of a pupil who has attained the age of eighteen, the pupil himself." This use of the word "include" would appear to mean that when a pupil attains the age of 18 he or she assumes the same rights which are afforded to his or her parents and not that the pupil assumes the rights in place of his or her parents. The lack of involvement of children under the age of 18 was criticised by the reporting committee of the UNCRC when it reported in 1995.[112] In spite of the criticism the legislation has not been amended to give pupils a separate right to be heard in exclusion decisions.

GROUNDS FOR EXCLUSION

7.49 There are no specific statutory restrictions on the grounds for which a pupil may be excluded from school. All of the Schemes for Suspension and Expulsion stress that it is an exceptional disciplinary measure which should be used only as a last resort and for serious incidences of misbehaviour. However, there is no guidance from the Department as to which behaviours are serious enough to merit exclusion. Although the Department plans to produce guidance to encourage a more consistent use of suspensions (see above), it is not clear whether this will address the grounds for imposing an exclusion. Departmental guidance for England and Wales suggests that an expulsion would be inappropriate where: the pupil has poor attendance; is unable to comply with dress codes through no fault of his or her own; or where the pupil is pregnant.[113] In the latter case, it could be argued that an expulsion amounted to a breach of the Sex Discrimination (NI) Order 1976. The guidance in England and Wales also sets out the factors which are relevant to a decision to permanently exclude. These include: the age and health of the pupil; the previous record; the pupil's circumstances (e.g. domestic situation); parental or peer pressure, the frequency of the occurrence and likelihood of it reoccurring; whether the behaviour will impair the normal functioning of the pupil or other pupils at the school; the degree of severity of the behaviour; whether or not it occurred on school premises or when the pupil was in the charge of school staff; the degree to which the behaviour was a violation of the school's policy; whether the behaviour was perpetrated by the pupil on his or her own or as part of a group; and whether consideration has been given to seeking the support of other agencies.[114] One of the recommendations of the Social Exclusion Unit's report was that this guidance should be put on a statutory footing.[115] This will undoubtedly clarify the obligations for schools but may result in an increased level of legal challenge.

7.50 In spite of the lack of regulation in this area, there are lessons to be drawn from the numerous judicial review actions which have followed decisions to expel in England and Wales. As a result of the Northern Ireland

---

[112] *Concluding Observations of the Committee of the Rights of the Child: United Kingdom of Great Britain and Northern Ireland*, CRC/C/15/ADD 34 Centre for Human Rights, Geneva, January 1995 para. 32.
[113] DfEE Circular 10/94.
[114] *Ibid.*
[115] *Truancy and School Exclusion* The Social Exclusion Unit, The Cabinet Office 1997, para. 5.9.

decision, *In Re Kean*, these would also be relevant to decisions to suspend a pupil.[116] Clearly some consideration must be given to the pupil themselves; their previous character, their regret for the misbehaviour and the effect of the expulsion on their education. However, in *R v Camden LBC, ex parte H* the Court of Appeal considered that the primary consideration must be the need to maintain a disciplined school environment so as to safeguard the welfare and interests of the generality of the pupils.[117] In addition, the reported decisions would suggest that the following factors require particular consideration.

Proportionality

7.51 One factor which may be important in determining the reasonableness of an expelling authority's action is whether the punishment is proportionate to the offence. There has been some debate over whether proportionality constitutes a separate ground for challenging the legality of administrative decisions by way of judicial review or whether it is in fact simply an aspect of the overall reasonableness of the decision.[118] However, in either case, it has been accepted as relevant by the courts in judicial review actions challenging decisions to expel pupils from school. In *R v London Borough of Newham, ex parte X* the court suggested that an expulsion may have been a disproportionate punishment for a retaliatory attack which involved pulling a pupils trousers down.[119] However in *R v Governors of St Gregory's RC Aided High School, ex parte M* the court considered that swearing in the presence of (but not at) a teacher and then failing to own up to the conduct justified an expulsion.[120] In this case the court placed considerable emphasis on the specific circumstances of the school and in particular on the strict disciplinary regime. The court concluded that the decision could not be considered to be unreasonable (in the *Wednesbury* sense) and commented that "the decision would have been the same even if the principle of proportionality formed a part of the domestic law of our courts".[121] The approach in the *St Gregory's* case would appear to be consistent with that of the Court of Appeal in *R v Camden CC, ex parte H* in which the Court of Appeal placed emphasis on the school's need to maintain good discipline in the interest of other pupils.[122] Thus, although a decision to permanently exclude may be more severe than the specific misdemeanour of the pupil, it may still be a proportionate response to the need to maintain good order in the school.

One-off incidents versus repeated misdemeanours

7.52 One issue which appears to arise frequently is whether it is appropriate to expel a pupil for a series of minor misdemeanours or whether expulsion is only appropriate for a serious incident of misbehaviour. The

---

[116] There remains some doubt as to whether suspensions are justiciable through judicial review. See the discussion on suspensions at paras. 7.55-7.56.
[117] *The Times*, 15 August 1996.
[118] See for instance, Jowell and Lester, 'Beyond *Wednesbury*, Substantive Principles of Administrative Law' (1988) Public Law 368.
[119] *The Times*, 15 November 1994.
[120] *The Times*, 27 January 1994.
[121] *Per* Turner J.
[122] *The Times*, 15 August 1996.

evidence from teachers is that they are more concerned about persistent minor misbehaviour than the one-off incident.[123] Moreover, drawing a distinction between the two categories of behaviour can leave the persistent troublemaker in a better position than the child who becomes involved in a one-off incident. In spite of this, guidance given to schools in Great Britain suggests that expulsion is an inappropriate response in circumstances where there has been a series of minor breaches of the school's disciplinary code.[124] However, there is nothing in the legislation or reported cases to say that schools cannot expel a pupil as a result of the cumulative effect of a series of minor incidents. The disciplinary policy should, however, make it clear that expulsion may be the result if a pupil persistently misbehaves. Likewise, the Scheme for Suspensions and Expulsions should not restrict the measures to one-off incidents. However, even if schools are restricted in this way, it is still open to the expelling authority to consider the pupil's previous record of behaviour when making its determination.[125]

Effect on the victim and other pupils at the school

7.53 A relevant factor when determining whether a child should be excluded may be the effect on the victim of non-exclusion. In *R v Camden LBC, ex parte H* the court considered that, when undisciplined conduct had injured another pupil, a relevant factor was the effect which re-instatement would have on the victim and the other pupils at the school. Since 1998 expulsion appeal tribunals are directed to have regard to the interests of other pupils and the teachers at the school when deciding whether to expel a pupil.[126]

Conduct of the parent

7.54 In *R v Neale, ex parte S* the English High Court considered that a parent's conduct could be relevant to a determination that an exclusion should become permanent.[127] In that case the pupil's mother initially failed to sign a behaviour contract or to co-operate with other education agencies recommended by the school. When the pupil was suspended for digging his nails into a teacher's hand the mother took the child to the school along with an advice worker and forced him into the classroom. The headteacher subsequently made the exclusion permanent. An appeal tribunal ordered the school to re-admit the pupil. However, the school did not fully comply with this (possibly because the teachers took strike action at the pupil's proposed re-instatement). The parent sought judicial review claiming that the school's decision to expel and to comply with the direction of the tribunal was unlawful. The court dismissed the application, concluding that the mother's attitude, as expressed by her defiant conduct, was of necessity relevant to the decision to exclude permanently.

---

[123] The Elton Report, *op cit* n. 8 at p. 60.
[124] DfEE, Circular 10/94, para. 25.
[125] *R v Camden CC, ex parte H, The Times*, 15 August 1996.
[126] Schools (Expulsion of Pupils) (Appeal Tribunals) Regulations (NI) 1994, Sch. 2, para. 5 as substituted by reg. 2 of the Schools (Expulsion of Pupils) (Appeal Tribunals) (Amendment) Regulations (NI) 1998.
[127] [1995] ELR 198.

SUSPENSIONS

7.55 A suspension is a temporary exclusion from school. A pupil can only be suspended by the principal or if the principal is absent the person performing the duties of principal.[128] Schools cannot avoid their obligations under the regulations by calling a suspension something else such as 'sending the child home'. Any period during which the school refuses to provide a registered pupil with an education on its premises is arguably a suspension necessitating compliance with the procedures described below. The legislation does not prohibit an immediate suspension. However, in such cases a school would be advised to make arrangements for the pupil's safe delivery to his or her parents. The initial period of suspension cannot exceed five days. A pupil cannot be suspended for more than 45 days in any school year.[129] Until 1998 schools were only permitted to exclude pupils for a maximum of 15 days in any one term. Although the total period has not increased, the spread across the whole school year gives schools more leeway to determine what it proposes to do during a suspension. The longer period was considered to be necessary to cover serious breaches of discipline when expulsion is being considered.

7.56 Where a pupil has been suspended the principal must immediately give written notice of the reasons for the suspension and the period of the suspension to the parent of the pupil, the ELB, the chairman of the Board of Governors and in the case of a Catholic maintained school the local diocesan office of the CCMS. The principal must also invite the parent (or pupil if aged 18) to visit the school and discuss the decision to suspend. The principal shall not extend the period of suspension without the prior approval of the chairman of the Board of Governors and must notify the reasons for the extension to the parent, ELB, and in the case of a Catholic maintained school, the CCMS. The school is still under an obligation to provide an education to a pupil who has been suspended. This would normally be achieved by setting work which the pupil can do at home.

Challenging a decision to suspend

7.57 There is no statutory right of appeal against a decision to suspend a pupil. There is the possibility of a complaint to the Department under article 101 of the 1986 Order.[130] However, this is restricted to complaints about ELBs and Boards of Governors acting unreasonably in the exercise of their statutory functions and does not extend to the actions of principals. It could be argued that a Board of Governors which, having been consulted by the principal, allows the principal to suspend a pupil inappropriately, has failed to discharge its statutory functions.

7.58 The final possibility is an action by way of judicial review. In one Northern Ireland case, *In re Kean*, a pupil successfully challenged a decision to suspend her on the grounds that the procedures employed had operated

---

[128] Reg. 3(A) of the Schools (Suspension and Expulsion of Pupils) Regulations (NI) 1995.
[129] *Ibid* reg. 3(C) as substituted by the Schools (Suspension and Expulsion of Pupils) (Amendment) Regulations (NI) 1998.
[130] See paras. 2.63-2.72.

unfairly.[131] The principal had imposed an immediate suspension for what he had considered to be a serious breach of discipline - the pupil had allegedly kicked her foot through a glass door. In view of the immediate suspension, the pupil had not been given an opportunity to respond to the statements of witnesses and the principal had not invited her parents to discuss the suspension in line with the school's published procedures. The court considered the decision to have been taken unfairly but stressed that it rested on the specific circumstances of the particular case.

7.59 The decision in *In re Kean* is somewhat surprising in that it had previously been thought that decisions to suspend a pupil would not be subject to judicial review. The reasons for this were two-fold. First, the decision to suspend is taken by the principal (not the Board of Governors) and secondly, suspensions, although operating within statutory procedures, could be considered to be part of the internal disciplinary arrangements within the school. In effect, there is a strong argument that a decision to suspend is not a public law issue and therefore one on which the court on judicial review has no jurisdiction. The court itself acknowledged its disinclination to find that the "day to day exercise of his disciplinary powers by a professional teacher would be subject to the unwieldy and time consuming supervision of the law". In determining that the court had jurisdiction, the judge was influenced by the "statutory underpinning of the powers" and the "nature of the issues involved". However, there is little discussion of either in the judgment. Instead the judgment cites a number of English authorities on expulsions. No attempt is made to distinguish expulsions from suspensions in spite of the significant differences between the two (not least in terms of the consequences of the decision for the pupil). Moreover, it might be questioned why the statutory right to appeal a decision to expel to an independent tribunal was not extended to suspensions. The somewhat anomalous effect of the decision in *In re Kean* is that a pupil who has been suspended may go directly to judicial review whereas a pupil who has been expelled must first seek redress through a statutory tribunal.

EXPULSIONS

7.60 The ultimate disciplinary action is an expulsion. An expulsion is a permanent exclusion from a particular school. Given the implications of an expulsion, the measure should only be used by a school in exceptional circumstances. An expulsion will not only leave a child temporarily without an education but will leave a permanent blemish on their school record. For this reason some schools offer parents the opportunity to withdraw their child before an expulsion. There is nothing in the legislation to prohibit this. However, if undue pressure is placed on parents to withdraw the child, it could be argued that the school was acting unlawfully by attempting to avoid its statutory obligations in relation to expulsions. This might provide grounds for a complaint to the Department under article 101 of the 1986 Order.

---

[131] [1997] NIJB 109.

The pre-expulsion meeting

7.61 The procedure governing expulsions is specified in the Schools (Suspension and Expulsion of Pupils) Regulations (NI) 1995. A pupil cannot be expelled unless they have first served a period of suspension.[132] Before a pupil can be expelled, there must be a consultation between the principal, the parent of the pupil, the Chief Executive of the ELB or someone authorised by him, the chairman of the Board of Governors and in the case of a Catholic maintained school, the Director of the CCMS or someone authorised by him. A pupil can be expelled even if his or her parent neglects or refuses to take part in the consultations. The consultations must include discussion about the future provision of suitable education for the pupil concerned. There is, however, no obligation to come to any decision about the pupil's future education.

The decision of the expelling authority

7.62 A pupil can only be expelled by the expelling authority. The body who has ultimate responsibility for the decision depends on the status of the school. In controlled schools the decision to expel is taken by the ELB acting on the recommendation of a sub-committee. In voluntary schools and grant-maintained integrated schools the decision is taken by the Board of Governors. The decisions of ELBs and Boards of Governors in this area are subject to judicial review.[133] There have been a series of cases in the English courts challenging expulsion decisions. These must be viewed with a degree of caution in Northern Ireland because the systems operated are quite different. In particular, in Great Britain the initial decision to expel is taken by the principal and is later reviewed by the Board of Governors. Nonetheless the judgments shed some light on what is required of expelling authorities.

7.63 The expelling authority should be careful to ensure that there is no appearance of bias in its procedure for making a determination. In *R v Stoke Newington School, ex parte M* the court considered that the Board of Governors reviewing the decision should not have included a teacher who had had direct responsibility for the child as a year head.[134] This might also be appropriate if the teacher governor was involved in the incident which prompted the consideration of the need for an exclusion. Similarly, the parent governor should not be part of the decision-making body if his or her child's future is being considered or if his or her child has been directly affected by the behaviour of the pupil concerned. The role of the principal should also be considered carefully. In *R v Board of Governors of London Oratory, ex parte Regis* the court expressed concern about the fact that the principal had acted as clerk to the Board during the expulsion meeting (although he had withdrawn before the determination was made).[135] This is particularly significant in Great Britain because the principal's decision is reviewed by the Board of Governors. Although this is not the case in Northern Ireland, it is still

---

[132] Schools (Suspension and Expulsion of Pupils) Regulations (NI) 1995, reg. 3.
[133] *R v Board of Governors of London Oratory, ex parte Regis*, The Times, 17 February 1988.
[134] *R v Stoke Newington School, ex parte M* (unreported).
[135] *The Times*, 17 February 1988.

important that the principal's role in any discussion or determination is considered carefully so as to avoid the appearance of bias.

EXPULSION APPEAL TRIBUNAL

7.64 Where the pupil has been expelled the principal shall immediately give written notification to the parent of the pupil of his or her right to appeal the decision, the time limit for lodging an appeal and the place where the appeal may be lodged. Each ELB is required to make arrangements for an appeal against any decision to expel from a grant-aided school in its area. The parent of a pupil or the pupil himself where he has attained the age of 18 may appeal to this appeal tribunal against a decision to expel.[136] The procedure for appeal is set down in the Schools (Expulsion of Pupils) (Appeal Tribunals) Regulations (NI) 1994.

Composition of the appeal tribunal

7.65 The appeal tribunal can have three or five members drawn from a panel selected by the ELB.[137] The panel is comprised of three categories of people: (i) persons representing the interests of controlled schools in the area of the ELB; (ii) persons representing the interests of voluntary schools and grant-maintained schools in the area of the ELB; and (iii) persons who have experience in education, are acquainted with the educational arrangements in the ELB area or are parents of registered pupils at a school. The appeal tribunal must have at least one member in each of these categories. The chairperson is elected by the members of the tribunal. Certain people are excluded from membership of appeal tribunals. First, the tribunal cannot include any person employed by the ELB apart from full-time teachers. Secondly, the tribunal cannot include those who were involved in the original decision or discussions to exclude the pupil. Finally, teachers at the school are not permitted to sit on the tribunal if the tribunal is considering whether to re-admit the child to the school.

Procedure

7.66 A parent or pupil who wishes to appeal the decision must give notice in writing setting out the grounds on which the appeal is made.[138] There are no specific grounds of appeal, although an important factor will be whether the school's procedures were properly followed. The person appealing has a right to make written representations to the tribunal and to appear and make oral representations. The tribunal may also allow the appellant to be accompanied by a friend or to be represented. The authority which has expelled the pupil is also entitled to make written representations and to attend and make oral representations. In controlled schools (where the expelling authority is the ELB), the Board of Governors may also make written representations and a

---

[136] Art. 49(6) of the 1986 Order.
[137] *Ibid* Sch. 1 to the 1994 Regulations.
[138] Sch. 2.

representative of the Board of Governors may appear and make oral representations.[139] Otherwise the appeal is heard in private.

The determination

7.67 In considering the appeal the tribunal must have regard to all the circumstances of the case and in particular three things: (i) any representations made to it by the parent, pupil, expelling authority or the ELB; (ii) whether the procedures in relation to the expulsion of the pupil from the school were properly followed; (iii) the interests of other pupils and teachers in the school.[140] The appeal is determined by a simple majority of votes cast. The appeal tribunal may dismiss the appeal or allow the appeal and direct that the pupil be re-admitted to the school. If the tribunal directs that the pupil be re-admitted to the school, the Board of Governors of the school must comply with this direction.[141] The decision is communicated in writing to the appellant and to the authority which took the decision to exclude.

7.68 Two or more appeal tribunals may sit at the same time. Where the issues raised are substantially similar, the ELB may determine that those appeals be combined and dealt with in the same proceedings. This might be appropriate where two pupils are expelled as a result of involvement in the same incident. The ELB is under a duty to determine all other procedures to be followed on appeal. In particular, it must set time limits for the hearing of the appeal and in doing so must ensure that appeals are disposed of without delay.

EDUCATIONAL ARRANGEMENTS FOR EXPELLED PUPILS

7.69 The parents of expelled pupils continue to be under a duty to ensure that their child receives a suitable education.[142] However, schools are understandably reluctant to admit pupils who have been expelled from another school. Given that this could result in a child being left without access to education, there are several provisions designed to ensure that the child's educational needs are addressed. First, when a school is taking a final decision to expel it must consider the options for the child's future educational provision.[143] This will be discussed with the ELB. Secondly, on appeal, the tribunal can direct that the child be readmitted to the school but only if it does not uphold the decision to expel. Thirdly, parents still have a right to apply to another school for the admission of their child. A school cannot refuse to admit the child if it has vacant places. If it has its full enrolment number, it may refuse to admit the child on the basis that admission would prejudice the provision of efficient education or efficient use of resources in the school.[144]

---

[139] Schools (Suspension and Expulsion of Pupils) Regulations (NI) 1995, Sch. 2, para. 5 as substituted by the Schools (Suspension and Expulsion of Pupils) (Amendment)) Regulations (NI) 1998, reg. 2.
[140] *Ibid.*
[141] Art. 49(9) of the 1986 Order.
[142] *Ibid* Art. 45.
[143] Reg. 3 of the Schools (Suspension and Expulsion of Pupils) Regulations (NI) 1995.
[144] See generally para. 4.19.

7.70 The Social Exclusion Unit has recommended that all LEAs in England and Wales should be required to provide education for children who have been out of school for more than three weeks.[145] However, it is proposed that this 'duty' should be implented through guidance rather than regulations. Northern Ireland does not have an equivalent obligation either in law or guidance. Thus, the ELB in whose area the child resides is not under a specific duty to ensure that a child who has been expelled receives a suitable education. In practice, however, education welfare officers from the ELB will assist the parents in their attempts to get the child admitted to another school. In 1996 ELBs were given the power to direct schools to admit a child who has been expelled from another school.[146] An ELB may issue such a direction if a child has been refused admission to or expelled from each school which provides a suitable education and which is a reasonable distance from his or her home. In such cases the ELB may issue a direction specifying a grant-aided school which is a reasonable distance from the child's home and from which the child has not been expelled. Before giving a direction the ELB must consult the parent of the child, the Board of Governors of the school it proposes to specify; if the school is in another ELB's area, the other ELB; and if the school is a Catholic maintained school, the CCMS. If the ELB makes a direction to admit it must notify in writing the Board of Governors of the school. The Board of Governors cannot refuse to admit a child who is the subject of a direction. Finally, in cases where an ELB is satisfied that a child is unable to attend school for the purpose of receiving an education, it must make such special arrangements as it considers suitable for the child to receive education outside of school.[147] This could mean that a child is given home tuition or is sent to a Pupil Referral Unit. It is important that some form of educational provision is arranged for the child. A failure to do so may amount to a breach of Article 2 of the First Protocol of the ECHR which states that " no one shall be denied the right to education".[148]

7.71 A separate issue may arise as to the interim arrangements to be made for a child who has been expelled but who is appealing that decision to the local appeal tribunal or is challenging the decision by way of judicial review. In *R* v *London Borough of Newham, ex parte X* the court directed that a child should be returned to the school pending an appeal committee's decision which was due to take place three weeks later.[149] The court appeared to be influenced by the fact that the child was 15 years of age and involved in GCSE coursework at the time of the expulsion. The court stated that it took its decision bearing in mind "how critically important every day and certainly every week is in the education of a child of this age". However, the court stressed that this was an exceptional case. It is clear that each decision of this kind will be considered on its own facts. In a subsequent case the English High Court refused to make an order sending the child back to school as a full judicial hearing of the issue was due to take place within a few weeks.[150]

---

[145] *Op cit* para. 5.23.
[146] Art. 42 of the 1996 Order.
[147] Art. 6(3) of the 1986 Order amended by art. 36 of the 1993 Order.
[148] See generally, paras. 1.51-1.52.
[149] *The Times*, 15 November 1994.
[150] *R* v *Staffordshire CC, ex parte A, The Times,* 29 August 1996.

DISCIPLINARY RECORD

7.72 The pupil's school record will normally contain details of any serious disciplinary action, including exclusions or expulsions. It is important that the information contained in the record is accurate. In particular, schools should be careful how they record allegations or suspicions which have not been fully substantiated. If the record is stored manually parents (or the pupil themselves once aged 18) have a right under the Education (Pupil Records) Regulations (NI) 1998 to see the record and to request that any inaccurate information be corrected. Similar rights exist in relation to computerised records under the Data Protection Act 1998. An expulsion will stay on a school record permanently. This can be contrasted with a record of a criminal offence which will in most instances be removed after a fixed period of time.

PROVISION FOR CHILDREN WITH BEHAVIOURAL DIFFICULTIES

7.73 ELBs are required to prepare a statement setting out the arrangements to be made or proposed to be made in connection with the education of children with behavioural difficulties.[151] This provision was introduced by the 1998 Order. It mirrors a similar provision in England and Wales which was intended to ensure a greater degree of co-operation between LEAs and schools in disciplinary matters so as to minimize the need for exclusions.[152] The arrangements to be covered in this statement must include four things. The first is the arrangements made by the ELB for the provision of advice and resources to schools in its area and other arrangements made with a view to meeting the request by schools for support and assistance in connection with the promotion of good behaviour and discipline. The second is the arrangements for assisting schools to deal with general behavioural problems and difficulties with individual children. Thirdly, the ELB must detail the arrangements which it has made in relation to pupil referral units as required by article 86(1) of the 1998 Order. Finally, the ELB statement must set out the arrangements which will be made by the ELB to assist children with behavioural difficulties to find places at suitable schools. The ELB may revise the statement at any time but must review it every year. The ELB is required to consult other ELBs and all schools in its area when preparing or reviewing the statement. It is also required to publish the statement, send a copy to all Boards of Governors in its area and ensure that copies are available for inspection at ELB headquarters.

7.74 The statements document the general provision to be made by ELBs and should not be confused with statements of special educational needs which are made for individual children under article 16 of the 1996 Order.[153] There is inevitably some overlap since some children with behavioural difficulties will also be considered to have special education needs and these needs will be addressed in their statement. The legislation specifically

---

[151] Art. 6 of the 1998 Order.
[152] See generally Monk, 'School Exclusions and the Education Act 1997' (1997) 9/4 *Education and the Law* 277, at 284.
[153] See paras. 8.46-8.49.

explains that the ELB's statements about provision for children with behavioural difficulties must deal with the interaction between those arrangements and those made by the ELB in relation to pupils with behavioural difficulties who have special educational needs.[154]

INDEPENDENT SCHOOLS

7.75 The law in relation to discipline in private schools is very different to that in grant-aided schools. This is largely a result of the fact that the relationship between private schools and parents is considered to be contractual. In *R v Fernhill Manor School, ex parte A* the court stated that:

> " the relationships between the private schools and those who attend them are founded on the contract which is made between the school and those who are paying for the teaching and education of the pupils of the school. That contract is a completely private contract and is not underpinned by statute."[155]

Parents who send their children to private schools should be informed of the school's disciplinary rules which are in effect terms of the contract. If the parent objects to a particular form of discipline he or she should make that clear at the outset in which case it might be considered to have been excluded from the terms upon which the child is accepted as a pupil.

Exclusions

7.76 The legislation relating to exclusions does not apply to independent schools. Moreover, a parent cannot challenge a decision to exclude by way of judicial review because independent schools are not considered to be public bodies. In independent schools the power to exclude is determined by the contract. The information provided to parents should clearly state the grounds on which a pupil might be excluded and the procedure which will be followed. Although the public law principles of natural justice are not applicable in independent schools, in *R v Fernhill Manor School, ex parte A* the court considered that there might be an implied term in the contract that a decision to expel could not be taken except by a process of adjudication which complied with the principles of natural justice.[156] This would require the school to follow a fair procedure when making the decision to exclude. If these principles are not adhered to, the parent (but not the pupil who would be considered to be a third party to the contract) may be able to sue for breach of contract. The practical difficulty with such a course of action is that the parents will have to finance such an action privately.

Corporal punishment

7.77 The statutory prohibition on corporal punishment does not apply to pupils who are privately funded at independent schools. It does apply to pupils who are receiving publicly-funded grants to attend private schools. The legal position on the use of corporal punishment in private schools is still

---

[154] Art. 6(3) of the 1998 Order.
[155] *R v Fernhill Manor School, ex parte A* [1993] 1 FLR 620.
[156] *Ibid.*

determined in the main by the common law cases which preceded article 49 of the 1986 Order. These acknowledge a teacher's authority to administer reasonable punishment. However, the use of corporal punishment in private schools has been successfully challenged in the European Court of Human Rights on the grounds that it amounted to inhuman and degrading treatment under Article 3 of the Convention.[157] As a result of this, article 49 (1A) of the 1986 Order states that where in any proceedings it is shown that corporal punishment has been given to a pupil by or on the authority of the member of staff, the punishment cannot be justified if it was inhuman or degrading. The meaning of this phrase was considered earlier at paragraph 7.40. However, there have been several cases which have determined what inhuman and degrading treatment means in the particular context of corporal punishment in private schools. In *Costello and Roberts* v *UK* the European Court of Human Rights found that the "slippering" of a seven year old on his clothed buttocks three days after the misbehaviour did not amount to inhuman or degrading treatment.[158] However, in *Y* v *UK* the European Commission considered that a caning which left the pupil with weals on his buttocks as well as swelling and bruising amounted to degrading treatment.[159] Relevant factors will include: the severity of the punishment; the physical and mental effects; the sex of the person inflicting the punishment; whether the punishment was carried out in front of others; and the delay between the incident and the administration of the punishment.

---

[157] See *Y* v *UK* (1992) 17 EHHR 238.
[158] (1995) 24 EHRR 250.
[159] (1992) 17 EHHR 238.

CHAPTER EIGHT

SPECIAL EDUCATIONAL NEEDS

INTRODUCTION

8.01 It is estimated that approximately one fifth of all children will have special educational needs at some stage while they are at school (SEN).[1] In spite of this, until recently education legislation contained limited provision for such children. The Education and Libraries (NI) Order 1972 placed local authorities under a duty to have regard to the need for securing that provision was made for pupils suffering from "disability of mind or body". However, there were no formal procedures for identifying and providing for such children. In 1978 a committee headed by Lady Warnock conducted an inquiry into educational provision for children with disabilities.[2] It recommended that the scope of provision should not be restricted to the physically and mentally disabled but should be extended to include all children with "learning difficulties"; that there should be established procedures for identifying, assessing, recording and reviewing individual cases; and that parents should be involved to a greater extent in the decision-making process. The Warnock Report's recommendations formed the basis for the Education Act 1981 in England and Wales.[3] Northern Ireland introduced similar provisions in 1986.[4] In 1991 special educational needs fell for further consideration as part of the government's general review of education.[5] As a result, the Education Act 1993 introduced reforms designed to increase parental involvement and to provide an independent means of challenging decisions. Similar reforms are contained in the Education (NI) Order 1996. The result is that special needs provision is now one of the most highly regulated areas of education.

8.02 The current legal provisions do a number of things. First, they define the children who fall within the ambit of special educational provision. Secondly, they establish procedures for identifying and assessing children who have special educational needs. Thirdly, they set down procedures for determining appropriate educational provision where the ELB assumes responsibility for the education of such children. Finally, the legislation provides parents with a means of challenging certain decisions regarding their child's education. The Special Educational Needs Tribunal (SENT) began

---

[1] This figure derives from the Warnock Report, *Report of the Committee of Enquiry into the Education of Handicapped Children and Young People*, (1978) Cmnd 7212. It is now widely used by ELBs as a target figure for identifying children with special educational needs.
[2] *Ibid.*
[3] For an analysis of this legislation, see Hannon, 'The Education Act 1981: New Rights and Duties in Special Education' (1982) *Journal of Social Welfare Law*, p. 275. The author highlights the differences between the Warnock Report's recommendations and the legislation implemented.
[4] Education (NI) Order 1984, art. 16. This was later consolidated in the Education and Libraries (NI) Order 1986, arts. 29-36. See DENI Circular 1987/21.
[5] See DfEE *Choice and Diversity* (HMSO, 1991).

operating in Northern Ireland in 1997. Its remit and operation are considered at paragraphs 8.64-8.61. In addition to the statutory provisions, there is a Code of Practice on Special Educational Needs which is intended to provide guidance to ELBs and Boards of Governors on the exercise of their statutory duties. The Code of Practice is not in itself legally binding. However, it is one of the most important documents in the area so its scope and legal effect are considered at paragraphs 8.19-8.25.

8.03 The key distinction made by the legislation is between children for whom a statement is maintained and children who have special educational needs but for whom no statement is maintained. A statement is a document setting out the child's needs and the provision which will be made. A statement will only be made where the ELB considers it necessary that it assumes responsibility for the child's educational provision. This will normally only be the case in relation to approximately two per cent of children - those children whose needs are particularly severe or unusual. The responsibility for the vast majority of children with special educational needs (approximately 18% of all pupils) lies with the Boards of Governors in ordinary schools. The key focus of the legislation is on the procedures for statutory assessments and for statementing by ELBs. The provision for children without statements is less regulated and is considered separately at paragraphs 8.85-8.89.

8.04 Whether or not a statement is maintained there is a duty to secure appropriate provision for children with special educational needs. In practice, the most important factor in determining the nature of the education to be provided will be the individual needs of the child. However, this is by no means the sole determinant. Two other factors may have a significant influence in the decision making process. The first of these is the wishes of the parents. The provision to be made for children with special educational needs is an issue on which parents will often have very strong feelings. Parents generally want the best for their child. However, their feelings can be even more potent when the child is starting with some sort of disadvantage. Furthermore, there is no standard response. Some parents want their child to be educated in an ordinary school. Other parents may feel that an ordinary school is not meeting their child's needs and want them to attend a special school. Some parents may have difficulty accepting that their child has special needs. Other parents may feel that their child's difficulties are not being given due recognition. The legislation gives parents the right to express a preference as to their child's education and to have their views heard. It does not give them an unqualified right to choose the education which they consider most appropriate. This is underlined by the second factor which impacts on decision-making; the resources available to meet the child's needs.

8.05 Needs which depart from the educational norm will inevitably mean extra expenditure. Both ELBs and Boards of Governors are under a duty to secure provision only to the extent that it is "reasonably practicable" and is compatible with "the efficient use of resources".[6] The legislation does not provide parents with an unqualified right to choose the form of education. This was emphasised in a judgment of the English Court of Appeal:

---

[6] Arts. 7-8 of the 1996 Order.

> "There is no question of Parliament having placed the local authority under an obligation to provide a child with the best possible education. There is no duty to the authority to provide such a Utopian system, or to educate him or her to his or her maximum potential."[7]

The scope for conflict between parental wishes and the availability of resources makes this one of the most potentially litigious areas of education law. Many of the disputes will centre on parents' dissatisfaction with the type of educational provision being made for their child. Most of these will now be dealt with by the Special Educational Needs Tribunal. However, the legal significance of the area has been further underlined by the House of Lord's decision in *X* v *Bedfordshire CC*.[8] The case involved a claim for damages for "impairment of development" on the grounds that the local authority had failed to identify and provide for the plaintiff's special educational needs pursuant to its statutory duties. The House of Lords stated that the Education Acts did not in themselves give rise to a statutory claim for damages. However, it accepted the validity of a possible claim for negligence at common law against individuals employed by the authority for failure to exercise care in the fulfillment of their normal professional duties. The case is significant in that education authorities may now be vicariously liable if someone employed by them negligently fails to identify or make appropriate provision for a child with learning difficulties. Its scope and impact are considered at paragraphs 8.97-8.101.

8.06 Special educational needs is one of the areas which has fallen for review under the Labour government's plans for education reform. In 1997 the government issued a green paper, *Excellence for All Children - Meeting Special Educational Needs*.[9] This included proposals to define national criteria for making statements; to introduce a contract between schools and parents for children at stage three; to introduce conciliation procedures for parents dissatisfied with local education authority decisions; and to increase the role of education authorities in the monitoring of school expenditure on SEN. The proposals have not yet been enacted in England and Wales. However, it might be anticipated that Northern Ireland will replicate whatever reforms are introduced. Special educational needs is one area where the law in Northern Ireland is virtually identical to that in England and Wales. There is, however, one notable exception to this and that relates to the time limits by which ELBs are required to act. In England and Wales, the maximum time limit from a parent's request for an assessment to the issue of a statement is normally 26 weeks. In Northern Ireland the only statutory time limit is that an ELB must issue a copy of the proposed statement within 18 weeks of the notice of its proposal to make an assessment or the parent's request for an assessment. The Code of Practice does include various recommended time scales which are noted at relevant points of the chapter. However, these do not have statutory force.

---

[7] *R* v *Surrey County Council, ex parte H* [1983] LGR 219, *per* Slade LJ.
[8] [1995] 3 All ER 353.
[9] (1997) Cm 3785.

LEGAL RESPONSIBILITIES

The Department of Education and the Education and Library Boards

8.07 The Department is responsible for: producing the Code of Practice; making appointments to the Special Educational Needs Tribunal; and approving special schools. ELBs are more actively involved in the delivery of special educational needs provision. For instance, ELBs are under a statutory duty to produce and keep under review a policy on special educational needs in their area.[10] They are also required to conduct the statutory assessment process and to make, maintain and review statements. Most significantly, perhaps, when a child is statemented, the ELB is under an obligation to ensure that the child is receiving the educational provision which they require.[11] This applies even where the child is educated in a mainstream school.[12]

Duties on Boards of Governors

8.08 The Boards of Governors of mainstream schools also have a range of duties in relation to children with special needs. First, they must ensure that the school has a policy on the provision of education for children with special educational needs.[13] This must be compatible with the various statutory provisions in relation to education (particularly those concerning special needs).[14] Moreover, the Board of Governors must have regard to its policy when carrying out its functions under the Education Orders.[15] The Board is also required to include information about special educational needs in its annual report. For instance the annual report must include: information about the special arrangements for the admission of children without statements; the steps taken to prevent pupils with SEN being treated less favourably than other pupils; and the facilities provided by the school to assist access for pupils with SEN.[16] The annual report must also describe what steps have been taken to secure the implementation of the school's policy in relation to the provision of education for children with SEN.[17]

8.09 Boards of Governors are also under some obligations towards individual children with SEN. First, the Board of Governors is under a duty to ensure that the child's needs are made known to all those who are likely to teach him or her.[18] More significantly, the governors are also under a duty to use their best endeavours to secure that registered pupils with special needs are receiving the educational provision which their learning difficulty calls for.[19] This may mean providing the child with a classroom assistant or

---

[10] Art. 6 of the 1996 Order.
[11] Art. 16 (1) of the 1996 Order.
[12] *R v Secretary of State for Education and Science, ex parte E* [1992] 1 FLR 377.
[13] Art. 9 of the 1996 Order.
[14] *Ibid* art. 9(3).
[15] *Ibid* art. 9(4).
[16] *Ibid* art. 8(3)-(4).
[17] *Ibid* art. 9(5).
[18] *Ibid* art. 8(1)(b).
[19] *Ibid* art. 8(1)(a).

remedial teaching. The duty is not qualified by a clause prevalent in other areas of education law which makes the performance of a duty conditional upon compatibility with the efficient education of other children at the school and the efficient use of resources. Such a qualification would, arguably, be inappropriate - if a school cannot make appropriate provision, there is an argument that the child should have been statemented thus transferring responsibility to the ELB. However, the duty is not absolute; it is required only to use its best endeavours to secure suitable provision. In a House of Lords' debate on the draft legislation this phrase was described as a "powerful duty", and interpreted by Baroness Blatch as meaning that "governors must do everything that they possibly can to secure the provision".[20] Insofar as this gives the impression that governors are all but compelled to secure appropriate provision, it is probably an over generous interpretation of the extent of the obligation. The phrase "best endeavours" inevitably allows some scope for argument as to what it is realistic to expect a Board of Governors to provide, since the governors can only do as much as their resources permit.

Principle of integration

8.10 The importance of the integration of children with learning difficulties together with children who do not have such difficulties has long been recognised as a key concept in the field of disability rights.[21] Integration is considered to be especially important during the formative years and is therefore of particular significance for children with disabilities. Article 23(1) of the UNCRC requires contracting parties to "facilitate the [disabled] child's active participation in the community". An important facet of that integration relates to the child's education. It is widely accepted that being educated along with his or her peers will best prepare children with SEN for life after school. One of the key conclusions of the Warnock Report was that as many children as possible should be educated in mainstream schools along with their peers and this is now recognised to some extent in the state education system. The legislative obligations in relation to integration are considered in the next paragraph. Moreover, one of the key principles of the Code of Practice is that children with SEN should, wherever appropriate, be educated alongside their peers in mainstream schools.[22] The difficulty is that integration can be problematic in two ways. First, it may be costly, for instance where the child needs assistance from a personal classroom assistant. An education authority may consider it would be more cost-effective if the child were to be placed in a special school so that the money saved could be allocated in other ways. Secondly, problems can arise where the child's needs are such that meeting his or her needs has such an impact on the general school processes that it affects the education of the other children. Thus, although the legislation contains a number of presumptions regarding integration, the relevant obligations are heavily qualified.

---

[20] HL Deb, vol. 545, col. 504, 29 April 1993.
[21] See generally, The Snowdon Report, *Integrating the Disabled* (1976) published by the National Fund for Research into Crippling Diseases.
[22] Para. 1.6.

8.11 The principle of integration is embodied in the legislation in a number of ways. First, in respect of children who are statemented, ELBs and Boards of Governors are required to secure that the child is educated in an ordinary school.[23] However, this duty only applies where educating the child in a mainstream school is compatible with him or her receiving the special educational provision which his learning difficulty calls for: the provision of efficient education for the children with whom he will be educated; and the efficient use of resources.[24] In *Graeme v United Kingdom*, a case taken under Article 2 of the First Protocol of the ECHR, the European Commission on Human Rights gave the United Kingdom a wide discretion in determining the type of provision which was suitable for an individual child.[25] In that case, the parents of a child who was epileptic and had a series of other problems wanted him to attend a mainstream rather than a special school because they had a principled objection to non-mainstream education. The Commission considered that the child's right to an effective education prevailed over the parents' views on non-segregated education to the extent that those views represented a philosophical conviction. Secondly, if a child is educated in a mainstream school, Boards of Governors are under an obligation to ensure that the child engages in the activities of the school together with children who do not have special educational needs.[26] However, this duty is also qualified so that those concerned do only what is "reasonably practicable" and compatible with the child receiving the special educational provision which his or her learning difficulty calls for, the provision of efficient education for the children with whom he or she will be educated and the efficient use of resources. In one case, the European Commission on Human Rights considered that a refusal to install a lift in a mainstream school for a child in a wheelchair did not amount to a denial of the right to education under Article 2 of the First Protocol.[27] The Commission stated that the legitimate aim of the LEA's policy was to provide educational facilities in a manner that was consistent with the practical and efficient use of resources and public funds and that the refusal to provide a lift was not disproportionate in the light of the available resources and the other measures which had been taken to assist the applicant.

8.12 While the legislation specifically embodies the principle of integration, in practice whether a child is fully mainstreamed depends on a series of external factors which include not just his or her needs but also the needs of his or her peers as well as what is considered to be a proper rationing of resources. The issue of resources can be controversial. For instance, it can be difficult to estimate the relative costs of keeping children in mainstream schools as opposed to placing them in special schools. It has been suggested that there may be little difference in terms of cost. However, this might be difficult for a parent who wants mainstream education for their child to prove

---

[23] Art. 7(1) of the 1996 Order.
[24] *Ibid* art. 7(2).
[25] (1990) 64 DR 158. See further para. 1.52.
[26] *Ibid* art. 8(2).
[27] *McIntyre v United Kingdom* (1998) Application No. 29046/95.

to an ELB or the SENT.[28] The Northern Ireland Forum has recommended that children with SEN should not be prevented from being educated in mainstream classes because of a lack of support by ELBs and that the Department might provide additional resources to enable special schools to provide more outreach work to children in mainstream classes.[29]

DEFINITION OF SPECIAL EDUCATIONAL NEED

8.13 The legislation on special educational needs applies to children under the age of 19 who are registered at school.[30] However, a person who attains the age of 19 during the school term is deemed to be aged 18 until the day after the end of the school term.[31] A child is considered to have special education needs if "he has a learning difficulty which calls for special educational provision to be made for him".[32] In effect, this involves a two-stage test. First, does the child have a learning difficulty? If so, does he or she require special educational provision?

Learning difficulty

8.14 The term "learning difficulty" applies to a broad range of circumstances. In particular, it is not limited to those who have physical or mental disabilities but can apply to children with no disability who are not developing at a similar rate to other children of their age. The statutory definition of learning disability focuses on the child's abilities in comparison to other children of the same age. A child will be considered to have a learning difficulty in one of three circumstances:

(i) The child has a significantly greater difficulty in learning than the majority of children his age.[33]

The terms "significantly greater" and "a majority of children" are not defined. In practice, a range of tests are employed by the ELBs to determine whether a child falls into this category. A child should be considered to have a learning difficulty if he or she is placed in the lowest 20 per cent of children on these tests. The definition covers children with a range of problems such as Down's Syndrome and dyslexia[34] to children who for no medically-diagnosed reason are slow learners.

---

[28] See, The Audit Commission , *Getting in on the Act - Provision for Pupils with Special Educational Needs - The National Picture* (HMSO, 1992).
[29] NI Forum for Political Dialogue, *Special Educational Provision for School-age Children in Northern Ireland* (1998) p. 31.
[30] Art. 3(6) of the 1996 Order.
[31] *Ibid* art. 3(7).
[32] *Ibid* art. 3.
[33] *Ibid* art. 3(2)(a).
[34] *R v Hampshire Education Authority, ex parte J* [1985] 84 LGR 547.

(ii) The child has a disability which either prevents or hinders him from making use of the educational facilities of a kind generally provided in schools for children of his age.[35]

This covers children with a range of physical disabilities, including blindness, deafness and restricted mobility. It was also found to cover a highly intelligent child with dyslexia whose parents wished him to attend a special independent school.[36] The court found that his dyslexia was a disability which "hindered" him in using the educational facilities of the school.

(iii) The child has not attained the lower limit of compulsory school age and is, or would be if special educational provision were not made for him, likely to fall within either of the two heads above.[37]

The first two tests are defined in relation to other children or school facilities. This may not be appropriate when the child is not yet at school and therefore in a position to be compared to other children. The third head of learning difficulty catches young children who are not yet of school age but whom it is anticipated will have learning difficulties when they are of school age. It is a general principle that early intervention reduces the needs later in the school career and this definition ensures that children are identified and provided for even before they start school.

8.15 The term learning difficulty does not include children whose problems arise solely because the language (or form of language) in which he or she is, or will be, taught is different from a language (or form of a language) which has at any time been spoken in his or her home.[38] This means that children who are experiencing learning difficulties because English is not their first language do not fall within the scope of the legislation and the Code of Practice. Their difficulties must be addressed within the school system but they will not be considered to have special educational needs in this context.

Special educational provision

8.16 The second limb of the special educational needs test is that the child's learning difficulty calls for special educational provision to be made for him or her. A child may well have learning difficulties but not require special educational provision to assist him or her. Special educational provision is defined as educational provision which is "additional to, or otherwise different from, the educational provision made generally for children of his age in ordinary schools".[39] In the English High Court, Taylor J stated that "the phrase 'made generally for children of his age' means provided to the general run of normal children, to the normal majority".[40] He rejected the argument that for provision to be special educational provision it would have to be unavailable generally in ordinary schools. On this basis the

---

[35] Art. 3(2)(b) of the 1996 Order.
[36] *R v Hampshire Education Authority, ex parte J* [1985] 84 LGR 547.
[37] Art. 3(2)(c) of the 1996 Order.
[38] Art. 3 (3) of the 1996 Order.
[39] *Ibid* art. 3(4((a).
[40] *R v Hampshire Education Authority, ex parte J* [1985] 84 LGR 547, at p. 555.

correct test would appear to be whether ordinary children need this form of educational provision and not whether ordinary schools provide it. Thus for example, a child whose reading ability is below that of his or her peers may be considered to require special educational provision even though most schools have a remedial teaching class. The definition places the focus on the child's ability relative to other children of the same age and not on what is actually available in schools. In practice however, the two will be related because school provision will inevitably mirror the actual needs of the majority of children.

Scope of the definition

8.17 The definition of special education needs covers children whose difficulties vary both in their range and degree. For example, it includes children whose difficulties range from moderate problems with reading to profound deafness and severe mental disability. In terms of the nature of the learning difficulties covered, the Code of Practice envisages seven categories: (i) low educational attainment; (ii) specific learning difficulties such as dyslexia and dyscalcula; (iii) emotional and behavioural difficulty; (iv) physical disability; (v) hearing impairment; (vi) visual impairment; (vii) and learning problems arising from illnesses (such as epilepsy, asthma, or cystic fybrosis).[41] However, within each of these categories it is anticipated that there may be a wide variation in the degree of difficulty experienced. For example, the category "emotional and behavioural difficulties" includes children who are "withdrawn and lack confidence" as well as children who are "bizarre, obsessive, violent or severely disruptive". Since it is recognised that the term "special educational needs" embraces one-fifth of the school population, it is clear that the children who fall within the scope of the definition may differ considerably in the degree of assistance that they require. The legislation acknowledges this by distinguishing those children who are affected most severely through the statementing procedure. Children whose needs are particularly severe or complex receive a statement from their local ELB which will undertake responsibility for ensuring that they receive the education that they require.

Educational?

8.18 There has been some dispute as to when provision is "educational", particularly where there is an overlap between the child's educational and medical needs.[42] For instance, an issue arose over whether speech therapy could be considered to be a form of educational provision. Initially this was not considered to fall within the scope of the legislation.[43] However, the English Court of Appeal has since stated that speech therapy can amount to

---

[41] These are set out in the appendix to the Code of Practice at pp. 69-86.
[42] There has also been an issue over whether a religious requirement can be a special educational need. The English courts have concluded that in certain instances it can, for instance where a child from a strictly religious background would not cope in a secular school. See *R v Secretary of State for Education and Employment, ex parte E* [1996] ELR 312.
[43] *R v Oxfordshire County Council, ex parte W, The Times*, 12 November 1986.

educational provision depending on the facts of the case.[44] The Court of Appeal gave this illustration:

> "To teach an adult who has lost his larynx because of cancer might well be considered as treatment rather than education. But to teach a child who has never been able to communicate by language ... seems to us as much educational provision as to teach a child to communicate by writing."[45]

The Code of Practice now makes specific reference to speech difficulties.[46] However, there will be other instances when it is unclear whether provision is deemed to be educational rather than medical. The Court of Appeal's judgment makes it clear that the fact that the appropriate provision is normally provided as part of the health service does not necessarily mean that it is not educational for the purposes of this legislation.

THE CODE OF PRACTICE

8.19 The 1996 Order places the Department under a duty to produce and publish a Code of Practice which gives the ELBs and Boards of Governors "practical guidance" in respect of the discharge of their statutory functions".[47] The Northern Ireland Code of Practice came into operation in September 1998. The Code of Practice was made after consultation with relevant bodies and was subject to the affirmative resolution procedure.[48] ELBs and Boards of Governors are under a duty to have regard to the provisions of the Code when exercising these functions.[49]

The content of the Code

8.20 The Code is intended to provide practical guidance to ELBs and Boards of Governors on the exercise of their statutory duties. The Code outlines five stages for the assessment and provision of children with special needs, the first three of which are school-based and relate to children for whom no statement is maintained. The stages are distinguished from one another by the degree of intervention on the part of the school or ELB. Stage One applies when children are identified and initial action is taken by their teacher. At Stage Two the school's special education needs co-ordinator (SENCo) takes responsibility for co-ordinating the child's special educational needs provision. At Stage Three the teachers and the SENCo are supported by external specialists.

8.21 Stages One to Three should cover most children with special educational needs being educated in mainstream schools. The Code recommends that at each of these stages the SENCo should produce an "individual educational plan" which should include details of the following: the nature of the child's learning difficulties; the special educational provision to be provided; help to be given by parents at home; targets to be achieved;

---

[44] *R v Lancashire CC, ex parte M* [1989] FLR 279.
[45] *Ibid* at p. 301.
[46] At pp. 83-84.
[47] Art. 4(1)(4) of the 1996 Order.
[48] *Ibid* art. 5.
[49] *Ibid* art. 4(2).

pastoral care or medical requirements; monitoring and assessment arrangements; and review arrangements. Stages Four and Five relate to the statutory assessment and statementing procedures respectively.

The principles of the Code

8.22 The fundamental principles underlying the Code are as follows:

- The needs of all pupils who may experience learning difficulties during their school careers must be addressed; there is a continuum of needs and a continuum of provision which may be made in a variety of forms.
- Children with special educational needs require the greatest possible access to a broad and balanced education, including the Northern Ireland Curriculum.
- The needs of most pupils will be met in mainstream schools, and without a statutory assessment or statement. Children with special educational needs, including those with statements, should, wherever appropriate and taking into account the wishes of their parents, be educated alongside their peers in mainstream schools.
- Even before a child reaches compulsory school age, he or she may have special educational needs requiring the intervention of ELBs as well as the health services.
- The knowledge, views and experience of parents are vital. Effective assessment and provision will best be secured where there is partnership between parents and schools, ELBs and other agencies.

Essential practices and procedures

8.23 The essential practices and procedures which the Code embodies are as follows:

- Children with special educational needs should be identified as early as possible and assessed as quickly as is consistent with thoroughness.
- Provision should be made by the most appropriate agency. In most cases this will be the child's mainstream school, working in partnership with the parents, and no statutory assessment will be necessary.
- ELBs should complete assessments and statements as quickly as thorough consideration of the issues allows.
- ELBs must produce clear and thorough statements, setting out the child's educational and non-educational needs, the objectives to be secured, the provision to be made and the arrangements for monitoring and review. They must ensure that there is an annual review and that educational targets are monitored and revised.
- The ascertainable wishes of the child should be considered in the light of his age and understanding.

- There must be close co-operation between all the agencies concerned and a multi-disciplinary approach to the resolution of the issues.

The legal status of the Code of Practice

8.24 The Code of Practice is pivotal to the operation of special needs provision in schools. Its legal status is therefore worthy of comment. At the outset it should be stressed that the Code itself is not legally binding. However, article 4(2) of the 1996 Order states that it shall be the duty of ELBs and Boards of Governors "to have regard to the provisions of the code". This means that decision-makers should not make any decision without first having considered the matters covered by the Code. In Parliament the significance of the equivalent Code of Practice in England and Wales was described as follows:

> "By law, those who must have regard to the Code cannot ignore it. If they do so, they will be in breach of a duty. They do not, however, have to follow the Code to the letter and in every particular. But any departure from the Code will be challenged, require justification to parents in the first instance and then, depending on the circumstances, to the Secretary of State if the matter at issue is the subject of an appeal."[50]

It is clear that the provisions of the Code do not have the force of law and that ELBs and schools are not therefore bound to follow them in all circumstances. The question arises as to when an ELB or Board of Governors would be justified in departing from the guidance given in the Code. Essentially, they should be able to do so any time that they consider the situation requires a departure. There are three types of possible variations: (i) improved provision; (ii) different but equally beneficial provision; and (iii) less beneficial provision. It is unlikely that parents will be unhappy if ELBs or schools improve on the provision set out in the Code. However, a dispute may arise where a parent requests something which is additional to what is set out in the Code. If the parent can establish a good reason for this extra provision, the authority should consider it and not reject it simply on the basis that it does not form part of the Code. The Code cannot properly be regarded as some sort of statement of the maximum provision to be offered. It would seem that the second type of situation, equal but different provision, is also an option. In the debate on the legislation in the House of Lords, Baroness Blatch made the following statement:

> "In justifying their actions, those to whom the Code applies will have to show that the alternative action produced results which were at least as beneficial as those which would have resulted from their following the Code."[51]

The implication of this statement is that these are the only types of situation when departure from the Code would be justified. However, the basis for such an approach is not clear from the statute. It is submitted that there may be occasions when an ELB or Board of Governors have regard to the Code but

---

[50] HL Deb, vol. 545, col. 487, 29 April 1993.
[51] *Ibid.*

feel obliged to pursue a different and less beneficial procedure, for instance there may be occasions when the time limits cannot be complied with for reasons not anticipated in the Code. This will not inevitably give rise to a valid challenge on appeal. A failure to follow the guidance laid out in the Code may influence the SENT on an appeal but will not necessarily invalidate any decision made or action taken.

8.25 Research commissioned by the Department prior to the introduction of the Code of Practice indicated that schools in Northern Ireland were concerned about the implications of the Code.[52] The research also indicated that the practice in schools in Northern Ireland was often not in conformity with the fundamental principles of the Code (e.g. SEN provision often occurs outside mainstream classrooms). This would suggest that schools will at least initially have difficulties implementing the Code. However, the legislation does not provide parents with a specific means of redress if a school or educational authority fails to abide by the guidance given in the Code of Practice. However, the legislation does underpin the significance of the Code in a number of ways. First, the Special Education Needs Tribunal is required to have regard to any provisions of the Code which appear to it to be relevant on appeal.[53] This should provide a considerable incentive for schools to follow the Code. However, it should be noted that it is of less significance for children without statements who have limited rights of appeal to the SENT. Secondly, the status of the Code is further underlined by the fact that schools will have to demonstrate that they are fufilling their duties in regard to the Code during an inspection by the Education and Training Inspectorate. Finally, the Code of Practice may attain increased significance in negligence actions following *X* v *Bedfordshire County Council*.[54] The Code of Practice is undoubtedly the benchmark of the procedures which a reasonable education authority would have followed in relation to a child with special educational needs.

IDENTIFICATION OF CHILDREN WITH SPECIAL EDUCATIONAL NEEDS

8.26 It is important that children who may have special educational needs are identified so that appropriate provision can be made quickly. A failure to identify a child with special needs may result in an action for negligence.[55] ELBs are placed under a general duty to identify children who have special educational needs and who may require a statement.[56] This duty applies to all children in its area who are registered pupils in grant-aided schools. It does not apply to children who have special educational needs but who are unlikely to require a statement. Nor does it apply to those who are attending independent schools. The ELB's obligations also extend to children aged over two but

---

[52] DENI Research briefing RB/98, *Practice in Mainstream Schools For Children With Special Educational Needs*.
[53] Art. 4(3) of the 1996 Order.
[54] See paras. 8.97-8.101.
[55] *Ibid.*
[56] Art. 13 of the 1996 Order.

under compulsory school age who have been brought to the ELBs attention, for instance by a local social services office or by the child's parents.[57]

8.27 In practice special needs are likely to come to light when the child attends school. For this reason schools have a number of obligations which should encourage the identification of children with special needs. First, the school's SEN policy must state how such children will be identified. In addition Boards of Governors are under a duty to ensure that teachers in a school are aware of the importance of identifying children who have special educational needs.[58] In some cases it will be apparent before the child attends school that he or she has special needs. Moreover, less obvious learning difficulties are likely to come to light through the newly introduced baseline assessments and the various other assessments which are undertaken at each Key Stage of the curriculum. The Code of Practice suggests that children will be identified at Stage One by their teacher or because parents have expressed concern.

STATUTORY ASSESSMENT

8.28 The Code of Practice details procedures for assessing children at Stages One to Three. Stage Four contains the guidance for the conduct of the Statutory Assessment under article 15 of the 1996 Order. This assessment is of key significance because it is the primary determinant of whether the child will be statemented. A child will not be statemented unless he or she has been subject to a statutory assessment. On the other hand not all assessments will result in statements.

8.29 The decision to assess a child can arise in one of two ways. First, the ELB can take the decision to assess. This will usually be prompted by the school having expressed concern about the child's educational progress. In most cases the child will have proceeded through Stages One to Three of the Code of Practice. However, there is no legal restriction on a child who is attending a mainstream school being subject to a statutory assessment without having gone through the first three stages although it is anticipated that such cases would be rare.[59] The ELB must conduct an assessment if it is of the opinion that the child has or probably has special educational needs and that it is (or probably is) necessary for the ELB to determine the type of educational provision which is called for.[60]

8.30 Alternatively, the parents may request that the child is formally assessed.[61] In such cases the ELB must notify the health and social services authority and the principal of the child's school that a request has been made.[62] The ELB should comply with the parent's request if an assessment has not been made within six months and the ELB considers it necessary to comply with the request. There will be occasions when the ELB might not consider it necessary to conduct an assessment: for instance when the school provides

---

[57] *Ibid* art. 13(3)(b).
[58] Art. 8(1)(c) of the 1996 Order.
[59] Code of Practice, para. 3.17.
[60] Art. 15(1) of the 1996 Order.
[61] *Ibid* art. 20.
[62] Reg. 4(3) of the Education (SEN) Regulations (NI) 1997.

evidence that the child is progressing normally; or where an assessment has been conducted recently and there is no evidence of a change in circumstances. However, if it decides not to make a formal assessment, it must notify the child's parents and inform them that they have a right to appeal the decision to the SENT.[63] There is no statutory time limit by which an ELB has to respond to a parental request for assessment when it decides not to assess. The Code suggests that parents should be informed immediately. In contrast, legislation in England and Wales requires LEAs to inform parents within six weeks of receipt of a request for assessment.[64]

Notices to parents regarding proposed assessments

8.31 Where the ELB proposes to conduct a formal assessment it must first notify the child's parents.[65] This notice must contain the following information: that the ELB proposes to make an assessment; the procedure to be followed in making the assessment; the name of the officer of the ELB from whom further information can be obtained; and the parent's right to make representations and submit written evidence to the ELB within a specified period. The period in which the parent can make representations must be at least 29 days beginning with the date on which the notice is served.[66] If, after serving a notice that it proposes to assess under article 15(1) of the 1996 Order, the ELB decides not to assess, it must give notice in writing of that decision and the reasons for making it. If, however, when the original notice period has expired, the ELB is still of the opinion that the child has or is likely to have special educational needs, it will arrange for an assessment.[67] At this point the ELB must notify the parents of its decision to make an assessment and the reasons for making it.[68]

Advice to be sought

8.32 When it is making an assessment under article 15 an ELB is under an obligation to seek advice from a number of different sources. These include: (i) the child's parent; (ii) educational advice; (iii) medical advice; (iv) psychological advice; (v) social services advice; (vi) and any other advice that the ELB considers appropriate for the purposes of arriving at a satisfactory assessment.[69] An ELB does not have to seek advice from anyone other than the parent if it has obtained such advice within the previous 12 months provided that the ELB, the parent and the person from whom the advice was obtained are satisfied that the existing advice is sufficient for the purposes of arriving at a satisfactory assessment.[70] The requirements relating to the advice sought are set down in the Education (Special Educational Needs) Regulations (NI) 1997. These regulations describe in detail the advice to be sought. They attempt to ensure that all relevant information is before the ELB when it takes

---

[63] Art. 20(2) of the 1986 Order.
[64] Education (SEN) Regulations 1994, reg. 11.
[65] *Ibid* art. 15(1) of the 1996 Order.
[66] *Ibid* art. 15(1)(d).
[67] *Ibid* art. 15(3).
[68] *Ibid* art. 15(4).
[69] Reg. 5(1) of the Education (SEN) Regulations (NI) 1997.
[70] *Ibid* reg. 5(5).

its decision. This is clearly in the child's interests. Moreover, it also serves to ensure that ELBs which abide by the regulations will be protected from actions for negligence.

8.33 The advice to be sought must cover: the educational, medical, psychological or other features of the case which appear to be relevant to the child's needs (including his or her likely future needs); how those features could affect the child's educational needs; and the provision which is appropriate for the child in light of those features of the child's case, whether by way of special educational provision or non-educational provision.[71] It should not include any matter which is required to be specified in a statement by virtue of article 16(4)(b) of the 1996 Order (i.e. the name of the school which the child should attend). Any person from whom advice is sought may consult other people whom he or she considers expedient and must consult people whom the ELB has specified as having relevant knowledge or information concerning the child.[72] When the ELB is seeking advice, it must supply the person from whom the advice is sought with any representations made by the parent and any evidence submitted by or at the request of the parent.[73]

8.34 In addition to the above general requirements regarding advice, there are a number of specific provisions relating to particular kinds of advice to be sought.

Parental advice

8.35 There are no legal provisions governing the advice to be received from the parents. The Code of Practice suggests that parents might find it helpful to talk to the Named Board Officer.[74] It also gives guidance notes to help parents collect some of the information which would be relevant to the assessment process.

Educational advice

8.36 Educational advice is to be sought from the principal of each school which the child is currently attending or has attended at any time within the preceding 18 months. If this is not possible (e.g. the child is not attending a school), advice should be sought from a person whom the ELB is satisfied has experience of teaching children with special educational needs or knowledge of the differing provision which may be called for in different cases to meet those needs. In the latter case, the ELB should ensure that they also have advice from a person who is responsible for the child's educational provision. However, in each case, the advice must be sought from a qualified teacher. Advice sought from a principal must, if the principal has not taught the child within the preceding 18 months, be advice after consultation with a teacher who has taught the child. The advice sought from the principal shall include advice relating to the steps which have been taken by the school to identify

---

[71] *Ibid* reg. 5(2).
[72] *Ibid* reg. 5(3).
[73] *Ibid* reg. 5(4).
[74] Para. 3.44.

and assess the special educational needs of the child and to make provision for the purposes of meeting those needs.

8.37 Where it appears that a child is hearing impaired or visually impaired or both, and the person from whom the educational advice is sought is not qualified to teach children with these impairments, then the advice must be given after consultation with a person with the relevant qualifications.[75] A person will be considered to be appropriately qualified if he or she is employed at a school as a teacher of a class for pupils who have these impairments otherwise than to give instruction in a craft, trade or domestic subject.

Medical advice

8.38 Medical advice will be sought from the health and social services authority which shall obtain the advice from a registered medical practitioner. This advice may include advice from the child's general medical practitioner and the school doctor, nurses, health visitors etc. It may also include private reports obtained by the child's parents. The advice should state the likely consequences for the child's education.[76]

Social services advice

8.39 The Health and Social Services Trust should give the ELB any relevant social services information which it may have. This may include details of any Child Care Plan or information from placements if the child is living in a residential or foster home.[77] If the family is not known to social services, the Trust should say so. However, Trusts can also combine an assessment of a child in need under the Children Order 1995 with statutory assessment under the education legislation to check what assistance might be provided to the family.

8.40 Where an ELB has requested advice from a health and social services authority under regulation 5(1)(c) or (e) the authority must comply with the request within six weeks of the date on which it receives it.[78] An authority need not comply with this time limit if it is impractical to do so for one of the following reasons: (i) exceptional circumstances affect the child or his or her parent during the six week period; (ii) the child or his parent is absent from the area of the authority for a continuous period of not less than four weeks during the six week period; (iii) the child fails to keep an appointment for an examination or a test made by the authority during the six week period; or (iv) the authority has not prior to the service of a copy of the notice produced or maintained any information or records relevant to the assessment of the child.[79]

---

[75] Reg. 6(5) of the Education (SEN) Regulations (NI) 1997.
[76] Para. 3.51 of Code of Practice on Special Educational Needs.
[77] *Ibid* para. 3.54.
[78] Reg. 9A(4) of the Education (SEN) Regulations (NI) 1997 as substituted by the Education (SEN)(Amendment) Regulations (NI) 1998, reg. 2.
[79] Reg. 9A(5) of the 1997 Regulations.

Psychological advice

8.41 The psychological advice must be sought from a person who is regularly employed by the ELB as an educational psychologist or engaged by the ELB as an educational psychologist in the case in question.[80] The advice sought shall be given after consultation with another psychologist if the person has reason to believe that another psychologist has relevant knowledge of other information relating to the child.

The child's views

8.42 Article 12 of the UNCRC requires Member States to take account of the views of children in all matters pertaining to them. The 1996 Order does not require the ELB to consider the child's views. However, the Code of Practice requires ELBs to seek wherever possible to establish the views of children on their needs and the way in which they may be met.[81] If such views are available, they should be set out separately from the views of parents and professionals.

Formal examinations

8.43 As part of the assessment process the ELB may require the child to attend for a formal examination.[82] In such cases it may serve the parent with a notice requiring attendance for examination. This notice must specify: the purpose of the examination; the time and place of the examination; the name of the officer of the ELB from whom more information may be obtained; the parents' right to submit information; and the parent's right to be present at the examination.[83] Failure to comply with the requirements of the notice without reasonable excuse is a criminal offence if the notice relates to a child under compulsory school age at the time of the examination.[84]

The nature and purpose of assessment

8.44 When it is making an assessment the ELB must take into account any representations and any written evidence submitted by or at the request of the child's parent under article 15(1)(d) of the 1996 Order and any advice obtained under regulation 5.[85] The assessment process is essentially for one purpose - to determine whether the ELB should assume responsibility for determining the type of education which should be provided for the child. In effect, the process is used to determine whether a child should be statemented or not. The Code of Practice states that the central question for the ELB is whether there is convincing evidence that, despite relevant and purposeful action by the school, with the help of external specialists, the child's learning difficulties remain or have not been remedied sufficiently.[86] If the ELB assumes responsibility, it will make and maintain a statement of the child's

---

[80] *Ibid* reg. 8.
[81] Para. 3.59.
[82] Sch. 1, para.4 to the 1996 Order.
[83] *Ibid* Sch. 1, para.4 (3) to the 1996 Order.
[84] *Ibid* Sch. 4, para.5.
[85] Reg. 9 of the Education (SEN) Regulations (NI) 1997.
[86] Para. 3.21.

needs. If it does not assume responsibility, the child's education will be the responsibility of the Board of Governors at the school where he or she is a registered pupil. In cases where the ELB decides not to issue a statement, it may issue a notice in lieu of a statement setting out the child's needs and the provision which should be made.[87] This may assist parents' requests within the child's school and may therefore be a good tactical reason for seeking a statutory assessment.

The consequences of assessment

8.45 If, having conducted an assessment, the ELB is of the opinion that it is necessary for it to make a statement, it will proceed to issue a copy of the proposed statement.[88] However, if the ELB decides not to issue a statement, the Code recommends that the ELB should inform the parents "immediately".[89] In contrast, in England and Wales, an LEA is required by statute to decide within two weeks of completing an assessment whether a statement is necessary and to notify parents accordingly.[90]

THE STATEMENT

Definition and legal effect

8.46 The Warnock Committee recommended that particular provision should be made for children with "severe, complex and long-term disabilities" who were judged by their local education authority to require provision not generally available in ordinary schools.[91] The special provision for such children was to be based on a system of assessment and recording which would produce a "detailed profile of their needs prepared by a multi-professional team".[92] When the Warnock Committee's recommendations were translated into legislation in the form of the Education Act 1981, the records of special educational needs were termed "statements" and, in line with the Committee's recommendations, children were only issued with statements when their needs were so severe as to necessitate provision not normally available to ordinary schools.

8.47 The word 'statement' is not given a statutory definition. It refers to the document which sets out the needs and educational provision which will be made for a child for whom the ELB has assumed responsibility. An ELB must make a statement only if it considers it necessary for it (rather than the child's ordinary school) to determine the special educational provision which the child's learning difficulty calls for.[93] In determining whether to make a statement, the main consideration will be whether all the special educational provision necessary to meet the child's needs can reasonably be provided

---

[87] Code of Practice, paras. 4.12–4.15.
[88] See para. 8.50.
[89] Code of Practice, para. 4.14.
[90] Education (SEN) Regulations 1994, reg.11.
[91] *Committee of Enquiry into the Education of Handicapped Children and Young People* (1978) Cmnd 7212, at para. 3.31.
[92] Code of Practice, para. 3.15.
[93] Art.16(1) of the 1986 Order.

within the resources normally available to ordinary schools in its area.[94] This will include specialist provision provided to the school by the ELB such as peripatetic teaching. If this is not the case the ELB will make a statement. As has already been stated, this will usually only apply to around two per cent of all pupils.[95]

8.48 The statement does not have any legal effect in its own right. However, if an ELB maintains a statement a number of statutory responsibilities ensue. First, the ELB is required to arrange the special educational provision indicated in the statement.[96] Where some of that provision is in an ordinary school, the ELB is under a duty to ensure that the school makes the provision required.[97] The ELB may also (but is not obliged to) arrange any non-educational provision as it considers appropriate.[98] The ELB's obligation to arrange the provision specified in the statement does not apply if suitable arrangements have been made by the child's parents. The ELB should, however, take steps to ensure that the education is suitable. Moreover, the obligation to maintain the statement persists and must be reviewed annually.

8.49 If a grant-aided school is named in the statement the Board of Governors is required to admit the child to the school.[99] This is notwithstanding the fact that the admission of the child may cause them to exceed their statutory admissions or enrolment number. In such cases, the Board of Governors does not have to apply for Departmental approval to exceed its number. The duty to admit the child does not, however, affect their power to expel or suspend a child who is already a pupil at the school.

PROCEDURE FOR MAKING A STATEMENT

Copy of proposed statement

8.50 Before it makes a statement, the ELB must serve the child's parent with a copy of the proposed statement and a written notice which explains the procedure to be followed including the parent's right to express a preference as to a school and to make representations.[100] The notice which accompanies a copy of the proposed statement must be in a form corresponding to that set out in Part A of the Schedule to the Education (Special Educational Needs) Regulations (NI) 1997.[101] The copy of the proposed statement should not specify the school which the ELB considers appropriate or any other provision other than in a school or institution.[102] If the ELB were to specify the provision which it considers appropriate, it might pre-empt the exercise of parental choice.

---

[94] Code of Practice, para. 4.1.
[95] *Ibid* para. 2.2.
[96] Art. 16(5) of the 1996 Order.
[97] *R v Secretary of State, ex parte E* [1992] 1 FLR 377.
[98] Art.16(5)(a)(ii) of the 1996 Order.
[99] Art. 10 of the 1997 Order.
[100] Sch. 2 para. 2 to the 1996 Order.
[101] Reg. 10 of the Education (SEN) Regulations (NI) 1997.
[102] Sch. 2 para. 2 to the 1996 Order.

Time limits

8.51 There are statutory time limits which prescribe when a copy of the proposed statement must be issued. If an ELB considers it necessary to make a statement, it must serve the child's parent with a copy of the proposed statement within 18 weeks from the date on which it served a notice of a proposed assessment under article 15(1) of the 1996 Order or received a request from a parent for an assessment under article 20(1).[103] An ELB does not have to comply with the time limit if it is impractical to do so because: (i) after receiving advice under regulation 5, it is necessary for the ELB to seek further advice; (ii) the child's parent has indicated that he or she wishes to provide advice after six weeks from the date on which the request for advice was received and the ELB has agreed to consider such advice before completing the assessment; (iii) the ELB has requested advice from the principal of the school during a period beginning one week before any date on which the school was closed for at least four weeks and ending one week before the date it re-opens; (iv) the ELB has received advice from a health and social services authority and the authority has not complied with the request within six weeks; (v) exceptional circumstances affect the child or his parent within the 18 week period; (vi) the child or his parent is absent from the area of the ELB for a continuous period of not less than four weeks during the 18 week period; or (vii) the child fails to keep an appointment for an examination or test during the 18 week period.[104] A report by the Comptroller and Auditor General found that in the periods 1994 - 1995 and 1996 -1997, no ELB had an average which came remotely near this target period.[105] In the light of this, the Northern Ireland Affairs Committee has recommended that ELBs should review their practices and procedures immediately with a view to ensuring that as many cases as possible are completed within the 18 week time limit.[106]

Preference as to school

8.52 One of the key objectives of the 1996 reforms was to increase parental involvement in the statementing procedure. Parents must be given an opportunity to express a preference as to the grant-aided school that they wish their child to attend along with the reasons for that preference.[107] This preference must be expressed within 15 days of the notice of the proposed statement or a meeting with the ELB.[108] The ELB must comply with the parent's preference unless the school is unsuitable for the child or the child's attendance would be incompatible with the provision of efficient education for other children at the school or the efficient use of resources.[109]

---

[103] Education (SEN) Regulations (NI) 1997, reg. 9A(1)-(2) as substituted by the Education (SEN) (Amendment) Regulations (NI) 1998, reg. 2.
[104] *Ibid* reg. 9A(3).
[105] Comptroller and Auditor General for Northern Ireland, *Report on Special Educational Needs* HC898 (1997-1998), paras. 3.35-36.
[106] Northern Ireland Affairs Committee, *Public Expenditure in Northern Ireland*, Session 1998-99, HC33 and 317, 1032 i-ii (1997-98), para. 35.
[107] Sch. 2, para. 3(1) to the 1996 Order.
[108] *Ibid* Sch. 2, para. 3(2).
[109] *Ibid* Sch. 3, para. 3(3).

8.53 The legislation places a qualified duty on ELBs to offer children with special needs integrated education in ordinary schools. ELBs are under a duty to provide education in an ordinary school provided that this is suitable to the child's needs and compatible with the interests of other pupils and the efficient use of resources.[110] In certain circumstances parents may have strongly held opinions that their child should attend a special school rather than an ordinary school. However, in a judgment of the English High Court, Slade J suggested that where the conditions about the child's needs and efficiency are satisfied it is "the statutory duty of the local authority to secure the education of the child at an ordinary school; no question of sending a child to a special school in these circumstances can arise".[111] On the other hand, the statutory emphasis on provision in ordinary schools may be of some assistance to parents who want their child to attend ordinary schools. However, the broad scope of the qualifications may mean that the ELB may legitimately determine that the child should be educated in a special school rather than a mainstream school.

8.54 Before it specifies a grant-aided school in a statement the ELB must consult the Board of Governors of that school.[112] Boards of Governors cannot refuse to admit a child if the school is specified in the statement. It will not usually be appropriate that a child with special educational needs will specify a grammar school. However, it is possible, for instance where a child with normal intelligence has physical disabilities. If the school is outside the ELB's area it must also consult the ELB responsible for that area.[113]

Parental representations

8.55 The parent has a right to make representations to the ELB about the content of the statement. These must be made within 15 days of the written notice of the proposed statement or the meeting with the ELB. The parent may also request a meeting with an officer of the ELB. The request must be made within 15 days of the written notice of the proposed statement. If, after the meeting, the parent disagrees with any part of the assessment the parent can request that the ELB arrange a meeting with the person responsible for advising the ELB on the child's needs.[114] Such a request must be made within 15 days of the original meeting with the ELB.[115]

Making the statement

8.56 The ELB cannot make a statement until it has considered parental representations.[116] This means that the ELB must wait until 15 days after the notice or any meetings. The statement may be in the form proposed or may be amended in the light of the representations. A copy of the statement must be served on the child's parent.[117] The ELB must also give the parent written

---

[110] *Ibid* art. 7.
[111] *R v Surrey County Council, ex parte H* [1983] LGR 219, at p. 231.
[112] Sch. 2, para. 3(4) to the 1996 Order.
[113] *Ibid* Sch. 2, para. 3(4).
[114] *Ibid* Sch. 2, para. 4.(2).
[115] *Ibid* Sch. 2, para. 4(6).
[116] *Ibid* Sch. 2, para. 5.
[117] *Ibid* Sch. 2, para. 6.

notice of his right of appeal to the SENT and the name of the person from whom he can seek information and advice about the child's special educational needs. The ELB is not under any statutory time limit to complete the statement. The Code of Practice recommends that it should be completed within eight weeks.[118] In contrast in England and Wales LEAs are under a statutory duty to produce a final copy of the statement within eight weeks of the issue of the proposed statement.[119]

FORM AND CONTENT OF THE STATEMENT

8.57 A statement made under article 16 of the 1996 Order must be in a form which substantially corresponds to that in Part B of the Schedule to the Education (Special Educational Needs) Regulations (NI) 1997. In *R v Secretary of State for Education, ex parte E* the statement was likened to a medical diagnosis and prescription.[120] This is because the content of the statement falls into one of two categories. The first is the ELB's assessment of the child's needs. The second is the educational provision which will be made to provide for those needs.[121]

8.58 The statement usually has six categories: (i) an introduction containing personal details; (ii) details of the learning difficulties; (iii) special educational provision; (iv) the type of placement required to meet the special educational provision; (v) the child's non-educational needs; and (iv) non-educational provision. All advice obtained during the assessment process must be attached as appendices to the statement. The statement should include details of all special needs provision to be made for the child, even where some of that provision is to be made by an ordinary school.[122]

8.59 The Code of Practice states that ELBs should draft "clear, unambiguous statements".[123] However, questions can arise as to the level of detail contained in the statement. In *L v Salford CC, ex parte L* the Court of Appeal said that the statement should not be too specific or too precise.[124] It is accepted that the statement may be less specific about the provision to be made when the child is to be educated at a special school.[125]

---

[118] Para. 3.37.
[119] Education (SEN) Regulations 1995, reg. 14.
[120] At p. 388.
[121] Art. 16(3) of the 1996 Order.
[122] *R v Secretary of State for Education and Science, ex parte E* [1992] 1 FLR 377 where the child had literacy and numeracy skills but the statement only referred to the literacy skills because the problems with numeracy could be met by the school.
[123] Para. 4.19.
[124] [1998] ELR 28.
[125] *R v Coupland* (1996) unreported.

CHANGES TO THE STATEMENT: REVIEW, AMENDMENT AND TERMINATION

Review

8.60 A statement must be reviewed at least every 12 months.[126] The reviews are intended to assess the child's progress, review the special provision to be made for the child and consider whether it might be appropriate to cease to maintain or to amend the statement.[127] The precise requirements regarding review depend on the age of the child (i.e. whether they are over or under the age of 14) and whether or not they attend school. If a child does not attend school, the review will be organised by the ELB.[128] School principals are required to arrange a review for children aged under 14 attending their school.[129] Children aged over 14 have a special review which will prepare a transitional plan for the child's post school years.[130]

Amendments

8.61 The ELB may only amend the statement if it follows the procedure set out in the legislation.[131] The ELB must serve a notice on the parents which informs them of the proposed amendment and their right to make representations. The parent may make representations within 15 days. The ELB must consider these representations and then give the parent written notice of its decision. It must also notify the parents of their right to appeal if the ELB has amended the description of the assessment of the child's needs or the special educational provision. Any amendment must be made within eight weeks of sending the letter of proposal to the parents

8.62 Parents can request that the school named in the statement is changed to another grant-aided school chosen by them.[132] Such a request can only be made 12 months after: the service of the copy of the original statement; a previous request for a change of school; the service of a notice of amendment to the statement; or the conclusion of an appeal to the SENT, whichever date is later. The ELB must comply with the request unless the school is unsuitable for the child or the child's attendance would be incompatible with the provision of efficient education for the other pupils or the efficient use of resources. If the ELB proposes to comply with the request it must consult the Board of Governors for the school and, if the school is outside its area, the ELB in whose area the school is situated. If the ELB decides not to comply with the request, it must notify the parents and inform them of their right to appeal to the SENT. In either case there is no statutory requirement as to the time within which the ELB should respond to the request. The Code states that

---

[126] Art. 19(5)(b) of the 1996 Order.
[127] Code of Practice, para. 6.3.
[128] Reg. 15 of the Education (SEN) Regulations (NI) 1997 and Code of Practice, paras. 6.17 and 6.18.
[129] Reg. 13 of the Education (SEN) Regulations (NI) 1997 and Code of Practice, paras. 6.4-6.16.
[130] Reg. 14 of the Education (SEN) Regulations (NI) 1997 and Code of Practice, paras. 6.35-6.48.
[131] Sch. 2, paras. 9-10 to the 1996 Order.
[132] *Ibid* Sch. 2, para.8

parents should normally be told within eight weeks.[133] In England and Wales this is a statutory requirement.[134]

Termination of the statement

8.63 The ELB will cease to maintain a statement in a number of circumstances.[135] The first is at the end of the term during which a school pupil attains his or her nineteenth birthday. The second is where they are directed to cease to maintain the statement by the SENT. In addition, the ELB can decide not to maintain the statement where it considers that it is no longer necessary to maintain it.[136] In such cases it must give the parents two months notice of its decision and inform them of their right to appeal this decision to the SENT.

SPECIAL EDUCATIONAL NEEDS TRIBUNAL

8.64 The 1996 Order established a new independent tribunal, the SENT, to which parents can appeal many of the decisions relating to the statements of children with special educational needs. The SENT has been in operation in Northern Ireland since September 1997. Prior to that dissatisfied parents had a right of appeal to the Department under Schedule 11 to the 1986 Order. This was generally considered to be unsatisfactory given the complexity of the issues involved. The new tribunal is different from the education tribunals operated by ELBs in a number of respects. The tribunal operates centrally under an independent President; the chairpersons are legally qualified; and the tribunal's powers and procedure are set down in regulations.

8.65 It is too early to ascertain the impact which the SENT will have in Northern Ireland. However, some indication of its likely success can be derived from its sister tribunal which has been operating in England and Wales since 1994. A major survey into its operation in 1996 found that as a whole the tribunal was "making an important contribution to enabling many more parents and...their children than before to secure access to justice in respect of disputes for SEN issues".[137] There were, however, some concerns about the tribunal's operation including the variation in practice between tribunals as well as the impact on education authority resources of tribunal decisions.

Composition

8.66 The SENT is headed by a President of the Tribunal appointed by the Lord Chancellor.[138] The current president is Mr Aidan Canavan. The tribunal has three members, a legally-qualified chairperson and two other members. The chairman is appointed by the Lord Chancellor and the lay members are appointed by the Department.[139] At each hearing the chairman may be the

---

[133] Para. 6.4.
[134] Education (SEN) Regulations 1994, reg. 14(5).
[135] See the Code of Practice, paras. 6.28 and 6.29.
[136] Sch. 2, para. 11 to the 1996 Order.
[137] Harris, *Special Educational Needs and Access to Justice* (1997) p. 193.
[138] Art. 22(2) of the 1996 Order.
[139] *Ibid* art. 22(2)(b)-(c).

President or a person selected from the chairman's panel by the President. The lay members will also be selected by the President.[140] If, at or after, the commencement of any hearing a member of the tribunal other than the chairman is absent, the hearing may, with the consent of the parties, be conducted by the two other members. In that event the tribunal shall be deemed to be properly constituted and the decision of the tribunal shall be taken by the two members.[141]

Grounds for appeal

8.67 A child's parent can appeal to the SENT on one of five grounds:

(i) The ELB has refused to assess the child[142]

Parents do not have a right to appeal a decision by an ELB to assess a child under article 15 of the 1996 Order. The need to understand the child's educational abilities overrides the parents' wishes in this respect. Parents do, however, have a right to appeal a decision by an ELB not to assess. This arises where the parents have asked the ELB to assess the child's needs and there has not been an assessment in the previous six months.[143] The right of appeal includes a request where the child already has a statement. On appeal the SENT can dismiss the appeal or order the ELB to arrange a statutory assessment. The European Commission on Human Rights did not intervene in a case where an LEA decided not to assess a child.[144]

(ii) The ELB has decided not to make a statement[145]

ELBs are not under a duty to make a statement for every child who has special educational needs.[146] Moreover, there is no specific statutory test for determining which children will be the subject of a statement and which children will not. The legislation gives ELBs a broad discretion to determine whether "it is necessary for the board to determine the special educational provision which any learning difficulty he may have calls for".[147] However, it seems clear that the ELB will only make and maintain a statement when it considers that it should make arrangements for the child's needs and that will normally only be the case where the child's needs cannot be met in the resources available to ordinary schools.[148] In a judgment of the English High Court, Dillon J described the position in relation to statements as follows:

> "The issue of a statement is an indication that the authority accept that the child's needs are such as to require their

---

[140] Reg. 4 of the Special Educational Needs (Tribunal) Regulations (NI) 1997.
[141] *Ibid* reg. 28(5).
[142] Art. 20(2)-(3) of the 1996 Order.
[143] *Ibid* art. 20(3).
[144] *SP v United Kingdom* (1997) 23 EHRR 139.
[145] *Ibid* art. 17(2)-(3).
[146] *R v Secretary of State for Education and Science, ex parte Lashford* [1988] 1 FLR 72.
[147] Art. 16(1) of the 1996 Order.
[148] However, see *R v Secretary of State for Education and Science, ex parte E* [1992] 1 FLR 377, where Staughton LJ suggested that a statement could be made even where the ordinary school was able to provide for the child wholly from its own resources.

intervention to secure provision which is not normally available in ordinary schools in the area."[149]

The Code makes it clear that this will normally only apply to around two per cent of children. A parent who wishes to appeal on the basis that their child should be the subject of a statement would have to try to establish that the special educational provision which their child's learning difficulty calls for cannot be met by ordinary schools and requires some intervention by the ELB.

(iii) *The parents are dissatisfied with the contents of the statement*

The content of the statement can be appealed when the statement is first made or when it is amended or where, after a statutory assessment, the ELB decides not to amend the statement.[150] On appeal the SENT may dismiss the appeal, order the ELB to amend the statement or order the ELB to cease to maintain the statement. There are various aspects of the statement which may give rise to dispute: the appeal may relate to the description of the assessment of the child's needs; the educational provision indicated in the statement; or the fact that no school is named in the statement. In practice, parents are most likely to be unhappy with some aspect of the provision being made. This could be the level of provision, for example the number of hours of remedial teaching the child is receiving. However, the one aspect of the statement which appears to have given rise to most of the litigation in England and Wales is the choice of school. This is considered separately below.

(iv) *The choice of school*

There are two ways in which a parent can appeal the school named in the statement. The first arises under article 18 of the 1996 Order which is described in the previous paragraph. In such appeals the SENT will not order the ELB to specify a school in the statement unless the parent has expressed a preference for that school under the procedures in Schedule 2, paragraph 3 to the 1996 Order or if during the proceedings the parent, ELB or both have proposed the school. In effect this means that the tribunal cannot name a school for the child on its own initiative. The second way in which an appeal arises is under Schedule 2, paragraph 8 to the 1996 Order where a parent applies for a change in the school named in the statement and the ELB refuses. In such cases the tribunal may dismiss the appeal or order the ELB to substitute the name of the school specified by the parent.[151]

Parents will often have very strong feelings about the school that they wish their child to attend. ELBs must consider the parents' representations before making any determination.[152] Moreover, the legislation gives parents a specific right to express a preference for the grant-aided school which they wish their child to attend. The ELB must comply with this preference unless the school is unsuitable to the child's age, ability or aptitude or to his special educational needs or the attendance would be incompatible with the provision of efficient education for the children with whom he would be educated or the efficient

---

[149] *R v Secretary of State for Education and Science, ex parte Lashford* [1988] 1 FLR 72.
[150] Art. 18(1) of the 1996 Order.
[151] *Ibid* Sch. 2, para. 8(5).
[152] *Ibid* Sch. 2, para. 5(1).

use of resources.¹⁵³ ELBs are also under a duty to ensure that the child is educated in an ordinary school provided that this is compatible with him receiving the special educational provision which his learning difficulty calls for, the provision of efficient education for the children with whom he will be educated and the efficient use of resources.¹⁵⁴ Disputes can arise in a number of ways.

First, parents may wish their child to attend a different grant-aided school from that proposed or named in the statement. In such cases due regard will be had to the reasons for their preference, for example religious convictions, siblings, travelling distance. Secondly, parents may wish their child to attend an ordinary school but the statement specifies a special school. In such cases parents will be assisted by the statutory duty in article 7 of the 1996 Order. However, it will be open to the ELB to show that: it is not suitable for the child; not fair to the other children at the school children; or not financially viable. Thirdly, parents may wish their child to attend a special school but the statement specifies an ordinary school. In such cases the parents will have to prove that the child's needs cannot be met in an ordinary school even with extra resources from the ELB. Finally, an issue may arise over the parent's desire to send their child to a private fee-paying school. The duty to comply with the parental preference only applies to grant-aided schools. However, ELBs have a discretion to pay expenses for a child attending a private school. This is contained in articles 11 and 12 of the 1996 Order which are considered further at paragraphs 8.102-8.105. A strong case would have to be made that education at an independent school was the best or only way of meeting the child's educational needs. However, it should be noted that the ELB is not under a duty to finance the best education possible. At the same time it must not rule out consideration of independent options.¹⁵⁵

There have been several instances in which parents have complained that a refusal to provide their child with a place in a particular school or type of school has amounted to a breach of Article 2 of the First Protocol of the ECHR. None of these cases have met with success before the European Commission on Human Rights. In particular, it has not been considered to be a breach of the ECHR for the United Kingdom to refuse to pay for a dyslexic child to have an education in a private school¹⁵⁶ nor to place a child with special needs in a special rather than mainstream school.¹⁵⁷

(v) The ELB has decided to cease to maintain the statement

An ELB may cease to maintain a statement only if it is no longer necessary to maintain it.¹⁵⁸ The parent's arguments in such cases will therefore be similar to those considered above under the appeal concerning a failure to make a

---

[153] *Ibid* Sch. 2, para. 3.
[154] Art. 7 of the 1996 Order.
[155] See *R v Hampshire Education Authority, ex parte J* [1985] 84 LGR 547, where it was successfully argued in relation to English legislation that the authority had fettered its discretion in refusing to consider independent schools unless it could be shown that grant-aided schools were unsuitable.
[156] *Simpson v United Kingdom* (1989) 64 DR 188.
[157] *PD v United Kingdom* (1989) 62 DR 292 and *SP v United Kingdom* (1997) 23 EHRR 139.
[158] Sch. 2, para. 11 to the 1996 Order.

statement. The difference in such cases will be that the parents will often be arguing that circumstances have not changed sufficiently for the statement to be withdrawn. The tribunal can dismiss the appeal or order the ELB to continue to maintain the statement in its existing form or with such amendments as the tribunal may determine.[159]

The procedure for appeal

Notice of appeal by the parent

8.68 In order to initiate an appeal, the parent must serve a signed notice of appeal which indicates that the notice is a notice of appeal and which includes personal details, the name of the ELB which made the decision and the date on which the parent was notified of it, the grounds of appeal and, if the parent is looking to change the school in the statement, the name and address of the proposed school.[160] The notice must be accompanied by a copy of the notice of the disputed decision and where the appeal relates to the content of the statement or a change of the named school, a copy of the statement.[161] The notice of appeal must be delivered to the secretary of the tribunal no later than the first working day after the expiry of two months from the date on which the ELB gave notice that he had a right of appeal.[162] The parent may at anytime before the hearing of the appeal withdraw his appeal by sending the secretary to the tribunal a signed notice stating that he withdraws the appeal. He may also withdraw the appeal at the hearing.[163]

Representation at hearing

8.69 The notice of appeal may state the name, address and profession of any representative of the parent to whom the tribunal should send notices or replies concerning the appeal instead of the parent.[164] Where this has not been included in the notice, the parent can notify the secretary to the tribunal of the use of a representative any time before the hearing and may change the representative at any time.[165] The parent may also conduct the case themselves with assistance from one person (if so desired) or may be represented by one person. The President may give permission before the hearing or the tribunal may give permission at the hearing for the parent to be assisted or represented by more than one person.

The reply by the ELB

8.70 An ELB which receives a copy of the notice of appeal must deliver a written reply to the secretary of the tribunal acknowledging service of the notice of appeal.[166] This must state whether or not it intends to oppose the appeal and the grounds on which it relies and the name and profession of the

---

[159] *Ibid* Sch. 2, para. 11(3).
[160] Reg. 7(1)(a) of the Special Educational Needs (Tribunal) Regulations (NI) 1997.
[161] *Ibid* reg. 7(1)(b).
[162] *Ibid* reg. 7(3).
[163] *Ibid* reg. 9.
[164] *Ibid* reg. 7(1)(c).
[165] *Ibid* reg. 11.
[166] *Ibid* reg. 12.

ELB representative dealing with the appeal and the address for service. The reply must also include a statement summarising the facts relating to the disputed decision, the reasons for the decision and all the written evidence which the ELB wishes to submit to the tribunal. The reply must be signed by an officer of the ELB and delivered to the secretary not later than 20 working days after the date on which the notice of appeal was received by the ELB. The reply may be amended and further evidence submitted in exceptional cases with the permission of the President before the hearing or the tribunal at the hearing.[167] If no reply is received by the secretary within the specified time or if the ELB states in writing that it does not intend to resist the appeal or if it withdraws its opposition to an appeal, the tribunal will determine the appeal without a hearing or hold a hearing at which the ELB is not represented.[168]

Parent's response to the reply

8.71 If an ELB delivers a reply to the notice of appeal the parent may submit a written response to that reply within 15 days from the date on which the parent receives a copy of the reply.[169] This will include all written evidence which the parent wishes to submit at the tribunal. However, in exceptional cases, the parent may with the permission of the President before the hearing or the permission of the tribunal at the hearing amend the notice of appeal or any response or submit further evidence.

Pre-hearing procedures

8.72 The secretary of the tribunal is responsible for acknowledging the notice of appeal and for serving the relevant documents.[170] The secretary must ensure that the notice of appeal is correct and that the appeal is within the tribunal's jurisdiction. The secretary is responsible for making a number of enquiries including whether the parties intend to attend the hearing, be represented, wish the hearing to be in public, intend to call witnesses, require the assistance of an interpreter or wish any other person to be in attendance if the hearing is to be in private.[171] The President has a number of powers which enable him to give directions requiring additional material and the production of documents as well as the summoning of witnesses.[172]

The hearing

8.73 The tribunal may determine an appeal or any particular issue on an appeal without a hearing if the parties agree in writing, where the parties have not complied with directions and where the ELB does not resist the appeal or withdraws its opposition to the appeal.[173] In such cases the issues will be determined on the basis of the written evidence submitted to the tribunal.[174] In all other cases there will be an oral hearing.

---

[167] *Ibid* reg. 13.
[168] *Ibid* reg. 14.
[169] *Ibid* reg. 8.
[170] *Ibid* reg. 16.
[171] *Ibid* reg. 17.
[172] *Ibid* regs. 20-23.
[173] *Ibid* reg. 25.
[174] *Ibid* reg. 27(2).

8.74 The hearing may be held in public if both the ELB and the parent request this or the President orders it before the hearing or the tribunal orders it at the hearing. In practice this is unlikely to occur as the parties are usually keen to protect the child's privacy. Hearings are therefore normally held in private, that is only the authorised parties will attend.[175] Apart from the parties their representatives and witnesses, those in attendance may include parents who are not parties to the appeal, the clerk and secretary to the tribunal, the President and any tribunal members not sitting, any person undergoing training as a panel member or clerk and an interpreter. The tribunal may with the consent of the parties present permit other persons to attend the hearing. None of those attending apart from the parties, the clerk and an interpreter may take any part in the hearing or the deliberations of the tribunal. The tribunal may exclude any person whose conduct has disrupted or is likely in the opinion of the tribunal to disrupt the hearing.[176]

8.75 The legislation does not mention the child whose needs are subject to discussion. The child does not therefore have an automatic right to be present at the hearing, a position which is arguably in contravention of Article 12 of the United Nations Convention on the Rights of the Child.[177] In practice, the child can attend a hearing in one of two ways: (i) as a witness; or (ii) as a person whom the tribunal has allowed to attend at the request of the parent under regulation 17(b) of the Special Educational Needs (Tribunal) Regulations (NI) 1997. Evidence from Great Britain indicates that few children do attend hearings.[178] In fact, there is some dispute as to whether it is advisable for a child to attend hearings. On the one hand, the child may well have a significant input into the proceedings and their attendance will give the tribunal a chance to directly observe the child. On the other hand, tribunal venues may not cater for children and young children may become restless during the procedures and disrupt the hearing. More significantly perhaps, there are concerns over the psychological impact which the evidence of a child's learning difficulties may have on the child.[179] As a compromise some advisers recommend that a child with sufficient understanding should send a letter or a video to the tribunal outlining their views as part of the written evidence.

8.76 If a party fails to attend or be represented at a hearing the tribunal may adjourn the hearing or if it is not satisfied that there is sufficient reason for the absence, determine the hearing in the party's absence.[180] If the tribunal is disposing of the appeal in the absence of any party it will consider any written submissions made by the party along with notice of appeal, replies by the ELB and responses by the parent.

---

[175] *Ibid* reg. 26.
[176] *Ibid* reg. 26(4).
[177] See further para. 1.48.
[178] In one study, children were present in only 10 out of 118 hearings observed. See, Harris, *Special Educational Needs and Access to Justice* (1996) p. 146.
[179] See, House of Commons Education Committee, Second Report (1995-6), *Special Educational Needs: The Operation of the Code of Practice and the Tribunal*, HC 205, *Minutes of Oral Evidence, per* T. Aldridge QC, President of the GB SENT.
[180] Reg. 27 of the Special Educational Needs (Tribunal) Regulations (NI) 1997.

Procedure at hearing

8.77 The conduct of the hearing is at the discretion of the tribunal which must, in so far as it is appropriate, seek to avoid formality in the proceedings.[181] The tribunal will determine the order in which the parties are heard and the issues determined and shall explain this to the parties at the beginning of the hearing. The tribunal may, if it is satisfied that it is just and reasonable to do so, permit a party to rely on grounds not stated in his or her notice of appeal, reply or response and to adduce evidence not presented to the ELB before or at the time it took the disputed decision.

8.78 The tribunal may receive evidence of any fact which appears to the tribunal to be relevant. The parties are entitled to give evidence, call and question witnesses and to address the tribunal both on the evidence and generally on the subject matter of the appeal.[182] Neither party is entitled to call more than two witnesses to give evidence orally unless the President has given permission prior to the hearing or the tribunal gives evidence at the hearing. Evidence may be given orally or by written statement but the tribunal may at any stage of the hearing require the personal attendance of the maker of any written statement.[183] The tribunal may require any witness to give evidence on oath or affirmation or may require any evidence given by written statement to be given by affidavit.

Decision of the tribunal

8.79 When the tribunal is arriving at its decision it must order all parties to withdraw except for those employed by the tribunal or attending for training. The decision may be taken by a majority and where the tribunal is constituted by two members the chairman will have a casting vote. The decision may be given orally or reserved and shall be recorded in a document which will include a statement (in summary form) of the reasons for the decision. In practice oral decisions are not given. The decision should not indicate that a decision was taken by a majority, if that was the case. The decision will be recorded and a copy sent to each party accompanied by guidance about the circumstances in which there is a right to appeal and the procedures to be followed. It is notable that the legislation does not give the tribunal a specific means of enforcing a decision. If the ELB fails to implement a decision, one possible avenue of redress for parents would be a complaint to the Department under article 101 of the 1986 Order.

Review of the tribunal or President's decision

8.80 A party may apply to the secretary of the tribunal for the decision of the tribunal to be reviewed on the grounds that: it was wrongly made as a result of an error on the part of the tribunal staff; a party who was entitled to be heard at a hearing but failed to appear or be represented had good and sufficient reason for failing to appear; that there was an obvious error in the

---

[181] *Ibid* reg. 28.
[182] *Ibid* reg. 29.
[183] Evidence can only be given by written statement if it was submitted with the notice of appeal or in accordance with regs. 8, 12 or 13 (the response, reply or amendments respectively).

decision of the tribunal; or the interests of justice require.[184] The tribunal may also of its own motion review its decision on any of these grounds. An application for review must be made within 10 working days of the decision being sent to the parties and shall state the grounds in full. An application may be refused if it has no reasonable prospect of success. If it is not refused the review will be determined by the original tribunal or if that is not practicable, another tribunal appointed by the President. On review the tribunal may set aside its previous decision and substitute such decision as it thinks fit or order a rehearing before either the same or a differently constituted tribunal.

8.81 The President may review his decision on the application of either party or his own motion if he is satisfied that the decision was: wrongly made as a result of an error or the part of tribunal staff; there was an obvious error in the decision; or the interests of justice require.[185] An application for review must be made within 10 working days of the date of notification stating the grounds in full. The parties are entitled to be heard on any application or proposal for review. The review will be determined by the President who may vary the decision or set it aside.

APPEAL FROM THE TRIBUNAL

8.82 The decision of the SENT may be appealed to the High Court on a point of law.[186] Alternatively, the parent can ask the SENT to sign and state a case for the opinion of the High Court. The procedure to be followed is not specified in the legislation. However, it appears that an action should be brought under Order 56 of the Rules of the Supreme Court.[187] In such cases an appeal must be made within 21 days of the notice of the SENT's decision. The parties to the appeal will be the parents and the ELB. The child is not a party to the appeal.[188] In an English case it was suggested that the appropriate respondent was the chair of the tribunal not the tribunal itself.[189]

8.83 There are no specific grounds for appeal other than that there must be a point of law rather than an issue of fact in dispute.[190] In *Russell* v *London Borough of Kingston* the jurisdiction of the court in SENT appeals was described as follows:

> "...whether the tribunal, in making its decision, applied the correct principles of law, whether it failed to take account of any relevant matter, whether it took into account any immaterial factor and whether it reached a decision which was irrational, in other words on which no tribunal could reasonable have reached."[191]

---

[184] *Ibid* reg. 31
[185] *Ibid* reg. 32.
[186] Art. 24 of the 1996 Order.
[187] Order 94 of the Rules of the Supreme Court (NI) 1980) as amended by art. 7 of the Rules of the Supreme Court (NI) (Amendment) Order 1999.
[188] *Ibid*.
[189] *S and C* v *SENT* [1997] ELR 242. See Oliver and Austen, *Special Educational Needs and the Law* (1996) p. 154.
[190] *Joyce* v *Dorset County Council*, unreported, 25 January 1996.
[191] [1996] ELR 400.

The appeal may also concern allegations of breach of the duty of fairness.[192] The appeal to the High Court covers many of the same issues which might previously have been challenged by way of judicial review. One consequence of this is that applications for judicial review will usually not be permitted where the statutory right of appeal exists.[193] In particular, the court may not permit an application for judicial review which is intended to evade the 28 day time limit under Order 55 or to allow the applicant to claim legal aid.[194] There may, however, be exceptional cases where an application may lie by way of judicial review.[195] Moreover, applications for judicial review will still be entertained in areas where there is no appeal to the High Court from its decision. One example of this is where the parties wish to challenge a decision of the secretary of the tribunal (e.g. the power to strike out an appeal on the grounds that it is vexatious).

8.84 One of the key issues which will determine how often the procedure is used will be the availability of legal aid. In judicial review cases the applicant is the child and it is the child's resources which are assessed for the purposes of determining eligibility for civil legal aid. However, in *S v Special Educational Needs Tribunal* the court considered that because the right to appeal is vested in the parent by statute, it is the parent's income which will be relevant for the purposes of calculating entitlement to civil legal aid. This has been criticised by the House of Commons Select Committee on Education.[196] In spite of this, a private members bill to rectify the position by giving the child an independent right of appeal was unsuccessful in Parliament.[197]

CHILDREN FOR WHOM NO STATEMENT IS MAINTAINED

Children without statements

8.85 Approximately one fifth of all school children are expected to have special educational needs at some time in their school career. Although schools and ELBs have responsibilities to all children with SEN, the legislation draws a distinction between the two per cent of children who are statemented and the 18 per cent of children who are not. Children without statements are not readily identifiable either at law or in practice. The term "unstatemented" refers to children sandwiched between two imprecise legal boundaries: (i) the definition of special educational needs under article 3; and (ii) the decision to statement under article 16 of the 1996 Order.

---

[192] *R v SENT, ex parte F* [1996] ELR 213.
[193] *R v SENT, ex parte South Glamorgan* [1996] ELR 326; *R v SENT, ex parte F* [1996] ELR 213.
[194] *R v SENT, ex parte F* [1996] ELR 213 and *R v SENT, ex parte South Glamorgan* [1996] ELR 326.
[195] For instance, an appeal to the High Court on a point of law is not considered to cover a breach of the duty to give reasons. *S v SENT* [1995] 1 WLR 1627.
[196] Second Report (1995-96) *Special Educational Needs: The Working of the Code of Practice and the Tribunal* p. 47.
[197] Education (Special Educational Needs) Bill 1996 introduced by Lord Campbell of Alloway QC. See generally, (1996) 3 *Education, Public Law and the Individual* 59.

Provision for children without statements

8.86 Although unstatemented children comprise the vast majority of children with SEN, the provision which is made for them is much less regulated than that of children with statements. The primary responsibility for meeting the needs of children who have special educational needs but are not statemented will fall on the Board of Governors of the school which the child attends. These obligations were considered earlier in this chapter.[198] Essentially a Board of Governors is under duty to use "its best endeavours" to ensure that the child's needs are met. One problem is that the phrase "best endeavours" inevitably qualifies the obligation with the effect that governors are only required to do what resources permit. Thus, in contrast to children with statements, provision for children without statements is determined largely through the Code of Practice. The first three stages of the five stage approach relate to the provision for non-statemented children in ordinary schools. While the Code of Practice is useful and sensible it concentrates mainly on procedure and even then is not in itself legally binding.[199]

8.87 Problems can arise when parents are dissatisfied with the provision being made for their child. One difficulty is that parents do not have a legal right to a document which sets out the nature of the provision which the school intends to provide. While the Code of Practice requires schools to prepare individual education plans, these are drawn up by the school for the school. Parent's views may be taken into account in determining the content of the plan but otherwise parents have no particular property in them. There is a very real danger that these plans may reflect what the school is currently doing rather than what the child's needs require. This danger is compounded by the funding arrangements for SEN. While resources for children with statements are ring-fenced, all schools receive a proportion of their funding for meeting the needs of children without statements. Schools have a wide discretion as to how this money may be spent. Disputes can arise if the school states that it does not have the resources to provide additional support for the child but the ELB is satisfied that the child should not be statemented.[200]

Avenues of redress for dissatisfied parents

8.88 The legislation does not provide the parents of non-statemented children with a specific right of appeal if they are dissatisfied with the provision that is being made for their child. When this general lack of accountability towards children without statements was queried in the House of Commons Education Committee, the Department of Education argued that procedures existed for ensuring proper provision; in particular it pointed to the fact that schools are required to have a policy on special education and report on that policy at annual parents' meetings, and that schools would be

---

[198] See paras. 8.08-8.09.
[199] See para. 8.24.
[200] House of Commons Select Committee on Education, Second Report (1995-6) *Special Educational Needs: The Working of the Code of Practice and the Tribunal* (HC 205,1996) at p. vi.

inspected every four years.[201] The Committee was not satisfied with the Department's response; it considered the meetings were too sparsely attended and inspections too infrequent to have a significant impact on the level of accountability. Moreover, the general nature of the meetings and inspections is unlikely to be of significant benefit to a parent with a grievance about the treatment of an individual child. However, in spite of a lack of designated means for challenging decisions about children without statements, there are a number of strategies a dissatisfied parent might adopt.

8.89 The obvious way to effect change would be to get the child statemented. Parents have a right to appeal to the SENT if they think that their child should be the subject of a statement and the ELB has refused to make a statement.[202] In most cases there will be little prospect of a statement being made. Instead, an appeal against a refusal to issue a statement may - along with a request for a formal assessment of the child's needs - have more value as a tactical move since the information gathered in the assessment process may inform, and perhaps exert subtle pressure on a school in relation to the decisions to be taken by the school about the child's needs. Secondly, there may be a possibility of a complaint to the curriculum appeal tribunal.[203] The legislation specifies that each pupil should be "taught" the compulsory contributory subjects within each area of study.[204] Pupils may only be excepted from such study in prescribed circumstances. In situations where the child's special needs are such that he is not able to participate or be "taught" in accordance with the Northern Ireland curriculum, the parents might be able to complain to the curriculum complaints tribunal that the Board of Governors has failed to discharge its statutory duties. Thirdly, the parents may complain to the Department where the ELB or a voluntary school has acted unreasonably or failed to discharge its functions.[205] Fourthly, there may be a possibility of an action for judicial review if the Board of Governors has acted unlawfully, unreasonably or unfairly. The success of such an action, however, will be hindered by the broad scope of the statutory obligations towards children who are not the subject of a statement. In any case the judicial review process is unlikely to lead to a prompt resolution of the issues, which is probably the primary objective for parents of children in this situation. Finally, the parents could begin proceedings for an action in negligence, an option which is considered at paragraphs 8.97-8.101. Again the limitations of this type of action are apparent; tortious actions may result in compensation, but it is in the interest of all the parties that appropriate remedial action is taken to avoid the need for compensation

THE RESOURCE ISSUE

8.90 One of the key considerations in any decision or dispute about the provision for children with SEN will be resources. For instance, the main decision which is taken about children with SEN - the decision to statement -

---

[201] House of Commons Select Committee on Education, Third Report (1992-3) *Meeting Special Educational Needs: Statements of Needs and Provision* (HC 287-1 1993) at para. 46.
[202] Art. 17 of the 1996 Order.
[203] Under art. 33 of the 1989 Order. See paras. 5.87-5.94.
[204] Art. 6 of the 1989 Order.
[205] *Ibid* art. 101. See paras. 2.63-2.74.

is essentially a question of resources. A child will only be statemented if the ELB thinks it is necessary for it to make provision for the child and this will only be the case where the child's school does not have the resources to meet his or her needs. One consequence of this is that the funding system for children varies depending on whether or not the child is statemented. If a child who is statemented attends a mainstream school, the school will be given additional resources to meet the child's needs. This money is ring-fenced and can only be used to meet that child's needs. In spite of this, disputes can arise between parents and the ELB as to the level or type of support being provided. In such cases, parents have a right to appeal the contents of the statement to the SENT. In contrast, the position of children without statements is much less regulated. All schools have specific elements of their budgets reserved for children with special educational needs. This is intended to cover the needs of children without statements. However, once allocated schools have a wide discretion as to how to apply this money and there is little supervision of how the money is spent. Problems can arise if the ELB is satisfied that it has allocated sufficient resources to the school but the school says that it cannot provide the additional support that the parent wants. The Northern Ireland Affairs Committee has recommended that schools should be required to publish details of how they have used the part of the delegated budget allocated for special educational needs.[206]

Statutory restrictions on resources

8.91 The issue of resources is addressed twice in the SEN legislation. Both restrictions apply to children with statements. The first is in relation to the "qualified" duty under article 7 of the 1996 Order to secure education in mainstream schools for statemented pupils. This applies only in so far as educating the child in an ordinary school is compatible with the "efficient use of resources". The second restriction arises in relation to parental choice of school. When making a statement ELBs are under an obligation to specify the parent's choice of school unless the attendance of the child at the school would be incompatible with the "efficient use of resources".[207] In *R v Surrey CC, ex parte P* the court considered that for attendance to be incompatible with the efficient use of resources it has to result in significant additional expenditure.[208] In no other part of the special needs legislation is this qualification used expressly. However, the issue of resources has arisen in other contexts and in particular in areas where the word "necessary" appears in the legislation.

The resource issue in the courts

8.92 The issue of resources can arise in a number of instances: (i) when provision is being determined, that is whether a child should be statemented; and (ii) if he or she is statemented how much help he or she should receive. In *R v Surrey CC, ex parte H* the Court of Appeal considered that education

---

[206] Northern Ireland Affairs Committee, *Public Expenditure in Northern Ireland*, Session 1998.99, HC33 and 317, 1032 i-ii (1997-98) para. 47.
[207] Sch. 2, para. 3(3)(b) to the 1996 Order.
[208] [1997] ELR 516.

authorities were only obliged to meet the needs of the child, not provide the best possible help.[209] Slade J considered that "there is no question of parliament having placed the local authority under an obligation to provide such a Utopian system, or to educate to his or her maximum potential".[210]

8.93 It was generally accepted that resources could not be used to determine what help was needed but instead could only be used to choose the most cost-effective form of provision from a series of alternatives.[211] However, the issue was re-opened following the judgment of the House of Lords in *R v Gloucestershire CC, ex parte Barry*.[212] This case, which was not an education case, concerned a local authority's statutory duty to make arrangements for domiciliary services when satisfied that it was "necessary" to do so in order to meet the needs of disabled person. The House of Lords considered that the words "necessary" and "needs" were relative concepts which had to be considered in the context of the other needs and resources available. This meant that the authority could lawfully set eligibility criteria and prioritise its services according to its budget.

8.94 The House of Lords' judgment in *Barry* has clear implications for SEN decisions regarding the making and content of statements given that both fall within the broad remit of social welfare provision and that the terminology used in the relevant statutes is similar. In particular, article 16 of the 1996 Order only requires ELBs to make and maintain a statement if it is "necessary" for the ELB to determine the SEN provision which any learning difficulty calls for. The issue was considered directly in one SEN case prior to the House of Lords' decision in *Barry*. In *R v Hillingdon LBC, ex parte Governing Body of Queensmead School*, which followed the Court of Appeal ruling in *Barry*, the court concluded that financial constraints could be considered when determining how a child's needs were to be met provided that they were met.[213] It is unclear whether the House of Lords would interpret the words "necessary" differently in the SEN context.

8.95 Some guidance may be taken from the House of Lords' decision in *R v East Sussex County Council, ex parte Tandy*.[214] This decision, which is considered at paragraph 2-37, concerned a clear duty to provide suitable education otherwise than at school for a child who was unable to attend school through illness. The House of Lords considered that resources were irrelevant to the issue of what amounted to "suitable" education. One of the factors which helped them to reach this decision was that resource limitations were expressly included in other parts of the SEN legislation (i.e. choice of school and duty to integrate). This is, of course, also true in relation to the decision to statement under article 16 of the 1996 Order and may be sufficient to distinguish it from the statutory duty which was considered in *Barry*.[215]

---

[209] (1985) 83 LGR 219.
[210] At p. 235.
[211] See *R v Hillingdon LBC, ex parte Governing Body of Queensmead School* [1997] ELR 331.
[212] [1997] 2 All ER 1.
[213] [1997] ELR 331. See paras. 2.37-2.39.
[214] [1998] ELR 80. The equivalent Northern Ireland legislation is art. 86 of the 1998 Order.
[215] For further discussion of this, see McManus, *Education and the Courts* (1998) pp.58-9.

8.96 Problems may arise if the courts are to apply the *Barry* ruling in the SEN context, particularly after the *Tandy* case. If it were to be concluded that resources were relevant to the determination of issues under article 16, children without statements educated outside school under article 86 of the 1998 Order would be in a stronger position than children with statements. Commentators have warned that education authorities under financial pressure might be tempted to divert funds from statementing in order to discharge their obligations in relation to children educated otherwise than at school.[216] This could not be what Parliament intended and may well be further grounds for a different approach to the meaning of "necessary" in the SEN context.

ACTIONS FOR NEGLIGENCE

8.97 A failure to identify and provide for children with special educational needs may result in actions for negligence. The door to such litigation was opened by the House of Lords' landmark decision in *X v Bedfordshire CC*.[217] This was a multiple action claiming damages for breach of statutory duty in five cases. Three of these were concerned with education and two concerned a local education authority's failure to diagnose and provide for a child with special educational needs. The court found that the LEAs did not themselves owe a duty of care to the children involved. Moreover, it considered that an individual did not have a right of action for breach of the LEA's statutory duties in relation to SEN. However, the House of Lords did consider that other people working with the child such as educational psychologists and teachers could have a common law duty of care in such cases and that the LEA could be vicariously liable for the negligent actions of its employees. The import of this is that an ELB or other educational employer may be vicariously liable if one of its employees fails to identify and make appropriate provision for a child with special educational needs.

8.98 One of the cases which emanated directly from the House of Lords' decision was *Christmas v Hampshire CC*, in which the plaintiff sought damages for an LEA's failure to detect and address his dyslexia.[218] The High Court dismissed the claim for damages because it was not convinced on a balance of probabilities that there was a want of care on the part of the LEA's advisory teacher service. However, in a different case *Phelps v London Borough of Hillingdon*, an LEA was ordered to pay damages of over £45,000 to a former pupil whose dyslexia one of its educational psychologists had failed to diagnose.[219] The High Court's decision was subsequently overturned in the Court of Appeal.[220] The Court of Appeal cited a number of policy reasons in support of its conclusion. These included: the costs of vexatious claims; the involvement of parents in the procedures; the availability of alternative remedies; and the danger that schools might engage in defensive teaching. In a subsequent appeal the House of Lords reinstated the award for damages, dismissing the argument that such cases should be excluded on the

---

[216] See Richards, 'Resources, Rights and Special Educational Needs' (1998) 3/2 *Education, Public Law and the Individual* 24.
[217] [1995] 3 All ER 353.
[218] [1998] ELR 1.
[219] [1998] ELR 38.
[220] [1998] ELR 587.

grounds of public policy alone.[221] Lord Slynn of Hadley considered that, although such cases might be difficult, there was no reason in principle to rule them out. In his view the recognition of the duty of care did not of itself impose unreasonably high standards on the educational professionals and, in fact, the "...professionalism, dedication and standards of those engaged in the provision of educational services are such that cases of liability for negligence will be exceptional".

8.99 The first hurdle in actions such as these is for a plaintiff to establish that the defendant has failed to exercise the degree of care and skill to be expected of an ordinarily competent member of their profession. This will involve proving that a duty of care exists (i.e. it was reasonably foreseeable that if the person did not take care that harm would result) and that there was a breach of the duty. Moreover, the test in *Bolam* v *Friern Hospital Management Committee* is applicable in these cases, that is that the educational staff involved are only bound to exercise the skill and care that a reasonable colleague would have exercised at that time.[222] In the *Phelps* case the Court of Appeal considered that the High Court had imposed too high a standard of care upon the educational psychologist involved in the case. Stuart Smith LJ considered that it was not fair, just or reasonable to impose a duty of care upon an educational psychologist "unless it is quite clear that in addition to performing her duty to her employers, she assumed personal responsibility to the plaintiff".[223] This was rejected by the House of Lords. Lord Slynn of Hadley was of the view that:

> "...where an educational psychologist is specifically called in to advise in relation to the assessment and future provision for a specific child, and it is clear that the parents acting for the child and the teachers will follow that advice, *prima facie* a duty of care arises. It is sometimes said that there has to be an assumption of responsibility to the person concerned. The phrase can be misleading in that it can suggest that the professional person must knowingly and deliberately accept responsibility...the phrase means simply that the law recognises that there is a duty of care. It is not so much that responsibility is assumed as that it is recognised or imposed by law."[224]

8.100 A second problem for plaintiffs in these cases will be establishing that there was demonstrable damage as a result of the breach of duty. In *X* v *Bedfordshire CC* the House of Lords considered that even if a child had been denied provision, if the child was so seriously disadvantaged that no provision could have improved his or her quality of life or job prospects, then the carelessness had caused relatively little harm and no, or very little, compensation could be paid. This would suggest that the children with the most severe learning difficulties might be likely to receive least compensation where their needs have not been addressed. Moreover, in the Court of Appeal

---

[221] *Phelps* v *London Borough of Hillingdon, Anderton* v *Clyde CC, In Re G (A Minor), Jarvis* v *Hamshire CC*, unreported decision of the House of Lords, 27 July 2000.
[222] [1957] 1 WLR 582.
[223] [1998] ELR, 587, 606.
[224] *Phelps* v *London Borough of Hillingdon, Anderton* v *Clyde CC, In re G (A Minor), Jarvis* v *Hamshire CC*, unreported decision of the House of Lords, 27 July 2000.

in *Phelps,* Stuart Smith LJ said that it was wrong to categorise dyslexia or a failure to ameliorate or mitigate its effects as an injury. Similarly, Otton LJ was of the view that:

> "Any plaintiff with a congenital condition faces formidable difficulties in proving failure to diagnose and/or treat appropriately, particularly in relation to future earning capacity."[225]

However, the House of Lords in *Phelps,* approved the approach of the High Court judge who found that a failure to mitigate the adverse consequences of a congenital defect could amount to a personal injury to a person.[226] Lord Slynn of Hadley stated:

> "...psychological damage and a failure to diagnose a congenital condition and to take appropriate action as a result of which a child's level of achievement is reduced (which leads to a loss of employment and wages) may constitute damage for the purpose of the claim."

8.101 Problems also arise over the level of damages to be awarded. There is little difficulty calculating the amount of damages needed to cover the cost of tuition which the plaintiff might otherwise have received at school. In the *Phelps* case the High Court awarded £2806.50 for loss in respect of past tuition and £3750 in respect of future tuition. However, problems arise when attempts are made to estimate the lost advantages (e.g. reduced wage levels) which have ensued from an inferior education. In *Phelps* the High Court considered the issue of whether there could be damages for a 'lost gain' and concluded that damages could be awarded on the basis that it was foreseeable that the plaintiff's dyslexia could have been mitigated by earlier diagnosis and appropriate treatment. The court awarded £25000 in respect of lost opportunity of employment at a higher rate, and general damages of £12500 in respect of the loss of congenial employment. These latter figures were considered to be moderate in view of the uncertainties involved. Although the Court of Appeal cast a shadow on the method of calculation used, the House of Lords reinstated the award of damages.

8.102 There is no doubt that the House of Lords' decision in *Phelps* will encourage more actions of this kind in spite of the Court's view that successful cases would be rare. One result of this will be that the Code of Practice will take on increased significance since adherence to it will be an indicator of what the reasonable professional should do in relation to any child with special educational needs. This can only be a good thing. It is much better that children are identified and provided for as early as possible. While compensation is important when things have gone wrong, most parents would prefer to have their child's needs provided for at the appropriate time rather than receiving compensation years later. Moreover, as Robinson points out, education authorities still have every reason to fight claims and "the question

---

[225] [1998] ELR, 587, 618.
[226] *Phelps* v *London Borough of Hillingdon, Anderton* v *Clyde CC, In re G (A Minor), Jarvis* v *Hamshire CC,* unreported decision of the House of Lords, 27 July 2000.

which faces a pupil, and his or her parents (and advisers), is whether a claim justifies the stress and uncertainty in raking over the distant past".[227]

ASSISTANCE WITH EDUCATION AT NON GRANT-AIDED SCHOOLS

8.103 Northern Ireland does not have many private institutions providing specialist education to children with special needs. However, worldwide there are numerous institutions providing specialist educational services to children with particular disabilities. Some parents will be keen for their children to attend these institutions but many will be unable to afford to pay for this education themselves. The 1996 Order makes provision for ELBs to fund the education of children with special needs at private institutions either within or outside Northern Ireland. To qualify for assistance at an independent institution within Northern Ireland the institution must be approved by the Department and the Department must give its consent to the child being educated there.[228] To qualify for assistance outside Northern Ireland the institution must specialise in providing for children with special needs.[229] This latter provision has been referred to as the 'Peto' clause because its existence is due in some part to pressure from parents for local authorities to fund their child's education at the Peto Institute in Hungary.

8.104 In both cases, the ELB has the power (N.B. not the duty) to contribute or pay for expenses relating to the child's attendance at the institute. he ELB may pay all or part of the fees charged by the institution. If the institution is in Northern Ireland the ELB may also provide the following: all or part of the expense of board and lodging where the ELB considers this necessary; transport to facilitate his attendance; and equipment and services to the institution.[230] If the institution is outside Northern Ireland the ELB may pay all or part of the following costs: costs reasonably incurred in maintaining him; travelling expenses; and the expenses reasonably incurred by any person accompanying him while he or she is travelling or staying at the institution.[231]

8.105 The legislation does not specify any entitlement to have a child educated at an independent school. However, the issue has been the subject of extensive litigation in England and Wales. Essentially the parents will usually have to persuade the ELB or SENT that a child's needs cannot be met at a grant-aided school.[232] Where the ELB cannot meet the child's needs at a grant-aided school, it is under an obligation to pay for the provision at an independent school.[233] Moreover, if the ELB is proposing a grant-aided school and the parent is expressing a wish for an independent school, the ELB should decide the issue on purely educational grounds if there is no extra cost

---

[227] Robinson, 'Damages for a pupil's academic under-performance - thus far, but how much further?' [1998] Vol. XX(1) *Liverpool Law Review* 95 at p. 114.
[228] Art. 12(1) of the 1996 Order. The approval procedure is in art. 26.
[229] *Ibid* art. 11(1).
[230] *Ibid* art. 12(2).
[231] *Ibid* art. 11(3).
[232] *S v SENT* [1995] 1WLR 1627.
[233] *R v Kent, ex parte W* [1995] ELR 362.

involved (e.g. because a private benefactor is subsidizing the child's education).[234]

8.106 It should be noted that a failure to send the child to their preferred school is not considered to be a breach of Article 2 of the First Protocol of the European Convention on Human Rights. In *Simpson* v *UK* the applicant argued that the education authority's failure to pay for him to attend a private school for dyslexics amounted to a denial of his right to education.[235] The Commission refused the application on the basis that as there was a place available in a state school which had special facilities for teaching disabled children he had not been denied his right to education.

---

[234] *R* v *Cheshire CC, ex parte C, The Times*, 1 August 1997.
[235] No. 14888/89, (1989) 64 DR 188.

CHAPTER NINE

INTEGRATED EDUCATION

DEFINITION

9.01 In the United Kingdom the concept of integrated education is unique to Northern Ireland. The Education Orders do not provide a statutory definition of an integrated school. However, article 64 of the 1989 Order describes integrated education as: "The education together at school of Protestant and Roman Catholic pupils". Some controlled and voluntary schools have pupils of both religions but would not be classified as integrated. The difference between these schools and integrated schools is that integrated schools are under a legal obligation to ensure that the student body reflects a balance of both religions in the population. Thus the Boards of Governors of all integrated schools are required to use their best endeavours to ensure that "the management, control and ethos of the school are such as are likely to attract to the school reasonable numbers of both Protestant and Roman Catholic pupils".[1] The legislation does not define what is meant by a "reasonable" number of Protestant or Catholic pupils, an omission which has been criticised by those involved in integrated education.[2] The Department's guidance suggests that the school should have at least 30 per cent of its enrolment from the relevant minority religion.[3] This is considerably lower than the 40 per cent figure used by integrated schools themselves. The rationale underlying their choice of 40 per cent as the relevant balance is that "in any culturally mixed group where there is a minority smaller than 40 per cent of the total, the minority feels, behaves and is perceived as a minority; and conversely, where a group amounts to 60 per cent of the total they feel, behave and are perceived as a dominant group".[4] This approach forms the basis for admission to integrated schools. It should be noted from this that integrated schools are not attempting to reflect the actual proportions of both religions in the population in general (this is still estimated to be 62% Protestant, 38% Catholic[5]). What integrated schools are trying to achieve is a balanced pupil intake from both communities in Northern Ireland and it is this feature which most characterizes and distinguishes them from other schools in the grant-aided sector in Northern Ireland.

---

[1] Arts. 66 and 88 of the 1989 Order.
[2] Smith, 'Shared Governance, Maintaining Shared Participation in Integrated Schools', Chapter 12 in Moffat (ed), *Education Together for a Change* (1993) at p. 144.
[3] See, *Integrated Education: A Framework for Transformation* (DENI, 1997) at p. 2.
[4] Stephens, 'Integrated Education in Northern Ireland', Chapter 1 in Moffat (ed) *Education Together For A Change* (ed.) (1993).
[5] *Northern Ireland Annual Abstract of Statistics* (HMSO, 1997).

INTRODUCTION

9.02 Northern Ireland's school system is religiously segregated to a large extent.[6] Controlled schools are attended mainly by Protestant pupils and voluntary schools are attended mainly by Catholic pupils. This religious segregation dates back to the 1930s when many schools which had previously been managed by the Protestant churches transferred control to the state in return for full public funding and a significant say on the Board of Governors of the school.[7] The Catholic church was reluctant to transfer control of its schools to the new Northern Ireland state and remained in the voluntary sector, receiving as a consequence more limited state funding. Catholic parents continued to send their children to Catholic schools while Protestant parents sent their children to the new state schools which now make up the controlled sector. Over time these choices became embedded with the result that there is now little movement between the two sectors (although there are a few non-Catholic schools in the voluntary grammar sector which attract an increasing number of Catholic pupils).[8] The move for an integrated system of education began in the early 1970s with the formation of pressure groups such as All Children Together. These were founded by parents who were concerned at the effects of the segregated nature of the Northern Ireland school system as well as parents who wanted a religion-free education for their children. The first statutory recognition of the desire for integrated education appeared in 1978 through a procedure which allowed existing schools to convert to controlled integrated status and thus qualify for mainstream funding.[9] The 1978 legislation had a limited influence on the development of integrated education as its scope was restricted to allowing existing schools to convert to controlled integrated schools.[10] The legislation did not provide any mechanisms for the establishment of voluntary integrated schools or for starting a school from scratch. Nor was there any provision which enabled parents to take the initiative in the process of the conversion of an existing school. In spite of this, the integrated movement continued to develop outside the statutory framework through the establishment of independent schools which then applied for grant-aided status. The first school to achieve public funding was Lagan College which in 1986 was recognised as a voluntary maintained school.

9.03 In 1988 the government published proposals for the radical reform of the Northern Ireland education system.[11] One of the key objectives of the reforms was to accommodate parental preference in the choice of their child's

---

[6] See further Chapter 1.
[7] See further Dunn, 'A Short History of Education in Northern Ireland', in the *Fifteenth Report of the Standing Advisory Commission on Human Rights* (HMSO, 1990).
[8] See further, Mc Ewen, 'Segregation and Integration in Northern Ireland's Education System', in Caul (ed.) *Schools Under Scrutiny, The Case of Northern Ireland* (Macmillan Education, 1990).
[9] Education (NI) Act 1978, referred to as the 'Dunleath Act' after the Private Member who introduced it.
[10] For a discussion of the limitations of the 1978 Act, see Mullan, 'Never the Twain Shall Meet: Legal and Practical Difficulties in the Establishment of Integrated Schools in Northern Ireland' (1987) 38 *Northern Ireland Legal Quarterly* 342.
[11] *The Way Forward* (DENI, 1990).

school. This included recognition of the growing demand in Northern Ireland for integrated education.[12] A further key reform proposed was the introduction of a new category of school - the grant-maintained school - which would be funded directly by the Department. This proposal mirrored reforms which had just been implemented in Great Britain. The policy of allowing schools to 'opt out' of local authority control, introduced by the Conservative Government in 1988, was intended to give individual schools greater autonomy and to reduce the potential for political influence which accompanied local authority control in Great Britain.[13] The original intention in the Northern Ireland proposals was that all schools would be able to opt for grant-maintained status. However, the proposals were not well received in Northern Ireland, albeit for different reasons than in Great Britain. For a start the churches were hostile to the concept of 'opting out' given the potential reduction in their influence in individual schools. There may also have been (an undocumented) concern that schools in certain areas could be effectively taken over by political or paramilitary influences. The Department appears to have recognised the concerns and withdrew its plans to extend the option of grant-maintained status to all schools in Northern Ireland. However, what the traditional educational sectors in Northern Ireland rejected the integrated movement welcomed, fully aware of the potential for development which this new option would provide. As a result of the concerns expressed the proposals were amended so that the option of grant-maintained status would be confined to integrated schools. In consequence, the Education Reform (NI) Order 1989 provided specific procedures for establishing grant-maintained integrated schools both by converting existing schools and by starting a school from scratch. The legislation also revised the procedure through which existing schools could convert to controlled integrated status.

9.04 The extent of the new commitment to integrated education is now reflected in the statutory duty placed on the Department "to encourage and facilitate the development of integrated education".[14] There is no corresponding duty on ELBs, a point of contention in the integrated movement given that ELBs are primarily responsible for ensuring the sufficiency of schools in their area.[15] Moreover, some advocates of integrated education argue that the law should go even further and give all parents who want it the right to have their children educated in integrated schools. Support for this is derived from the 1960 UNESCO Convention against Discrimination in Education which requires that attendance at religious schools should be optional.[16] However, in theory, provision in Northern Ireland complies with this Convention since all controlled schools are non-denominational and parents who do not wish their child to attend religious education have an

---

[12] For a discussion of some of the background to the 1989 Order, see Cullen, 'Parent Power: Building Bridges in Northern Ireland' (1991) 3 *Education and the Law* 27.

[13] Harris, *Law and Education: Regulation, Consumerism and the Education System* (1993) p. 47.

[14] Art. 64 of the 1989 Order.

[15] See for instance the Introduction in Moffat (ed), *Education Together for a Change* (1993) at p. 13.

[16] Article 2(b) of the UNESCO Convention against Discrimination in Education, adopted by the General Conference of the United Nations, Paris, 14 December 1960.

absolute right to withdraw them from religious education classes and periods of collective worship.[17] In spite of this, critics would point to the *de facto*, though not *de iure*, reality that controlled schools are essentially Protestant in ethos and are perceived as such by the general population in Northern Ireland. Likewise, the jurisprudence to the European Court of Human Rights gives states a large degree of discretion in determining educational provision.[18] In interpreting Article 2 of the First Protocol, the European Court of Human Rights has stressed that the right of access is to existing schools rather than a right to have the specific provision that the parents wish to have.[19] The second sentence of Article 2 to the First Protocol gives parents a right to have their child educated in accordance with their religious and philosophical convictions. However, even if a desire for integrated education was seen as a "philosophical conviction", the United Kingdom's reservation would allow it to argue that the present arrangements (whereby integrated schools are funded when they are deemed "viable" according to the Department's criteria) falls within the boundary of the reservation.[20]

9.05 While the supporters of integrated education feel that the 1989 legislation does not do enough to facilitate integrated education, there are others involved in education in Northern Ireland who consider that the 1989 legislation may have gone too far in its support of integrated schools to the disadvantage of the existing schools in the publicly-funded sector. From the outset the 1989 changes were not well received by some of the local churches who objected to the preferential treatment which the government appeared to be giving to integrated schools and who were concerned about the potential impact on existing grant-aided schools. In *In re Daly* the 1989 legislation was challenged by the Catholic bishops by way of judicial review on the ground that it discriminated against those attending Catholic schools and was therefore invalid under the Northern Ireland Constitution Act 1973.[21] The argument in support of the contention that the new provisions discriminated against Catholics was framed in a number of ways. Two areas were of particular concern. First, it was argued that integrated schools were receiving preferential funding which was not available to other schools and which would ultimately disadvantage those remaining in the voluntary sector. Secondly, concern was expressed about the fact that a small group of parents could effectively convert a Catholic school into an integrated school thus removing the option of a Catholic education from other parents. The court found that the legislation did not discriminate against any particular religious group because its adverse effects (if any) were not limited to those who favoured schools with a religious ethos. MacDermott LJ stressed that if the 1989 Order favoured integrated schools, any disadvantage ensuing would affect not only those attending schools with a particular religious ethos but also those in non-denominational schools and those with no religious beliefs or whose religious beliefs did not require them to send their children to a

---

[17] Art. 21 of the 1986 Order. See further para. 5.49.
[18] See paras. 1.51-1.52.
[19] *The Belgian Linguistics Case* (1968) 1 EHRR 252. See further para. 1.52.
[20] See paras. 1.53-1.56.
[21] Unreported judgment of the Northern Ireland High Court, 5 October 1990.

school with a denominational ethos.[22] In its evidence to the court, the Catholic bishops re-iterated the duty of Catholic parents under Canon Law to send their children to Catholic schools but stressed that they would not obstruct or oppose the efforts of people who favoured the integrated option. It is, however, clear that the Catholic church will not actively assist the development of integrated schools. One illustration of this is its refusal to nominate representatives to serve on the Board of Governors of controlled integrated schools. Although the Protestant churches are prepared to participate in the integrated sector to this extent, they have similar reservations about the development of integrated education. The Transferor Representatives' Council, an independent voluntary body which represents the four main Protestant traditions on educational issues, has expressed its concern about the impact which the growth in integrated schools has on the controlled sector and in particular on the reduced influence of transferor representatives when schools opt for integrated status. [23]

9.06 In spite of perceived limitations of the legislation and the lack of positive endorsement by the main church bodies in Northern Ireland, the integrated movement has undoubtedly been successful in harnessing the potential for growth offered by the 1989 Order. In 1999 the number of children educated in integrated schools was approximately three per cent of the school population and this figure is rising steadily. The primary momentum for the move to integrated schools lies with parents. However, they are assisted in this process by the Northern Ireland Council on Integrated Education (NICIE), a voluntary organisation which receives core funding from the Department. NICIE acts as both a focal point and facilitator of the integrated movement. It assists the planned development of integrated education by co-ordinating voluntary and statutory support and providing advice and guidance to parents who want integrated education for their children. It has published a Statement of Principles Charter to which integrated schools adhere. This defines integrated education as follows:

> "Education together in school of pupils in approximately equal numbers from the two major traditions with the aim of providing for them an effective education that gives equal recognition to and promotes equal expression of the two major traditions."

Since 1990 there has been a steady rise in the numbers of integrated schools. In 1998/99 there were a total of 36 integrated schools of which 10 were controlled integrated and 26 grant-maintenance Integrated schools. Of these, 24 are primary schools and 12 secondary schools (referred to as colleges). The trends look set to continue. Each year there a number of proposals for new integrated schools and for existing grant-aided schools to transform to integrated status.

9.07 The organisation and management of an integrated school is for the most part the same as for any other school. However, there are a few key differences. The composition of the Board of Governors and the arrangements for funding are both different from other grant-aided schools and are

---

[22] P. 17 of the transcript.
[23] See 'Integrated Education', Appendix 2 in The Transferors Representatives' Council, Annual Report 1996-1997.

considered in Chapter 3. This chapter is divided into three sections. The first describes the two main categories of integrated school. The process for establishing an integrated school is detailed in the second section. The final section highlights specific issues in relation to the management of an integrated school.

CATEGORIES OF INTEGRATED SCHOOL

9.08 There are two types of integrated schools: (i) controlled integrated (CI) and grant-maintained integrated (GMI). CI schools are under the control of ELBs. A proportion of the representatives on the Board of Governors is made up of nominees of the local churches (both transferors and representatives of the Catholic church). CI status is only open to existing grant-aided schools. GMI schools are funded directly by the Department.[24] A proportion of the Board of Governors is reserved for foundation governors, that is those responsible for establishing the school. Schools which already have public funding can apply for either grant-maintained or CI status. However, GMI status is the only option open to schools which do not have existing funding (i.e. because they have been operating as independent schools or because they are being established from scratch by a body other than the ELB).

The choice between transformation of an existing school and establishing a new school

9.09 Parents who want the option of integrated education in their area have the choice of trying to set up a new integrated school from scratch or of trying to get an existing grant-aided school in the area to transform to integrated status. Transformation is an option for all schools with existing state funding. However, given the composition of the Board of Governors and general ethos in Catholic maintained schools, it is extremely unlikely that a Catholic maintained school will ever seek integrated status.[25] In practice, it is only ever controlled schools which seek to transform to integrated status. The advantage of transformation is that the school will already have its buildings and equipment, personnel and pupil base. The initial difficulty in transformation will be in convincing the Board of Governors or parents that integration is a good idea. Moreover, even if the initial legal hurdle is satisfied and parents ballot to seek integrated status, the road to integration can be difficult.[26] Most of these schools have been attended by mainly Protestant pupils and staffed by mainly Protestant teachers and it may be difficult to show that they will be able to attract sufficient Catholic pupils on transformation.[27] Moreover,

---

[24] The 1998 Order includes provisions which will transfer the funding responsibility from the Department to the ELB.
[25] This was openly acknowledged in *In re Daly*, (unreported judgment of the Northern Ireland High Court, 5 October 1990) although it was still presented as theoretically possible to advance the argument in relation to the adverse effects which the 1989 Order could have on Catholic children.
[26] See McGaffin, 'The Development of an Integrated School', in Caul (ed.), *Schools under Scrutiny - the Case of Northern Ireland* (1990) p. 57.
[27] For a description of the difficulties faced by one school, see Moffat and Lemon, 'The Transformation Option', in Moffat (ed.) *Education Together for a Change* (1993) p. 112.

integrated schools strive for not only a balanced pupil intake but also a balance in staff and the Board of Governors. This can make it difficult to move to the new ethos of integrated education when there has been an established Protestant tradition.

9.10 Many parent groups prefer the option of starting a new integrated school from scratch. This gives them a carte blanche to establish religious balance throughout the school from the very beginning. In this case, the difficulties are essentially financial and practical: finding premises; financing the purchase or rent of property and equipment; recruiting staff. Since 1989 new integrated schools are able to seek recognition from the Department and funding for certain running costs from day one. This includes books, salaries, telephone, heating and light. If an application for recognition is refused, some schools begin operating in the independent sector and then seek funding when they are in a better position to demonstrate their viability. In either case, schools are assisted in this process by the NICIE. In particular, NICIE manages a trust fund for integrated education which can be used by new schools to underwrite loans for capital costs until such time as the Department recognises the school and takes responsibility for capital costs.

9.11 In spite of the apparent difficulties which face parents who want to establish a new school, the option has proved itself to be very popular, a trend which the Department appears to wish to halt. In 1997 the Department published proposals aimed at encouraging the "transformation" of existing schools rather than the establishment of new integrated schools.[28] The reasons underlying this shift in policy were "increased responsiveness, the utilisation of existing facilities and increased cost-effectiveness". It is quite clearly less expensive for existing schools to transform than for the Department to have to cover capital costs in additional schools. Moreover, the transformation option will normally have less impact on the other non-integrated schools in the area. In an attempt to emphasise the transformation option, the Department has made the viability criteria for new schools more stringent by raising the qualifying enrolment numbers.[29] In spite of this, the interest in integrated education is such that parents' groups appear to have little difficulty in meeting the approved enrolment criteria which are needed to satisfy the Department and new integrated schools continue to be established this way.

The choice between controlled or grant-maintained status

9.12 Schools which are already grant-aided can choose to opt for either controlled integrated or grant-maintained integrated status. Although the latter takes them out of the direct influence of the ELB and allows for the appointment of new governors who are committed to integrated education, some schools opt to retain controlled status. It is to be assumed that their reason for doing so is that this is the operational structure with which they are most familiar and which they therefore feel best placed to work within at a time when the school is undergoing so many other significant changes. The potential disadvantage in CI schools is that there are also reserved places on the Board of Governors for representatives of the churches and the ELB.

---

[28] DENI, *Integrated Education, a Framework for Transformation* (February 1996).
[29] See paras. 9.26-9.28.

Church appointments can be difficult. Although the transferors will nominate representatives of the Protestant churches, the Catholic church has declined to do so. This could leave the Board of Governors of the school religiously unbalanced, something which integrated schools strive to avoid. Since 1989 the situation can be remedied to some extent by the ELB who have the power to nominate any person whom they consider suitable if the nominating authorities fail to make a nomination within the required period.[30] However, it has been questioned whether the ELB is the most appropriate body to make such nominations. Appointments from the ELBs have not been without difficulty, particularly where those appointed were not sympathetic to the concept of mixed schooling.[31] In view of this there is now a statutory obligation on ELBs to appoint only those who are "committed to the continuing viability of the school as a CI school".[32] In contrast the choice of GMI status gives schools a free hand in the appointment of the Board of Governors. In particular, there are no reserved places for the nominees of the main churches. There is also a larger proportion of places on the Board for parents.

PROCEDURE FOR ACQUIRING INTEGRATED STATUS

9.13 The procedures for establishing a publicly funded integrated school are set down in Part IV of the 1989 Order. The process is virtually identical for both GMI and CI schools. The key difference arises at the proposal stage and will be highlighted at paragraph 9.24. The procedure for establishing an integrated school also varies depending on whether the objective is to convert an existing grant-aided school, convert an independent school, or establish an integrated school from scratch. If a person wishes to convert an existing grant-aided school all of the steps detailed below must be followed. If, however, a person wishes to convert an independent school or establish an integrated school from scratch, the required procedure begins with the drafting of a proposal to be considered by the Department. It is worth noting that the procedures which will be described below were based on the legislation in Great Britain which deals with opting for grant-maintained status. It is easy to see why this approach was attractive to the Department. In each case, the point of the exercise is to ensure that there is a significant level of parental support for the change in status which the school may undergo. However, it will be seen that it may not have been wholly appropriate to apply the same procedures in the context of integrated education in Northern Ireland, particularly when the change proposed involves the transformation of an existing school. On the other hand, taking a more pragmatic view, the operation of identical statutory procedures in Great Britain on what is undoubtedly a hotly contested issue, means that there are a number of reported decisions on the legislation in Great Britain which are of potential significance in Northern Ireland. These will be referred to at relevant points.

---

[30] Sch. 4. para. 6(1) to the 1986 Order, substituted by art. 89 of the 1989 Order.
[31] See, Moffat, 'The Transformation Option', in Moffat (ed) *Education Together for a Change* (1993).
[32] Sch. 4. para. 6(2)(a) to the 1986 Order, substituted by art. 89 of the 1989 Order.

Eligibility for transformation

9.14 Article 68 of the 1989 Order specifies that all existing controlled, voluntary and independent schools are eligible for grant-maintained integrated status. Existing controlled and voluntary schools (but not independent schools) are eligible for CI status (art. 90 of the 1989 Order). These general rules are subject to three exceptions: (i) nursery schools; (ii) special schools; and (iii) voluntary primary schools which have never been maintained. In addition, a voluntary school is not eligible if the trustees have served notice of intention to discontinue the school to the Department although the notice can be withdrawn to allow the request for integrated status to proceed. Similarly, a controlled or voluntary school is not eligible for integrated status if a proposal to wind the school down has been approved by the Department. This latter provision is clearly intended to prevent schools which are being closed though insufficient enrolments making a last ditch effort to change status and survive. It should be noted that the prohibition only applies when the Department has approved the notice to discontinue. It is still open to schools who are faced with closure to submit a proposal prior to any formal decision being taken. It has been suggested that parents' views should be sought about the possibility of transformation in rural areas where the local controlled and Catholic maintained school both face closure as a result of falling attendances.[33] The intention here seems to be to allow one school to transform on an informed assumption that children attending the other school would then transfer to it. The proposal has clear attractions; parents might well prefer to have a local integrated school rather than have to send their children some distance to the nearest controlled/maintained school. An alternative would be to enable a number of schools to make a joint application for integrated status. Arrangements of this kind would clearly be more complicated than single applications. However, the difficulties are not insurmountable; in Great Britain the nettle has been grasped and since 1994 there has been provision for enabling schools to acquire grant-maintained status as part of a cluster.[34]

The resolution or request

9.15 In an existing grant-aided school, the process of acquiring integrated status can begin in one of two ways: (i) through a resolution by the Board of Governors; or (ii) after a request by the parents of registered pupils. A resolution is the most convenient way of starting the process towards integration and is the norm where the Board and the parents are in broad agreement about the desirability of integrated education. The request method will be appropriate where the Board of Governors refuses to pass a resolution to hold a ballot but there are a significant number of parents who support the proposal. The request process ensures that integration cannot be blocked by a Board of Governors where there is a significant amount of parental support for the idea.

---

[33] This point was made by Moffat in a submission to the Northern Ireland Forum Education Committee, "Comments on 'The Framework for Transformation'" (1996).
[34] Education Act 1996, s. 346 and the Education (Groups of Grant-Maintained Schools) Regulations 1994.

Resolution

9.16 The Board of Governors can decide by a resolution passed at a meeting of the Board to hold a ballot of parents as to whether the school should seek integrated status.[35] Under the original provisions of the 1989 Order, the Board of Governors of the school was required to pass a second resolution but this additional hurdle was removed in 1996 so as to make the process towards integration somewhat easier and quicker.[36] The resolution is simply to hold a ballot of parents. It is not a resolution to seek integrated status. The legislation does not specify the proportion of votes needed to determine such a resolution. It is to be assumed from this that the voting arrangements will be determined by the scheme of management. Nor does the legislation place any restrictions on the members of the Board who are eligible to vote on the resolution. In Great Britain equivalent resolutions to seek grant-maintained status were challenged on the basis that the teacher governors had a pecuniary interest in the outcome of the vote.[37] Although these challenges were not successful the legislation in Great Britain now specifies the eligibility of teacher governors to vote on the resolution.[38] While it is unlikely that teacher governors in schools considering a transformation to integrated status would be deemed to have a pecuniary bias in the outcome of the resolution, a specific amendment to the Northern Ireland legislation to the same effect would clarify the issue.

Request

9.17 The process of applying for integrated status can be initiated by a request from parents to the Board of Governors.[39] In this case the request must be endorsed by a number of parents of registered pupils which is at least 20 per cent of the registered pupils on the date on which the request is received. To facilitate the process of compiling the request, any parent of a registered pupil is entitled to inspect and be supplied with a copy of a list containing the names and addresses of the other parents of registered pupils provided that the request is in connection with the proposal for a ballot or the holding of the ballot. However, the Board of Governors may not release this information without the consent of each parent in writing. If a parent does not give his or her consent, his or her name will be excluded from the list. The Board of Governors can charge for the cost of supplying the lists.

Ballot of parents

9.18 If there has been a resolution or valid request, the Board of Governors must arrange for a ballot to be held within a specified period.[40] The ballot must not take place earlier than 28 days after the date of the resolution or request. It must, however, take place within two months unless the Department gives its

---

[35] Art. 69(1)(a) and art. 91 of the 1989 Order.
[36] Art. 36 of the 1996 Order.
[37] See *R v Governors of Small Heath School, ex parte Birmingham City Council, The Times*, 14 August 1989.
[38] Education Act 1996, s. 186.
[39] Art. 69(1)(b) and (2) and art. 91 of the 1989 Order.
[40] Arts. 70 and 91 of the 1989 Order.

approval to a longer period. The Departmental guidance indicates that the ballot must be held within three months of the resolution or request.[41] The Board of Governors is required to inform the following bodies that a ballot is being held: the relevant ELB; if a school is a voluntary school, the trustees; and if the school is a Catholic maintained school, the CCMS.

9.19 The Board of Governors is under a duty to make the necessary arrangements for a ballot. First, it must take steps to ensure that those entitled to vote are supplied with such information about the procedure for and consequences of integrated status as may reasonably be expected to enable them to form a proper judgment as to whether or not such status should be sought for the school.[42] This must include: a general explanation of the procedure for acquisition of integrated status; the constitution and powers of the Board of Governors of the school; the conduct and funding of the school; the date included in the proposal; and any other information which the Department may direct. Similar information must be made available for inspection by all those employed to work in the school. The legislation neither requires nor prevents the Board of Governors from expressing its views as to the desirability or otherwise of the proposal for integrated status. However, the Departmental guidance on the issue strenuously recommends that material which argues the case for integrated status should not be distributed with ballot papers.[43] Instead, the Department suggests that a Board of Governors can offer its own view as to the implications of the change in status when it is writing to inform parents of the resolution to hold a ballot. This is essentially the statutory position applicable in Great Britain where the legislation explicitly permits governors to "promote" the case for opting out provided that this is done separately from any communications about the ballot.[44]

9.20 The ballot must be a secret postal ballot with the necessary arrangements being made by the "prescribed body".[45] The prescribed body for these elections is the Electoral Reform Society (ERS). The ERS must be given the electoral roll - the name and address of every person recorded on the school register as being a parent of a pupil at the school. It will then send each of these parents the ballot papers and count the votes. A person is eligible to vote if he is known to be a parent of a registered pupil at the school and is named in the school's register on a date not later than 14 days after the original resolution or request for the first ballot was passed. A "parent" is defined in the legislation as any person who has parental responsibility for a child.[46] This includes: parents who were married at the time of the child's birth; unmarried mothers; unmarried fathers where they have had parental responsibility; guardians; and persons in whose favour a residence order is made. The effect of this wide definition is that more than two people can have parental responsibility for a child. Each of these are entitled to vote in the election. Article 69(10) of the 1989 Order states that it is for the Board of Governors to determine any question as to whether a person is a parent of a

---

[41] DENI, *Acquisition Procedures for Integrated Status, Notice of Advice for Governors* (1996).
[42] Art. 70(3)-(5)) of the 1989 Order.
[43] *Ibid*.
[44] Education Act 1996, s. 189(6).
[45] Art. 70(8) of the 1989 Order.
[46] Substituted by the Children (NI) Order 1995.

pupil registered at the school. This decision could only be challenged if the Board of Governors' decision as to eligibility is such that no other Board of Governors paying due regard to its responsibilities could have reached the same decision. The legislation does not specify how many votes a parent should have if he or she has more than one child at the school. However, the Departmental guidance states that "every parent has the right to participate in the ballot, though each has one vote only, regardless of the number of other children he or she may have in attendance at the school". Boards of Governors are required to take this guidance into account under article 70(6) and (7) of the 1989 Order.

9.21 In order for the ballot to pass there must be a simple majority of votes cast. There is no provision as to what should be done in the event of a tie. This seemingly unlikely result actually occurred in Great Britain during a ballot on grant-maintained status with the result that the legislation there now requires a second ballot in the event of a tie.[47] If the total votes cast is less than 50 per cent of those eligible to vote, the Board of Governors must arrange a second ballot. This second ballot must be held within 14 days of the day on which the total number of votes cast in the first ballot was determined.[48] The Board of Governors does not have to supply information about the ballot again but it must inform those eligible to vote that they are entitled to do so and must give every parent an opportunity to vote again. Even if fewer than 50 per cent of those eligible vote in the second ballot, the result of the second ballot stands. Departmental guidance specifies that the second vote is "decisive, irrespective of the turnout".[49] If the vote is against the move to integration another ballot cannot be held in that school year unless the Department gives its consent in writing for a new ballot to be held.[50]

9.22 If the Department is not satisfied with any of the arrangements in relation to the ballot it may require the Board of Governors to conduct a further ballot on a specified date.[51] The Department may intervene in this way in one of three circumstances: (i) the statutory requirements in article 70 of the 1989 Order have been contravened; (ii) the arrangements for the ballot did not accord with any guidance issued by the Department; or (iii) the Board of Governors acted unreasonably in the discharge of its duties. A difficulty may arise as to the determination of those eligible to vote if the re-arranged ballot is held in a subsequent school year. The legislation does not specify whether the ballot is open to those who participated in the first ballot or whether only those who are parents of pupils at the time of the re-arranged ballot are eligible. The issue arose in Great Britain in 1992 after the Secretary of State directed that the original parents should be re-balloted in the subsequent school year, a decision which had the effect of depriving the parents of the

---

[47] Education Act 1996, s. 186.
[48] Art. 70(8) of the 1989 Order.
[49] *Acquisition Procedures for Integrated Status, Notes of Advice for Governors* (DENI, 1996) p. 3.
[50] Art. 69(5) of the 1989 Order.
[51] *Ibid* art. 70(11). The Department may pay or reimburse the Board of Governors in respect of the whole or part of any expenses occurred in respect of the ballot.

newly admitted children of a vote.[52] The legislation in Great Britain now specifies that it is parents of registered pupils at the time of the fresh ballot who are eligible to vote.[53]

9.23 It has already been pointed out that the balloting procedures described here were copied from the procedures which are used by schools in England and Wales who are looking to opt out of local authority control. However, one significant difference is that governors in Great Britain are required by statute to consider whether to hold a ballot at least once a year, a provision which was designed to keep the possibility of a change in status on the agenda. Differences such as this aside, the fundamental procedures are the same in both jurisdictions. Given that the legislation on grant-maintained status was introduced by a government which was vigorously supporting a policy of opting out, the requirements for a successful ballot are not particularly demanding. In theory, a school could be required to seek integrated status in a situation where just over 25 per cent of the parents of children at the school voted for it on the first ballot. Moreover, this figure could be considerably lower in a second ballot if a large number of parents are indifferent to the idea and fail to register a vote. In spite of this, there have been a number of criticisms of the balloting arrangements and in particular the field of eligibility to vote. In Great Britain concern has centred on the fact that the ballot takes no account of the wishes of the parents whose children will attend the school in the first year after the conversion. In 1992 the legality of this was challenged by way of judicial review on the grounds that the exclusion of the new parents frustrated the purpose of the legislation and was irrational.[54] These arguments were rejected by the High Court which considered that all electoral rolls are likely to be out of date to some extent and that this did not necessarily mean that there was a flaw in the democratic process. Different concerns have been expressed in Northern Ireland about the pool of people who are eligible to vote. It is clearly important that considerable weight should be attached to the views of the parents of existing pupils. They chose to send their child to the school on the understanding that the school was a controlled, non-integrated school and it would be patently unfair to change this position in the course of their child's education without the majority of parents being in support of the idea. However, it remains a fact that a successful move to integration depends not just on the support of the parents of existing pupils but more particularly on the views of the other group of parents who have not traditionally sent their children to the school. Current legislative provision takes no account of their views, a situation which has been criticised by those attempting to bring about a transformation.[55] Finally, on a more general point, it is worth noting that no account whatsoever is taken of the views of the pupils at the school, a situation which is potentially in breach of the government's obligation under Article 12 of the UNCRC to give children the right to express their views in all matters affecting them.

---

[52] For an account of this incident see, Harris, *Law and Education: Regulation, Consumerism and the Education System* (1993) p. 125.
[53] Education Act 1996, s. 192.
[54] *R v Governing Body of Irlam and Cadishead Community High School, ex parte Salford CC*, unreported decision of the English High Court, 1992.
[55] See Moffat's submission to the Forum's Education Committee, *op cit.*

The proposal stage

9.24 Article 71 of the 1989 Order governs proposals to acquire GMI status while article 92 covers proposals for CI status. The proposal is the key to the success of the procedure. It is at this point that the procedure for acquiring grant-aided status begins for independent schools and integrated schools being established from scratch. If an existing controlled or voluntary school passes a ballot to establish a CI school, it is the ELB who must draft the proposal. Likewise, proposals to establish a new CI school from scratch are the responsibility of the ELB. If the parents in a controlled or voluntary school have voted for the acquisition of GMI status the Board of Governors must submit a proposal to the ELB. The submission of a proposal to the ELB is also the first stage in the procedure for independent schools and those wishing to establish a GMI school from scratch. In an independent school the proposal must be submitted by the proprietor of the school. Where the proposal relates to a new school the duty is on the person who is proposing to establish the school. The proposal must be in the form prescribed by the Department as it may impose. The ELB must within 21 days of receiving the proposal submit it to the Department. The ELB must submit its views on the proposal within two months.

The advertisement

9.25 Once the ELB has received the proposal or drafted the proposal, it must publish a notice in one or more newspapers circulating in the relevant area.[56] The advertisement must state: that a proposal has been made; where a copy can be inspected; and that objections can be made to the Department within two months of the date of the advertisement. In addition the ELB must supply a copy to any person who requests one but subject to a reasonable charge.

Approval by the Department

9.26 The Department will then consider the proposal, paying particular attention to the objections and to the views of the ELB.[57] It may make such modifications as it considers necessary after consultation with the Board of Governors or the person making the proposal (in the case of an application for GMI status) or the ELB (in the case of an application for CI status). The Department may approve the proposal in which case it will inform the Board of Governors or the person making the proposal. The Department may also give its approval subject to such conditions as it thinks fit. If it rejects the proposal of an existing controlled or voluntary school it may require the Board of Governors (grant-maintained) or ELB (controlled) to submit a further proposal within a specified time.

9.27 The Department must not give its approval to any proposal unless it is satisfied that the school would be likely to be attended by reasonable numbers of Protestant and Catholic pupils.[58] There are no other statutory grounds for

---

[56] Arts. 71(6) and 92 (4) of the 1989 Order. Art. 71(6) was substituted by art. 37 of the 1996 Order.
[57] Arts. 71(7) and 92(5) of the 1989 Order.
[58] *Ibid* arts. 71(8) and 92(6).

approval. However, the Department makes its decisions based on pre-established policies about the viability of the proposal. The Department will consider a range of issues such as the existing viability of the school and an assessment of the school's commitment to, awareness of, and preparation for the process of integration. The specific criteria used vary depending on whether the proposal is for transformation of an existing school or a proposal to establish a new school. These have been changed by the Department following a review of its procedures for assisting the development of integrated education. The outcome of the review was that the Department has embarked on a policy of encouraging existing schools to transform to integrated status where possible in preference to assisting the development of new integrated schools. Their reasoning which is set out in a published document "Integrated Schools: A Framework for Transformation", was discussed earlier in the chapter.[59] However, the primary means by which this is to be achieved is through the new arrangements for approving proposals.

New schools

9.28 Until 1996 new schools were expected to achieve a minimum starting ratio of 75:25 between the majority and minority religions in the area. In July 1996 this was changed to 70:30. Specified enrolment figures were also raised making it more difficult for new schools to demonstrate viability.[60] The revised conditions for a new integrated primary school are an opening enrolment of 25 pupils and a long-term enrolment within the range of 150-175 pupils. The required enrolment figures for new secondary schools are an opening enrolment of 100 with a long-term enrolment of 500 pupils. (The previous requirements were 15/100 for primary schools and 60/300 for secondary schools.) In addition, the Department will consider: the potential impact on existing integrated provision; whether existing integrated schools could be expanded to meet the projected additional demand; and the possibility of transformation of existing controlled or maintained schools in the area.

Transformation

9.29 The Department's revised policy on transformation to integrated status is set out in "Integrated Education: A Framework for Transformation". The key consideration will be whether the existing school will be likely to achieve a reasonable balance between religious groups. Schools are not required to demonstrate any pre-existing level of integration.[61] However, they will be required to achieve a minimum of 10 per cent of their intake from the minority community in their first year. The objective is that over time this would increase to no less than 30 per cent. In addition, the Department will seek evidence of the school's efforts to address the implications of integration including enrolment criteria, the curriculum and religious education, pastoral care and education and training. Finally, it will consider the impact of any change in status on other schools in the area.

---

[59] See para. 9.09.
[60] Northern Ireland Information Service, 17 July 1996.
[61] The Department had previously proposed a requirement of at least 1% pre-existing integration and/or 5% in the first year.

9.30 It remains to be seen whether the new criteria will encourage more schools to transform. The new enrolment criteria for new GMI schools are unlikely to constitute a major hurdle to groups of parents who want to set up a new school. Past experience shows that they have little difficulty in meeting the required enrolment criteria, a fact which the Department itself recognises.[62] However, even if parents are able to demonstrate that they can reach the target enrolment figures, it seems that the Department may not approve the proposal if it considers that the demand for integrated schools can be met in a more efficient way through existing provision.

Transition to integrated status

9.31 Transitional measures will be put in place in the period between the approval of the proposal and incorporation. One of the first tasks will be to establish a Board of Governors for the school. The composition of a Board of Governors of an integrated school is set out in Chapter 3. The provision for arrangements during the transition period are different for grant-maintained and controlled schools. In a controlled school the ELB makes all the necessary arrangements in the transition period.[63] In a grant-maintained school the provision depends on whether the proposal is for a new school or an existing school. Under article 71(12) of the 1989 Order, when a proposal for a new grant-maintained school is approved, the Department may by order make such provision as it considers appropriate in connection with the establishment of the school and the constitution of the Board of Governors prior to incorporation. The provisions on the transitional arrangements for existing schools are set out in Schedule 6 to the 1989 Order. This gives the Department the power to issue an order making such provision as it considers appropriate in connection with the school's transition to grant-maintained status and for the transfer of responsibility for the management and control of the school to the new Board of Governors. This provision is stated to include: arrangements for the constitution of the Board of Governors; the exercise of specified functions such as appointments and entering into contracts; and a requirement that the new Board of Governors is consulted or given the opportunity to participate in certain functions. The Department has the power to pay grants to the new Board of Governors in respect of any expenditure incurred by it in the exercise of any provision made under such an order.

Incorporation

9.32 The final stage of the procedure is the incorporation of the Board of Governors on the proposed date of implementation.[64] This means that the Board is a body corporate and can then exercise all of the functions and powers reserved for Boards of Governors. On incorporation an existing school ceases to have its previous status as a controlled school, voluntary school or independent school.[65] On the date of incorporation all land and property which

---

[62] This was recognised by Michael Ancram, MP, when announcing the revised criteria for new schools. Source: Northern Ireland Information Service, 17 July 1996.
[63] Art.92(9) of the 1989 Order.
[64] Arts.72 and 92(9) of the 1989 Order.
[65] *Ibid* art. 75 (8)-(10).

was used for the purposes of the school transfers to and vests in the Board of Governors.[66] All rights and liabilities under the property also transfer. Similarly, articles 76 and 96 of the 1989 Order preserve the rights of existing employees of a school on incorporation. The legislation states that the contract of employment with the former employer will have effect as from the incorporation date as if originally made between the employee and the Board of Governors of the integrated school. All contractual obligations are transferred and the Board of Governors will be liable for the previous employers actions. The protection in article 76 of the 1989 Order applies to all those employed by the Board of Governors, ELB or CCMS. It excludes people whose contracts have terminated on the day before the incorporation date, those reassigned by the ELB or CCMS, and those who have withdrawn from employment.

Management of the school while the procedures are pending

9.33 Once the procedure for seeking integrated status has begun there are a number of provisions which restrict the process of decision-making for the school. These are designed to ensure that the school does not undergo major changes during the time which it takes to complete the proposal for the acquisition of integrated status. The restrictions apply during any period when the procedure for acquiring integrated status is pending. The procedure is deemed to be initiated when the relevant ELB receives notice of a valid resolution or request to hold a ballot.[67] The procedure is deemed to have terminated if: the ballot does not show a majority in favour; the proposal is not approved by the Department; the proposal is withdrawn; or the Board of Governors is incorporated.[68]

9.34 Where the procedure for acquiring GMI status is pending schools are restricted from making a resolution or request to seek CI status and vice versa.[69] In the case of a voluntary school the trustees may not dispose of property or enter into a contract to dispose of property without the consent of the Department.[70] This restriction does not, however, apply to any contract entered into before the procedure was initiated in relation to the school. Moreover, in cases where the trustees do make a disposal or enter into a contract in contravention of these provisions, the agreement will not be considered invalid or void and any person acquiring property does not have to enquire whether the Department's consent was obtained.[71]

9.35 If an ELB intends to formulate a proposal for a controlled school which is eligible for GMI or CI status it must consult the Board of Governors.[72] The ELB cannot submit a proposal for alteration to a controlled school under article 14(1)(c)(d) or (e) of the 1986 Order once the proposal for acquisition of integrated status has been approved. This covers proposals to discontinue,

---

[66] *Ibid* arts. 75(1) and 83(1).
[67] *Ibid* arts. 73(3) and 93(3).
[68] *Ibid* arts. 73(4) and 93(4).
[69] *Ibid* arts. 73(3) and 93(10).
[70] *Ibid* arts. 73(7) and 93(7).
[71] *Ibid* arts. 73(9) and 93(9).
[72] *Ibid* arts. 74 and 94.

make a significant change in character or any other change which would have a significant effect on a controlled school. If two proposals are being considered by the ELB at the same time, the Department will consider them both together but will not determine the proposal under article 14 until it has made a determination about the proposal for integrated status. This is designed to give the application for integrated status priority. However, where a proposal for a significant change in character is approved before the procedure for acquiring integrated status is approved but not implemented, the proposal under article 14 of the 1986 Order will be deemed to be a proposal under article 79 or article 97 of the 1989 Order, that is, an approved change in the character of an integrated school.

MANAGEMENT ISSUES SPECIFIC TO AN INTEGRATED SCHOOL

Scheme of management

9.36 Articles 66 and 88 of the 1989 Order state that the scheme of management of an integrated school will require the Board of Governors to "use its best endeavours to ensure that the management, control and ethos of the school are such as are likely to attract to the school reasonable numbers of both Protestant and Roman Catholic pupils". This means that the Board should take steps to ensure that the school is accessible to both sides of the community, for example by arranging appropriate religious instruction. Moreover, it should not do anything which might alienate one tradition or the other. The NICIE Statement of Principles states that integrated schools should be places where "parents feel secure knowing that the religious and cultural values and beliefs of their families will be respected in the school". This necessarily involves the identification of activities which accommodate cultural differences but which do not leave pupils from one community feeling threatened or undermined. For instance it may be appropriate for an integrated school to offer pupils Gaelic games and cricket lessons but not appropriate for it to insist that all children participate. In addition to this general responsibility, there are a number of management issues which require particular consideration in the context of integrated schools. They are: admissions criteria; the curriculum; and the employment of staff.

Admissions criteria

9.37 All schools are required to determine their admissions according to pre-published admissions criteria.[73] In drafting its admissions criteria an integrated school must try to achieve a reasonable balance of pupils from both religions. It has been seen that one of the difficulties with the 1989 legislation is that it does not define what is meant by a reasonable balance. The policy of the Northern Ireland Council on Integrated Education is that the balance should not fall below 60/40 of either religion. In integrated schools admissions criteria are used to achieve a form of positive discrimination where one community is under-represented in applications to the school. Integrated schools had previously got into legal difficulty when they defined their criteria

---

[73] See para. 4.29.

in such a way as to restrict themselves to certain percentages of pupils. In *In re Patton*, a school's criteria had stated that the Board of Governors would seek to reflect an overall balance between traditions of no more than 40 per cent of either tradition. The school in fact admitted 63 per cent Catholic and 32 per cent Protestant.[74] The court considered that when one of the two main traditions reached 40 per cent, the other criteria should have been suspended until a balance was achieved. Integrated schools now use criteria which are less prescriptive about the precise numbers of pupils from each tradition. The process normally involves separating admissions from each of the two communities and admitting children to each group on the basis of other prescribed criteria, for example contributory schools, catchment area, sibling attendances. The Board of Governors of an integrated school must also be careful in drafting admissions criteria not to upset the balance of intake for instance by defining the school's catchment area or contributory schools in such a way as to reduce the number of applications from one religion. A further 20 per cent of places are normally reserved for children from neither tradition. If those places are not filled, the remaining places are distributed equally between the two main traditions.

9.38 The legal validity of admissions criteria which positively favour one religion over another has not yet been considered by the Northern Ireland courts. Previous challenges have focused on the way the criteria were applied rather than the substance of the criteria themselves. The fact that the criteria have not been challenged on their substance must be due to some extent to the lack of a clear basis to found such a challenge. A case would have had to be mounted around section 76 of the Northern Ireland Act 1998. The possibility of this type of challenge in the context of school admissions criteria was discussed at paragraphs 4.36-4.39. Integrated schools are clearly in a slightly different position from other schools. They select on religion overtly and in fact must do so in order to meet their statutory obligation to ensure that the school is attended by reasonable numbers of Protestant and Catholic pupils. However, if the school receives a much higher proportion of applications from pupils of one tradition than the other, it is undoubtedly more difficult for pupils of the majority tradition in the area to gain admission. It might be argued that this amounts to a form of direct discrimination. It might also be difficult, in the face of factual evidence, for a court to adopt a similar approach to that of the court in *In re Daly* discussed earlier, that is that the effect of the criteria was the same for both religions.[75] So far the issue has not been tested in the courts. However, if a challenge of this nature were to be successful, legislative intervention would be necessary to allow schools to select pupils on this basis and thus preserve the distinctive ethos of integrated schools.

The curriculum

9.39 Integrated schools are subject to the general requirements of the Northern Ireland curriculum in the same way as other schools. One exception relates to the teaching of religion in CI schools. In controlled schools the

---

[74] Unreported judgment of the High Court of Northern Ireland, 30 September 1994.
[75] Unreported judgment of the High Court of Northern Ireland, 5 October 1990.

teaching of religious education must normally be non-denominational.[76] However, CI schools are exempt from this.[77] This allows them to provide their pupils with denominational religious instruction. The exception is important in allowing integrated schools to attract pupils of both religions. It is also in keeping with the ethos of integrated education in that it specifically recognises and provides for the diversity of its pupil body. This means that integrated schools can organise separate religious instruction classes for pupils of different denominations.

Employment of staff

9.40 Boards of Governors of integrated schools are under an obligation to ensure a balanced pupil intake. One criticism of this provision is its exclusive focus on the student body and its resultant failure to include a requirement that the staff and Board of Governors should also contain a balance of both religious traditions. It is clear that integrated schools want to achieve a balance in their employment of staff. There is currently no legislative prohibition to stop them employing affirmative action to achieve this since schools are exempted from the Fair Employment and Treatment (NI) Order 1998. However, in controlled schools the ELB will normally insist that the applicant's religion is not taken into account on staff appointments. This has been criticised for its tendency to hamper controlled schools which have transformed from attaining a religiously balanced staff. However, the education exemption to the Fair Employment legislation is subject to ongoing review. If the exception were to be removed there would be a case for allowing integrated to schools to make affirmative appointments in its efforts to secure the integrated ethos of the school.

---

[76] Art. 21(2) of the 1986 Order.
[77] Art. 13(1)(b) of the 1989 Order.

CHAPTER TEN

SCHOOL TRANSPORT

INTRODUCTION

10.01 The seemingly mundane issue of school transport is in fact a highly controversial aspect of education law. An indication of this is the fact that the legal provisions on school transport have been considered by the House of Lords not once but twice[1] and that related issues are considered regularly by the English Court of Appeal.[2] Although there has only been one recent case in which a written decision has been given in Northern Ireland,[3] the area of home to school transport has always been a major source of contention in this jurisdiction with the result that further litigation would not come as a surprise to anyone involved in the system's administration. The potential for legal action is fuelled by two factors: (i) the complexity of the legal provisions; (ii) and the strength of parental feeling on the issue.

10.02 The law surrounding school transport provision is complicated for a number of reasons. First, the legislation contains a number of terms (such as "suitable" and "appropriate") which are inherently imprecise and thus provide a breeding ground for uncertainty. However, more problematically, the legal position involves the interplay of two separate statutory provisions: (i) article 52 of the 1986 Order (the ELB's obligation to make arrangements to facilitate attendance at school); and (ii) Schedule 13, para.3(2), (the parents' defence of lack of suitable transport in cases of non-attendance at school).[4] These provisions do not employ precisely the same terms. However, they must logically have a relationship. This was the view taken by the House of Lords in *George v Devon CC*, where it considered that it would be unreasonable for a local education authority not to provide free transport if this would mean that the parents were not under a legal obligation to secure their child's attendance at school.[5] Moreover, to complicate the legal picture further, two other statutory provisions are of potential significance: (i) article 44 of the 1986 Order (the principle that a child should be educated in accordance with the wishes of his or her parents); and (ii) article 45 (the parental duty to secure the child's education). It will be seen that the equivalent English provisions have given the courts in that jurisdiction much to grapple with.[6] The result is a series of quite complex and often contradictory decisions. If similar issues were to come before the Northern Ireland courts there is a wealth of

---

[1] *Rogers v Essex CC* [1986] 3 All ER 321, *George v Devon CC* [1988] 3 All ER 1002.
[2] See for instance, *R v Essex CC, ex parte Bullimore* unreported 26 March 1997, *R v Dyfed CC, ex parte S*, [1995] 1 FCR 113, *R v Essex CC, ex parte C* [1994] Fam Law 128.
[3] *In Re Martin's Application*, unreported decision of the Northern Ireland High Court, 8 May 2000. See para. 10.08.
[4] See further paras. 6.18-6.19.
[5] *Op cit* n. 1.
[6] In England and Wales the equivalent to art. 52 is contained in the Education Act 1996, s. 509.

authorities which will assist the representations which are likely to be made by each side.

10.03 Parental feelings about school transport run high because the amounts involved can accumulate over a child's school career into considerable sums of money.[7] Moreover, dissatisfaction is generated by the type of case often highlighted in the media where children living in the same street have been treated differently by ELBs. The fact is that 100 yards can make the difference when it comes to measuring statutory walking distances. Moreover, this is not the only source of dissatisfaction. Even where assistance is provided parents may be unhappy with the type of transport being used, the length of the journey, or the fact that the child is not left closer to their home. In 1997 the potential for parental dissatisfaction increased further as a result of a change in the Department's policy on the provision of free transport.[8] Since September 1997 free transport has been restricted to the nearest suitable school rather than to any school of the parents' choice. The change does not affect children who had previously received assistance. While it is clearly fair that the existing entitlement of these children should be protected (their parents chose the school on the assumption that assistance with transport would be provided), an unfortunate consequence of the change is that one child in a family may receive assistance which is denied to his or her younger sibling if the school which he or she attends is not deemed to be the nearest suitable school. The combined result of the inherent complexity of the law, perceived inequities in its operation, and the recent shift in policy is that the area is ripe for litigation.

10.04 At present the combined cost of the home to school transport schemes in the five ELBs totals over £38 million per year.[9] This represents approximately six per cent of each ELB's annual budget, a significant proportion of the schools budget for a service which is not concerned with the delivery of core education.[10] In view of the considerable costs involved it is important to understand why the ELB is bound by statute to provide this ancillary service. In fact state provision of home to school transport can be traced to the commencement of compulsory schooling in 1923.[11] At a time when many parents were reluctant to send their children to school it was considered important that the expenditure/difficulty involved in getting children to the classroom could not be used as a defence to non-attendance. However, while accepting the motivation underlying the provision at that time it might now be questioned whether the time is right for change. Societal attitudes towards education have moved on, for instance, the principle of compulsory schooling is now almost universally accepted. Moreover, access

---

[7] The average annual cost per child assisted is £350.
[8] DENI Circular 1996/41.
[9] In 1995/96 the total expenditure on Home to School Transport was £38,112,211. *Statements and Summary of the Education and Library Boards' Accounts* (April 1995 - 31 March 1996) Cm 3717 (The Stationery Office, 1997), p. 12.
[10] See for example the WELB which spent £10,106,686 on school transport out of a total budget for recurrent expenditure of £197,264,878. *Ibid*, pp. 118 and 152
[11] The Education Act (NI) 1923, s. 30 required education authorities to provide "suitable means of conveyance for a child between "a reasonable distance of its home and a public elementary".

to transport both public and private has increased dramatically since the requirement to provide assistance was first conceived. In view of the spiralling expenditure (at a time when ELB budgets are under severe strain) it might be questioned whether there is a need to redefine the criteria for assistance.

10.05 It will be seen that the legal limitations on the provision which is made (through the statutory walking tests) are not only imprecise but result in a series of anomalies.[12] Given that the actual distances used are no more than a legal fiction (few children walk more than a mile to school irrespective of their age), it might be appropriate to seek a new means of defining those children who need assistance with the costs of home to school transport. The anomalies in the school transport system were highlighted in an Audit Commission report in 1990.[13] The report did not make specific recommendations for reform but suggested that consideration should be given to both means-testing and the introduction of a set of flat fares for the public transport of school children.[14] An obvious change would be to reduce the walking distance to something more realistic and to target assistance on families with low income (i.e. those receiving means-tested benefits). The government is promoting the idea of 'affluence testing' in other areas of social provision. In this context too it can be queried whether it is sensible to continue to provide this service to parents who are in position to pay for it themselves. The reality is that assistance can be provided to the children of well-to-do parents whose children use the system infrequently (because the parents leave them to school in their cars) while the children of parents on social security benefits living just within the statutory limits use public transport at their parents' expense.

10.06 Finally, the whole issue of transport to school might be approached from a different perspective, for instance by re-examining the way in which children travel to school. Possibilities such as dedicated cycle tracks might be promoted as an economic, safe and healthy way of getting children from their homes to their schools. This type of strategy looks increasingly likely since the government's recently published White Paper on transport, *A New Deal for Transport: Better for Everyone*.[15] This specifically identifies the 'school run' as one of the major transport problems of today. The White Paper argues that the concern about the use of cars for school journeys goes further than the need to reduce congestion in the morning and includes a need to encourage children to walk and cycle more for their own health.[16] The report recommends reducing the need for children to be driven to school by encouraging safer routes for walking and cycling and giving greater priority to public transport. The government intends to set up a School Travel Advisory Group in England and Wales to disseminate best practice and to develop policy in this area. Reform of the statutory home to school transport schemes is not mentioned in the White Paper. The only specific recommendation for

---

[12] Liell, 'Home to School Transport: Anomalies and Anachronisms' [1997] 2 *Education, Public Law and the Individual* 37.
[13] *Home to School Transport: a System at the Cross Roads*, The Audit Commission (1990).
[14] *Ibid.* p. 33.
[15] Cm. 3950 (1998).
[16] *Ibid* p. 145.

legislative change is a proposal to strengthen the powers of school crossing patrol officers so that they can help children below school age and adults.[17]

OBLIGATION TO PROVIDE FREE TRANSPORT

10.07 Each ELB is under a duty to make arrangements for transport which will facilitate the attendance of pupils at grant-aided schools.[18] The key legal provisions are contained in article 52 of the 1986 Order which was substituted by article 23 of the 1997 Order to accommodate the change in policy outlined in DENI Circular 1996/41. The precise scope of the obligation on ELBs is not specified. Article 52 of the 1986 Order simply requires ELBs to make such arrangements as it considers "necessary" or as the "Department may direct". The arrangements are subject to approval by the Department.[19] In practice all ELBs will provide assistance with transport where the child's school is not within walking distance of the child's home. They will usually also provide transport for children with special educational needs or in other exceptional circumstances. If the ELB is under an obligation to facilitate attendance (i.e. it considers it "necessary") the assistance given must be provided free of charge. However, the ELB also has the power to provide transport or assistance with travelling expenses for other pupils for whom it is not required to provide free transport.[20] In such cases it may charge the parents for all or part of the transport costs.

Who is entitled to free school transport?

10.08 There are no specific restrictions in the legislation in relation to the categories of pupil who are entitled to free transport. Article 52 refers simply to facilitating the attendance of "pupils at grant-aided schools". In *In re Martin's Application*, the Northern Ireland High Court considered that ELBs did not have the power to provide transport to children attending non-grant aided schools, in this case an Irish medium primary school.[21] The court did not regard it as absurd that subsidised school transport should be restricted to those attending grant-aided schools. However, Departmental guidance states that no assistance will be provided to two categories of pupil: (i) children under compulsory school age (who may nevertheless gain admission a year early); and (ii) children who pay tuition fees (such as those attending the preparatory departments of grammar schools).[22] The legal basis for the restriction on children under compulsory school age is not readily apparent. The term "pupil" is defined to mean "a person of any age for whom education is provided under the Order".[23] On the face of it this specifically includes children under school age. It must be assumed that the restriction is founded on the Department's power to direct the "arrangements" which might be made under article 52(1). However, there is a possible argument that the Department's power is limited to the physical "arrangements" for the

---

[17] P. 146.
[18] Art. 52 of the 1986 Order substituted by art. 23 of the 1997 Order.
[19] Art. 52(3) of the 1986 Order.
[20] *Ibid* art. 52(3)-(4).
[21] Unreported decision of the Northern Ireland High Court, 8 May 2000.
[22] DENI Circular 1996/41, para. 3.1.
[23] Art. 2 of the 1986 Order.

provision of transport and does not permit them to limit the type of pupil who may receive assistance since the term "pupil" is referred to without restriction in article 52(1)(a). Similarly, the only possible legal basis for excluding children at preparatory schools is that these are not "grant-aided" and do not, therefore, fall within the ambit of article 52. However, the 1986 Order defines a grant-aided school as a school "to or in respect of which grants are made under this Order". Preparatory schools are subsidised by the Department although it is somewhat unclear whether this arises under the 1986 Order.

Free transport for children who live outside the statutory walking distances

10.09 All ELBs will make provision for children who live outside statutory walking distances. In *George* v *Devon CC* the House of Lords considered that to do otherwise would be unreasonable. Keith L.J stated that "...a local education authority would be acting unreasonably if it decided that free transport was unnecessary for the purpose of promoting their attendance at school, because if it were not provided the parents of these children would be under no legal obligation to secure their attendance".[24] In Northern Ireland this defence arises under Schedule 13 to the 1986 Order.[25] This states that a child will not be considered to have failed to attend school regularly:

> "if the parent proves-
>
> (i) that the school at which the child is a registered pupil is not within walking distance of the child's home; and
>
> (ii) that the child is one for whom the board is required to make provision under Article 52(1) but no suitable arrangements have been made by the board for his transport to and from school; and
>
> (iii) that no suitable arrangements have been made by the board for boarding accommodation for the child at or near the school or for enabling him to become a registered pupil at a school nearer to his home."

Schedule 13 defines the one situation in which an ELB must consider it necessary to provide assistance with transport. If a parent can satisfy the three conditions above, he or she will have a defence to their child's non-attendance at school. An ELB must provide assistance with transport if it wishes to secure the child's education. Thus article 52 and Schedule 13 must be read together. At one level this has been useful since Schedule 13 inserts a specific obligation into the otherwise vague language of article 52. However, it will be seen that the use of Schedule 13 as a means of interpreting the extent of the duty under article 52 has not been without its problems. Some of these difficulties could be avoided if article 52 were to be amended so as to include a precise obligation to provide assistance to children living outside the statutory walking distances.

---

[24] *Op cit* n. 1 at p. 1006.
[25] Amended by art. 23(2) of the 1997 Order.

Statutory walking distances

10.10 Walking distances are set at two miles for a child at primary school and three miles for other children.[26] The legislation does not specify where the measurement should begin and end. In particular it is unclear whether it should be taken from door to door or gate to gate. In one of the first reported decisions on the issue the measurement was taken from the school porch to the house porch.[27] This would seem fair given that the extra yards between a school gate and the school entrance are part of the overall journey to school and may make the vital difference in borderline cases. The distances are measured by the nearest available route. In *Shaxted* v *Ward* the court considered that the nearest available route was one which the child could normally walk.[28] It did not matter if the route was sometimes unsafe. Lord Goddard stated that "Parliament has not substituted safety for distance as the test".[29] However, in *Rogers* v *Essex CC* the House of Lords determined that the nearest available route is the route along which the child could walk to school with reasonable safety when accompanied by an adult.[30] A route does not therefore fail to qualify as available because of dangers which would arise if the child was unaccompanied. It is, however, still arguable that a route would not be available if it is dangerous for both parent and child (e.g. because of the danger of sectarian attacks).

10.11 The statutory walking distances can be controversial mainly because they are not widely regarded as being realistic. Few parents would expect a primary school child to walk two miles to and from school, or a secondary school child to walk three miles. A further difficulty has been created by the House of Lords' endorsement of the principle of parental accompaniment. Given that few parents will remain at the school for the entire day, there is an assumption that parents may be expected to walk distances of nearly 60 miles a week accompanying their child to and from school. There are not many parents who would be willing to do this even if their circumstances permitted it (i.e. they do not work, are physically capable and do not have other care commitments which preclude them from accompanying their child). However, if the child lives within walking distance and there are other factors which preclude accompaniment and the route is too dangerous for the child to walk alone, an argument might be made that assistance with transport is "necessary", an option which is explored at paragraphs 10.19-10.21.

Restrictions on provision for children living outside the walking distances

10.12 The policy of open enrolment means that parents can apply to any school to admit their child. It does not have to be close to the parental home. If the child is accepted and registered at the school the parent is under an obligation to secure attendance.[31] As has been seen, parents will have a

---

[26] Sch. 13(3), para. 6.
[27] *Hares* v *Curtin* [1913]2 KB 328.
[28] [1954] 1 All ER 336.
[29] At p. 338.
[30] *Op cit.*
[31] Sch. 13, para. 3 to the 1986 Order.

defence to non-attendance if the school is outside the statutory walking distance and no arrangements have been made by the ELB to facilitate attendance. However, the defence involves a third condition - that the ELB has not made *suitable* arrangements for the child through boarding accommodation or by enabling them to become a registered pupil at a school nearer his or her home. It is this third arm to the statutory defence which provides ELBs with a means of restricting the provision which it makes. Arrangements for boarding accommodation are rare. In practice this occurs for a small number of secondary school children who live off-shore and would have to travel by boat to return home each day. Instead, it is the provision of suitable arrangements for enabling a child to register at a school nearer home which allows education authorities to restrict the levels of assistance.

10.13 It is clear that education authorities can limit the provision which they make to children living outside walking distances if they can show that they have made "suitable arrangements" for enabling the child to become a registered pupil at a school nearer to his or her home. However, in England and Wales disputes have arisen over the precise nature of the restrictions and in particular the meaning of the phrase "suitable arrangements". A key issue is whether an authority must show whether the particular school which it is proposing is objectively suitable for the pupil or whether the suitability relates simply to the other administrative arrangements. The issue has been before the English courts on a number of occasions and there has been a series of conflicting judgments on the point. In *R v Rochdale Metropolitan Borough Council ex parte Schemet* in which Roch J was of the opinion that "arrangements will not be suitable unless the school is suitable for the particular pupil".[32] However, in *R v East Sussex County Council, ex parte D* Rose J refused to infer a requirement that the education authority considers the suitability of the school.[33] The conflicting authorities were considered by Jowitt J in *R v Essex County Council, ex parte C* who opted for the latter judgment, commenting that "the suitable arrangements do not, in my judgment, describe the quality of the school and could not do so without suspending the rules of grammar".[34] However, the decision was challenged in the Court of Appeal where Staughton LJ took the opposite view. He considered that "Arrangements for unsuitable transport, or unsuitable boarding accommodation or an unsuitable school nearer home, are in my judgment unsuitable arrangements". This did not, however, determine the issue once and for all. In a subsequent decision of the Court of Appeal, *R v Dyfed County Council, ex parte S* Butler-Sloss LJ dismissed the comments in *ex parte C* as obiter dicta and took the view that "suitable" related to the arrangements and that this did not include the school.[35] All of the above authorities were reviewed in the case of *R v Bedfordshire County Council, ex parte DE* in which Collins J considered himself bound by the decision of Butler-Sloss in the *Dyfed* case even though he was more persuaded by the line of argument favoured by *Schemet*.[36] That said, he took a pragmatic view that few education

---

[32] [1993] 91 LGR 425.
[33] Unreported, 15 March 1991.
[34] [1994] Fam Law 128.
[35] [1995] 1 FCR 113.
[36] Unreported 1 July 1996.

authorities would rely on the provision so as to require a child to go to a school which it considered to be unsuitable and if it did it would be considered to be acting perversely.

Significance of parental preference

10.14 Many of the English cases cited in the previous paragraph commenced because children were not provided with transport to the school of their parent's choice. Although each of the LEAs had a different policy on the schools to which it would provide transport, most would only provide it to the nearest maintained school. This did not always allow for factors such as grammar school education, Welsh-speaking schools and denominational schools. In several instances counsel for the parents argued that parental preference should take primacy in determining whether home to school transport should be provided. Instead, the English courts have adopted the pragmatic position that the education authority should have regard to parental preferences, but that it is not an overriding factor. In the *Schemet* case Roch J stated that "the wishes of the parents are an important consideration but they are not the sole consideration, and the local education authority may reach the conclusion that they can make suitable arrangements for the child to be a registered pupil at a school nearer to his home despite the fact that it conflicts with the stated preference of the child's parents, provided that the local authority have taken the parent's preference into consideration when reaching that decision".[37] This was also the view of the Court of Appeal in *R v Essex County Council, ex parte C*.[38] In that case, the parents of a child with severe learning difficulties argued that the local education authority had to give primacy to parental wishes in determining whether to make transport arrangements. Steyn LJ rejected this because he considered that such an approach would "emasculate" the LEA's power to nominate a nominate a suitable alternative school under the equivalent of Schedule 13, paragraph 3(2). Moreover, although article 44 of the 1986 Order requires ELBs to have regard to the principle that children should be educated in accordance with the wishes of their parents, the duty applies only in so far as this is compatible with the avoidance of unreasonable public expenditure. The ELB may, having taken into account all the circumstances of the case, including the parents' reasons for their choice of school, conclude that the expenditure is unreasonable and make suitable arrangements for the child to attend a school closer to home. The parents do not, of course, have to send their child to the school proposed by the ELB. However, if they keep the child at the school of their choice they will have to make their own arrangements for the child's transport.

Policy in Northern Ireland: DENI Circular 1996/41

10.15 Prior to 1997 ELBs provided transport to the school which a child had been admitted even if it was not the nearest school of its type. However, from September 1997 ELBs have imposed restrictions on the circumstances in which they will finance travel arrangements when there is a suitable school closer to the child's home. This is a direct result of Departmental guidance

---

[37] *Op cit.*
[38] [1994] Fam Law 128.

designed to restrict the provision of free transport to the nearest suitable school.[39] For these purposes ELBs have divided schools into specific categories and sub-categories:

Primary: maintained, controlled, integrated, Irish-Medium

Secondary: maintained, controlled, integrated, Irish-Medium

Grammar: denominational and non-denominational

In practice parents can apply for a place in a school in more than one of these categories in each school sector and for grammar and secondary schools. In order to qualify for transport assistance to a school outside the statutory walking distance, application must first be made to all of the schools in the same category that are within statutory walking distance before a preference is expressed for a more distant school.[40] To be eligible for assistance, children attending a more distant school must be able to show that they were unable to gain a place in a school in the same category within statutory walking distance of their home.

10.16 When compared to some of the policies which have been challenged in the English courts, the Department's categorisation of the nearest suitable schools provides a generous view of the factors which would influence parental choice. It allows for decisions based on denominational, language, ability and integrated grounds.[41] The decision in *R* v *Dyfed CC* considered earlier would suggest that ELBs are not bound in law to ensure that the alternative school proposed is "suitable" in all these respects.[42] Thus, the Department's policy might be considered to be a relatively wide interpretation of the legal obligation placed on ELBs. In adopting this approach to the issue of alternative schools the Department will undoubtedly have headed off many of the types of challenge which have predominated in England and Wales.

10.17 The Department's guidance states that these are the only options open. In particular, it suggests that a desire for single sex or co-educational schooling will not be taken into account.[43] In 1998 an attempt was made to challenge the legality of the policy on single sex schools by parents who wanted their child to attend an all-girls school. The substance of the challenge was that the refusal to provide home to school transport to such schools discriminated against female pupils who generally did better in single sex schools.[44] The evidence for this assertion is somewhat conflicting. It appears that legal aid was refused with the consequence that the applicants did not proceed with the claim. However, there are other ways in which this aspect of the policy might be challenged, for instance it is clear that ELBs cannot completely fetter their discretion in this way. They have to consider all factors in determining whether it is "necessary" to provide assistance. The limitation is only possible on the basis that the ELB has been "directed" not to make

---

[39] DENI Circular 1996/41.
[40] *Ibid* para. 3.6.
[41] Parents in the "Dickson Plan" area (Craigavon) also have a right to express a preference for a grammar school outside the area.
[42] [1995] 1 FCR 113.
[43] *Ibid*, para. 3.5, note i.
[44] *McAteer* v *DENI* which appears to have been withdrawn prior to hearing.

such arrangements by the Department under article 52. The question is whether such a direction might be open to challenge.

10.18 The obvious basis for challenge would be on the meaning of "suitable arrangements" in Schedule 13 as discussed at paragraph 10.13. There is a possibility that the Northern Ireland courts might prefer the interpretation placed on this in *R v Rochdale Metropolitan Borough Council, ex parte Schemet* case and approved in *R v Essex CC, ex parte C*. If this were to be the case, the ELB would have to be satisfied that the nearest school proposed was "suitable" for the child and might be prepared to take into account factors such as a need for single sex or co-educational schooling. Alternatively, there might be on the facts of a particular case an argument that the Department's policy was irrational, for example if an ELB were to refuse transport assistance to a co-educational school for mixed-sex Siamese twins. Likewise, there might be compelling circumstances in which a parent would want single sex schooling, for example where a child has been the victim of a sexual assault which has left them with a fear of the opposite sex. It is unlikely that cases of this sort would reach the courts. It might be anticipated that such issues would be handed sensitively by ELBs with the approval of the Department. Nonetheless, it is worth remembering that ELB policy and Departmental guidance are not immune from challenge and that relevant considerations other than those in the circular must be considered.

Free transport for children living within the statutory walking distance

10.19 An ELB may be under an obligation to provide a child who lives within statutory walking distances with free transport. This arises because article 52 places ELBs under an obligation to provide such transport as it considers "necessary". In *George v Devon CC* the House of Lords stated that it would be wrong to assume that Parliament expected all pupils living within walking distances to walk to school. Lord Keith stated: "The intention of Parliament was that pupils living outside the statutory walking distance would in all cases be provided with transport, and that pupils living within that distance would normally walk to school but would be provided with free transport if the local education authority considered it necessary for facilitating their attendance".[45] The question is when an ELB will consider it "necessary" to facilitate attendance if the child lives within statutory walking distances.

10.20 The wording of article 52 is deliberately broad and gives ELBs considerable discretion in determining whether assistance is "necessary". In *George v Devon CC* the House of Lords defined this to mean "really needed".[46] In that case, the local authority were considered to be entitled to refuse assistance to a nine year old boy who lived 2.8 miles from the school and who had to travel along a track used by agricultural vehicles. The Court considered that it was lawful for the education officer to take into account the fact that the child's step-father was unemployed and therefore available to

---

[45] [1988] 3 All ER 1002, at pp. 1006-1007.
[46] *Op cit* p. 1006.

accompany him to school. The House of Lords described the duty on the education authority as follows:

> "The question is whether the authority considers arrangements for free transport to be necessary for facilitating their attendance. Obviously free transport will make the attendance of every such pupil easier, however close to the school he or she happens to live. But that cannot determine the matter. It is for the local authority and no one else to decide whether free transport is really needed for the purpose of promoting the attendance at school of a particular pupil. That must depend on the authority's view of the circumstances of the particular case...The authority's function in this respect is capable of being described as a 'discretion', though it is not of course an unfettered discretion but rather in the nature of an exercise of judgment."[47]

In practice, the largest group of pupils who live within statutory walking distances but nonetheless receive transport assistance are children with special educational needs. The need for assistance with transport will usually be specified in their statement of special educational needs.[48] This is acknowledged in the Department's guidance which specifies that the general arrangements in Circular 1996/41 do not apply to pupils with statements of special educational needs.[49]

10.21 Children with statements are not the only children living within the walking distances who may be entitled to assistance. The Department's Circular provides no guidance on this point beyond the statement that "transport assistance will not *normally* be provided for any pupil who lives within statutory walking distance of the school...".[50] ELBs have defined school transport policies in order to assist them in making decisions as to the cases in which transport arrangements are "necessary". These normally make provision for children who have medical conditions which affect their mobility. However, this does not mean that no other cases can be considered. ELBs cannot restrict the exercise of their statutory obligation by rigid adherence to their transport policy. Each case must be fully considered and that includes considering the possibility of an exception being made to the policy. Relevant factors might include the child's physical and mental capabilities, the parents' ability to accompany the child and the nature of the route. For instance, in *George v Devon* CC, the House of Lords was of the opinion that the LEA had properly considered the child's age, the nature of the route and the availability of his parents before coming to a determination that assistance was not necessary.[51] Interestingly, in *R v Bedfordshire CC, ex parte DE* Collins J expressed considerable doubt over an LEA policy which stated that there was no scheme on the grounds of low income or hardship.[52] In his view:

---

[47] *Ibid.*
[48] See further para. 8.58.
[49] Para. 6.
[50] Para. 3.1.
[51] [1988] 3 All ER 1002.
[52] Unreported decision of the English High Court, 1 July 1996.

"If that is a blanket approach so that low income and hardship are never taken into account in deciding whether free transport should be provided, then it seems to me that is wrong. First of all, it fetters the discretion generally. But, more importantly, it may well result in discrimination in relation to the exercise of parental choice... I do not say, of course, that the mere fact that they cannot afford is itself sufficient to require that a grant be given where a choice has been exercised, but it is surely a factor that should be taken into account."[53]

It is possible to envisage a situation where a child is living within the statutory walking distance; the route is unsafe without accompaniment; the parent(s) is unable to accompany because of other care responsibilities (or because he or she is accompanying another child along a different route to a different school at the same time); and the parent(s) is unable to afford the fare for the bus which can take their child to his or her school safely. If an ELB were to refuse assistance in such a situation it might be considered to be acting unlawfully or unreasonably.

TYPE OF PROVISION WHICH MUST BE MADE

10.22 The legislation does not specify the type of assistance which must be given. Article 52 simply refers to "arrangements for the provision of transport and otherwise". In practice this will involve the use of buses, taxis, private hire coaches, ferries etc. ELBs all have their own in-house bus services. However, as a matter of policy, they will use public transport wherever possible. This may restrict the transport arrangements to set hours and routes as determined by the transport company, a factor which can lead to parental dissatisfaction with assistance being provided.

General principles

10.23 The obligation placed on the ELB is simply to "facilitate attendance". In *George v Devon CC* this was defined as meaning "make easy" or "promote".[54] Article 52 goes no further. However, reading article 52 with Schedule 13(3), it is arguable that the arrangements must also be "suitable" in cases where the child lives outside the statutory walking distances (otherwise a parent will have a defence to the child's non-attendance at school). If the arrangements offered were plainly unacceptable (e.g. a young child had to change buses on route, thus crossing a busy road and waiting an hour for the second bus to arrive) it could be argued that the ELB was not "facilitating attendance" or that the arrangements were not "suitable" under Schedule 13(3).

10.24 In *R v Hereford and Worcester CC, ex parte P*, McCullagh J considered that an LEA was under a duty to make such arrangements as it considered necessary for a child to reach school without "undue stress, strain or difficulty" which might prevent him from taking advantage of the education

---

[53] But note however, the view of Lord Keith in *George v Devon CC* [1988] 3 All ER 1002 where he considered that the relevance of parental means was "open to serious doubt" (at p. 1009).

[54] *Ibid* p. 1006.

that the school had to offer.[55] He also considered that the LEA should make arrangements in which children could travel in safety and reasonable comfort. In determining whether the transport arrangements provided are acceptable in these respects, the authority must look at all the circumstances. The child's age and physical and mental abilities will be of particular significance. However, there a number of other factors which are relevant when determining whether the arrangements are appropriate.

Particular factors

Duration of the journey

10.25 One key factor in the determination of the suitability of the arrangements is the total time taken in the journey. In *R v Hereford and Worcester CC, ex parte P* the court considered that it was unacceptable that the journey should last an hour each way.[56] The pupil was a child with Downs' Syndrome and the journey time was extended by the fact that the bus had to stop at a number of other routes along the way. The parents sought judicial review basing their submission on the legality of the contents of the statement and in particular the section covering non-educational provision. The court considered that it was implicit that the authority should make such arrangements as it considered necessary for a child to reach school without undue stress, strain or difficulty so that he could benefit from the education on offer at the school. On the facts, the child had a journey which lasted an hour each way. His parents asserted that the maximum journey time should be 45 minutes. The education authority wished to continue with the existing arrangement which allowed them to use one bus for 12 children attending three different schools. The court declined the parents' application on the basis that the decision was not so unreasonable that no other reasonable education authority would have taken the same decision. However, the court stressed that the transport provisions require the education authority "to do what is necessary, not to do what is considered affordable" and suggested that an application might have been successful had it been argued that the authority took into account an irrelevant consideration when it prioritised resources when determining its transport provision for the child.

Door to door?

10.26 One of the key queries parents have is whether the ELB is required to take the child from the door of their home to the gate of the school. This will be of particular concern to the parents of young children who will otherwise have to bring the child to or meet them at the designated bus stop. Further problems can arise where the child is still left a considerable distance from his or her home with the result that the parents consider the overall journey (transport and walking) to be onerous. When LEAs are measuring the distance between home and school for the purpose of determining statutory walking distances, they will measure from the door of the house to the door of the school.[57] However, if a decision is taken to provide transport assistance, it

---

[55] [1992] 2 FLR 207.
[56] *Ibid.*
[57] See *Hares v Curtin* [1913] 2 KB 328.

does not have to be provided door to door. In *Surrey CC* v *Ministry of Education* the court considered that it was not sufficient for an authority to provide transport so as to limit the journey to two or three miles (i.e. to bring them within the statutory walking distances).[58] Lynsley J considered that the transport should be provided from "a point reasonably near his home to a point reasonably near the school - I do not say the school door, but reasonably near thereto". Departmental guidance reflects this. It states that "A board has no obligation to assist with travel for the whole of a journey, provided that the remainder of the journey does not exceed the statutory walking distance and the board is satisfied, having regard to the length and time of the total journey, that the remainder of the journey is not excessive".[59] Thus, if a child had to wait 20 minutes on a bus, the journey took 30 minutes and the child still had to walk two miles home, a court might consider the overall journey to be excessive with the result that the ELB might be considered to have failed to comply with their statutory obligation to "facilitate attendance".

Supervision

10.27 There is no statutory requirement for ELBs to provide supervision on school buses. However, a failure to provide supervision may in certain cases be considered to be negligent and thus give rise to a civil action for damages if a child is injured on a bus where there is no or inadequate supervision. In one such case, *Jacques* v *Oxfordshire CC*, the court considered that an education authority should provide whatever level of supervision was appropriate bearing in mind the children's ages and standard of behaviour.[60] Thus one might expect an ELB to provide adult supervision where a large number of young children or children with learning difficulties are being transported. Supervision might also be required where it is known that a certain group of children are particularly boisterous or undisciplined. In the *Jacques* case the court refused to award damages against the education authority when a child was injured during some pellet throwing on a bus which was supervised by school prefects. The court considered the standard of care to be that of "reasonable parent (applying his mind to school life where there is a greater risk of skylarking)". The court placed emphasis on the fact that there was no evidence that the children were particularly boisterous and undisciplined.

Safety obligations

10.28 There are a number of detailed provisions which govern Public Service Vehicles. These require those driving Public Service Vehicles to have special licences.[61] They also require buses carrying school children to display special signs.[62] However, the issue which appears to most concern parents in relation to school transport is that of seat-belts. Not all buses are required to have seat-belts. In buses where seat-belts are not required, three children count

---

[58] [1953] 1 All ER 705.
[59] Para. 3.1.
[60] (1967) LGR 440.
[61] Part II of the Road Traffic (NI) Order 1981 as amended by art. 3 of the Road Traffic (NI) Order 1991.
[62] Road Vehicles Lighting (Amendment) Regulations (NI) 1995, reg. 17 as substituted by the Road Vehicles Lighting (Amendment) Regulations (NI) 1997, reg. 4.

as two passengers,[63] a situation which has been criticised by parental pressure groups. ELBs will not be considered to have acted unreasonably when they do not provide seat-belts in circumstances not required by the legislation.[64]

Parental input

10.29 While it is clear that an ELB can be under an obligation to facilitate attendance, the responsibility for getting the child to school does not necessarily fall upon it entirely. Article 45 of the 1986 Order is of some relevance in this context. It places an onus on parents to "cause" their child to receive full-time education. In *George* v *Devon CC* the House of Lords described the parental obligation as follows:

> "In general, the parent must do these things which are reasonably practicable to be done and which an ordinary prudent parent would do. This may include accompanying the child in situations where it would be unsafe for the child to go to school unaccompanied. In a case where a child lived 100 yards from the school but the route involved crossing a busy trunk route, and the parent, although available to do so, refused to accompany the child and refused to allow him to go to school on the ground that it would be dangerous, there can be no doubt that the parent would be guilty of an offence."[65]

The fact that ELBs are under an obligation to facilitate attendance does not absolve the parents of all obligation in relation to securing their child's attendance at the school of their choice.

WITHDRAWAL OF ASSISTANCE

10.30 ELBs are required to make "such arrangements for the provision of transport and otherwise as they consider necessary, or as the Department may direct, for the purpose of facilitating the attendance of persons receiving education...at schools". It has been seen that this rather broad duty has been the subject of much litigation as regards the circumstances in which an education authority is bound to provide assistance with transport. However, disputes arise not only about the situations in which the authority should assist but on the situations in which it might wish to discontinue assistance which has previously been provided. The key difficulty here is that the legislation does not specify the circumstances in which an authority might withdraw assistance. It must be assumed therefore that it may (and indeed should) withdraw assistance when it considers that it is no longer "necessary" for it to provide assistance so as to facilitate the child's attendance at school.

10.31 There are a number of occasions on which an ELB might wish to withdraw assistance with transport. The most commonly occurring of these is where there has been a change of circumstances (for instance the child moves house or school) with the result that the authority no longer considers assistance to be necessary. In such instances, provided the child's parents notify the authority of the change in circumstances, the removal of entitlement

---

[63] Reg. 61(2)(b) of the Public Service Vehicles (Carrying Capacity) Regulations (NI) 1995.
[64] *Harris* v *Gwent CC*, unreported 6 April 1995.
[65] [1988] 3 All ER 1002.

will be unproblematic. However, there are a number of other situations in which the withdrawal of assistance might result in parental dissatisfaction and consequently become a breeding ground for litigation. These arise where there has been a mistake as to the facts, a change in policy or where the transport company refuses to carry a child on account of the child's behaviour during the journey. At the outset it should be noted that litigation in such cases is likely given that most people will have strong feelings about the removal of a benefit previously enjoyed (compared to one never experienced). Moreover, in the case of home to school transport, the sense of injustice goes further since parents' original understanding of their child's entitlement may well have been a determining factor in the choice of school.

Mistake as to the facts

10.32 Difficulties may arise where the assistance has been granted previously because of a mistake (innocent or otherwise) as to the facts. In *Rootkin* v *Kent* an LEA had provided the applicant's child with assistance for three months when it discovered that the route was 175 yards less than the statutory walking distance of three miles.[66] The LEA withdrew assistance and the applicant sought judicial review arguing first, that the authority had no power to withdraw assistance once it had been provided and secondly, that the authority was estopped from removing assistance. The Court of Appeal considered that the LEA did have the power to discontinue the assistance. In fact Lawton LJ was of the view that the authority was duty bound to reconsider the matter once it discovered the mistake of fact. Moreover, the Court of Appeal was unanimous in the view that the doctrine of estoppel could not be used to prevent the authority from exercising its discretion to refuse assistance and that, in any event, the applicant's position had not been altered sufficiently to enable her to rely on the doctrine.

10.33 It is clear therefore that assistance can be withdrawn if the original decision has been based on a mistake as to the relevant facts. In *Rootkin* v *Kent* the mistake was the LEA's own fault; the first measurement was taken by the mileometer in a private car, the second was taken by a special machine called a 'Trumeter' which (living up to its name) gave a more accurate reading. It goes without saying that assistance can also be withdrawn if the authority has been misled as to the facts by the parents. This could arise where parents have given false addresses so as to show that a child is living within the catchment area for a particular school, a situation which it has been suggested has become increasingly common.[67] Such situations may, of course, also result in civil actions to recover monies lost and criminal proceedings for fraud.

Change in policy

10.34 Each ELB has a published policy on the provision of home to school transport. This sets out the situations in which the ELB is prepared to meet the costs of school transport and outlines any exclusions. ELBs can easily get into legal difficulty for over rigid adherence to their policies. However,

---

[66] [1981] 2 All ER 227.
[67] See Ward, 'The Parents who cheat for their Children', *The Independent* 17 April 1997.

problems can also arise where the ELB decides to implement a change in policy. This is increasingly more likely given the financial pressures on education authorities; transport assistance is an ancillary service and consequently one which is vulnerable to review when ELBs are experiencing difficulty managing their budgets. The most effective way of reducing the money spent on transport costs is to restrict the criteria for assistance.

10.35 While ELBs are able to change policy and thus remove existing entitlement to assistance they would be advised to consult widely about the changes. In *R v Rochdale Metropolitan Borough Council, ex parte Schemet* an LEA changed its policy so as to refuse assistance to children travelling to extra-district schools to receive denominational education.[68] It did not consult parents before or during the change. The applicant's daughter had previously received assistance to attend such a school. The court considered that the parents of children at extra-district schools already receiving passes had a legitimate expectation that the benefit would continue until there had been communicated to them some rational grounds for withdrawing it on which they had been given the opportunity to comment. The court stated that the withdrawal of a travel pass might mean that a child would have to change schools so it was right and sensible that the LEA should pay some regard to the effect on the child before finally deciding to withdraw its assistance. The court refused to issue an order of certiorari quashing the decisions of the council to change the policy since to do so would have affected the budget of the education authority for the previous two years. Instead, it issued a declaration that the decisions were unlawful and that the parents had a legitimate expectation that the passes would continue until such time as they had been properly consulted.

Indiscipline

10.36 The final situation in which an ELB might wish to withdraw assistance is where the pupil is behaving badly on the means of transport with the result that he is a danger to himself, the driver or other passengers. If the carrier is a public transport company, it might refuse to carry the child, thus forcing the ELB to reconsider the assistance provided. The problem is that the legislation does not give ELBs the power to withdraw assistance on grounds of misbehaviour alone and it is difficult to see how an argument might be sustained that transport was no longer "necessary" because of the child's misbehaviour alone. A child's behaviour may be relevant to what is "necessary…for the purpose of facilitating attendance" when an ELB is considering whether to make a positive grant of assistance, for example there may be cases where a child cannot be controlled on a public footway even with adult supervision. However, it is difficult to mount an argument that a child's unruly behaviour while being transported can be a factor in determining that assistance is not necessary. It would appear therefore that if the ELB is under an obligation to provide free transport (i.e. if it considers it to be necessary), it must make alternative arrangements (e.g. provide a private taxi) if the child is not permitted on public transport because of their actions. A countervailing argument is that once the ELB has made the arrangements to

---

[68] [1993] 91 LGR 425.

facilitate transport (e.g. secured the annual ticket from the local bus operator) it has fulfilled its statutory obligation and need do no more if the child's behaviour means that they are unable to avail of the assistance provided.

10.37 Although the legislation does not give the ELB the power to impose sanctions for misbehaviour, the education authority could inform the child's school in the hope that it might take disciplinary measures. The head teacher's power to discipline extends to incidents occurring outside the school premises.[69] This is generally accepted to include the journey to and from school.[70] In serious cases of indiscipline a head teacher could suspend the pupil for the misbehaviour. This might act as a deterrent and should at least give the ELB time to make alternative arrangements for transport.

10.38 What is not included in article 52 of the 1986 Order may be as problematic as what is. In particular, the lack of prescribed circumstances in which an education authority might withdraw assistance can cause difficulty. ELBs would undoubtedly find it useful to have a subsection providing them with a list of defined circumstances in which they might withdraw assistance. The money which is used to defend litigation often outweighs the money which in spent meeting the costs of transport in individual cases. This would be particularly useful when a pupil has been banned from the transport which has been provided as a result of their own misconduct.

COMPLAINTS

10.39 There are a number of ways in which a parent who is dissatisfied with the operation of the home to school transport provisions might complain. Clearly parents should raise the issue with the ELB in the first instance. However, if still dissatisfied there are a number of avenues of address. The first is a complaint to the Department under article 101 of the 1986 Order.[71] This provides a means of complaint if a parent considers that there has been an unreasonable exercise of the statutory functions. A complaint to the Department should be the first port of call for dissatisfied parents since an application for judicial review may not be entertained if parents have failed to raise the issue with the Department. In *R v Essex CC, ex parte Bullimore* Lord Bingham refused to consider an application for judicial review because the parents had not first taken the issue to the Secretary of State (the GB equivalent of a complaint to the Department in NI).[72] Lord Bingham stated that "in all circumstances, it is preferable that the decision on this matter should be made on the merits by the political authority entrusted with responsibility for the operation of the educational system". An application for judicial review remains an option where the parents are unhappy with the Department's decision. Moreover, if the parents are unhappy with the administrative handling of the application for transport assistance, they might have grounds for complaint to the Ombudsman.[73]

---

[69] *R v Newport Salop Justices, ex parte Wright* [1929] KB 416.
[70] See *R v London Borough of Newham, ex parte X, The Times*, 15 November 1994, where a pupil pulled a fellow pupil's trousers down in a retaliatory attack.
[71] See further, paras. 2.68-2.72.
[72] Unreported, 26 March 1997.
[73] See further, paras. 2.73-2.74.

APPENDIX

Table 1: Voting Members on Boards of Governors[1]

Controlled Schools (other than Controlled Integrated Schools)

	Primary	Secondary Intermediate	Grammar, Special & Nursery
General	4 (nominated by transferors or superseded managers)	4 (nominated by Boards of Governors of contributory schools)	
ELB	2	2	3
The Department			2
Elected parents	2	2	2
Elected teachers	1	1	1
Total	9	9	8

Table 2: Voluntary-Maintained Schools

	100 per cent Capital Funding	**85 per cent Capital Funding**
General	4 nominated by managers/trustees of the school	6 nominated by managers/trustees of the school
ELB	2	2
The Department	1	
Elected parents	1	1
Elected teachers	1	1
Total	9	10

---

[1] The numbers in the Tables represent the minimum number for a Board of Governors. The number of governors may be doubled or tripled but the proportions of base nominations and other appointments must stay constant.

Table 3: Voluntary Grammar

	100 per cent Capital Funding	**85 per cent Capital Funding**	**No Capital Funding**
General	4 (as set out in scheme of management)	6 (as set out in scheme of management)	(as set out in scheme of management)
ELB	3 balance depending on the agreement	2 balance depending on the agreement	
The Department			
Elected parents	1	1	1 or 2 depending on the size of the Board
Elected teachers	1	1	1 or 2 depending on the size of the Board
Total	9	10	no fixed number

Table 4: Integrated Schools

	Controlled Integrated Primary Secondary	**Controlled Integrated Grammar** (or an integrated school that was previously a voluntary school but not a Catholic maintained school)	**Grant-Maintained Integrated School**
General	2 - nominated by transferors or superseded managers 2 - nominated by trustees of Catholic maintained schools		6 Foundation governors including at least 2 parents
ELB	4	4	
The Department		4	4
Elected parents	4	4	4
Elected teachers	2	2	2
Total	14	14	16

INDEX

Acts of the Northern Ireland Assembly
    legislative competence 1.22, 1.23
    voting arrangements 1.24
Admission appeal tribunal
    appeal, grounds of 4.87
    composition of 4.88
    decision of 4.93
        challenges to 4.94- 4.95
    function 4.91
    powers 4.92
    procedure 4.89-4.90
Admission to school
    admission numbers 4.18-4.21
    age 4.12-4.15
    appeals 4.86-4.95
    attendance/behaviour requirements 4.55-4.56
    catchment area 4.51
    complaints 4.96
    contributory schools 4.52
    disabilities, children with 4.85
    enrolment number 4.17
    information on 4.09-4.10
    Irish language 4.54
    litigation 4.06-4.07
    open enrolment, policy behind 4.02-4.04
    parental preference 4.22-4.23
    procedures for 4.24-4.28
    residence in Northern Ireland 4.53
Admissions criteria
    ability and aptitude 4.64, 4.67-4.69
    age 4.65
    duty to draw up 4.29-4.33

family connections	4.46-4.49
gender	4.40-4.41
grammar schools	4.70-4.84
boarding pupils	4.80
key stage 2 assessments	4.84
performance in the transfer procedure	4.71
primary school reports	4.83
special circumstances	4.72-4.79
tests held by or on behalf of Board of Governors	4.81-4.82
integrated schools	9.37-9.38
nursery schools	4.62
order of parental preference	4.50
primary schools	4.63-4.65
ability and aptitude	4.64
age of the child	4.65
race	4.45
religion	4.36- 4.39
secondary schools	4.66- 4.69
ability and aptitude	4.67- 4.69
selection by	
date of birth	4.60
date/time of application	4.61
lot	4.59
last available place	4.57-4.61
unworkable criteria	4.34

Age

compulsory school age	6.12-6.13
primary school, admission to	4.12, 4.65
secondary school, admission to	4.13-4.15, 4.65

Attendance

admission to school, criteria for	4.55-4.56
attendance orders	6.33 –6.37
care orders	6.52-6.57
education supervision orders	6.42-6.51, 6.54-6.57
monitoring of	6.05-6.09
non-attendance	
criminal prosecution for	6.38-6.41

defences to 6.15-6.23
parental duty to secure 6.10-6.13, 6.30-6.32
registration at school 6.05-6.06
regular attendance 6.14
Belfast Agreement
Irish language 5.38
underlying principles 1.21
Board of Governors
annual report 3.40-3.41
annual parents' meeting 3.42
appointment of 3.08- 3.22
    eligibility 3.23
appointments, duration of 3.24
composition 3.07
decisions, potential for bias 3.30-3.33
disputes with ELB or the Department 3.60-3.61
functions 3.39-3.43
    delegation of 3.35
finance 3.44-3.57
joint responsibility .... 3.36 –3.38
legal status 3.58-3.59
meetings .... 3.28 – 3.30
reforms to, 1989 .... 3.01-3.06
scheme of management 3.26
school development plan 3.42-3.43
special educational needs, obligations in relation to 8.08-8.09
voting rights 3.34
Catholic Church
integrated education, response to 9.05
voluntary schools, influence in 1.09, 1.10, 1.15, 1.16
Changes to schools
changes in the size or character .... 2.49 – 2.53
consultation 2.43-2.44
Departmental approval 2.45
discontinuance 2.48
new school, establishment of 2.46
proposals 2.42

    recognition as a grant-aided school 2.47
    significant effect on another grant-aided school 2.54
Commissioner for Complaints ....2.73 - 2.74
Council for Catholic Maintained Schools
    background 1.15, 2.12
    composition 2.15-2.16
    functions 2.13, 2.17-2.18
Controlled schools
    background 1.09
    Board of Governors, composition of 3.07-3.22
    description 2.20
    finance 3.46-3.49
Curriculum
    areas of study and compulsory contributory subjects 5.13
    assessment arrangements 5.19
    background to 5.01-5.03
    charging for 5.56-5.76
    complaints tribunal 5.87- 5.94
    discrimination 5.40-5.44
    educational themes 5.10-5.11
    exemptions from the Northern Ireland curriculum 5.21-5.26
        development work and experiments 5.26
        special educational needs 5.22
        temporary individual exceptions 5.23-5.25
    inspections 5.95-5.99
    integrated schools 9.39
    Irish language 5.34-5.39
    key stages 5.12
    political/cultural issues 5.45
    redress for poor quality education 5.101
    religious education 5.46-5.55
        children's rights 5.52-5,53
        collective worship 5.48
        parental rights 5.50-5.51
        teacher's rights 5.54
    sex education 5.27-5.33
    statement of curricular policy 5.08

target setting 5.100
Department of Education
   functions 1.25, 1.26, 2.06
   complaints to 2.63-2.72
   special educational needs, obligations in relation to 8.07
Department of Education for Northern Ireland (DENI)
   abolition 1.18, 2.05
Discipline
   admission to school, relevance of 4.55-4.56
   appearance 7.18-7.20
   behaviour outside school 7.21
   behavioural difficulties, provision for children with 7.73-7.74
   block punishments 7.31
   confiscation 7.42
   corporal punishment 7.02, 7.10, 7.33-7.37
   degrading punishments 7.43
   detention 7.38- 7.41
   exclusions .... 7.45-7.68 *see* **Exclusions**
   expulsions 7.60-7.63
   independent schools 7.75-7.77
   investigating misbehaviour 7.22- 7.32
      accomplices 7.29
      identification of culprit 7.30
      searches 7.28
   isolation 7.44
   parental wishes 7.10-7.11
   punishment, reasonableness of 7.08-7.09
   record 7.72
   restraining pupils, power of members of staff 7.36-7.37
   school transport, misbehaviour on 10.36-10.37
   statement on discipline 7.12-7.15
   suspensions 7.55-7.59
   teacher's authority, basis of 7.07
Discrimination
   disability
      admissions 4.56
      curriculum 5.43-5.44

race 2.61-2.62
    admission to school 4.45
        curriculum 5.42
        school uniform 7.20
religious belief or political opinion 1.36-1.37, 2.59-2.60
    admission to school 4.36-4.39
schools, in the provision of 2.55-2.62
sex discrimination 2.57–2.58
    admission to school 4.40-4.41
        curriculum 5.41
        school uniform 7.19

Education at home 6.24-6.29

Education and Library Boards
    background 2.07
    composition 1.07, 2.09-2.10
    duty to provide sufficient schools .... 2.32 – 2.36
    functions 2.11
    plan to reduce number 1-13, 1.20
    special educational needs, obligations in relation to 8.07

Education for Mutual Understanding 5.04
    parental objections to 5.45

Education otherwise than at school 2.37-2.39

Equality Commission 1.31, 1.34
    statutory equality duty 1.32- 1.35

European Convention on Human Rights
    Acts of NI Assembly, compatibility with 1.22
    attendance at school 6.02, 6.23
    corporal punishment 1.53, 7.02
    integrated schools, funding of 1.60, 9.04
    parental rights in education 1.53-1.56, 5.37, 6.02, 6.23
    religious education 5.53
    right
        fair trial, to 1.57
        freedom of expression, to 1.59
    not to be discriminated against in enjoyment of
        other rights... 1.58,4.39
    not to be subjected to torture, inhuman or degrading treatment ..1.59

    not to be denied education 1.52, 6.02, 6.23
    respect for privacy and family life, to 1.59
  sex education 5.30
Exclusions
  expelled pupils, arrangements for 7.69-7.71
  expulsions 7.60-7.63
  expulsion appeal tribunal 7.64-7.68
  grounds for 7.49-7.54
  scheme for suspension and expulsion 7.47-7.48
  suspensions 7.55-7.59
    challenging a decision to suspend 7.57-7.59
    procedure 7.55-7.56
Finance
  Board of Governors, responsibility for .... 3.44 – 3.56
  changes to funding arrangements for voluntary schools 1.16, 1.41
  curriculum, charging for 5.56-5.76
  voluntary contributions 5.76
Grammar schools
  admission to 4.70- 4.84
  charges 5.71-5.75
Grant-maintained schools
  opting out of LEA control 1.05, 1.08
Grant-maintained integrated schools
  Board of Governors, composition of 3.07-3.22
  description 2.23
  finance 3.55-3.57
Human Rights *see also* **European Convention on Human Rights**
  Human Rights Act 1998 .... 1.22, 1.61
  protection for, ...1.28-1.30
Information
  annual school reports 5.78
  pupil achievement, on 5.77-5.86
  pupil records 5.82-5.86
  records of achievment 5.80-5.81
  reports at end of key stages 5.79
Integrated education
  admissions criteria 9.37-9.38

background to 9.02-9.09
controlled integrated schools 9.12
curriculum 9.39
definition 2.30, 9.01
employment of staff 9.40
establishment of new schools 9.09-9.11
grant-maintained integrated schools 9.12
incorporation 9.32
procedures for acquiring integrated status ....9.13 - 9.31
scheme of management 9.36
transformation of existing schools 9.09-9.11

Irish language
admission criteria 4.54
curriculum 5.35-5.39
duty to encourage and facilitate 5.38
right to Irish language education 5.37-5.38

Irish medium schools
curriculum 5.36
definition 2.31

Independent schools
description 2.24
special educational needs 8.102-8.105

Judicial Review
grounds for review 2.78
procedural requirements 2.77
remedies 2.79
significance in education law 2.80

Minister for Education
appointment under D'Hondt 1.19
control over decision-making in NI Act 1998 .... 1.25, 1.26
controversy over appointment 1.19, 1.27

Northern Ireland Human Rights Commission
advice and assistance 1.30
advice on Acts of NI Assembly 1.23
Bill of Rights for Northern Ireland 1.29
functions 1.28
UNCRC *see also* **UNCRC**..1.50

Index

Nursery schools
    admission to 4.62
    definition 2.29

Ombudsman .... 2.73 – 2.74

Parents
    annual meeting for, ...3.42
    ballot of, in establishment of integrated schools 9.18-9.23
    Boards of Governors, membership of 3.18, 3.20
    conduct of, relevance to exclusion 7.54
    discipline, significance of parental wishes 7.10-7.11
    school transport
        parental input 10.29
        parental preference, significance of 10.14

Parental rights
    admission to school 4.50
    child's education, to choose nature of 2.34-2.36, 5.45
    curriculum, complaints about 5.97-5.88
    detention, notice of 7.39
    educate child at home, to 6.24-6.29
    expulsion
        right to appeal against 7.66
        right to be consulted prior to 7.61
    policy on 1.04
    pupil records 5.82
    religious education 5.50-5.51
    sex education 5.29-5.30

Primary schools
    admission to 4.63-4.65
    definition 2.26

Pupil records 5.82-5.86,
    discipline 7.72

Religion
    admissions criteria 4.36-4.39
    curriculum 5.49
    religious segregation 1.09, 1.10

SACHR
    school finance, research on 1.41

selection on ability, call for reform of 4.08
Secondary schools
    admission to 4.66-4.69
    definition 2.27
Selection on ability *see also* **Grammar Schools**
    admissions criteria, ... 4.64, 4.67-69
    background 1.11
    prospect of reform 1.20
Special educational needs
    assessment, statutory 8.28-8.45
    attendance orders 6.37
    background 8.01
    Code of Practice 8.19-8.25
    curriculum, exemption from 5.22
    definition of 8.13-8.18
    Department of Education, obligations on 8.07
    education at non-grant aided schools 8.102-8.105
    integration, principle of ....8.10-8.12.
    negligence 8.97-8.101
    resources 8.90-8.96
    statements of special educational need
        changes to 8.60-8.63
        definition 8.46-8.47
        form and content ....8.57 - 8.59
        legal effect 8.48-8.49
        procedure for making 8.50-8.56
        provision for children with out statements 8.85-8.89
    1996 reforms 1.43
Special Educational Needs Tribunal
    appeal
        grounds for 8.67
        High Court 8.82-8.84
        procedure for 8.68-8.72
    composition 8.66
    decision 8.79-8.81
    establishment 1.43, 8.64
    hearing 8.73- 8.78

Special schools
    definition 2.28
    finance 3.50-3.51
Transferor's representative council
    influence in controlled schools, ... 1.10, 1.15
    recognition as a statutory body, argument for 2.14
Transport
    charging for 5.66
    complaints 10.39
    defence to non-attendance at school 6.16-6.19
    free transport to school, obligation to provide 10.07-10.21
    parental preference 10.14
    policy on 10.15-10.18
    provision which must be made 10.22-10.24
        door to door? 10.26
        duration of the journey 10.25
        parental input 10.29
        safety obligation 10.28
        supervision 10.27
    statutory walking distances 10-09-10.13, 10-19-10.21
    withdrawal of assistance 10.30-10.38
United Nations Convention on the Rights of the Child
    enforcement 1.49
    influence 1.50
    religious education 5.53
    right to be heard 1.48
    right to education 1.47
    sex education 5.32
United Nations Universal Declaration of Human Rights
    attendance at school 6.01-6.02
    right to education 1.46
Voluntary grammar schools
    composition of Board of Governors 3.07-3.22
    description 2.22
    finance 3.52-3.54
Voluntary maintained schools
    composition of Board of Governors 3.07-3.22

description 22.21
finance 3.46-3.49